CHALLENGES
TO
EQUALITY

CHALLENGES TO EQUALITY

POVERTY AND RACE IN AMERICA

CHESTER HARTMAN
Editor

Foreword by John Lewis

M.E. Sharpe
Armonk, New York
London, England

Library of Congress Cataloging-in-Publication Data

Challenges to equality : poverty and race in America / edited by Chester Hartman
   p.cm.
  ISBN 0-7656-0726-3 (alk. paper) — ISBN 0-7656-0727-1 (pbk. : alk. paper)
   1. Equality—United States. 2. Social stratification—United States. 3. United
States—Race relations. 4. Poverty—United States. I. Hartman, Chester W.

HN90.S6 C48 2001
305′.0973—dc21   00-049249

Printed in the United States of America

BM (c) 10   9   8   7   6   5   4   3   2   1
BM (p) 10   9   8   7   6   5   4   3   2   1

Contents

Foreword

Congressman John Lewis

As a college student, I became a part of the movement that Dr. Martin Luther King had inspired in the Montgomery Bus Boycott. We challenged the system of segregation that had dominated the lives of black people since the days of slavery.

I found myself in a community of people who were willing to disobey social custom and defy the law. These people were willing to suffer beatings, go to jail, and give their lives for a higher purpose.

In 1961, we began the Freedom Rides. We rode from Washington, DC to Mississippi. We challenged segregation in interstate travel. We captured the imagination of the nation and effectively opened the doors to public travel facilities for all races.

We had a dream that we could eliminate racism and the division between human beings and build the Beloved Community—a community of peace, justice, and brotherhood. It was a dream whose time had come.

The struggle continues. As a nation and as a people we have made great strides in protecting the rights of each and every American, but we still have more work to do. As long as wages are not fair and livable, as long as families cannot afford decent health care, and as long as our country is still torn and divided by the color of one's skin, there is still much work to do.

It is not fashionable to talk about integration today. Yet, it will take a coming together of all people—nationally and globally—to address the injustices and inequalities of our nation. We cannot run away from anyone or leave behind anyone—not the poor, not the sick, not the disenfranchised.

We are one community living in one house. Perhaps we are in different rooms, but we are within the same walls and under the same roof. If one section of the house begins to rot, the entire structure is in danger of collapsing. We must work together if we want to lift this nation.

President Franklin D. Roosevelt once said, "The only limit to our realization of tomorrow will be our doubt of today. Let us move forward with a strong and active faith." This strong and active faith has moved our nation forward. We have weathered many storms. We have heard the thunder roll, and the rain beating down on this house we call America. At times, the very foundation of the American house has been shaken. Nevertheless, a faith that embraces the principles of social and economic justice can hold our American family together. A faith that forms our courage and gives us the strength to stand up for what is right is a faith that can never, never be dimmed.

Within these pages, leaders of our country engage in conversations on race, poverty, education, the environment, and democratic participation. They examine the foundations of injustice in our country. It is important that these discussions take place and be at the forefront.

Introduction

Chester Hartman

This is the second volume containing the best articles and symposia from *Poverty & Race*, the bimonthly newsletter journal of The Poverty & Race Research Action Council (PRRAC), a Washington, DC-based national public interest organization. The first collection, published by M.E. Sharpe in 1997, was *Double Exposure: Poverty and Race in America*; it contained sixty-one contributions, with a preface by NAACP Board Chair Julian Bond and a foreword by former U.S. Senator Bill Bradley. This new book, reprinting pieces published in *P&R* between 1997 and 2000, is considerably larger and contains an even one hundred contributions. Contributors to these two volumes represent the best of progressive thought on America's two most salient, and seemingly intractable, domestic problems.

While the full range of important issues around the intersection of race and poverty cannot be treated in a single volume, this collection focuses on what we regard as key questions as the new century begins: the possibility of true racial integration (as distinguished from desegregation), especially in the most meaningful and therefore difficult areas—housing and schooling; the various ways poverty manifests itself and the promise (or lack thereof) of recent antipoverty policies; education in its role as potential counter to structural, intergenerational poverty, by creating opportunities and ending isolation; the need to create true democratic process and participation in the political system; the relatively new focus on environmental justice; shining a race-poverty spotlight on a number of areas and issues where such focus is needed and useful, yet neglected or insufficiently emphasized; and what a true attack on racism requires—framed in the context of critical commentaries to President Clinton's disappointing Initiative on Race.*

---

* An orthographic note: With regard to terminology on race and racial categories, we opted to let each author use whatever is her or his word, punctuation, capitalization preference; such usage embodies issues that, for many, have levels of meaning well beyond mere style, and we chose not to impose any arbitrary single format or rule.

PRRAC, the organization that I have headed virtually since its inception in 1990, was founded by committed advocates from the legal services and antipoverty communities who were seeking progressive solutions to what we term "the intersectional trap": the ways our society creates and maintains a large stratum of the population that is both poor and subject to subordination by the dominant white majority. A list of our present and past Board of Directors and Social Science Advisory Board appears starting on page 363.

As our name conveys, PRRAC deals not only with the intersections of race and poverty, but also with the intersection of research and advocacy. We seek to enhance collaboration between those whose research is relevant to the fight against racism and poverty and those activists who use the tools of litigation, community organizing, public education, and legislation in that fight. We hope to encourage and facilitate more, better, and relevant social science research useful to activists, and to persuade activists to shape their work in light of what relevant research can impart regarding problems and solutions.

Among PRRAC's many activities is funding social science research on the intersections of race and poverty that is designed to support a planned advocacy agenda. PRRAC's oversight task is to ensure that the methodology is sound and the researchers are competent (which does not necessarily mean having traditional credentials). What we have found over the years is that such research, even if carried out by not disinterested parties, can provide credible, compelling evidence that legislators, the courts, the media, and the general public must take seriously. We also have found that relatively small grants (our maximum grant is $10,000, our average grant $7,500) can yield first-rate products when the recipients/doers are those who want and need the results for their advocacy work. A complete list of PRRAC-funded projects and their products is available on request, and is posted on our website: www.prrac.org. PRRAC can be reached at 3000 Connecticut Ave. NW, #200, Washington, DC 20008, 202/387–9887, info@prrac.org.

We are grateful to all the contributors for their prompt and careful responses to our requests to review and, as appropriate, update their original articles. PRRAC staff members Melissa Best, intern Mark Iriye, and Sandra Paik helped with some of the mechanical and proofreading tasks. Most especially, PRRAC is indebted to Jana Rumminger, our 2000 Mickey Leland Hunger Fellow, whose good judgment, omniskills, and perseverance in assisting with the multiple tasks involved in compiling this book have been nothing short of stellar. We thank the Mickey Leland Hunger Fellows Program of the Congressional Hunger Center for bringing Jana to us and wish her the best as she begins law school.

CHALLENGES
TO
EQUALITY

Part 1

Integration

Civil Rights, Now and Then

Julian Bond

At the turn of the century, the great scholar and activist W.E.B. DuBois predicted that "the problem of the twentieth century will be the problem of the color line." Not only was he right, but one regrettably may conclude that it will be also the problem of the century just begun.

This is a time when the leadership of the House and Senate is more hostile to civil rights than in recent memory. On a civil rights report card prepared by the National Association for the Advancement of Colored People (NAACP)—with 100 percent as a perfect score—they fail, averaging 21 percent in the House and 36 percent in the Senate.

It is also the aftermath of Supreme Court decisions sharply attacking affirmative action, limiting the scope of the court's historic 1954 decision in *Brown v. Board of Education*, and restricting the Voting Rights Act, and in a climate in which trashing affirmative action substitutes for dialogue on race.

In the current formulation, it is black people who hold the key to racial progress, but the door to justice is double-locked. White people keep their keys in their pockets, and many deny that they have a key at all.

Everywhere, we see clear racial fault lines, which divide American society as much now as at any time in our past.

Some Bright Spots

The picture we see is not without its brighter side. Taken over several decades rather than in snapshot moments, our portrait shows clear progress throughout the twentieth century. No more do signs read "white" and "colored." The voters' booths and schoolhouse doors now swing open for everyone, no longer closed to those whose skins are dark. Despite popular thinking to the contrary, the battle to preserve affirmative action is being won, not lost. Nearly twenty states have tried to place anti-fairness referenda on their ballots and all, but two, have failed. The two which succeeded did so by deceiving the public: in California 27 percent of voters said they thought a vote for Proposition 209 was a vote for civil rights; Washington State's Initiative 200 was a California copycat.

Three times in 1998, Congress voted on affirmative action measures, and three times bipartisan majorities voted to keep vital protections for minorities and women.

3

But. . . .

But for many, despite the successes, today's civil rights scene must seem like an echo of the past.

Many stand now in reflection of that earlier movement's successes, confused about what the next steps should be. The task ahead is enormous—equal to if not greater than the job already done.

Today we are three-and-a-half decades past the second Reconstruction, the modern movement for civil rights that eliminated legal segregation in the United States, and thirteen decades past the first Reconstruction, the single period in American history in which the national government used armed might to enforce the civil rights of black Americans.

Then, as now, scientific racism and social Darwinism were in vogue. Then, as now, a race-weary nation decided these problems could be best solved if left to the individual states. Then, as now, racist demagogues walked the land. Then, as now, minorities and immigrants became scapegoats for real and imagined economic distress.

Then a reign of state-sanctioned and private terror, including ritual human sacrifice, swept across the South to reinforce white supremacy. That is when the heavy hand of racial segregation descended across the South, a cotton curtain that separated blacks from education and from opportunity, but not from hope.

As we recall the struggles of the recent past, many of us are confused about what the movement's aims and goals were, what it accomplished and where it failed, and what our responsibilities are to complete its unfinished business today.

The movement's origins were in a bitter struggle for elementary civil rights, but it largely became, in the post-segregation era, a movement for political and economic power, and today black women and men hold office and wield power in numbers we only dreamed of before.

But despite impressive increases in the numbers of black people holding public office, despite our ability to sit and eat and ride and vote and attend school in places that used to bar black faces, in some important ways nonwhite Americans face problems more difficult to attack today than in years before.

The 1960s–1980s

Much of the origins of today's distresses are found in the recent past and came to climax in the 1980s.

Over time, opposition to government, especially Washington government, succeeded opposition to Communism as a secular religion. The United Nations, Washington bureaucrats, gays and lesbians, and supporters of minority and women's rights replaced the Soviet Union as the "evil empire," and together, these became the energies driving the callous coalition that captured Congress in 1994.

As long ago as 1964, Republicans had begun to remake their party as the white people's party, and they found a winning formula at the intersection of race and opposition to activist government. For much of the 1980s, America was presided over by an amiable ideologue whose sole intent was removing government from every aspect of our lives. He brought to power a band of financial and ideological profiteers who descended on the nation's capital like a crazed swarm of right-wing locusts, bent on destroying the rules and laws that protected our people from poisoned air and water and from greed. But nowhere was their assault on the rule of law so great as in their attempt to subvert, ignore, defy, and destroy the laws that required an America that is bias-free.

Today, thanks to judicial appointments by Presidents Reagan and Bush, the greatest threat to affirmative action comes from the courts—not, as the media would have us believe, from the anti-affirmative action preferences of the people.

Then, as now, they unleashed a gang of financial sociopaths to raid and ravage the national treasury.

Then, as now, they forced a form of triage economics upon us. Then it produced the first increase in infant mortality rates in twenty years and pushed thousands of poor and working poor Americans deeper into poverty.

By the mid 1980s, the Census Bureau reported that the number of Americans living in poverty had increased over the previous four years by 9 million, the biggest increase since these statistics were first collected over two decades ago. In the late 1960s, three-quarters of all black men were working; by the end of the 1980s, only 57 percent had a job.

Today's Conditions

Today, a significant portion of our population faces permanent privation, with the percentage of people living in poverty growing from 12.8 to 13.7 percent between 1989 and 1996.

Although we hear a lot these days about how well our economy is doing, we do not hear much about how poorly the average person does. Between 1990 and 1995, median family income actually declined while the number of people with a net worth over $1 million more than doubled.

The United States today is the most economically stratified of all industrial nations, the gap between rich and poor larger than in Britain, Italy, Canada, Germany, France, Finland—greater and rising faster than anywhere else.

Those years then were what these years now promise to be—a kind of festive party, thrown for America's rich.

Since 1979, the wages of the bottom 20 percent of workers have dropped nearly 12 percent. Workers at the bottom half of the wage scale make 75 cents less per hour than they did twenty years ago.

This at a time when the average executive earns 220 times what the average production worker is paid.

And for those workers whose skins are black or brown, the gap is greater and their prospects bleaker. Today, the net financial assets of black families in which one member has a postgraduate degree are lower than the assets of white families in which the highest level of education achieved is elementary school.

In 1968, the Kerner Commission, appointed by President Johnson to investigate the causes and prescribe the cures for the 1967 riots, concluded that "white racism" was the single most important cause of continued racial inequality in income, housing, employment, education, and life chances between blacks and whites.

Within a few short years, the growing numbers of blacks and other minorities and women, pushing for entry into and power in the academy, the media, business, government, and other traditionally white male institutions, created a backlash in the discourse over race. The previously privileged majority exploded in angry resentment at having to share space with the formerly excluded.

Opinion leaders began to reformulate and redefine the terms of the discussion. No longer was the Kerner Commission's description of the problem acceptable.

Any indictment of white America could be abandoned, and a Susan Smith defense was adopted—black people did it, did it to the country, and did it to themselves. Black behavior, not white racism, became the reason why whites and blacks lived in separate worlds. Racism retreated and pathology advanced. The burden of racial problem-solving shifted from racism's creators to its victims. The failure of the lesser breeds to enjoy society's fruits became their fault alone. In a kind of nonsensical tautology we heard again and again: these people are poor because they are pathological, they are pathological because they are poor.

Pressure for additional civil rights laws became special pleading. America's most privileged population, white men, suddenly became a victim class. Aggressive blacks and pushy women became responsible for America's demise.

All this occurred despite almost daily incidents of racial attack, and a series of public opinion polls that demonstrate most white Americans believe racial minorities are less than equal human beings, lacking in thrift, morality, industriousness, and patriotism.

Most Americans do not just believe minorities are suspect; they believe there are more of them than there actually are.

According to a Gallup Poll, the average American thinks that 18 percent of all Americans are Jewish; the real figure is 3 percent. The average American thinks that 21 percent of all Americans are Hispanic; the exact number is 8 percent; most Americans think that 32 percent of all Americans are black; the real figure, of course, is 12 percent.

For the average American, then, minorities are the majority: 71 percent of the national population.

The New Racism

This exaggeration of the other, this blame-shifting and role-reversal, where victim becomes perpetrator and minorities become majorities, this perversion of reality occurred as a result of an organized campaign that continues to this day.

It is led by a curious mix of whites and a few blacks, academics, journalists, and policymakers. Its aim is the demobilization of effective insurgent politics, the depoliticizing of discussions of our gross misdistribution of income, and the adoption of reactionary and punitive social policy.

Its adherents profess strong support for equal rights while opposing every tool designed to achieve this goal. They attack and discredit affirmative action, not simply because it threatens ancient white-skin privilege, but because it serves as a handy symbol of despised government intervention, and feeds the myths of black-caused white disadvantage.

For these new racists, equal opportunity is a burden that society cannot afford to bear. Their less than subtle message is that including blacks and women excludes quality.

The continuing disparity between black and white life chances is not a result of black life choices; it stems from epidemic racism and an economic system dependent on class division.

Abundant scholarship notwithstanding, there is no other possible explanation—not family breakdown, not lack of middle-class values, not lack of education and skills, not absence of role models. These are symptoms. Racism is the cause; its elimination is the cure.

But racism was no rationale for bad behavior even when it legitimized slavery and made people property; it ought be no excuse for anyone's failure to strive to live with decency now.

We must be careful not to define the ideology and practice of white supremacy too narrowly. It is greater than scrawled graffiti and individual indignity, the policeman's nightstick, the job or home or education denied. It is rooted deeply in the logic of our market system, in the culturally defined and politically enforced prices paid for different units of labor, and it is deeply entrenched in our national psyche.

Black Political Gains

The strategies of the 1960s movement were litigation, organization, mobilization, and civil disobedience, aimed at creating a national political constituency for civil rights advances.

In the 1970s, electoral strategies began to dominate, prompted by the increase in black votes engendered by the 1965 Voting Rights Act. The numbers of locally elected black officials multiplied, coinciding with a decline in political party organization, and, for many, the number of black voters sufficient to elect them became voters enough.

Forgotten in the wave of inaugurations of new black mayors was the plight of blue-collar blacks. Just as black workers began to win access to industrial jobs and organized labor, the jobs went offshore and labor declined in power and influence. President Nixon's plan to promote black capitalism as a cure for underdeveloped ghettoes was embraced by a growing generation of politically connected black entrepreneurs, and their cause gained ascendancy.

Some black elites joined white elites at the feeding trough.

Since the heady days of the 1960s, too many have concentrated too much on enriching too few, while the large numbers of working-class black Americans, like their counterparts in the larger society, have seen their plight ignored, their incomes shrink, and their jobs disappear.

Martin Luther King lost his life supporting a garbage workers' strike in Memphis; the right to decent work at decent pay remains as basic to human freedom as the right to vote.

"Negroes," King said in 1961, "are almost entirely a working people. There are pitifully few Negro millionaires and few Negro employers."

That there are more black millionaires today is a tribute to the movement King led; that there are proportionately fewer blacks working today is an indictment of our times and our economic system, a reflection of our failure to keep the movement coming on.

Everywhere black Americans face conditions different from but just as daunting as the bus back seats, fire hoses, and billy clubs of three decades ago.

On streets and sidewalks where many black Americans live, crime and violence are a frequent rule. As angry white men blow up buildings, angry black men blow each other away. These are not drive-by shootings or stranger shooting stranger; in most of these deaths, the killer and the victim knew each other. These are friend shooting friend.

Black Children

In America today, compared with a white child, a black child is one and a half times more likely to grow up in a family whose head did not finish high school.

> That child is two times as likely to be born to a teenage mother.
>
> That child is two and a half times more likely to be born with low birth weight.
>
> That child is three times more likely to live in a single-parent home.
>
> That child is four times more likely to have a mother who had no prenatal care.
>
> That child is four and a half times more likely to live with neither parent.
>
> That child is five times as likely to depend solely on a mother's earnings.
>
> That child is nine times as likely to be a victim of homicide as a teenager or young adult, the end of a long, winding, uphill struggle to beat the racial odds against success.

In life chances, life expectancy, and median income—by all the standards by which life is measured—black Americans see a deep gulf between the American dream and the reality of their lives.

Affirmative Action

For the last thirty-five years—the period of the second Reconstruction—the most effective tool for advancing entry into mainstream American life has been affirmative action.

Opponents now try to tell us that it does not work, or it used to work but it does not now and is not needed now; when it does work, it only helps people who do not need it. Their real problem is that it does work, and despite limits, where it works it works well.

These opponents argue that the beneficiaries of race-centered affirmative action are "profiting" from it, as if its goals were comparable to an investment shared by a greedy few, a sub-tribe of dusky Donald Trumps and ebony Ivan Boeskys trading up life's ladder.

There is never "profit" in receiving right treatment. Receiving rights that others already enjoy is no benefit or badge of privilege; it is the natural order of things in a democratic society.

Affirmative action really is not about preferential treatment for blacks; it is about removing preferential treatment that whites have received through history, giving equal treatment to people who were denied equality in the past.

Affirmative action is not a poverty program, and ought not be blamed for failing to solve problems it was not designed to solve. It is a program designed to counter racial discrimination, not poverty. No one beat Rodney King because he was poor.

Affirmative action created the sizeable middle class that constitutes one-third of all black Americans today.

In the late 1960s, the wages of black women in the textile industry tripled. From 1970 to 1990, the number of black police officers more than doubled; the number of black electricians tripled and black bank tellers more than quadrupled. The percentage of blacks in managerial and technical jobs doubled. The number of black college students increased from 330,000 in the mid 1960s to more than 1 million eighteen years later.

These are not just numbers. They represent the growth and spread of the tiny middle class I knew as a boy into a stable one-third of all black Americans today, black women and men with jobs and homes, productive tax-paying citizens, able to provide for their families now and in the future.

Without affirmative action, both white and blue collars around black necks would shrink, with a huge, depressive effect on black income, employment, home ownership, and education.

"Color-Blind"

This is because racism is alive and all too well in America. Those who would have us believe otherwise, and who argue for a return to a color-blind America that never was, who would have us believe that their opposition to affirmative action is rooted in a desire for fairness and equality, are engaged in justification, rationalization, and downright prevarication. We have long heard these arguments from white racists—they are joined today by black self-haters and apologists, too.

They are color-blind, all right—blind to the consequences of being the wrong color in America today.

Let me tell you what they say. It is the fourth quarter of a football game between the white team and the black team. The white team is ahead 145 to 3. The white team owns the ball, the field, the goalposts, the uniforms, and the referees. They have been cheating since the game began. There are two minutes left to play. Suddenly, the white quarterback, who feels bad about things that happened before he entered the game, says, "Can't we just play fair?"

But in the double-speak used by the opponents of affirmative action, "fair" does not mean fair.

They just will not quit. They argue that affirmative action stigmatizes all blacks, making black beneficiaries and all others feel as if they have received some benefit they do not deserve.

Did you ever hear that argument made about the millions of whites who got into college as a "legacy" because Dad is an alumnus? Or the whites who got good jobs because Dad was president of the company? You never see them walking around with heads held low, eyes hidden, moaning that they have lost their self-esteem because everyone in the executive washroom is whispering about how they got their job.

As of the late 1990s, white males are 92 percent of the U.S. Senate, 80 percent of the U.S. House, 90 percent of the nation's newspaper editors, and 80 percent of the tenured faculty at the nation's colleges and universities. I seriously doubt if any of these men are suffering low self-esteem or other stigma because their race and gender helped them win these positions.

Affirmative action's poster child, Justice Clarence Thomas, argues that affirmative action makes black people feel bad. If that is so, why would 95 percent of Houston's black voters elect to retain a policy that made them feel bad? But Thomas may be right. Ever since he got his most recent affirmative action job, he has been in a foul and nasty mood.

As quiet as it is kept, Martin Luther King supported affirmative action. The critics like to quote his dream from 1963, that one day his children would be judged by the content of their character and not by the color of their skin.

It was a dream then; it is a dream now.

He said in 1963: "Whenever the issue of preferential treatment for the Negro is raised, some of our friends recoil in horror. The Negro should be granted equality, they agree: but he should ask for nothing more. On the surface, this appears reasonable, but it is not realistic."

In 1967 he said: "A society that has done something special *against* the Negro for hundreds of years must now do something special *for* him."

We tend today to look back on the King years with some nostalgia, as if those were the only years in which we were truly able to overcome.

Our inability to do so today is caused, at least in part, by the way we recall Dr. King. For most of us he is little more than an image seen in grainy black-and-white television films taken in Washington three decades ago, the gifted preacher who had a dream.

But King, of course, was much more than that, and the movement was much more than Martin Luther King.

We All Benefit

For too many people today, the fight for equal justice is a spectator sport, a kind of National Basketball Association in which all the players are black and all the spectators are white.

But in this true-to-life competition between good and evil, the players are of every color and condition, the fate of all the fans tied to the points scored on the floor. When good prevails, all the spectators win, too.

When four little girls died thirty-eight years ago in a Birmingham church bombing, astronaut Sally Ride won the right to shoot the moon.

Because young, black people faced arrest at Southern lunch counters thirty-five years ago, the law their bodies wrote now protects older Americans from age discrimination, protects Jews and Moslems and Christians from religious discrimination, and protects the disabled from exclusion because of their condition.

It took but one woman's courage to start a movement in Montgomery, and the bravery of four young men in Greensboro to set the South on fire. Surely there are men and women, young and old, who today can do the same.

Now the ancient forces of evil, appearing in new faces, threaten America again. They are determined to create an anorectic America, too starved and weak to protect the hungry, the forgotten, and the poor.

The current civil rights scene in the United States is dismal, but not without hope.

My grandfather James Bond's words, from 1892, might well be remembered here.

> The pessimist from his corner looks out upon the world of wickedness and sin, and blinded by all that is good or hopeful in the condition and progress of the human race, bewails the present state of affairs and predicts woeful things for the future.
>
> In every cloud he beholds a destructive storm, in every flash of lightning an omen of evil, and in every shadow that falls across his path a lurking foe.
>
> But he forgets that the clouds also bring life and hope, that the lightning purifies the atmosphere, that shadow and darkness prepare for sunshine and growth, and that hardships and adversity nerve the race, as the individual, for greater efforts and grander victories.

Greater efforts and grander victories. That was his generation's promise 109 years ago. That was the promise made by the generation that won the great world war for democracy five and a half decades ago. That was the promise made by those who brought democracy to America's darkest corners three and a half decades ago, and that is the promise we must seek to honor today.

This is an edited version of Bond's May 27, 1998, National Press Club speech.

"Preserving the Ways of My Ancestors" was the title of an 800-word letter to the editor in the February 6, 1999, Washington Post *from Jared Taylor, board member of the Council of Conservative Citizens, the organization built by supporters of the segregationist White Citizens Councils, the John Birch Society, and Alabama Governor George C. Wallace's 1964 presidential campaign. Taylor put forward the superficially reasonable argument that while Blacks and Hispanics do not have to apologize for forming caucuses, celebrating openly racial holidays, taking pride in their race, preferring the culture and company of other Blacks and Hispanics, "it is only whites who are forbidden to have an explicitly racial identity, and when they express loyalties non-whites take for granted, they are accused of 'bigotry.'" Taylor's words and claims had a familiar ring, echoing a passage from John Barry's superb 1997 book* Rising Tide: The Great Mississippi Flood of 1927 and How It Changed America. *Describing a speech by Ku Klux Klan organizer Colonel Joseph Camp at a Klan rally in Greenville, Barry writes: "[Camp] pumped his arms, pounded fist against lectern, strode the length of the platform and back, preaching pride: Pride in America! Pride in Mississippi! Pride in the white race! Then he began to preach hate. . . . Jews were organized! Catholics were organized! Niggers were organized! The only people in America who weren't organized were the Anglo-Saxons!"*

We asked sociologist Howard Winant of Temple University to provide a response to Taylor's claims, since such superficially reasonable arguments seem to be appearing regularly and attracting support.

Wake Up, Jared Taylor! America is a Democracy Now!

Howard Winant

Jared Taylor obligingly lists his "bigoted views" for our benefit in his letter, "Preserving the Ways of My Ancestors."

First, he informs us that "race is a significant biological characteristic of our species." But "race" is not a biological matter. It is a social concept, a way of classifying human beings into groups based on appearance or phenotype. Sure, people look different, but particular characteristics selected to do this classifying are arbitrary. Skin color counts, but height, say, does not. We could have a short people race (remember that Randy Newman song?), but we do not. Why not? Because historically, Europeans conquered the Americas and enslaved Africans. They needed ways of telling who was who, and so seized on certain physical characteristics to set up the necessary inequalities. At one time, poor immigrant groups like Irish and Jews were also considered to be "races."

A second type of bigotry is ethnocentrism. "It is natural and moral for people to prefer the society and way of life of people like themselves," Taylor claims. The idea here is that what is different is threatening; conversely, what is the same is reassuring and safe. Besides making exaggerated assumptions about human nature, how could people learn anything, meet strangers, maintain the variety necessary for healthy reproduction, or organize a democratic political life (just to pick a few counter-examples) if it were "natural," much less "moral," always to stick to themselves?

Bigotry number three is projection: by defining your adversary as the bad guy, you can make yourself look good. "Many blacks make race the centerpiece of their identities, as do many Hispanics. . . . It is only whites who are forbidden to have an explicitly racial identity." But if Taylor had stayed awake in his history class, he would have learned more about the centuries in which preservation of white identity was the top priority in America. There were antimiscegenation laws, for example. The "one-drop of blood" rule evolved to classify anyone with even a little "black blood" as all-the-way black. Scholars and politicians beat the drums against "primitive blacks" and the "yellow peril." Serious thought was devoted (in the racist eugenics movement) to the problem of how the supposedly "more advanced" whites could "outbreed" the inferior "lesser races." This tendency is not dead yet; look at the hogwash of *The Bell Curve*. So whites are as committed as anyone else to highlighting, preserving, and protecting their sacred racial identity. This is all the more true when you want to stay at the top of the heap.

Taylor's fourth and final bigotry is normalization: the idea that the way you do things, the way your group operates, is normal and regular. It is only those who are different from you, those "others," who are strange. "Why should whites hand over the country to people unlike themselves?," Taylor asks. Funny, I thought we whites had given up the idea that America was a "white man's country" a while back. It is ironic, not to say pitiful and profoundly wrong, that Taylor and his friends in the Council of Conservative Citizens (CCC) still think the country belongs to them, to whites, and that it could thus be "handed over" to others, to "people unlike themselves."

Wake up, Jared. After you pinch yourself a few times, go ahead and pinch Trent Lott, Bob Barr, and your other CCC friends too. This is the end of the twentieth, not the eighteenth century. Slavery is over. America is a democracy now. White, black, brown, yellow, and red can share the country peaceably. But to accomplish this we must overcome the remaining residue of white supremacy, the whiff of bigotry evident in your article, the legacy left you, no doubt, by some of your white ancestors.

Digging Out of the White Trap

Marian (Meck) Groot and Paul Marcus

In a television interview with Toni Morrison about her novel, *Paradise*, Charlie Rose asked whether Morrison thought she would ever stop writing about race. His question seemed to assume that books written about black people are about race, while books about whites written by white authors are not—an assumption Rose shares with the dominant white culture that white is generic and that white people's experience is universal. It is this assumption that is finally being recognized by a growing number of white people, though it has been understood by many people of color for as long as racism has been around. Morrison's response: there is no writing that is not about race.

There is a growing body of literature and analysis (see accompanying Resources box on page 18) that can help white people see that whiteness, though made to appear invisible to whites, is in fact a dynamic force that is used daily to oppress those who are not white and to privilege those of us who are. This invisibility is in large part what locks racism in place. As long as we do not have to see and acknowledge that we are given benefits and privileges simply because we are members of the dominant group, we can name racism as "black people's problem" or "Native Americans' problem" or the problem of some "Other." And as long as we can each assume an identity as an individual rather than as a member of the white race, we do not have to take any responsibility for racism.

Let us define a few terms. For us, race is not a biological category, but rather an economic, social, and political construct. Racism in the United States is the institutionalized power held by white people and kept in place by the authority whites have to make and enforce decisions, to set standards of acceptability, to name reality, and to access resources. Because it promotes the belief that white people and white culture are superior to all others, racism is the institutionalization of white supremacy.

As educators and organizers who have done antiracism work for many years, we find these definitions provide a useful analysis for our work. This definition of race allows us to talk about a white race, and the definition of racism allows us to talk about a white problem. But what is whiteness?

This question has become a subject of interest to an increasing number of activists, educators, scholars, and artists. That 300 people from cities around the United States, Canada, and Europe came to the second annual National Conference on Whiteness: Exploring Whiteness to End Racism (held in November, 1997, in Cambridge, Massachusetts) evidences the growing interest.

As we planned the conference, we began to see something of the range of perspectives on the meaning and relevance of whiteness. The question of whom the conference was for came up often and in different ways. Some of the conference planners believe that since racism is a product of whiteness, it is white people who need to confront it. Others believe that racism will only be eliminated when we create multiracial spaces that are truly multicultural. Some of us believe that the world is not ready for multiculturalism and will not be until white people deal with the legacy of whiteness. Others of us find no problem with monocultural spaces and communities, provided no community has the power to impose its way on others.

We believe that in terms of addressing issues of race and racism, white people and people of color have different work to do. Though it is important for us to check in with each other and to come together for some of our work, whites must wade through the layers of our racism in order to learn not to monopolize power and privilege, while people of color must wade through the layers of internalized racism to learn to claim power. In our experience, whiteness as a topic is not particularly attractive to many people of color; it was no surprise that they represented only 10 to 15 percent of participants at our conference.

In terms of class, we agreed that the conference needed to be accessible to people from all socioeconomic backgrounds. This was much harder in deed than in word. Conferences tend to attract those who have the luxury of time and space to think, talk, and write about their experience or the experiences of others. It is not clear how thinking, talking, and writing change the daily-lived reality of people most marginalized by racism and poverty. Conferences, by their very nature, do not attract working-class and poor people. Furthermore, in terms of class, it is hard to imagine why poor and working-class white people would be attracted to a discussion of whiteness, since typically there is the perception that only "trashy" white people need to claim their whiteness. The stereotypical white supremacist is a poor, uneducated, white person. This stereotype allows middle- and upper-class white people to see racism as a problem of poor whites. This excuses middle- and upper-class whites from their own racism, and further stigmatizes white poor people as being "beyond help." It is easy for us to accuse whites living in segregated housing projects in such places as South Boston, for example, of being racist, yet we do not typically make the same accusation of whites living in highly segregated wealthy suburbs such as Wellesley or Newton.

Schools of Thought

The group known as New Abolitionists argues that the white race is a historically constructed social formation that consists of all those who partake of the privileges of having white skin in our society. They believe that the solution to our social problems is to abolish the white race, i.e., to abolish white supremacy. Until this is accomplished, no real reform can occur because white influence permeates all issues in U.S. society. While they acknowledge that much of the work being done in whiteness studies comes from an antiracist perspective, they are concerned that by keeping whiteness as a category, we provide legitimacy to white nationalists.

Multiculturists tend to come in two categories. There are those who ignore power differences and believe we can solve our problems by bringing everyone to the table and having them get to know each other's cultures. They believe that in this process, prejudices and stereotypes will break down and disappear. Multiculturists with an antiracist perspective believe that multicultural space can only be created when all groups have equal access to power. Therefore, issues of institutionalized power and privilege for whites must be dealt with.

Critical Race theory, White Racial Identity theory, and Feminist theory on race are all academy-based examinations of race, racism, and racial formation. Critical Race theorists are interested in how white supremacy is written into the nation's laws. We are a nation of laws, and therefore examination of the ways in which racism is infused into our laws and legal institutions provides a deep understanding of how we as a people believe we ought to behave. White Racial Identity theory comes out of counseling psychology. It focuses on the stages whites go through in developing a positive white identity that includes confronting racism and oppression in daily life. Feminist theory is grounded in an examination of inequality between men and women, but also examines power differences among women because of differences in race, class, sexuality, etc.

While it is useful to list these various perspectives, our interest in them is the degree to which they help us as white people recognize our whiteness as well as its attendant privileges, and to create and follow through on strategies that seek to eliminate racism. While we believe that much of this work must be done by whites for whites, we also believe firmly in maintaining

Readings

Delgado, Richard and Jean Stefancic. *Critical White Studies: Looking Behind the Mirror* Philadelphia: Temple University Press, 1997.

Fine, Michele et al., eds. *Off White: Readings on Race, Power and Society.* New York: Routledge, 1997.

Frankenberg, Ruth. *White Women, Race Matters: The Social Construction of Whiteness.* Minneapolis: University of Minnesota Press, 1993.

————. *Displacing Whiteness: Essays in Social Change and Cultural Criticism.* Durham: Duke University Press, 1997.

Harris, Cheryl. "Whiteness as Property." In *Critical Race Theory: The Key Writings That Formed the Movement,* eds. Kimberlé Crenshaw et al. New York: New Press, 1995.

Hill, Mike. *Whiteness: A Critical Reader.* New York: New York University Press, 1997.

Ignatiev, Noel. *How the Irish Became White.* New York: Routledge, 1997.

Ignatiev, Noel, and John Garvey, eds. *Race Traitor.* New York: Routledge, 1996.

Lipsitz, George. *The Possessive Investment in Whiteness: How White People Profit from Identity Politics.* Philadelphia: Temple University Press, 1998.

Morrison, Toni. *Playing in the Dark.* New York: Vintage, 1993.

Roediger, David R. *The Wages of Whiteness: Race and the Making of the American Working Class.* New York: Verso, 1991.

Segrest, Mab. *Memoir of a Race Traitor.* Boston: South End, 1993.

Wray, Matt, and Annalee Newitz, eds. *White Trash: Race and Class in America.* New York: Routledge, 1997.

Organizations

- Center for the Study of White American Culture, 245 West 4th Ave., Roselle, NJ 07203; 908/241–5439; contact@euroamerican.org; www.euroamerican.org
- Sparking Powerful Anti Racist Collaboration (SPARC), 56 Lincoln Rd., Sudbury, MA 01776; 800/686–4809; lschecter@pobox.com
- People's Institute for Survival and Beyond, 1444 N. Johnson St., New Orleans, LA 70116; 504/944–2354; pisabnola@aol.com
- Challenging White Supremacy Workshop, 2440 16th St., PMB #275, San Francisco, CA 94103; 415/647–0921.

that whites get feedback from communities of color for the work we do and remain accountable as we push forward any agendas that have implications for all of us. Creating the systems whereby we do this with integrity is one of the major challenges before us as this movement swells.

Losing One's Identity

While we are trained to believe that the elimination of racism is something we do for people of color, it is also about what it does for us. Maintaining privilege at the expense of truth, integrity, and connection harms us as spiritual beings. In *The Fire Next Time*, James Baldwin writes to his nephew:

> They [white people] are in effect still trapped in a history they do not understand; and until they understand it, they cannot be released from it. They have had to believe for many years, and for innumerable reasons, that Black men are inferior to white men. Many of them, indeed, know better, but, as you will discover, people find it very difficult to act on what they know. To act is to be committed, and to be committed is to be in danger. In this case, the danger, in the minds of most white Americans, is the loss of their identity.

Losing one's identity is very scary. Much of the psychological violence of white supremacy can be described as targeting and creating a loss of identity among people of color. White people fear this and will take risks only if they can see the promise of a new identity to emerge from the old loss. We may not have to say what that identity is at this point; we simply assert that it is something we need to reach for.

Risking the loss of our identity as whites will take nothing less than spiritual transformation. This cannot be a head thing—though we will need our heads. The antiracist perspective we bring to our work is vital, but it is not enough. Each of us will have to find whatever spiritual resources will allow us to "accept equality, or die" (W.E.B. DuBois).

Response

Chip Berlet and Surina Khan

We agree with Marian Groot and Paul Marcus that White people need to take responsibility for (and redefine) Whiteness. However, a major stumbling block in discussions of racism and other forms of oppression is the lack of agreement over terminology. We find the definitions offered by Groot and Marcus narrow and confusing.

Racism around the world includes many forms other than White supremacy, which is the particular ideology of racism in the United States to justify disproportionate power and privilege accorded to White people. Yet there are other major forms of oppression that represent Eurocentrism (which has hegemonic influence over more U.S. institutions). These include sexism, heterosexism, Christian chauvinism, and a classism that champions idealized Darwinistic capitalism.

We would argue that an "ism" is an ideological worldview that may or may not be institutionalized or have dominant power in society. Oppression is generated when supremacy has power, and this power can exist on an individual and societal level; and when societal, may be institutionalized in customs and norms, or even codified in laws.

If the problem is largely a refusal of "white people" to acknowledge their dominance and their identity, maybe it is time for *Poverty & Race* (and the rest of us) to start capitalizing "White" when discussing the primary form of U.S. racism. More importantly, it is certainly time for White people to lead the discussion of White racism among Whites. The trick is to do this without patronizing people of color or displacing people of color leadership in the struggle for racial justice—and to recognize that most people calling for new White identity dream of Nordic festivals staging Wagner operas.

Race and Space

john a. powell

Through urban sprawl and racialized concentrated poverty, race plays a significant role in creating and maintaining fragmented metropolitan regions. The outer-ring suburbs of metropolitan areas are overwhelmingly white (although more recently minorities, in particular middle-class blacks, have participated in the move to the suburbs), and the inner cities are populated largely by people of color, especially blacks. The federal government alone has spent over a trillion dollars through sprawl subsidies to create and support the jurisdictional segregation that is now the norm in our metropolitan landscape. While the government paid for and subsidized white flight from central cities through Federal Housing Administration (FHA) and Veterans Administration (VA) mortgage insurance and guarantees, tax policies, and highway and other infrastructure investments, it also divested the inner cities of their resources and the people of color living in those cities of their opportunities.

This spatial and racial pattern makes sharing or fairly distributing regional benefits almost impossible. White suburbanites resist regional strategies, reluctant to embrace something that will have negative economic consequences for them—which is rational, albeit shortsighted. Blacks also resist regional solutions because they fear a loss of cultural control or identity and a loss of political power.

Ignoring these claims from the minority community is a serious mistake. Doing so makes a regional solution into just one more solution imposed by whites on people of color. Given the history of white and non-white relations in this country, particularly around the development of sprawl and metropolitan fragmentation, this is simply untenable. At a more practical level, in regions with a substantial minority population, regional approaches that do not engage the minority community will have difficulty gaining the necessary support. But regional solutions are imperative because a number of important inner-city problems are caused by regional forces, and thus can only be adequately addressed at the regional level. Failure to adopt regional strategies adversely affects the central cities; failure to address central city problems adversely affects the entire region.

We need a regional approach that gives cities or communities a way to maintain appropriate control of their political and cultural institutions, while sharing in regional resources and balancing regional policymaking. We need an approach that avoids the myopia of local, fragmented governance and the blunt regionalism exercised by an overarching unit of government, such as a county or state, which can suffocate local governments.

Some Race History

The economic and political isolation of poor minorities in the inner cities is caused by flight or sprawl, and fragmentation. The movement further away from the central cities to the suburbs is sprawl. The creation of rigid boundaries, which separate municipalities from each other, and more importantly from the central core, is fragmentation. As a result of these forces, minorities find themselves in neighborhoods of concentrated poverty, where four out of ten of their neighbors (or they themselves) are poor. Of the more than 8.2 million people who live in these areas, more than half are black, a quarter are Hispanic.

The residential segregation and concentration of poverty in neighborhoods inhabited by blacks did not come about accidentally. It was constructed and is perpetuated through historical forces, including government housing and transportation policies, institutional practices, and private behaviors. At the turn of the century, black Americans comprised 12 percent (almost 9 million) of the American population, and 90 percent (almost 8 million) of black Americans still lived in the Confederate Old South. While the same level of residential segregation that exists today did not exist at the turn of the century, blacks in the North and South were socially and economically segregated and subjugated by a number of practices, including Jim Crow laws and racial terrorism. Blacks were denied the right to vote, serve on juries, hold many jobs, and attend integrated schools. In short, blacks were not politically, economically, or socially equal to whites; they remained less than full citizens.

During the Industrial Revolution, the preferred labor pool of white European immigrants began to dry up, initially during World War I, then more severely during and after World War II. So the North began to hire blacks from the South. It was during this time that blacks started moving to Northern cities in record numbers. During the height of the Great Migration, the trickle of blacks from the rural South to the urban North became a torrent, as 5 million blacks moved to the North after 1940.

In the 1940s and 1950s, the FHA pursued an explicit policy against insuring mortgages for homes in minority or integrated neighborhoods, and preferred to back new construction rather than the purchase of existing units. Essentially, FHA paid whites to leave the central cities and confined blacks to the central cities, which were, in turn, divested by the federal government and private capital. The national highway program facilitated exit from the central cities and destabilized many urban neighborhoods. "Urban renewal" efforts destroyed stable black neighborhoods. Local governments have also contributed to the problems of segregation and concentrated poverty through the ongoing practice of exclusionary zoning (requiring large minimum lot sizes or banning multifamily housing), which makes it nearly impossible for poor families to find affordable housing in white suburban communities. Similar private measures included but are not limited to the practice of blockbusting by the real estate profession and the creation of racially restrictive covenants by homeowners.

The concentrated poverty that these kinds of policies create is usually ruinous to people's life chances. High levels of crime, drug use, and other social pathologies emerge and become self-perpetuating. In addition to this poor quality of life, residents experience severely limited social and economic opportunities. The quality of schools, housing, and municipal services, and the availability of transportation and employment are undermined.

The Role of the Courts

In 1950, 60 percent of Americans living in metropolitan areas still lived in the central cities. The city was still the regional hub for jobs, a strong tax base, decent housing, good schools, retail and other opportunities. This picture changed rapidly as the suburban population doubled between 1950 and 1970, and by 1990 the suburbs contained two-thirds of the metropolitan population, while only one-third remained in the central cities. Cities with many needs and few resources suffer from infrastructure deficit.

During the 1950s and 1960s, the Supreme Court, responding to the growing demands for racial justice, was beginning to break down a racial caste system inscribed in law. At the same time, however, the court, along with other powerful government and nongovernmental institutions, was establishing "American apartheid": racial segregation re-inscribed in jurisdictional boundaries. With the population shift from central cities to suburbs, a jurisdictional shift occurred as well. In 1950, 60 percent of America's metropolitan residents lived in just 193 jurisdictions. By 1990, almost 70 percent of the metropolitan population lived in 9,600 suburban jurisdictions, indicating the shift to a more fragmented regional structure. This process of land use planning has aptly been called "land use war."

Jobs also relocated to the suburbs, and the central city's strong tax base soon followed. It was no coincidence that these shifts occurred shortly after large numbers of blacks moved into urban areas. The fracturing of metropolitan areas is almost always a racially motivated method of excluding blacks. In order for this racial sorting to work, however, suburbs had to both attract whites and exclude blacks. Federal and state governments normalized these practices in our society by creating incentives for whites to move to the suburbs, while erecting barriers preventing blacks from doing the same. Barriers to the suburbs were not only economic but also racial, as many low-income whites were able to gain access to the suburbs while access was denied to blacks through redlining, racial steering, and discriminatory zoning practices. These numerous small white communities used their expanding autonomy to further capture resources and opportunities while excluding blacks and other minorities.

Although the Supreme Court supported desegregation within cities by ending *de jure* segregation, it simultaneously supported segregation of the region along jurisdictional lines through the constitutionalization of "local control." Federal courts made constitutional the concept of "local control" despite preexisting federal law that said cities were not entities unto themselves, thereby setting the stage for reestablishment of a racial hierarchy that reconfigured, but maintained, white supremacy and black subordination. "Local control" has been used to justify the segregated and fragmented jurisdictional structure of sprawl; it is the primary enforcement mechanism for racially exclusionary practices, and it appears to be a perfectly legal method of ensuring racial subordination under current federal law. Two areas of particular significance in the "local control" movement are land use practices or exclusionary zoning and protection of local control over education.

School desegregation litigation provides an example of how white suburbanization under the concept of "local control" has undermined the Civil Rights Movement. Despite almost fifty years of litigation since *Brown*, most black, and an increasing number of Latino, children attend racially and economically segregated schools in areas that have supposedly been desegregated under federal law. The Supreme Court fostered this arrangement by striking down explicit segregation at the intra-jurisdictional level while upholding it at the inter-jurisdictional level.

One of the most important rulings that supported this arrangement was the 1973 *Milliken v. Bradley* case. The Supreme Court, basing its decision on the importance of local control, would not allow the lower court to order a desegregation remedy for Detroit's discriminatory school district that included Detroit's suburbs. The court held that the suburban districts could not be incorporated into the desegregation remedy because they had not been found to intentionally segregate their districts—despite the fact that the Detroit school district was overwhelmingly comprised of students of color and the suburban districts were overwhelmingly white. The court ignored the claim that a segregated housing market on a jurisdictional level was causing inter-district school segregation. Instead, the court suggested that these segregative housing patterns were unexplainable and beyond the purview of the court.

Milliken sent a message to whites that neighborhood-level segregation within the city would not be acceptable, but the suburbs would be a safe haven from desegregation. And the message to blacks was that there were limits to how far the court would go to achieve racial justice, and those limits very closely matched the city limits.

This white suburban wall began to crack for middle-income blacks after passage of the Fair Housing Act of 1968. As a result, middle-income blacks have begun to move to the suburbs in record numbers. However, they are often resegregated in the suburbs and remain isolated from the more powerful white suburbs that still capture most of the opportunities and resources. During this same period, low-income people of color have been consigned to resource-depleted cities, isolated from the opportunities that brought blacks to the North fifty years ago. This isolation has caused an explosion of racialized concentrated poverty at the urban core. Growth in black and brown concentrated poverty at the urban core is almost always associated with white, upper middle-class, fragmented sprawl at the edge of the region. Racial subordination has taken on a different form: through the mechanisms of metropolitan fragmentation and sprawl, blacks have again been subordinated socially, politically, and economically. By racializing space through the spatial isolation of blacks and other minorities, we have achieved many of the negative racial conditions formally held in place with Jim Crow laws, thus frustrating the civil rights goals of the 1950s and 1960s.

The Metropolitan Area in Black and White

When one part of a region becomes dysfunctional, the entire area is compromised. This is what is happening with the inner cities and older suburbs through fragmentation and sprawl—their difficulties are negatively affecting entire regions. Among other things, a poor and racially segregated urban core harms the reputation of the metropolitan region as a whole and makes it less inviting to international, national, and local businesses, as well as to families looking for homes.

But white suburbanites have traditionally resisted claims like these that tie them to the inner city. The justification for this resistance changes over time. The current justification is that the "culture of poverty" found in the inner cities will infiltrate protected suburban enclaves—a justification that is simply a new name for a long-standing racism directed toward the central cities.

White segregationism, or resistance to regionalism, manifests itself in support of in-place strategies. Such strategies attempt to move resources and opportunities to low-income central city residents, and to generate improvements in urban neighborhoods of color, as opposed to mobility oriented schemes, which aim to disperse central city residents to existing opportunities. Whites want to keep minorities "immobile" and out of their suburban neighborhoods.

In-place strategies frequently receive support from minorities as well, though for different reasons. One motivation is the preservation of cultural identity. As Cornel West and others have argued, deconcentration of minorities can result in both assimilation of minorities who are pocketed in more affluent areas and dilution of culture in predominantly black areas.

Minorities also fear the erosion of political power and the loss of control over the political process if the political base of their communities diminishes or the minority population is dispersed throughout the region. Minorities would often rather retain this control even if opportunity structures were lacking in their communities. Political power is actually a very complex issue. On the one hand, the geographic concentration of minorities does not guarantee their political cohesion. Nor, given the challenges to majority-minority legislative districts, does it guarantee the election of minority candidates. (See "New Means for Political Empowerment," pp. 176–183.) Even if minority candidates do win office, they are likely to be isolated in the legislature. But on the other hand, mobility and the resulting dispersion of blacks throughout a metropolitan area may generate a backlash in some places, reducing black political power. There is evidence of a white backlash against black interests when the black population rises above 30 percent of a voting district. While a mobility strategy seems to be a better choice for the creation and maintenance of economic power for communities of color, it is likely to undermine political power.

In fact, both mobility and in-place strategies by themselves are limited, because they address only part of the problem. One proposes political and cultural control of areas isolated and starved of economic resources; the other proposes the possibility of access to resources at the cost of a stifled political voice and cultural assimilation or marginalization. These one-sided approaches must be rejected because they fail to address both the economic and concentrated poverty issues of the central core, while at the same time respecting the right to effective participation in political and cultural institutions.

Federated Regionalism as a Response to Minority Resistance

Federated regionalism attempts to balance both mobility and in-place approaches by allowing entities within a metropolitan region to cooperate on some levels and remain separate on others. It is based on two premises: (1) many important issues within the inner cities and older suburbs can be adequately addressed only at a regional level; and (2) some issues are local in nature and are thus more effectively addressed by a local government.

A federated approach recognizes the regional nature of racial and economic segregation and provides a solution that integrates regional policymaking with local governance. An example is tax-base sharing that, as practiced in Minnesota's Twin Cities, distributes the regional tax base according to regional needs without compromising local interests. Each city is allocated a certain share of the regional tax base but controls the tax rate for its residents, thereby maintaining authority and discretion over local issues. Another example is Portland, Oregon's regional housing strategy. There, the regional governing body sets requirements for affordable housing, but municipalities maintain responsibility for zoning and how they choose to meet their share of the regional housing need.

While strategies of federated regionalism such as these can provide a balance between local governance and regional concerns, not all federated strategies strike that balance. Those that fail to do so can actually perpetuate regional fragmentation. An example is Indianapolis's Uni-Gov, which made regional many areas of governance but left the schools under existing local segregated boundaries. The ideal balance between "local" and "federated" must be responsive to concerns of communities of color and the problems of concentrated poverty. It is critical that racial minorities participate in the effort to strike that balance.

Minorities have cause to be wary of regional solutions to the problems of segregation and concentrated poverty. What little political power they wield seems at risk of dilution if regionalism further fragments their communities. In searching for regional strategies, we must steer between two extremes. One is to be so jealous of local control as to preserve political and cultural control, but in areas that are isolated and starved of economic resources. The other extreme is a regionalism that offers access to resources at the cost of a stifled political voice and cultural assimilation or marginalization. We need a metropolitan approach that addresses both the economic and concentrated poverty issues of the central core, while respecting the right to effective participation in political and cultural institutions.

Tensions in metropolitan planning between local concerns and the needs of the whole metropolitan region are healthy. Structuring these tensions in a way that leads to true democratic cooperation in addressing fragmentation and sprawl—cooperation that transcends racial polarization—is the challenge.

Telling History on the Landscape

James W. Loewen

American history is taught so poorly in high school that it interferes with students' ability to think about contemporary race relations and poverty issues. I backed that sentence, which I hope got your attention, with three chapters of analysis in my 1995 book, *Lies My Teacher Told Me: Everything Your High School History Textbook Got Wrong*. After the Civil Rights Movement, authors did improve their treatments of slavery and Reconstruction. No longer do they portray slavery primarily as an acculturation tool that was toughest on the hardworking Master and Mistress. Now they even quote spirituals like "Nobody Knows the Trouble I've Seen."

Although slavery is over, racism—slavery's handmaiden—hardly disappeared in 1863 or 1865. It still haunts our society as slavery's legacy to the present. Racism is invisible in American history textbooks, however, and in most high school history courses taught from them. I surveyed twelve history textbooks to write *Lies My Teacher Told Me*. Only five of the twelve list racism, racial prejudice, or anything beginning with "race" in their indexes; I also searched under "white racism," "white supremacy," and every other heading I could imagine. Nor is this merely bad indexing, for I scrutinized the texts themselves, to no avail.

The mentions of racism in five textbooks are just that—mentions. Even more crippling to Americans' ability to think about race relations today is the omission, in high school American history courses, of causation. When history textbooks do mention racism, they do not relate it to any historical cause. Here is the longest treatment of racism in any of the twelve books I examined: "[African Americans] looked different from members of white ethnic groups. The color of their skin made assimilation difficult. For this reason they remained outsiders."

This passage is a retreat from history to lay psychology of a "human nature" sort. Unfortunately for its argument, skin color in itself does not explain racism. Jane Elliot's demonstrations in her Iowa classroom, made famous by the PBS *Frontline* video "A Class Divided," show that children can quickly develop discriminatory behavior and prejudiced beliefs based on eye color. Conversely, the leadership positions that African Americans frequently reached among Native American nations show that people do not automatically discriminate against others on the basis of skin color.

To comprehend racism, one must understand its role as rationale for race-based slavery. Not one textbook discusses the relationship of racism and slavery. Therefore, students are crippled from thinking rationally about this most emotional issue. Of course, treating slavery's enduring legacy today would be controversial.

Where might young Americans go to remedy this deficiency? Having been bored to tears by their high school history courses, five-sixths of them never take a course in American history beyond high school. Americans do, however, display considerable interest in their past, and one way is by stopping at historical markers and monuments and visiting historic sites. Accordingly, I have spent several years studying historic sites, as summarized in *Lies Across America: What Our Historic Markers and Monuments Get Wrong* (1999).

In some ways, historic sites are even worse than high school textbooks. Most historic markers and monuments in the United States tell heritage, not history. "The heritage syndrome," as described by Cornell historian Michael Kammen in *Mystic Chords of Memory* (1991), represents "an impulse to remember what is attractive or flattering and to ignore all the rest." Thus, most historic markers and monuments induce us to feel good, become more ethnocentric, and remain historically ignorant. Most of those that treat slavery—the "antebellum homes" that compete for tourist dollars—still present slave plantations basically as amiable communities. When they mention slaves at all, guides at most plantation homes minimize the horrors of slavery. No antebellum house shows that slavery was a penal system, resting ultimately on force and threat of force. Never have I seen on display a whip, whipping post, chains, fetters, or branding iron. Places like George Washington's Mount Vernon and Maryland's Hampton Manor never let slip that more than 90 percent of the people who lived there were held there against their will. Indeed, most slave sites mention slaves and slavery as little as possible. Everything gets done in the passive voice: this building "is where the laundry was done," while that "was for cooking." Or the master did it himself: "Thomas Jefferson was forever rebuilding Monticello."

About Reconstruction, the landscape is even less forthcoming. Indeed, Reconstruction goes almost unnoticed all across the South. Guides at antebellum plantations tell nothing about the economic and political changes that took place at their sites during Reconstruction. Reconstruction governors of Southern states get no statues; few even get historical markers.

Instead, monuments, markers, and historic sites across the South celebrate the white racist Democrats who during the 1880s and 1890s reversed the democratic policies that interracial Republican administrations enacted during Reconstruction. North Carolina, for example, boasts two white politicians who effectively ended black political participation: Zebulon B. Vance, who helped end Reconstruction, and Charles B. Aycock, who helped destroy the interracial coalition that briefly dominated North Carolina in the Fusion period. Statues of Vance, elected governor in 1876, and Aycock, elected governor in 1900, face each other in a plaza of honor on the grounds of the State Capitol in Raleigh. They are also North Carolina's two contributions to the National Statuary Hall in the United States Capitol.

The Wilmington Riots

Individuals and local groups can change how their communities tell history on the landscape, however. And some changes have happened. One of the more encouraging developments took place in October 1998 in Wilmington, North Carolina.

During the Civil War, Wilmington had been the only major port that the Confederacy controlled. In 1898, it was still the state's largest city, and in that year occurred the notorious Wilmington "race riot." The 1898 violence was crucial to the history of Wilmington and the state, and even had considerable national significance. After the end of Reconstruction, Southern politics entered the uneasy Fusion period. African Americans were still voting, but not freely. White Democrats did not want to risk federal enforcement of the Fifteenth (Voting Rights) Amendment, so they did not disfranchise blacks outright. Republicans tried to keep their party alive, but faced violence from nightriders; white Republicans also faced ostracism from their neighbors. Many whites were unhappy with the leadership of Democratic plantation owners; from time to time in various states coalitions emerged between Republicans and "Readjusters," "Regulators," and Populists.

In North Carolina, Republicans were still strong in the eastern part of the state, including Wilmington, where African Americans were in the majority. In 1894, Populists, mostly white, and Republicans, mostly black, formed a Fusion ticket, succeeded in portraying the Democrats as tools of big money interests such as the railroads, and won control of both houses of the state legislature. In 1876, to keep blacks from power in majority black areas, Democrats had put the state government in charge of many city and county governmental functions. In the process, whites had also lost local power. Hence, both elements of the Fusion coalition united to reestablish home rule. The Fusionists also passed laws making it easier for blacks to vote. In 1896, due to increased black voting, the Fusionists won every statewide race in North Carolina, increased their legislative majorities and elected a white Republican, Daniel Russell of Wilmington, as governor. In the 1897 municipal elections, the Fusion coalition elected six of Wilmington's ten aldermen and the town's mayor.

Democrats decided to fight back. Statewide, they mounted an overt white supremacy campaign in 1898, emphasizing the alleged lust that black males felt for white women. Vote Democratic, Charles Aycock and other party leaders urged, to keep your wives and sisters safe from black rapists. In Wilmington, Democrats planned a violent takeover. Red Shirts, the terrorist arm of the party in South Carolina, spread to North Carolina and menaced blacks and their white allies across the eastern part of the state. In Wilmington, the Red Shirts paraded throughout the downtown streets and then spent $1200 for a new Gatling gun.

In August, Alex Manly wrote an editorial in the local paper, the *Record*, opposing the call of Georgia's Rebecca Felton for white men to "lynch a thousand times a week if necessary" to protect white women from black men. Manly observed that not every liaison between black men and white women was forced. Democrats protested that he had defamed white womanhood and vowed to destroy him and his newspaper. On November 8 there was little election-day violence, but many blacks did not vote and the ballots of those who did may not have been tallied honestly. What had been a Republican majority of 5,000 votes in 1896 became a Democratic margin of 6,000 just two years later. Despite their victory, or flush with it, Democrats decided to take no chances. The next morning, they held a mass meeting led by Alfred Waddell in the courthouse that passed a "Wilmington Declaration of Independence." It declared, "We will no longer be ruled, and will never again be ruled, by men of African origin." The document also stated, "The negro" had "antagoniz[ed] our interest in every way, and especially by his ballot. . ." And it singled out "the negro paper" for "an article so vile and slanderous" that "we therefore owe it to the people . . . that the paper known as the *Record* cease to be published, and that its editor be banished from this community. . . . If the demand is refused, . . . then the editor Alex Manly will be expelled by force." Manly had already fled, but whites summoned thirty-two prominent African Americans to meet with them late that afternoon to receive the declaration.

When these men did not respond rapidly enough overnight, 2,000 whites paraded through down Wilmington on November 10 and demolished Manly's newspaper office. Some blacks armed themselves, and gun battles broke out in which whites killed at least eight blacks and drove many others out of town. White groups then moved into the black sections of town, some seeking specific political leaders, others just hoping to kill anyone still there. In all, probably twenty African Americans were killed.

Immediately, Waddell called a meeting to select a new city government; it chose him as the new mayor. The mobs threatened the Republican mayor and aldermen, who thereupon resigned, one by one, as did the entire police department. The next morning, white Democrats and soldiers found six black Republicans who had not already fled the city, walked them to the train station, placed them under guard on a rail car and banished them forever.

As Leon Prather, Sr., wrote in *Democracy Betrayed*, "the black exodus was not limited to those who fled immediately or were banished by the victors." By 1900, Wilmington was majority white. In that year, under Aycock's leadership, Democrats disfranchised blacks statewide.

The events in Wilmington in 1898 were important nationally because they proved that a Republican administration would no longer intervene in the South, even when white Democrats pulled a coup d'etat. During the Fusion period this had not been clear. Indeed, in 1890 Republicans fell just one vote short of passing a "Federal Elections Bill" whose goals were to achieve honest elections in the South. The new wave of imperialism that swept the United States in 1898 after the Spanish-American War effectively ended the already tenuous Republican commitment for black rights, however. Democrats had never had any.

Wilmington's New Historical Consciousness

For a century, Wilmington lived with the riot by forgetting about it (except in the black community) and maintaining white rule. In 1971, Wilmington again teetered on the edge of race war, with outbreaks of arson and gunfire from both blacks and whites. The 1990 Census showed Wilmington still quite segregated residentially, with an Index of Dissimilarity of 70. (The Index of Dissimilarity can range from 0—perfect equality, with every Census block group having the same racial makeup—to 100—apartheid, with all blacks in all-black block groups, all whites in all-white block groups.) Other North Carolina cities have indexes as low as 40, and the average for all U.S. cities was 64.

In 1998, however, a series of events, culminating in the placement of a new historical marker, may have helped Wilmington turn the corner. While some other American institutions were ignoring centennials that might have proven embarrassing—the Smithsonian, for instance, totally ignored our taking of the Philippines—Wilmington looked its past squarely in the eye. Blacks and whites met and set up an "1898 Centennial Foundation"; it adopted the slogan "A Community Effort for Remembrance and Reconciliation." During the year, hundreds of Wilmington residents from all social strata met in small dialogue groups. The public library discussed "The Wilmington Riot of 1898 in Fiction." The Foundation's Ministerial Roundtable held a workshop that drew more than fifty clergy from the area. A community theater company mounted an original play on the riot. Business leaders were involved because economic development was one of the goals of the program. Wilmington leaders also had the humility and wisdom to solicit outside expertise, including the Mayor of Tulsa, Oklahoma, which in 1996 had similarly observed the seventy-fifth anniversary of its own 1921 Tulsa Race Riot.

The highlight of these observances was the two-day seminar, "The 1898 Wilmington Racial Violence and Its Legacy," held at the University of North Carolina at Wilmington in late October. An impressive array of speakers participated, from descendants of victims of the violence to John Hope Franklin, fresh from his service chairing the Advisory Board of the President's Initiative on Race. Many panelists were contributors to a new book, *Democracy Betrayed: The Wilmington Race Riot of 1898 and Its Legacy*, published by the University of North Carolina Press on the occasion of the centennial.

Besides the book, the play, new connections among people and across groups, and new information imparted to audiences and participants in the year's events, the centennial also left a legacy on the landscape. North Carolina erected a new state historical marker which reads: "Alex Manly, 1866–1944—Edited black-owned *Daily Record* four blocks east. Mob burned his office, Nov. 10, 1898, leading to 'race riots' & restrictions on black voting in N.C." With this new marker, Wilmington began to tell more of its history.

The city's historical landscape had been overwhelmingly white supremacist, including Gutzon Borglum's dramatic bronze of "First Confederate Soldier to Fall . . . ," another Confederate monument, historical markers to Confederate General William W. Loring and Confederate spy Rose Greenhow, the Kenan Memorial Fountain donated by "a gallant soldier of the Confederacy," a statue of George Davis, Attorney General of the Confederacy, a historic marker commemorating the Cape Fear Club, founded in 1866 and still all-white in 1999, and Hugh McRae Park, named for a leader of the 1898 mob.

To learn more about how Wilmington did it, start with the website of the 1898 Centennial Foundation: www.1898Wilmington.org, which includes a particularly useful 1998 "People's Declaration of Racial Interdependence," in deliberate counterpoint to the racist 1898 "Declaration of Independence."

Perhaps the events in Wilmington in 1998 can prove as important as those of 1898. Certainly Wilmington has shown how to reach across racial and class lines, recognize wrongdoing on the landscape, and move forward as a community. All across America, other communities can now invoke Wilmington as a model in facing the points of shame and inhumanity in their own pasts.

"Don't Know Much About History. . . ." Quiz

James W. Loewen

ANSWERS ON PAGE 88.

1. The first black baseball player in the Major Leagues was Jackie Robinson.
   a. True
   b. False

2. George Wallace was considered racist for saying: "I have no purpose to introduce political and social equality between the white and black races. There is a physical difference between the two which . . . will probably forever forbid their living together . . . and I am in favor of the race to which I belong having the superior position."
   a. True
   b. False

3. White Americans forced roaming Indians to settle down and farm.
   a. True
   b. False

4. Who were the first non-Native settlers in what is now the United States? When?

5. What was the population of the Americas in 1492?

6. What percentage of the Native Americans of coastal New England was killed by a disease transmitted by Europeans and Africans three years before the Pilgrims landed?

7. Who segregated the federal government?
a. No one—it had always been segregated.
b. Abraham Lincoln in 1861
c. Ulysses S. Grant in 1871
d. Woodrow Wilson in 1913
e. Harry S. Truman in 1947

8. Which one statement about Christopher Columbus is true?
a. Most of his compatriots, like the scholars of the time, thought the world was flat.
b. He died never knowing he had "discovered" a new continent.
c. He and his men massacred and enslaved the Caribbean Indians.
d. He died alone and penniless.

Bilingual Education

Bebe Moore Campbell

When Henry Higgins took Eliza Doolittle under his wing in "My Fair Lady," the professor's challenge was to transform a street waif into a blue blood. Phase one was easy—a bath, a new coiffure, some fashionable clothes, and Eliza sure looked upper class. But then the child opened her mouth.

The rain in Spain falls mainly on the plain, all right, but the Cockney rendition and the King's English version are about as far apart as, say, somebody flipping burgers for minimum wage and the CEO of a Fortune 500 company. But the professor kept trying—this method, that method—and ultimately,

Eliza not only looked like a lady, she sounded like one, too. In the end, Eliza's proficiency in standard English garnered her a brand new life, filled with upward mobility and expansive possibilities—not to mention a man.

Here in America we do not have Cockneys, but we do have speakers of Ebonics and Spanglish. These dialects have been cobbled together by people who, by virtue of historic legalized and current de facto segregation in housing and schools, have been cut off from the mainstream, not unlike Eliza Doolittle.

Bilingual education gave newly arrived Latino immigrants greater access to learning the language that might transform their lives. That education is costly and is now almost assured of ending. The linguistic problems of some African Americans have never been adequately addressed by system-wide school programs.

Now California plans to mainstream native Spanish speakers, although mainstreaming has not improved the English proficiency of many poor blacks. Perhaps that is because the issue is not bilingual programs versus sink-or-swim total immersion. The real issue is how to motivate people to keep trying, when historically they have been denied the rewards that have gone to other groups that make their striving worthwhile.

How does one make speaking standard English attractive to people whose entire lives are ghettoized? In the early half of the twentieth century, European immigrants were motivated. They knew that if they exchanged the language and culture of their native lands for English and American ways, the society would reward them with success. But America has never promised her brown and black children that kind of access.

In the past, this nation has made it clear that the jobs reserved for dark-skinned people required less speaking ability than an aptitude for manual labor. Now that business is using new immigrants to push native-born blacks out of even America's dirty work; the broken English that some in both groups speak is coded with bile.

Would Eliza have persevered in her English studies if the rewards had been cleaning the professor's toilets for the rest of her life? Would Finns, Swedes, Italians, or Germans?

When Latino immigrants and poor black Americans truly believe that speaking correct English will improve their lives significantly, most will learn it, whatever way they can. To the extent that America reneges on that promise, the nation will be what it has always been: a house divided, unable to understand all who live within.

Bebe Moore Campbell's commentary was read on National Public Radio, May 28, 1998, just before the vote on California's Proposition 227, which passed, effectively ending that state's bilingual education program.

——Symposium——

Is Integration Possible?

It is indisputable that America has come a long way in fighting racism since the Jim Crow era. The Civil Rights Movement of the 1950s and 1960s, aided by the judicial system, succeeded in disestablishing the formal, legal structures of racial apartheid that replaced the slavery system in the post-Reconstruction era, and made serious inroads into the more informal tactics of terror and intimidation that elements of the dominant white society inflicted on African Americans. Anyone—particularly younger people—who has doubts on that score need only consult any of the many excellent histories of the previous era: Congressman/ former Freedom Rider and Student Non-Violent Coordinating Committee Chair John Lewis's first-rate 1998 autobiography, Walking With the Wind: A Memoir of the Movement *or Taylor Branch's two- (soon to be three-) volume* America in the King Years *(*Parting the Waters *and* Pillar of Fire*) are two such sources.*

But progress has stalled in the last decade or so. School integration, the promise and for a time the practice that followed issuance of the 1954 Brown v. Board of Education *Supreme Court decision, has given way to resegregation; and even where schools are nominally, statistically integrated, internal tracking systems recreate a* de facto *racially segregated community. Residentially, Blacks, and to a lesser extent, Latinos, are highly segregated from whites— Douglas Massey and Nancy Denton's classic 1993 study,* American Apartheid: Segregation and the Making of the Underclass, *is only one of many studies to document and lament this fact. The courts in recent years have consistently been rejecting integration measures. Conservatives have increasingly been propounding the position that the way to end racism is simply to stop paying so much attention to race.*

And so an important and legitimate question to raise is, "Is Integration Possible?" We were struck by a 1999 book coauthored by a white man and a black woman, colleagues on the faculty of American University in Washington, DC, with the intriguing title, By the Color of Our Skin: The Illusion of Integration and the Reality of Race *(Dutton). Both Leonard Steinhorn and Barbara Diggs-Brown, the authors, want to believe in the possibility of real integration, rather than mere desegregation: a true mixing of blacks, whites, and others, in residential areas, in schools, in workplaces. But the evidence they amass, from Census data, observations, opinion polls, and many other sources, says otherwise: real integration is an illusion—comforting, but not in the cards.*

That is of course a highly controversial position, and so we printed excerpts from their book and then asked a large number of thinkers and activ-

ists to put out their own views on the subject. Responses range from those who see continued progress, albeit not necessarily steady; those who support the Steinhorn/Diggs-Brown analysis; those who reject the concept of integration if it means assimilation; and those (white and black) who focus their anger on whites for continuing to support and profit from the system of white-skin privilege and racial hierarchy. Readers of the symposium that follows should be prepared to define and enunciate their own position on this volatile issue and what the consequences of such views are for how one functions in the society.

By the Color of Our Skin: The Illusion of Integration and the Reality of Race

Leonard Steinhorn and Barbara Diggs-Brown

There is a conventional wisdom about the 1960s that most writers and commentators follow. The story line is this: we came close, very close, to solving America's racial dilemma completely in the mid-1960s, until a number of factors stalled our progress and undermined the consensus. Great strides were made toward integration, according to this view, but unfortunately we now live with a bitter aftertaste. This version fits with the popular tendency to look at the early 1960s through the romance and nostalgia of Camelot and King, an innocent time when the great civil rights struggles united the black and white majority in America. We had a teachable moment for racial harmony, the story goes, and we squandered it. To liberals, blame for our current problems falls squarely on President Nixon's parochial and cynical strategy to build a silent majority from racial resentment and to draw discontented George Wallace voters into the Republican party—the southern strategy. It was a strategy that, liberals say, Ronald Reagan turned into a fine art. To conservatives, the villains include the black nationalists who fueled racial discontent and the liberal social engineers who rationalized violent crime and foisted divisive policies like busing, affirmative action, and group rights on well-meaning middle-class whites, deeply embittering them. To be sure, this type of finger-pointing is as much about present agendas as past events, but this fact should not obscure the similarity between the liberal and conservative points of view: that we had a chance to put this racial thing behind us if people had only put the national interest ahead of their special interest.

The trouble is, this view is not wholly accurate. The fact that some of us dreamed of integrating does not mean it was ever close to happening. The civil rights movement ended legal segregation in America. It created unprecedented opportunities for black political power and economic mobility. It established a social norm that no longer tolerated or condoned overt discrimination and bigotry. It was no doubt a crowning moment in American history, justifiably embraced and celebrated today by people of every political stripe. But it simply couldn't build an integrated America. As much as we like to blame the southern strategy, the silent majority, affirmative action, busing, race riots, multiculturalism, black power, or the precipitous rise of inner-city violent crime for poisoning the "beloved community," the evidence shows that the infrastructure of a separated America had already been established by the time any of these factors even entered the realm of race relations. The racially divided urban and suburban housing patterns of today were set in place in the early 1960s. So were the dynamics around desegregated schooling. Even the way we now interact and perceive each other was foreshadowed then. In November 1964, only four months after Congress passed the 1964 Civil Rights Act outlawing discrimination in employment, government programs, and public accommodations—a law whose purpose, as President Johnson stated, "is not to divide, but to end divisions"—the people of California, by a resounding two-to-one margin, approved a constitutional amendment for their state that overturned an open housing law and effectively allowed racial discrimination in housing. We may get misty-eyed when we think back to Martin Luther King's remarkable speech at the 1963 March on Washington, but barely two months later, Bower Hawthorne, the editor of two Minneapolis papers, the *Star* and *Tribune*, said, "We're getting increasing complaints from our readers that we are overplaying the integration story. Some of our white readers are getting tired of reading so much about it." We can accuse Nixon, Reagan, limousine liberals, black leaders, urban ethnics, or the social engineers of sowing discord, but they were merely acting out roles that in many ways already had been written for them in the early 1960s. To those who decry what they see as the balkanization of America by racial preferences today, the truth is that the boundary lines of today's balkanization were shaped long before racial preferences even became an issue. To those who fret over what they see as resegregation today, the sad truth is that there was never integration from which to resegregate. . . .

Many of these same [white backlashers] voted against real integration with their feet as early as the 1950s, and there was no shortage of overt backlash among self-proclaimed moderates even during the halcyon days of the civil rights era—before affirmative action, race riots, black power and busing supposedly alienated them. Praise for the bedrock fairness of America's middle class is a staple of political rhetoric these days, but the bottom-line is this: from the very beginning of the civil rights movement, from the moment desegregation became the law of the land, most whites were willing to accept and indeed applaud a degree of public interaction with blacks, but drew the line when it came to family, home, social life, school and work—the linchpins of real integration. Whenever and wherever blacks threatened to cross that line, whites first tried to flee and then, tired of running, resisted and fought. . . .

In October 1964, one of America's greatest political journalists looked into the crystal ball and wrote a prophetic, searing essay for *Life* magazine on white middle-class resistance to integration. Backlash, observed Theodore H. White, is "as invisible, yet as real, as air pollution." It would probably not show up in the 1964 presidential election results, he wrote, but it "is an unease whose impact will be felt not as much now as over the long range," particularly as whites see increasing black encroachment on their holy trinity of home, school and work. For the Democrats, the long-term peril of a divided party is clear, he noted. The Republican party, "born in racial strife, [must] choose whether it abandons its tradition and becomes the white man's party or refreshes its tradition by designing a program of social harmony." And so he concluded: "Only one political certainty can be stated now which will outlast next month's election: If, at this time when the nation is so rich and strong, both parties ignore the need for constructive answers to the question 'What Do They Want?' then disaster lies ahead—and backlash—the politics of chaos—will carry over, its snap growing in violence from 1964 to 1968 and all the elections beyond, until the question is answered. . . ."

Consider the many survey findings that herald the good news of white America's tolerance. A significant majority of whites say they would prefer to live in a mixed neighborhood, perhaps as mixed as half black, half white. But almost everywhere you look in every part of the country where more than a token number of blacks live, whites begin to flee from their communities the minute the first black family moves in. Often these are suburban communities where the new homeowners are middle-class or even affluent blacks. It is a classic case of the domino effect: each black family that moves in increases the likelihood that the remaining white families will leave. Integration exists only in the time span between the first black family moving in and the last white family moving out.

The very era that we applaud for racial progress tells a different story in communities like Sherman Park near Milwaukee, which lost 61 percent of its whites between 1970 and 1990; or Palmer Park, near Washington, D.C., which went from being virtually all white in the 1960s to virtually all black today; or the middle-class Philadelphia suburb of Yeadon, which doubled its black population in the 1980s, going from one-third to two-thirds black, and saw a corresponding decline among whites. Real estate agents will tell you that prospective white buyers show no interest in moving to these neighborhoods. . . .

The story is no different when it comes to schools. A majority of whites support mixed public schools, but apparently not for their own children. A 1993 survey of whites from the Minneapolis suburbs found that two-thirds favored sending white suburban children to the predominantly black Minneapolis public schools as a way to increase integration, but only 7 percent said they would send their own child. . . .

In Baltimore, every one of the nine all-white schools that were required to integrate in 1954 had become all black just seven years later. Roosevelt High School in northwest Washington, D.C., had 747 whites and no blacks in 1953, the year before desegregation; 634 whites and 518 blacks in 1955, the second year of desegregation; and 19 whites and 1,319 blacks in 1963, the tenth year of desegregation. White parents in Milwaukee even protested when some black children were transferred temporarily to white schools in 1963 while schools in predominantly black neighborhoods were being rebuilt. Years before busing roiled the educational waters, the pattern of school separation had been set. . . . In community after community, the story is the same: blacks make up a significantly larger proportion of schoolchildren than their percentage of the school-age population, which means that large numbers of whites begin to flee the system for private schools when the black student population inches above the token. . . . As of 1998, there were fewer than 4,000 white children left in Atlanta's public schools. Nor should we be misled if the numbers for an entire school district make it appear integrated; the actual schools themselves are often segregated by race. In Illinois, Michigan, New York, and New Jersey, almost three in five black public school students attend schools that have fewer than 10 percent whites. . . .

The dissonance between professed racial attitudes and actual racial reality should come as no surprise. Ever since the 1960s, as society began to shun overt bigotry and applaud gestures of racial tolerance, social scientists have found whites to exaggerate their contact with and support for blacks. As with any norm, people understandably want to be seen as conforming to it—in this case, they are evincing society's antiracist and tolerant attitudes. In exit polls after elections, for example, more whites say they vote for black candidates than actually do. One study compared the different responses offered when the phone survey interviewer could be clearly identified as white or black. On topics such as racially mixed schools, friendships with blacks, and who is to blame for current black problems, white survey respondents who were interviewed by blacks consistently provided a more liberal or integrationist response than whites who were interviewed by whites. . . .

The point here is not to deny the credibility of all polls, many of which can be useful in comparing black and white attitudes, but merely to show how powerfully the integration illusion defines our perceptions and self-image. Call it racial civility, decorous integration, or the politeness conspiracy—the bottom line is that our professed attitudes, symbols, and public expressions masquerade as integrated when our lives clearly are not. And what people say is less important than what they do. . . .

Whites are not blind to black anger and see it on or just below the surface. Part of white fear of black crime is the idea that black-on-white crime is not really random, that black rage toward whites actually leads to violence against whites. Whites describe how they consciously bite their tongues and refrain from obscene gestures when irritated with a black driver, but wouldn't show the same restraint if the other driver were white. Blacks know their anger frightens whites and pushes them even further away. That is why middle-class blacks work so hard to contain it when they are around white colleagues and employers. Other blacks take advantage of white fears by channeling their anger to arouse white guilt and perhaps obtain some short-term political benefit. Still others take silent pleasure in finally having a way to put white people on edge. Some young blacks even have fun with the anger, using it to intimidate whites in a nonverbal mind-game that seems momentarily satisfying when they are walking on the sidewalk or crossing the street—put on an attitude and see how they run. . . .

To be sure, let us not overlook an important area of consensus: blacks and whites share a nearly unanimous distaste for overt expressions of bigotry and blatant acts of discrimination. Considering the state of our nation just four decades ago, we should not underrate this accomplishment. We should be proud of establishing the norm and knowing it will not change. Beyond this, however, there is little consensus.

Most compelling are the different ways whites and blacks view the problem of discrimination. According to surveys on race conducted over the years, a substantial proportion of whites say that the civil rights gains of the 1960s largely ended the problem of discrimination in America. Whites see themselves as well meaning and concerned about racial equality. They believe themselves to be fair, if not color-blind, and they cannot imagine themselves as blatantly discriminating. With Jim Crow gone and outright bigotry diminishing, most whites just don't see discrimination as a major barrier for blacks any longer. They think Dr. King's integration dream is within reach. "Large majorities think blacks now have the same opportunities as whites in their communities in terms of obtaining jobs, housing and education," the Gallup Poll News Service reported in 1989. "Many whites are unable to name even one type of discrimination that affects blacks in their area." As columnist William Raspberry observed in 1995, "Younger whites know the cruder facts: that America once had slavery and Jim Crow and now has Colin Powell. Their sense . . . is of a problem confronted and mostly resolved." The problem is so resolved, most whites believe, that society has gone too far to accommodate blacks. Significant majorities of whites tell pollsters that prejudice harms blacks much less than affirmative action harms whites. Whites are not oblivious to the problems discrimination can cause blacks, but if anyone is to blame for black problems today, whites point the finger at blacks. They simply don't have the willpower or motivation to improve their lot, whites believe. All of these views are not of recent mint. . . . [T]hey actually began to form during the early civil rights days in the 1960s, before affirmative action and welfare became national issues. So it is safe to say that whites have a fairly static and consistent view of black life, which has developed over the past three decades: discrimination no longer unduly hobbles blacks, government has helped blacks at the expense of whites, and blacks have only themselves to blame for their problems. Given these assumptions, white opposition to affirmative action and other government programs seems logical. . . .

The discrimination may be more subtle today, but blacks feel it just as deeply. It is expressed not in the blatant 1950s style—"blacks need not apply"—but in the subtle cues and decisions that are made on a daily basis. Blacks also see how whites hear about jobs and opportunities—through their church, union, sports club, community group or fraternity network—and they know they will never be part of that. So as blacks see it, they have made progress in spite of these obstacles, with little help from whites. Their dream of the integration of truly color-blind equals remains precisely that, a dream. Blacks don't deny they are partly at fault for their problems, but they see society changing much less than whites think it has changed, and they see whites growing indifferent to racial problems altogether. . . .

These different views of discrimination spill over into the larger perception gap about life and politics in America. Generally speaking, whites believe that our nation's problems with racism and civil rights were solved three decades ago, while blacks see racial discrimination as an ongoing and daily obstacle to opportunity and equality. When blacks see discrimination, whites see equal opportunity. When blacks say civil rights, whites say special interests. When blacks support affirmative action, whites label it quotas, preferential treatment, and reverse discrimination. And where blacks see racism, whites respond that they are being overly sensitive. . . .

[M]ost politicians, especially most affirmative-action opponents, are unable to cite anything of King's other than his famous line in the "I Have a

Dream" speech: that his four little children "one day will live in a nation where they will not be judged by the color of their skin but by the content of their character." In their zeal to use these words for their own purposes, our politicians have reduced King's message to one line taken completely out of context. They have turned his vision of an ideal future into a prescription for color-blindness that should apply to the present. "I think the best means to achieve the ends of a color-blind society," conservative politician William Bennett said in 1986, "is to proceed as if we are indeed a color-blind society." The King who called for "discrimination in reverse . . . a sort of national atonement for the sins of the past" is nowhere to be found. Nor is the King who called for "radical changes in the structure of society," or for "a Bill of Rights for the Disadvantaged," or for "a policy of preferential treatment to rehabilitate the traditionally disadvantaged Negro." King wrote in his 1964 book *Why We Can't Wait*, "It is obvious that if a man is entered at the starting line in a race three hundred years after another man, the first would have to perform some impossible feat in order to catch up with his fellow runner." He realized that preferential treatment might make "some of our friends recoil in horror," but he also knew that "equal opportunity" without "the practical, realistic aid" to balance the equation was little more than a charade. "Giving a pair of shoes to a man who has not learned to walk is a cruel jest," he wrote. These were the very color-conscious ideas and policies that King thought might lead us to his promised, color-blind land. But they are too threatening to the integration illusion, too incompatible with what the largely white audience wants to hear, and too inconsistent with what the politicians want to say. So white politicians feed a denatured, neutralized King to their constituents, who want to see themselves—and their opposition to affirmative action—as truly color-blind and fair. It is rhetorical integration at its very best. . . .

If there is any doubt that the integration of blacks and whites is not working and may never work, it is instructive to compare blacks with the two other most prominent ethnic groups who also share the "minority" label, Hispanics and Asians. Because of comparable levels of poverty and disadvantage today, the plight of Asians and especially Hispanics is often equated with that of blacks. Government equal-opportunity laws make few distinctions among these groups, and they are often compared in terms of their educational, economic, and political achievements. But to lump them together based on a snapshot of today's economic circumstances is to overlook the more compelling evidence that these two recent immigrant groups are assimilating in ways that blacks have never been able to integrate. Indeed, it is a grievous error to lump blacks indiscriminately with Hispanics and Asians because it ignores the profoundly different relationships each has with the current American majority. Blacks are not immigrants and never have been, and the black experience is fundamentally at odds with the immigrant experience in America.

One hundred fifty years ago, the unmeltable ethnics, besides blacks, were the Irish and the Germans, and a century ago they were the Italian, Jews, Poles, and Russians. All were vilified, excluded, abused, and discriminated against and were portrayed at times as less than human, and always as less desirable than the Anglo-Saxon majority. All have assimilated, except for blacks. If the current assimilation patterns of Hispanics and Asians continue, it will be no different today. . . .

It has been the case throughout American history that a second-generation immigrant becomes an American while an eighth-generation black is still a black. Comedian Richard Pryor used to joke that the first citizenship lesson taught to new immigrants was the correct pronunciation of the word "nigger." Ethnic boundaries remain porous for immigrants, but virtually impermeable for blacks. "As to this country being a melting pot," wrote Supreme Court Justice Thurgood Marshall in 1978, "either the Negro did not get in the pot or he did not get melted down. . . ."

[R]eal integration depends on social engineering, constant vigilance, government authority, official attention to racial behavior, and a willingness by citizens to relinquish at least some personal choice for the greater good. And so we arrive at a fundamental dilemma of racial integration in America. The same factors that appear essential to successful integration run directly counter to some of our deepest beliefs about self-determination, authority, and individual rights. More than two centuries ago our nation was founded on a suspicion of vested power and an affirmation of individual liberty. The Declaration of Independence is as much about a king who abused his sovereignty as about the inalienable rights of humankind. This legacy remains as powerful today as ever. Most of us distrust authority, reject even a scent of social engineering, and must be dragged kicking and screaming to accept any limit on our personal freedoms. The reason better be good, very good, and it must produce unimpeachable results. Even then most Americans resist. Therefore, we cannot but conclude that what it takes even to break the integration ice in our country is largely unpalatable to most of our citizens. . . .

Integration is an ideal both of us would prefer to see realized in our lifetimes. A truly color-blind, integrated America is a vision we share. We believe it is in the best interest of all Americans, black and white. Part of us wants to buy in to the integration illusion, to praise the emperor's clothes, to embrace the hope of the dreamers that yes, it can work. We want a happy ending. But try as we might, the facts simply fail to accommodate our desires, and the racial reality stubbornly refuses to change. We must conclude, regrettably, that integration is an illusion borne of hope and desire, that our very devotion to the ideal ironically helps us avoid a real reckoning on race, and that for our nation to move beyond today's racial endgame we must relinquish the hope of ever reaching the racial Promised Land. . . .

From By the Color of Our Skin *by Leonard Steinhorn and Barbara Diggs-Brown, ©1999 by Leonard Steinhorn and Barbara Diggs-Brown. Used by permission of Dutton, a division of Penguin Putnam Inc.*

—— Commentaries ——

The Politics of Equality

Jerome Scott and Walda Katz-Fishman

Race and racial discrimination institutionalized within the structures and practices of American society since their beginning are surely not declining in significance as we enter the new millennium. On the other hand, social class—or the growing gap between rich and poor—is clearly increasing within all racial groups in the United States at a time when there is a vast abundance of goods and services to satisfy the basic human needs of people throughout the world.

We find persuasive the case made by Leonard Steinhorn and Barbara Diggs-Brown that race remains a reality and that the comprehensive integration of blacks into American society is an illusion. Our difference lies in the lessons we draw from American social history, and our vision and strategy for the future.

The enduring reality of race coupled with the deepening polarization of wealth and poverty suggests that the civil rights reforms of the 1950s to 1970s did not transform the fundamental economic and political structures of American society. The economic expansion of the post-World War II period was the context for the limited integration of blacks (along with other people of color and women) into the American class system. But blacks were always at the lower end of their respective classes and remain, as a whole, disproportionately at the bottom of the class structure.

In today's high-tech global economy, computers and automation are eliminating millions of good jobs and replacing millions of remaining jobs with contingent work (contract and part-time jobs, and jobs with few or no benefits). Americans of all races compete in a global labor force with over a billion un/underemployed workers. In the United States, more and more whites, along with their sisters and brothers of color, are excluded from good jobs and swell the ranks of the poor and near poor.

The reactionary policies of neo-liberalism have come home with the 1996 law eliminating welfare "as we knew it"; reversal of the civil rights gains of the reform era; the mushrooming prison-industrial complex; anti-immigrant legislation; and attacks on job security, public education and public housing, healthcare, and the environment.

All of this makes possible a new politics of equality that challenges the hierarchies of capitalist domination comprehensively and that has at its core the black radical tradition for our times. Such a politics challenges not only racism (and sexism), but the system of global capitalism in which they are embedded and which makes the condition of poverty for the many a condition for the creation of wealth for the few.

We in Project South are optimistic about such a bottom-up political movement growing and succeeding. In the southeast United States, we are part of a movement for racial and economic justice that is gaining strength daily and that is connected to struggles throughout the country, hemisphere, and world. The global economic human rights movement led by poor people and their allies (e.g., the March of the Americas spearheaded by the Kensington Welfare Rights Union in October 1999, the anti-WTO movement in Seattle in November–December 1999, the anti-International Monetary Fund (IMF)/ World Bank mobilization in Washington, DC in April, 2000, etc.) is on the move. This multiracial and multinational movement for structural equality is destined to fundamentally transform global corporate hegemony and to end its patterns of racial—and class and gender—inequality.

Equality Versus Integration

Herbert J. Gans

I agree with virtually all of Leonard Steinhorn and Barbara Diggs-Brown's analysis, but do not share their disappointment, since few of those of us who were around in the actual (rather than the now imagined) 1960s had any illusions or expected any miracles. Moreover, racial, and particularly residential, integration was then a priority mainly of affluent blacks and equally affluent liberal whites, for most blacks could not even afford to buy houses in white areas. One of the sensible points made by the early Black Power movement, which at times did speak for the mass of poor blacks, was that racial equality had priority over integration.

Not only does racial equality remain prior for many blacks, but also it should be so even for white advocates of integration. Until blacks obtain the opportunity to be more equal with whites economically, socially, and politically, most whites will not risk their property and status values to live with blacks. In fact, it may turn out that until the vast proportion of blacks is securely middle-class, white homeowners may continue to treat current middle-class blacks as surrogates for the poor ones that might move in right behind them. This is one reason why lily white suburbs and white flight continue.

Since blacks are a political as well as a numerical minority, universal policies that benefit all races will be needed. Greater economic equality should be the first priority, and one way to achieve it is aiming for full employment at decent incomes. The minimum and moderate-wage income jobs that have fueled the current economic boom are unequal jobs; their pay scales should be raised as much as economically and politically possible—and workfare turned into legitimate jobs. More economic equality is, after all, one way by which the unmeltable and swarthy ethnics of the early twentieth century became today's lily white Americans.

I wish the white-ethnic integration process could be repeated for blacks, but it cannot, since even swarthy ethnics were judged white by the time they were permitted to integrate. Blacks, especially African Americans, are not only dark-skinned, but they also suffer from modern forms of the hatreds and fears, the accusations of cultural or genetic inferiority, and the economic exploitation that originated in slavery. Why else, for example, are the blacks who were forced to compete for low-wage jobs with immigrants over a century ago expected to do so again with a new set of immigrants today? No one knows now how these aftereffects of slavery—too many created by ex-slave owners —can be eliminated, but it is high time to ask, both here and in other countries that permitted slavery.

One possible source of forward progress may turn out to be the rising level of intermarriage. Asians Americans, Hispanics, Native Americans, and other "nonblack" Americans are marrying whites at rapid rates. Even now the constantly increasing variety of ethnic and racial mixtures among young people, while still numerically small, suggests that finally, America may slowly be heading in the direction of a literal melting pot.

In the process, the hoary racial skin color scheme of white, yellow, red, and brown, as well as other differences in visible physical features, becomes less and less relevant in every generation until they finally fade into invisibility. Blacks will not immediately be part of that process, for although black-white intermarriage is also on the rise, it is only now approaching double-digit figures, as compared to 50 percent and more for some Asian Americans.

Still, it is possible to hope that if blacks are integrated economically, black-white intermarriage will also rise more quickly, and blacks will be admitted to the melting pot. In that case, eventually—and it is a far off eventuality—race may no longer be used by Americans to classify each other, and then racial discrimination will end as well.

Nonetheless, today's political struggle for racial integration has to continue. Concurrently, however, so must the pressure for more equality of all kinds, particularly that of income and wealth. In their wake, more political, educational, social and, yes, racial equality, can be achieved as well—and in the long run, more equality will also smooth the path toward racial integration.

Viable Integration Must Reject the Ideology of "Assimilationism"

John O. Calmore

While I think integration is possible, I nevertheless agree with Leonard Steinhorn and Barbara Diggs-Brown that "what it takes even to break the integration ice in our country is largely unpalatable to most of our citizens." They make an important point in observing that "our professed attitudes, symbols, and public expressions masquerade as integrated when our lives clearly are not." Even the masquerade, however, is fading, as whites become more comfortable with the segregated status quo.

Thirty years ago the Kerner Report characterized aspirations of African Americans as twofold: "to share in both the material resources of our system and enjoy its intangible benefits—*dignity, respect and acceptance*." What I am calling "viable integration" would at least entail reaching both of these aspirations. Viable integration must provide both the material and the intangible benefits. Beyond population mix and sharing space, integration—to be viable—must fundamentally address issues of equity, where each group is significantly represented, genuinely respected, broadly distributed, and sharing power and equality. Without incorporating these features, as Steinhorn and Diggs-Brown conclude, integration will remain an illusion, and our continued quest for this ideal will continue to cause us to "avoid a real reckoning" with racism.

A fundamental impediment to viable integration is the inability to define its operational features outside of the bounded ideology of "assimilationism." According to Christopher Newfield and Avery Gordon, assimilationism is not the benign road map used by immigrants to obtain the benefits of the economic, social, and political mainstream. Rather, assimilationism refers to "a specific ideology that sets the fundamental conditions for full economic and social citizenship in the United States." Any insurgent or critical multiculturalism must challenge this. The ideological dictates of assimilationism are at war with what I am calling viable integration. First, it demands that we adhere to core principles and behaviors, marginalizing those who do not. Second, it opposes race consciousness. Finally, it repudiates the distinctively cultural equity of diverse groups.

A viable integration will require people of color—all of our groups—to reject an identity that Elaine Kim characterizes as "the nonchoice between being either different and inferior or the same and invisible, between eternal alien and assimilated mascot." Thus, proponents of viable integration will have to struggle to renegotiate core principles that narrowly define America's common ground, shared values, and rules of the game. The dominant principles establish a conventional wisdom that is biased toward masking and reinforcing white supremacy and privilege. Color-blindness works hand-in-glove with these principles.

In response to Kim's observation, Steinhorn argues that her description of assimilation "sounds trendy and nice," but "it has little to do with people's lives." He then asks, "Do those who deride assimilation really believe that today's immigrants, if given the choice, would not want to follow the footsteps of the immigrants who came before them?" Steinhorn fails to appreciate that racism is a lived experience, and he should be less dismissive in critiquing a Korean woman's testimony about real lives of people of color. He fails to appreciate how racialized ethnicity really distinguishes the plight, historically and currently, of Asians and Latinos from the white groups he links them to, such as the Irish, Jews, Italians, Poles, and Russians.

The challenge to whited-in core principles and color-blind integration raises significant questions for all of us. What does a constructive concept of race consciousness mean? What does it mean not only for African Americans, but also for Latinos, Asians, Native Americans, and whites? How will people of color fight the new forms of racism that operate within partially integrated settings? What will motivate good-intentioned whites to move away from their presumed innocence and aversive racism? Can whites refocus their attention beyond the negative consequences of racism experienced by people of color and consider the advantages that accrue to whites from living within a system of racial inequalities?

Because people of color are almost forced to integrate, at least strategically, whites must become more involved in the integration project. Aside from hostile backlash, if good-intentioned whites remain so little concerned and inactive, the integration project cannot advance. White involvement must mean more than merely acknowledging white privilege, although this acknowledgment may be a first step toward reawakened accountability. Real integration is a two-way street. Whites must somehow come to see themselves not merely as the gracious hosts of integration, but, rather, as the hardworking, risk-taking joint agents of integration. They must push for it more, assume some of the risks, and carry a heavier load. They, too, will have to go through some changes.

Whites must stop demanding, or quietly supporting the demand, that people of color adapt to so-called universal expectations of what is proper behavior and presentment, when these race-neutral expectations really turn out to be white. Beyond the level of embracing token mascots, whites must admit that they are unwilling to incorporate people of color *as* people of color into their workplaces, seats of government, media, schools, neighborhoods, and social relations. This admission must lead whites to feel uncomfortable enough with their complicity in a segregated status quo that they seek not only a new way of relating to people of color, but also a different culture, a different set of institutional arrangements, and a different societal organization. A lot needs changing, because the segregated status quo has been so bad for so long.

We must come to realize that the presence of blacks and whites, properly mixed, may still fall short of constituting viable integration if Asians, Latinos, and Native Americans are missing. Similarly, people of color must look around not only for more of their particular groups, but also for the broader mix of all. Most importantly, colored people, must not be used against each other. Honorary whiteness is not worth it—not in the long haul.

If we all will not do these things, then we should simply admit that we do not support an integration that operates free of fear, division, individual self-interest, and the dictates of assimilationism. At least, then, we would stop waiting for (integration as) Godot.

A Wake-Up Call for Liberals

Richard D. Kahlenberg

Leonard Steinhorn and Barbara Diggs-Brown make a compelling case that integration remains an illusion, and, for that reason, the book is a powerful antidote to the happy talk of conservatives who tend to emphasize only the progress that we have made. But the authors' sobering evidence on the state of race relations might also be taken as a wake-up call to liberals. The policies that progressives have been pursuing for a generation have not worked nearly as well as hoped, and it is time to try alternatives.

While there is an undeniable logic to relying on race-sensitive policies (affirmative action, school desegregation) to remedy racial wrongs, there is also an undeniable downside to the explicit use of race: further balkanization and the reinforcement of race as a salient category. *By The Color of Our Skin* poignantly raises the question: what new policies might better promote the integrated society that so many of us desire?

Steinhorn and Diggs-Brown's discussion of Dr. Martin Luther King is instructive. They correctly point out that King was unsatisfied with merely passing antidiscrimination laws and calling it a day. In *Why We Can't Wait*, King wrote that he wanted a positive program to remedy "three hundred years" of discrimination. But the authors quickly glance over the significance of his actual proposal: a "Bill of Rights for the Disadvantaged." This is quite different than a Bill of Rights for People of Color. Indeed, King wrote, "While Negroes form the vast majority of America's disadvantaged, there are millions of white poor who would also benefit from such a bill . . . It is a simple matter of justice that America, in dealing creatively with the task of raising the Negro from backwardness, should also be rescuing a large stratum of the forgotten white poor."

Steinhorn and Diggs-Brown properly note that race-based programs, like affirmative action and school desegregation, did not create the white backlash, which predates those efforts. But these programs may well have kept the backlash going in a way that economic programs would not have. One of King's key advisors, Bayard Rustin, noted back in 1971 that poor and working-class whites often hold the swing vote in American elections, and that "The question is not whether this group is conservative or liberal, for it is both, and how it acts will depend upon the way the issues are defined."

Where racial efforts emphasize difference, class-based efforts—better schools, better health care, a leg up in college admission to poor and working-class students, expansion of the Earned Income Tax Credit—will all dispro-portionately benefit African Americans, helping to bring them into the economic mainstream, and at the same time will reinforce the notion that we are all in it together. Racial inequality is, of course, distinct as an issue from economic inequality, and antidiscrimination efforts will always be important in housing, education, and employment. But if the goal is greater fairness and integration, the programs that arouse the most opposition today—preferences and school desegregation—will work best if they apply to disadvantaged people of all races. The sooner the public disentangles race and class, the more likely we are to have a truly integrated society.

"Now We Are Engaged in a Great Civil War, Testing Whether That Nation, Or Any Nation So Conceived and So Dedicated, Can Long Endure"

Howard Winant

If Steinhorn and Diggs-Brown are correct that the elimination of Jim Crow did not really occur, then what *did* happen in the civil rights and post-civil rights era?

By the Color of Our Skin sounds quite familiar, perhaps because there is not anything really new here. Many academics and activists have made essentially the same points: critical race theorists such as Kim Crenshaw and Gary Peller, sociologists and historians such as Stephen Steinberg, Joe Feagin, Frances Piven and Richard Cloward, George Lipsitz, Robin Kelley, Manning Marable, and others too numerous to mention have all traveled this road before. Indeed, Steinhorn and Diggs-Brown's lament about the failure of integration may not be dolorous enough, for as many have pointed out, white racial intransigence is a virtual death sentence for democracy in the United States.

So let us stipulate to the fact that, with certain real exceptions (for example, voting rights), segregation and discrimination, prejudice and privi-lege, and white supremacy in general lived on after the high-water mark of the movement flood had been reached. Employment discrimination, educational discrimination, environmental discrimination, discriminatory immigration, taxation, health, welfare, and transportation policies (to name but the main dimensions of this issue) all continue in the present, at times ameliorated as a consequence of civil rights reform, but by no means uprooted or fundamentally altered from their pre-civil rights era configurations. The most egregious case of discrimination, that of *residential segregation*, was barely affected by civil rights reforms.

What *did* happen? A tremendous incorporation of political opposition. An adjustment of the previously dangerous imbalance between those with real, exercisable citizenship rights (whites) and those without such rights (particularly blacks, but also other "others": Native Americans, Latinos, and Asian Americans). This adjustment could not have been as successful as it was— speaking from the standpoint of the "power structure," the "establishment"—if it had been merely symbolic. It required real concessions, the redistribution of political and economic resources, to win acceptance, to readjust "racial hegemony," to defuse the radical potential of the black movement and its allies. Notably, too, the concessions made to the movement by means of the civil rights reforms were crucial maneuvers in the *international* political sphere, not just the domestic one. They were vital in the "twilight struggle" of the Cold War.

So there we have the real dilemma: not so much integration versus segregation, though of course I do not mean to disparage the importance of those issues. The more central questions that the black movement and its allies posed involved the readjustment of the balance of power in the United States. Put in starker terms, the movement called into question the national/state commitment to racial democracy versus racial dictatorship; it tested whether the "unstable equilibrium" of racial hegemony that had lasted for 350 years or so could be maintained. Perhaps most centrally, the movement tested the North American people. It questioned their commitments to democracy, equality, and social justice; they were asked to weigh these against the comforts and privileges, the majority of them derived from the racism on which the country had been founded. Would they accept substantial, let us call it social-democratic, redistribution of income and wealth? Would they agree to the wage cuts, the increased job competition, the increased taxation, and the massive cultural reorientation needed, at least in the short run, to achieve significant antiracist reform?

Most black people, significant numbers of other racially defined minorities, and an important but relatively small number of white people too, were willing to accept such radical changes, and were even poised to endure the upheavals that such a political program would have demanded. But most white people, significant numbers of other racially defined minorities, and an important but relatively small number of black people were unwilling to take the risks or make the sacrifices required. Hence the new "unstable equi

librium," or racial stalemate, of the post-civil rights era. Hence the continuation of DuBoisian "racial dualism," though obviously not on the same terms
as in the heyday of Jim Crow. This "dualism" cuts through the sensibilities
of us all now, through the minds and hearts of North Americans of every
color. Because the situation remains unstable, it can only result in further
social struggle. *A luta continua*!

The Morally Lazy White Middle Class

Robert Jensen

The invitation to write this commentary asked for reaction to the "sadly dour
view" on integration of Leonard Steinhorn and Barbara Diggs-Brown. Yet I do
not find the authors' view sad or dour; their conclusion that racial integration is
an illusion is honest and hopeful. Like the authors, it seems to me that the only
hope of progress toward racial justice in this country requires this kind of realistic assessment of the situation in which we find ourselves. Painful as it sometimes was, as I read I could see not only the lives of my fellow Americans in
their book, but my own life as well.

So, I could pick nits on a couple of points (most noticeably, I found their final
suggestion about an advertising campaign against racism to be strangely off the
mark). My most important reaction to the book, however, is not so much to the
authors' claims as to an underlying reality that struck me. As I read, I realized
that the American middle class, particularly the white middle class, is probably
the single biggest impediment to justice the world has ever known. While
Steinhorn and Diggs-Brown, noting how quickly they abandoned the dream of
integration, do suggest the magnanimity of middle class is overestimated, I think
the point needs to be stated even more bluntly.

In both domestic and international policy, it is the self-interested behavior or
the inattention to injustice on the part of the middle class that makes possible the
oppressive policies of the United States—the attack on labor unions and working people, the coddling of big business that produces obscene gaps in wealth
and privilege, the abandonment of the poor, and the assault for five decades on
any Third World movement that dared to strike out on an independent course.

While it is a much more elite class that plans, executes, and primarily benefits from those policies, it is a materially affluent, politically quiescent, and
morally lazy middle class that allows the elite strata to get away with it. In a

nominal democracy in which the use of direct coercion and violence against the middle class is virtually unheard of, the complicity of the middle class has to be faced honestly.

As Steinhorn and Diggs-Brown point out, that complicity on domestic race relations is clear: The white middle class has turned its back on residential and school integration, the linchpins of any true integration of racial groups. But I would go further, to highlight how racism and complacency allow other U.S. crimes to go unpunished. As I write this, for example, the United States continues to demand that the most comprehensive regime of economic sanctions continue to be imposed on Iraq, while also conducting a low-level bombing campaign. The predictable result of this starve-and-bomb strategy is that more than 1 million Iraqi civilians, at least half of them children under the age of five, have died as a direct result of U.S. policy in the past ten years, according to United Nations studies.

While one can argue about the underlying rationale for the policy, at the very least decent people should be able to see that making innocent civilians suffer and die at near genocidal levels to achieve the policy is a crime against humanity. Yet when I have confronted my middle-class cohort on this issue, I most often get a half-hearted shrug and a "that's the way the world works" comment. Usually unspoken, but often intimated, of course, is, "What's the big deal? They're just Arabs."

If anything, Steinhorn and Diggs-Brown may not be dour enough. The shameful moral and political performance of the middle class does not inspire confidence in the future for progressive politics. But, perhaps paradoxically, in the United States it may be that the middle class is our best hope for a progressive future. As hard as it is to imagine the middle class exhibiting the political will necessary for that future, it is even harder to imagine that future without the middle class taking an active role. Let us all commit to the self-reflection, dialogue, and activism necessary for that transformation.

Today's Integration Challenge

Angela E. Oh

Americans are confronted with the fact that we are a multiracial, multicultural society that has yet to define a new vision, strategy, or language that allows for the kind of transformation that integration once symbolized. A thorough and relevant assessment of our challenges in connection with race relations and integration today requires an analysis that moves beyond our temptation to resort to the traditional duality (black/white). We are in dire need of models that can allow Americans to continue to hold hope for the future, and make use of what has happened in the realm of race relations in the past three decades. Conversations such as the one shared by Leonard Steinhorn and Barbara Diggs-Brown do not allow us to make use of the intelligence we have gathered through organizing and advocacy efforts aimed at interracial justice. The experiences, insights, and analyses of those who are neither black nor white have added far more texture to what has been described as the "dilemma [of integration] facing America's democracy." In this respect, the discussion in *By the Color of Our Skin* falls short.

Steinhorn and Diggs-Brown provide us with yet another well-documented, accessible, and clear example of how the conversation between black and white can go on, ad infinitum, without getting any closer to breaking new ground. Theirs is a conversation that is familiar in that it celebrates the victories won when the politics of protest were effectively used to dismantle racial segregation and discrimination. It provides an analysis of how the lack of bold political leadership essentially missed an opportunity to transform American society, and ultimately it concedes the fact that most Americans are reluctant to sacrifice even a modest measure of personal choice for a greater good—in this case, integration. It is yet another good citation that can be used by those who wish to write about the black/white divide and the not-so-new revelation that blacks and whites see things differently in this society.

When it comes to the question of integration, however, we can no longer describe our dilemma as one that is black and white. Without diminishing the importance of the reports done by those who contributed to the work of the Kerner Commission and the McCone Commission in California, our current circumstances have developed well beyond what the analysts and policy experts in the 1960s ever imagined. Today's greatest challenges lie in divides that are intergenerational and intra-racial (not just between youth and elders but also between native and foreign-born). And these divides are made more complicated by the lack of progress in taking care of historical wrongs and by the rapidity with which this society has realized advances in the realms of telecommunications, technology, and media. Advancing the concept of integration in America and the goal of creating a truly color-blind society has just gotten tougher.

People of conscience, of all races, are looking for ways to create relationships that are productive and meaningful, not just integrated. Perhaps this is why integration has failed. Maybe it has less to do with resistance and the lack of trust among black people, white people, and other people in America and much more to do with the fact that we do not understand what "greater good" will be fulfilled by integrating. (This is where the lack of vision is glaringly clear.) A common understanding about the benefits of integration is absent. It has been almost four decades, and what we have learned is that integration sets up new patterns of migration. We have seen that integration has created new conflicts in old places like neighborhoods, schools, and workplaces. We have noted that those who integrate may ultimately assimilate—a concept that has in itself been debated so vigorously that the word, for many, is a pejorative. And if these are the lessons that have come from integration efforts to date, what makes us believe that integration in itself advances the interests of democracy?

We should open ourselves up to possibilities by examining the insights of those who offer a unique perspective on what a "color-blind" democracy in America may have to offer. This may mean looking for concepts, models, and values that do not reside in today's black/white world. In his new book *Interracial Justice*, Eric Yamamoto offers substance and a methodology by which fundamental and persistent race-based problems of inequality and conflict can be addressed from four dimensions that he describes as recognition, responsibility, reconstruction, and reparation. The concepts take into consideration both the historical and contemporary ways in which racial groups harm one another, take affirmative steps to redress justice grievances and restructure current relations. Examining integration, utilizing this approach and these concepts, could produce options that have yet to be considered.

The work of Steinhorn and Diggs-Brown can be appreciated as an important source of data and historical analysis concerning one aspect of this nation's experiences with integration. By no means has America reached any conclusions about the issue of integration and how it may reshape our democracy. To the contrary, the hardest questions we have ever had to confront are now emerging, and it will take principled, courageous, and creative individuals to introduce new concepts, dismantle old myths, and set new examples in order for answers to be found.

Half Full? Half Empty?

James W. Loewen

We all stare at the half-full glass of integration and racial justice. We all wish it were full. Leonard Steinhorn and Barbara Diggs-Brown and some others emphasize the empty top half, singling out neighborhoods and schools that have resegregated and stressing that white ethnic groups—"the Italian, Jews, Poles, and Russians"—have all assimilated, "except for blacks." This strategy offers ideological payoffs: social scientists can feel more honorable than those who admit to some satisfaction with the gains that have been achieved, can identify with militants who deny that any basic change has taken place, and can assure themselves that their expertise will be required until some distant future to help things get better or explain why they will not.

Three key problems still maintain America's racial hierarchy, almost without change. First, all-white or nearly all-white towns like Darien, Connecticut, still sit atop the social status hierarchy and pose as a goal for the rest of white America.

Second, schooling for the elite, whether at private schools or affluent suburban high schools like Darien, is far better than schooling for the poor, especially poor people of color. Race plays an important role in addition to class, because differential expectations are laid on the groups that John Ogbu calls "caste minorities"—African Americans, Mexican Americans, and Native Americans. These expectations afflict the performance of these groups within desegregated schools, as well as across schools and school districts, and to some degree have been internalized by the oppressed groups themselves.

Third, our social curriculum, by which I mean how we understand our country and our history—not just in school, but also as written in bronze and stone on our landscape and as celebrated or discussed in our public rhetoric—still largely derives from the "nadir of race relations." During that vicious era, from 1890 to about 1920, lynching reigned, and not just in the South; white clubs expelled Jews; Northern universities sequestered their black students; Major League baseball banished black players; the Kentucky Derby eliminated black jockeys; and Woodrow Wilson segregated the entire federal workforce. As my book *Lies Across America* shows, the legacy of this period is still visible even at John Brown's gravesite. Tentacles from this era still clutch at the minds of every child growing up in America, pulling ideas and beliefs toward white supremacy.

We must deal with each of these problems, which have proven intractable down to now.

At the same time, in at least three key areas, segregation and even racism are clearly on the run. One is the racial makeup of higher education and of workplace institutions. From the armed forces to, yes, Denny's, African Americans and other caste minorities are now hired to positions denied them before about 1960.

Second, and here we return to the glass metaphor, many neighborhoods and schools across America are desegregated. By 1990, according to research by Reynolds Farley and William Frey, many U.S. cities showed black/white residential segregation indexes from 32 to 50, not much higher than Italian/non-Italian residential segregation indexes (on a scale where 0 = totally equal dispersal and 100 = total apartheid). Nor were all these cities "new" ones like Anchorage and Honolulu and San Jose—also included were Fayetteville and Jacksonville, North Carolina. Other towns like Lincoln, Nebraska, and Bangor, Maine, hovered around 50. Yes, Chicago and Philadelphia and some Florida cities remain in the 80s, but even these show small declines in segregation levels.

Attitudes have changed to accompany this behavioral change. In the early 1960s, 60 percent of whites agreed with the sentence, "White people have a right to keep blacks out of their neighborhoods if they want to, and blacks should respect that right." By 1990, only 20 percent agreed. Of course, part of this change is hypocritical: elite whites especially know that giving the desegregated reply conveys status, just as living in a segregated neighborhood conveys status. However, there is a self-fulfilling aspect here: if most whites feel or at least say they feel that whites do not have the right to keep blacks out, it becomes difficult to mobilize the quick white response required to do it.

Herbert Gans (see "Equality versus Integration," pp. 46–48.) pointed out the third success: the rising level of intermarriage. Not only do interracial couples show that segregation has waned, they also prompt further waning. Their very existence challenges the system of white supremacy, just as their children challenge the system of racial classification in the Census.

A critical current battle ties one of the problems, unequal schooling, with one of the successes, college admissions. As affirmative action gets attacked, judicially and by voters, showing again that the glass is half empty, some whites are nominating "standardized" tests like the SAT as an allegedly racially neutral alternative. These tests are not racially neutral, partly owing to unequal schooling; and if they determine college admissions, they will largely destroy the progress made in this area.

It is critical, therefore, that we all keep our eyes on those areas in American life where the glass is largely empty or where reactionary forces threaten to empty it, rather than waste our time analyzing whether overall it is half full or half empty.

Needed: An Antiwhite Movement

Noel Ignatiev

Leonard Steinhorn and Barbara Diggs-Brown are right to conclude that integration of black and white must forever remain an illusion. Integration, in the sense they use the term, is incompatible with the existence of white and black as social categories. The society they envision requires not integration of white and black, but *dis*integration of the white race. My purpose in focusing on whiteness rather than "racism" is to move the discussion away from the ground on which whites are most comfortable—individual attitudes—and relocate it in social reality: the measurable whiteness gap that exists in every aspect of life.

The white race is neither a biological nor an ethnic group, but a hereditary aristocracy; without the privileges attached to the white skin, it would not exist. Any attempt to treat whites as a legitimate group with valid interests runs counter to the goal of transcending race. This is true whether the effort is made on traditional "racial" or on currently fashionable cultural grounds. As James Baldwin said, "So long as you think you are white, there is no hope for you."

But if whites cannot be absorbed into the common race of humankind, perhaps former whites can. There are more than 200 million people in this country "passing," claiming to be white in order to improve their chances. Why should they renounce something that gives them an edge in the rat race? The answer is, for many it costs more than it is worth. It is a question of class: like every modern society, the United States is divided into masters and slaves. The problem here is that many of the slaves identify with the masters because they consider themselves white. And that habit prevents them from acting consistently to build a new world. While there is a great deal of rebellion in the United States, there is very little real class politics, and what there is appears largely in a black face and is unrecognized as such by whites.

Class politics are not bi- or multiracial; they are nonracial. In America, nonracialism demands an assault on whiteness. Can the majority of oppressed whites be won to nonracial politics? In the ordinary course of events, probably not. Too many of their daily survival strategies depend on whiteness for them to imagine a world without it.

But abolishing the white race does not depend on winning over a majority of whites. What is needed is a band of people, including some nominally classified as white, who are determined to challenge, disrupt, and eventually break up the institutions that reproduce whiteness: the school system (including teachers' unions), the labor market, the criminal justice system (including the police unions), the welfare and health care systems, etc. The aim is not to win over individuals to secede from the white club (although that is great when it happens), but to make it impossible for anyone to be white. There are already enough "antiracists" to do the job.

The antislavery movement gave rise to movements for women's rights and against the Mexican War. The Civil Rights Movement stimulated new movements of women and youth, and a movement against the Vietnam War. Nothing offers so great a possibility of transforming the political climate of this country as an antiwhite movement.

Is Integration Possible? Of Course . . .

Florence Wagman Roisman

Not only possible, but absolutely essential.

Here are the "top eight" reasons for acknowledging that we cannot do without "racial" integration—and rejecting its opposite, segregation:

1. Racial segregation is inconsistent with civil democracy. The polity to which we aspire is premised on the equal worth of each human being. Putting us or other people into categories based on the color of their skin—or the color of some ancestor's skin—negates that fundamental principle.

2. Racial segregation is intellectually insupportable. As Audrey Smedley writes in *Race in North America: Origin and Evolution of a Worldview*: "Biological anthropologists, geneticists, and human biologists . . . no longer accept 'race' as having any validity in the biological sciences. [The concept of 'race' was] fabricated out of social and political realities" to impose "on conquered and enslaved peoples an identity as the lowest status groups in society." As we reject the goals of conquest and enslavement, we must reject also the tool by which they were achieved—the construction of "racial" identity.

3. Racial segregation is silly. It is ludicrous to consider that one knows anything about another human being when all one knows is the color of that person's skin—or the color of the skin of an ancestor of that person. As Benjamin Franklin wrote in *A Narrative of the Late Massacres . . .* , protesting the massacre of friendly Indians: "[S]hould any Man, with a freckled Face and red Hair, kill a Wife or Child of mine, [would] it . . . be right for me to revenge it, by killing all the freckled red-haired Men, Women and Children, I could afterwards anywhere meet with [?]"

4. Racial segregation is wasteful of human resources. One consequence of racial segregation is that the people who are considered "inferior" are confined to particular geographic areas, where schools, jobs, transportation, recreation, public facilities, and other opportunities are degraded. Among those who are so confined, and so deprived of the opportunities to develop their full human potential, are people who could discover cures for cancer, compose great symphonies, develop computers that do not crash, and make many other major contributions to human good. By cheating people of those opportunities, we cheat everyone of what those opportunities could produce.

5. Racial segregation is wasteful of natural resources. Racial prejudice is a principal cause of the abandonment of the cities and the push ever outward to the suburbs and beyond. [See "Race and Space," pp. 20–27] And this race-driven "urban sprawl" imposes immense costs in new highway development, with its destruction of farmland, dangers to biodiversity, increased air pollution (exacerbating respiratory illness and promoting climatic change), and social costs.

6. Racial segregation is expensive, as documented in The Leadership Council for Metropolitan Open Communities' 1987 study, *The Costs of Housing Discrimination and Segregation: An Interdisciplinary Social Science Statement*. Potential consumers and producers deprived of opportunities impose costs on society instead of contributing taxes to it. Douglas Massey and Nancy Denton, in their 1993 book *American Apartheid: Segregation and the Making of the Underclass*, teach us that residential segregation is the single central cause of the congeries of urban ills that we designate with the term "underclass."

7. Racial segregation is unfair. What one can make of one's life is largely dependent upon one's access to high-quality public institutions—schools, health care, transportation, recreation—and employment opportunities. There is considerable evidence that when integration does offer those opportunities, the minority people who move to better-served communities benefit from them. Studies of Chicago's Gautreaux Housing Mobility Program showed that moving to predominantly white suburbs "greatly improved adult employment, and . . . youth's education," according to James Rosenbaum in the 1993 *North Carolina Law Review*. Among suburban movers, many adults were employed for the first time in their lives. Compared with the city movers, the children who moved to the suburbs were more likely to be (1) in school, (2) in college-track classes, (3) in four-year colleges, (4) employed, and (5) employed in jobs with benefits and

better pay. As Rosenbaum and Leonard Rubinowitz write in *Crossing the Class and Color Lines: From Public Housing to White Suburbia*: "Contrary to the claim of 'culture of poverty' theorists, many participating low-income blacks showed the motivation and capacity to take advantage of the opportunities available in the predominantly white, middle-class, suburban communities to which they moved." Similar results have been shown by other studies of low-income people of color who moved to well-served, predominantly white communities.

8. Racial segregation is dangerous. Studies by Elliot Currie and Judith and Peter Blau indicate that the combination of residential racial segregation and concentrated poverty does not simply concentrate crime, disease, and other deleterious conditions, but actually enhances and augments them, increasing the amount of violent crime and contagious disease that damages whites as well as blacks. The likelihood is that dreams deferred will not, in Langston Hughes' words, "dry up like . . . raisin[s] in the sun"—they will explode. The riots of past years will seem tame to any of the new millennium. As the Milton S. Eisenhower Foundation recently reminded us (see *To Establish Justice, To Insure Domestic Tranquility*), the number of firearms in the United States "has just doubled to nearly 200 million—many of them high-powered, easily concealed models 'with no other logical function than to kill humans.'" Their report notes that violent crime is exacerbated by a "vast and shameful inequality in income, wealth, and opportunity. . . ." This reinforces the observation by John Duckitt in *The Social Psychology of Prejudice* that "prejudiced intergroup attitudes—with their potential for periodic eruption in overt intergroup conflict—have now become an extremely serious threat to the continued survival of human society and civilization."

We have no basis for concluding that integration is not possible. The material set out by Leonard Steinhorn and Barbara Diggs-Brown establishes not that integration is impossible, but that it is difficult and time-consuming. No one should have thought otherwise.

The racial and ethnic stereotypes—and the notion of white supremacy—that divide us from one another were created over a long period of time and buttressed by powerful societal forces. Although visionaries addressed these issues earlier, the general public and government actors did not begin seriously to undermine those societal forces and to root out the stereotypes until the 1960s, and our efforts have been sporadic since then. We have relied on under-funded, inconsistent programs and volunteer efforts to turn around a massive propaganda machine that serves potent institutions.

The foolish thing that many of us did in the 1960s was to think that the problems of racism and poverty would be solved in that decade. We now recognize that they may not be solved in our lifetimes. But—for all the inadequacy of the remedies—considerable progress has been made, and more will be made if we determine to do it.

Howard Zinn, interviewed by Susan Stamberg on National Public Radio in late 1999, said that the idea of the twentieth century that will last into the twenty-first is "the idea of non-violent direct action"—"precisely because it's been such a century of violence." In the same spirit, I would say that the twentieth century has demonstrated that racial separation is unacceptable: racial integration is the mandate of the twenty-first century.

What Is the Question? Integration or Defeat of Racism?

James Early

Research, principled discussion, and debate about how to address the racial reality of the nation should always be welcomed, as they help focus public attention and politics on what Peter Drucker identifies as "the basic American problem, race relations between white and black." A fundamental contemporary issue which he locates historically and qualifies in importance is his projection that ". . . the legacy of the sin of slavery has been the central American challenge for a hundred and fifty years and is likely to remain the central American challenge for at least another fifty or hundred years."

The excerpt by Leonard Steinhorn and Barbara Diggs-Brown connects to this important topic by reexamining one of the enduring philosophical and strategic attempts to define the nature of the problem: identify specific goals to be pursued and tactics to be employed. Integration, although a debated philosopy and strategy, inspired literally millions of people across racial and class backgrounds from the 1950s through the 1960s to actively enter in the watershed struggle to defeat American Apartheid. And so the integration philosophy and strategy played a critically important political role in confronting and defeating the reigning social, economic, and cultural forms of racial power that permeated every private and public aspect of national life. Steinhorn and Diggs-Brown acknowledge the social and transformative power embodied in the integration philosophy of that era as it galvanized a broad and diverse body of citizens to shatter social, legal, religious, and economic conventions.

However, their analysis and evaluation of integration and racial realities constitutes a rather "thin-skinned" treatment of the systemic nature of racism, and of the protracted struggle and varied strategies required to defeat it. Despite useful critical reflections about the miscalculations in the positive hopes and expectations many placed on integration, the authors' own faulty understanding of America's racial dilemma and how to address it is further compounded with their personal defeatist conclusion that integration can never be achieved. Their personal lament that integration will not be achieved in their lifetime is a diversion from their more important conclusion that continued devotion to the integration/assimilation strategy avoids a real reckoning on race.

The authors do appropriately challenge us to forthrightly consider that emphasis on stated idealistic hopes for "tolerance," "racial harmony," "color-blindness," and the contradictory life ways of whites provides little depth of understanding of the substantive realities of today's "America's racial dilemma." Shared values and ideals about integration among Blacks, whites, and other ethnic groups alike, important as they are to what racial progress has been achieved, nevertheless do not in and of themselves translate into concrete plans and actions required to resolve the ongoing nature and present forms of the social, political, economic, and cultural dimensions of race and racism in the United States (e.g., presumed innate racial and cultural superiority, educational inequities, job discrimination in private industry and government, redlining, police brutality and unjust incarceration, discrimination in access to capital, health care, and insurance, etc.).

The authors also make an important contribution by noting the stubborn nature of African American exclusion in relation to recent Hispanic and Asian immigrants who are assimilating in ways that Blacks have never been able to integrate. Little surprise to some of us who understand that the essentials of racism are historically evolved from white oppression and exploitation of Blacks. Thus, Black struggle became a crucible of American democracy on many fronts (and continues today)—an underrecognized factor in how other people of color are treated and what access they achieve. This history and ongoing particularity of white/Black relations sets the bases for the still dominant white/Black national social psychology, and underscores the centrality of African American struggles to the future of American democracy.

That we are trapped in an illusion of integration (a debatable conclusion certainly among the most discriminated) is less the issue than the fact that systemic racism, despite much racial progress, is alive, virulent, and destructive in American social life, corporations, local and federal governments, sports, the media, and even in liberal and left circles and institutions.

What then are we to do? Debate the ideals of an integrated society? Or work out the social and philosophical constructs as we confront and defeat racism in practice, building the social organization of the new society as we go. As an African American, I am more concerned with fairness, justice, and equality than the efficacy of one or another personal philosophy or defeatist conclusion. We will never be a color-blind nation. We can, however, through honest confrontation with racism, lower the negative valence attached to social constructions of race and physical characteristics. In doing so we will take a major step to becoming a new nation of diverse cultures who along the way construct new dominant values about the social individual and the social role of the state in public life.

There is no predetermined route or panacea to an integrated society. Nor is the path (or goal) merely integration of the excluded into the existing paradigm—a point the authors seem unable to consider.

Education and Incentives to Actualize Integration

Don DeMarco

The interracial team of Leonard Steinhorn and Barbara Diggs-Brown tell us that the integration glass is virtually empty. It is hard to argue against that, except by citing Shaker Heights, Ohio, Oak Park, Illinois, South Orange/Maplewood, New Jersey, Philadelphia's West Mt. Airy neighborhood, and the few other important exceptions to the rule of segregation. When they abandon integration as unattainable because it requires more engineering than they believe will be acceptable, that is where I part company totally. What is acceptable changes over time. We are not at the end of history.

By laissez-faire, color-blind means, racial integration may well be impossible, given the inertial force anchoring segregation. Neo-conservative policy will doom us to market segmentation by race and all the apartness derived from it.

Neo-liberal policy is no better. Funding minority and low- and moderate-income folks to form place-based community development organizations providing for their own kind in their own areas perpetuates, accommodates, and exacerbates separate and unequal living, even when done with a warm heart.

Racial integration in local school markets, housing markets, and civic life is possible and even likely, but not without pushing aside both liberal and conservative policies in favor of pro-integrative policy—that is, policy decisions informed by integration/segregation impact analysis and interracial commitment to favor options that will attract the race which is underrepresented, whether white or of color.

Whites tend to see racial balance where majorities and minorities are buying in numbers reflective of their regional presence and buying power. Blacks and Hispanics tend to see balance when their group is approximately half of the neighborhood population, school enrollment, or civic organization. These "what it's becoming" and "what it is" perceptions of balance beg for reconciling, not for being accepted as the end of history. Given these disparate inclinations and few or no education or incentive programs to foster compromise, it ought to be patently obvious that segregation has Big Mo(mentum) on its side, even without the actionable discrimination that is still with us.

In the near term, national housing policy is likely to continue favoring a diversity of racial ghettos—some white, others black or brown, some gritty and others glitzy, some long-established while others are just becoming. Devolution, local control, empowerment zones for people of color, and sprawl for whites have a firm grip on both for-profit conservatives and nonprofit liberals. But more and bigger islands of integration in the seas of segregation can be had right now. It takes an interracial commitment to pro-integrative principle and intentional effort for the indefinite future.

Economic and social rewards (e.g., wealth accumulation, mutual understanding, acceptance, and friendship) of integration are great, especially compared to resegregation. Some communities make the commitment while they have the human, financial, and time resources. The fact that long-term racially balanced living is relatively rare and never perfect is no reason to think it impossible or to devalue it.

Desegregation and tolerance are necessary preconditions on the way toward integration and acceptance. To disrespect the former, as Steinhorn and Diggs-Brown tend to do, is to thwart progress toward the latter. If we want choices beyond one sort of ethnic enclave or another, those who claim to value a broader choice must be challenged to develop a pro-integrative mindset and make personal, professional, and business choices that model pro-integrative behaviors. More leadership to supplant a culture of segregation with a culture of integration and a new interracial equilibrium is what we need now.

Should Racial Integration Be Pursued As the Only Goal?

Joe Feagin and Yvonne Combs

In practice, racial desegregation has often become a game of numbers, a game that does not serve well the basic needs and interests of the black community. Clearly, the end of legal segregation has meant increased housing, job, and education options for black Americans, especially those in the middle class. There has been some societal desegregation in many areas.

Yet, a token number of blacks in formerly all-white neighborhoods, schools, and workplaces has signaled to many whites that conditions for blacks are now the same as for whites, if not better.

However, what the omnipresent numbers on desegregation fail to show is the quality of this social change in everyday life. Many black Americans have not benefited much from racial desegregation.

They got some increased opportunities here and there, but they remain informally segregated and racially targeted across most institutions in society. Moreover, the quality of life for blacks in desegregated institutions is often negative and filled with racist obstacles. So-called integrated institutions have mostly incorporated blacks and other people of color in limited numbers without changing their white-washed character and culture; most are still run by white men according to the rules and norms established in the white interest long ago. Much research shows that today a majority of whites are still quite racist in their thinking about black Americans and that a majority will still sometimes discriminate—in areas like housing or promotions—when given the chance. Today, the white majority still gives the ideal of racial equality only lip service.

Given the failure to achieve large-scale integration and continuing white racism in all major institutions, many black Americans have shown a growing interest in community control and self-development strategies. In the mid-1990s, *New York Times* reporter Isabel Wilkerson interviewed several dozen middle-class blacks in Los Angeles and found them angry over police brutality and other racism issues. As a result, many were becoming more committed to black businesses and greater black community solidarity and separation from whites. In his important book, *Integration or Separation?*, leading black legal scholar Roy Brooks—formerly a dedicated integrationist —shows the defects in the integration strategy. As he sees it now, black Americans should keep integration as a strategy but couple it with strong community-focused strategies necessary for their short-term and long-term well-being. Working in the tradition of Malcolm X and W.E.B. DuBois, numerous scholars and community leaders have reiterated the importance of African values and understandings for African Americans in the strategy of building stronger communities and community control strategies.

In short, it is possible today to have safe neighborhoods, healthy homes, good economic activity, and successful school experiences within predominately black communities. Mere proximity to whites does not insure socioeconomic security or advancement. It is possible for African Americans to develop greater community control and a more independent infrastructure.

Consider, for example, the little known story of the prosperous "Black Wall Street" in Tulsa, Oklahoma, in the early twentieth century. Destroyed by white rioting and arson in 1921, this center of black prosperity is a possible prototype for greater economic independence. The money made in the community there, and in many other cities at that time, tended to stay in those communities.

As John S. Butler made clear in his research, many strong black communities existed on the heels of slavery—which clearly points to the ability of blacks to set their own agenda outside the confines of white society. A vicious war against these communities in the 1920s and 1930s—by whites at all class levels—and the impact of the Great Depression wiped out much of this black-controlled prosperity.

Some improvement in material circumstances for many black Americans, coupled with official desegregation of schools and neighborhoods, has failed to close the gap between black and white living standards. Indeed, in many ways, the socioeconomic gap now seems to be widening, and racial discrimination remains widespread.

In the long run, hopefully, the strategy of thoroughgoing racial desegregation and integration may still make sense for African Americans and for the larger society. However, it is an ideal still rejected in practice by most whites, who have the greatest power to implement it. In the meantime, one clear recommendation of a growing number of black voices is for black Americans to embrace the opportunity to develop greater solidarity and community control within black communities.

Progress in Integration *Has* Been Made

George C. Galster

Leonard Steinhorn and Barbara Diggs-Brown analyze contemporary American racial attitudes, behaviors, symbols, and politics and come to the pessimistic conclusion that black/white integration is impossible during our lifetimes. There is no doubt that the challenges of moving toward a racially integrated society are immense and longstanding. But there are trends in our metropolitan areas overall, and especially in certain communities, that suggest a less pessimistic future. Racial residential segregation is falling and integration is rising among black and white households.

Part of the picture is painted by trends in residential segregation indices provided by Professors Douglas Massey and Nancy Denton in *American Apartheid*. For example, in eighteen Northern and Western metropolitan areas with the largest black populations, the mean dissimilarity index fell 8 percent, from 84.5 in 1970 to 77.8 in 1990. Similarly, in twelve southern metropolitan areas with the largest black populations, the mean dissimilarity index fell 12 percent, from 75.3 in 1970 to 66.5 in 1990.

Professor Ingrid Gould Ellen provides a more detailed view, based on data from thirty-four large metro areas with black populations greater than 5 percent and Hispanic populations less than 30 percent in 1990. She notes several encouraging trends from 1970 to 1990:

- The percentage of the white population living in census tracts having less than 1 percent black population fell from 62.6 to 35.6.
- The percentage of the white population living in census tracts having between 10 and 50 percent black population rose from 10.5 to 15.6.
- The percentage of the white population living in census tracts where nonwhites comprised at least 10 percent of the population rose from 25.0 to 35.1.
- The percentage of the black population living in census tracts having between 10 and 50 percent black population rose from 25.7 to 32.4.
- The percentage of the black population living in census tracts having between greater than 50 percent black population fell from 67.1 to 53.9.

Moreover, Professor Ellen finds that the stability of racially mixed tracts has risen since 1970. During 1980 to 1990, the average loss of whites from tracts with more than 10 percent black residents was 10.5 percentage points, versus 18 percentage points during the prior decade. Between 1980 and 1990,

76.4 percent of the mixed tracts remained so, whereas only 61 percent remained so during the 1970s. Finally, the proportion of mixed tracts that did not lose whites between 1980 and 1990 was 53.3 percent, compared to 44.5 percent a decade earlier.

The causes for this increase in stable, racially diverse neighborhoods are undoubtedly multifaceted. But, one clearly is the effort by many nonprofit organizations, localities, and a few states to enact pro-integrative policies, which attempt to adjust racial patterns of demand for their communities in a way that diversity is encouraged and maintained. Many of these activities are documented in Juliet Saltman's book, *A Fragile Movement.*

Professors Steinhorn and Diggs-Brown may dismiss these efforts as wildly unpopular because they represent, in their words, "social engineering, . . . government authority, . . . and a willingness by citizens to relinquish at least some personal choice for the greater good." Yet, the aforementioned pro-integrative policies are overwhelmingly the results of municipalities, school boards, and neighborhood groups democratically fulfilling the wishes of their constituents. Most pro-integrative practices, like affirmative marketing and financial incentives, do not constrict freedoms. Far from constraining choices, such policies are the only means of providing a choice that many Americans clearly want—by words and actions: a stable, racially diverse community in which a high quality of life is maintained.

Unillusioned

S.M. Miller

How one evaluates the last four decades largely depends on one's expectations. My outlook in the 1960s was that an untroubled, clear, upward progression to real, full integration of African Americans would not occur. "Cost-free liberalism" was the somewhat caustic term I applied to the liberal confidence that economic growth would make everyone better off, alleviate strain, with the result that great social change would occur "on the (economic and political) cheap" with little disruption. I did not share that optimism.

When I went to work in 1966 at the Ford Foundation, I assigned myself the mission of moving the Foundation to broaden its civil rights activities in two ways. One direction was to support more activist organizations than the National Urban League. The other was to involve the Foundation in developing programs with Appalachian whites, Hispanics, and Native Americans.

My assumption was that the War on Poverty would not maintain support if it was regarded as an economic program to aid mainly black people. It had to be seen as also benefiting nonblack groups. My view, then and now, is that the United States is a politically conservative country with short liberal remissions. Race barriers are not easily overcome.

The 1960s was a great positive surprise to me. Greater change occurred than I had believed possible. Nevertheless, my belief was that a transformation in race relations would not come easily or swiftly.

Consequently, I am not disillusioned. I like to describe myself as unillusioned: I believe that enormous positive changes have emerged, while recognizing the difficult, disturbing barriers to integration that remain.

Since barriers, shortcomings, and regression are now familiar, I cite the gains. Occupationally, both black men and women are less concentrated in low-paying occupations than they were in 1960. Educationally, African American youth are graduating from high school at almost the same rate as white youth. These are not minor advances.

A more minor illustration of change is in major professional sports. In the 1960s they were just really opening up to black players; today, African Americans and Latinos predominate as players. And—miracle of miracles—as these "minorities" entered basketball, football, and baseball, salaries did not decline but jumped to unheard of heights. Yes, that is due to union organization and the courts, but also somewhat to changed attitudes.

Youth and, to a lesser extent, adult pop culture is dominated by black music, performers, themes, language. (That is different from the 1930s when white musicians like Benny Goodman predominated in playing black-derived music.) This is cultural integration—especially for white youth—although we do not know what to make of and do with it. But it does signify something positive in an entertainment-oriented period, not just a coloring of minstrel time.

While I do not accept as reality the General Social Survey's report that more than 50 percent of white respondents say that they have at least one black friend, I would not dismiss that finding as unrevealing. My interpretation is that whites feel that they "should" have African American friends. That is a big change in outlook if not in actual behavior.

This listing is not a "Pollyannaish" desire to ignore the extent of housing and educational segregation, the subtle and not-so-subtle discrimination in employment and policing, the intolerable incidence of poverty, the deterioration and neglect of cash and non-cash services. It is an effort to have a more balanced view so as to promote decisions that are shaped less by disillusion and more by creating new possibilities.

Two ideas of the 1960s might still be useful: to combat redlining and "white flight" as blacks move into white neighborhoods, improve public and school services in these changing localities. That is often the opposite of what now occurs. A second approach would attempt to deal with the economic component of the fear propelling white flight, that housing values would decline. Changing neighborhoods could be issued insurance policies that would guarantee the current value of owner-occupied homes. That could be done by federal or state agencies or by having them insure private insurers against losses. Improved services and a guarantee against loss might improve chances of having truly integrated neighborhoods.

john a. powell's efforts to affect the setting of schools and housing could be used in many areas to maintain or induce integration. (See "Race and Space," pp. 20–27.) A major issue is occupational concentration. Blacks are disproportionately in low-paying occupations. This situation is accentuated by the ending of "welfare as we know it." Getting on the job market ladder is insufficient if it is broken and one is stuck at the first step. Moving up quite a few rungs to a decent-paying occupational and industrial place is crucial. Training for entry-level jobs is only a beginning. What is needed is accessible, well-designed, subsidized training that will definitely lead to better jobs, an upward mobility program. Dead-end jobs—low-paid, hard, and boring work—as one's future do not encourage good work habits or motivation to act in positive ways.

Latinos and Asian Americans also experience the broken ladder, and so do the much larger number of whites who did not graduate from high school or have only a high school diploma, an increasingly devalued credential. Cross-race coalitions for an effective job mobility program might yield results. At present, race-oriented policies are not likely to win wide support. "Going it alone" is not a wise strategy for African Americans in a rapidly changing economy and society.

These suggestions and many others that are around will not lead to real integration. Progress has been made, but much remains to be done. Consequently, improving areas where African Americans live is important. That is happening through asset-building efforts that promote home ownership and entrepreneurship. Neighborhood improvement associations are making a difference. But these efforts and gains should not close out efforts to build toward a greater measure of integration. Without such a push, "separate but equal" will always be prey to separate but unequal.

A two-track approach is needed: improving black neighborhoods and integrating schools and neighborhoods. We should have expected a long struggle; we still should.

Keeping the Dream

William L. Taylor

Leonard Steinhorn and Barbara Diggs-Brown have made an important contribution with their trenchant analysis of where matters now stand in the long struggle for equality and racial integration. Sadly, race remains a seemingly intractable problem, an (perhaps *the*) American dilemma. W.E.B. DuBois's observation that the color line would be the American problem of the twentieth century is carrying over to the twenty-first. And one scenario offered by the authors—that some newer immigrant groups, even those of color, may be accepted and assimilated into society while black people continue to be excluded—is all too real a possibility.

But if those of us who consider ourselves advocates for racial and social justice are to be thoughtful and strategic in looking to the future, we must take into account another reality. We must understand how far we have come and how we got there. In conducting this examination, the measure should not be confined to "integration" as a narrow concept, but should include the progress black people have made in becoming part of the economic, civic, and political mainstream in the United States.

In my forty-five years as a civil rights lawyer I have seen some astonishing changes. Here are a few:

- Black people have entered into every business and profession. These include sectors such as banking, insurance, and communications in which they were once almost totally segregated, and jobs such as skilled construction work from which they were almost totally excluded. While discrimination and tokenism remain, the progress made has led to a great expansion of the black middle class.
- Black enrollment in colleges, universities, and professional schools increased greatly beginning in the late 1960s and 1970s, due in no small measure to the adoption of affirmative action policies. In addition to the obvious occupational and economic consequences, as William Bowen and Derek Bok have documented in *The Shape of the River*, black people who graduated from selective institutions are playing a larger role as civic leaders.
- Between 1970 and 1990, black teenagers cut the academic performance gap between themselves and white teenagers almost in half on the widely respected National Assessment of Educational Progress. There is strong

evidence that school desegregation and programs like Head Start contributed to these gains.

- Even in housing, where there is ample cause for discouragement, Douglas Massey and Nancy Denton, the chroniclers of *American Apartheid*, show gains in residential integration in many communities.
- Not least, the removal of voting barriers has led to political participation by blacks in regions of the nation where once they were virtually excluded.

The consequences of this accrual of political and economic power are worth pondering. In 1987, Robert Bork's nomination to the Supreme Court was defeated in large measure because of the growth of black political power. In the 1990s, while anti-affirmative action referenda prevailed in California and Washington, a Republican-dominated Congress several times voted down anti-affirmative action measures. Republican leaders fear that their chances of becoming and remaining a majority party will suffer if they alienate black voters. In 1999, when the NAACP protested the nonparticipation of blacks in television programming, heads of networks made at least some changes quickly, something that would not have happened in years past.

In short, the political and economic gains made by blacks have created a new reality that white Americans have had to accept regardless of their prejudices. It is telling that most whites feel impelled to respond to opinion polls by accepting the new norm of equality, even if, as Steinhorn and Diggs-Brown suggest, many may not mean it or live it. In fact, changes in behavior brought about by changes in law have led to some genuine reductions in biased attitudes. Racial stereotypes are continually challenged by the integration of black people into the mainstream. And even at the cosmetic level, it is interesting that conservative groups peddling such nostrums as school vouchers feel impelled to market their solutions as beneficial to black and poor children.

No, I am not suggesting that the millennium in civil rights has arrived. In addition to the old problems there are newer ones: the growing gap between the wealthy and poor that is seemingly exacerbated by the technological revolution and the nation's general prosperity; the increasing difficulty of focusing solely on a domestic agenda in the face of global economic injustice; the rising distrust of government's capacity to solve problems; the paradoxical fact that the communications revolution is in many ways leading to a decline in community life and increased isolation; and the political use of the progress that has been made to deny the need for more effort.

These challenges call for new ideas and strategies. But many of the fundamentals remain the same. Black people were not empowered politically or economically by laws. They used the laws to empower themselves through education and community and political action. These, along with coalition-building, will remain key to future progress.

Finally, there is the importance of ultimate goals. On this I disagree with the suggestion by Steinhorn and Diggs-Brown that integration is a chimera that may have to be abandoned as a goal in order to have a "real reckoning on race." In thinking about our aspirations today, we should be informed by the experience of four decades, stripping from the goal of integration old elements of paternalism and recognizing more clearly than we have the values of diversity. That said, it would be foolish to succumb to the thinking that told us in the 1960s that race riots were the result of raising the hopes and expectations of people too high. Any movement must have hopes and expectations that go beyond its short-term reach. No one I know has articulated the goals of racial and social justice and integration any better than Martin Luther King. His dream will have to do until a better one comes along.

No One Even Knows What Integration Is

John Woodford

Our struggle is about desegregation and justice, including recompensatory and reparative measures to make up for past systematic handicapping of our socioeconomic and political rights and privileges.

The goal is not and should not be termed as "integration." No one even knows what that is. It cannot be measured or defined. But desegregation and fairness are discernible and measurable. If integration is whatever happens after there is no racist repression and super-exploitation, then what will be will be. No one can say what form that will take as far as individual or group behavior may go. So it is not worth talking about, other than to say people should be free to associate however they choose.

But to declare integration "impossible," in view of the connotation the word has today, where it also implies desegregation, is really a defeatist cop-out, and such a slogan or program is an attempt to lull Afro-Americans into a defeatist and hopeless mind-set. Scholars have never been able to predict the future. But they can abuse their presumed authority to engage in psychological warfare. What you describe here is psychological warfare against Blacks.

We Aspire to Integration and Practice Pluralism

Frank H. Wu

Of all the prophecies for the new millennium, demographic predictions will come true the earliest. Within the foreseeable future, our society will make a transition that has never before and nowhere else occurred peacefully, much less successfully: we will cease to have a single identifiable racial majority and instead will begin to create a racially mixed new world. W.E.B. DuBois may have been as premature as he was prescient in declaring that the problem of the twentieth century would be the color line.

Everybody says they are in favor of diversity, but nobody has thought about the concept. Whether our diversity becomes a dream or a nightmare depends on the interpretation we give to the popular term. The left especially should take care to avoid arguments that can be appropriated.

Perhaps the defining characteristic of American exceptionalism and optimism is our ability to celebrate and embrace contradictory principles. We aspire to integration and practice pluralism. Each claims to be a form of equality, but they are as dissimilar as possible.

Progressive leaders of a generation ago proclaimed racial integration as a goal. They had in mind African Americans more than any other group, but white ethnics who only a generation ago would have portrayed themselves and in turn been perceived as less white and more ethnic have passed much more readily into this paradigm. The claim of integration is this: I am an individual who is like the next individual, and I demand to be treated as he is treated.

More cynical writers today doubt that the abstract promise of assimilation can be achieved, and they even suggest it is a false hope that must betray its beneficiaries. After all, the guarantee of a perfectly distributed assortment of peoples throughout the spheres of daily life virtually assures that in any given group of ten people the African American will always stand alone.

Another tradition of thinkers has declared cultural pluralism as an ideal. They have been concerned with American Jews more than any other group, but their values have been invoked as readily by Latinos, Asians, Arabs, Africans, and especially the immigrants among them who wish to form a diaspora community rather than lead a lonely life as an exile. The claim of pluralism is this: we are a group who are unlike the other groups, and we deserve to be respected as they are respected.

Contemporary commentators wonder whether the fragmentation into factions will lead to hatred and backlash, or if it can be nothing better than a superficial combination of tacos, sushi, hummus, and grits. The common core, as a unifying myth if not quite a shared reality, has given our citizenship its convention

The problem may be that we use diversity too casually and not critically enough. Like equality, diversity can have many meanings.

Because it can be defined for the context and has not yet become controversial, it is easy enough to substitute "diversity" for other terms: "integration" and "pluralism" are old-fashioned; "multiracial" and "multicultural" too trendy. These are not synonyms, though.

An institution can be multiracial without being multicultural, and vice versa. Race and culture correlate very roughly. A company could have its own buttoned-down protocol which accepted individuals of any skin color, but demanded submission to the prevailing norms. Or a college could be predominantly black, but encompass multiple national origins, geographical influences, class backgrounds, religious faiths, and ethnic traditions.

Treating everyone identically produces its own unfairness, because any standard that is chosen is bound to favor somebody. Even perfect neutrality, if it could be attained, has the vice of forcing everyone toward its sameness.

Encouraging dissent in all its forms creates anarchy. Almost nobody really intends to welcome each and every conceivable form of rebellion and opposition.

People who are eager for diversity in theory may not enjoy it in practice. The trouble is that any substance can be inserted into the label.

Essentially, diversity means difference. An advocate for diversity—genuine diversity—is an advocate for difference. If difference for the sake of difference is actually the goal, then every variation is worthwhile. One person's difference is another's damnation.

Supporters of diversity, for example, if they are to be true to the banner they fly, must at least acquiesce to the claim of the Ku Klux Klan member who insists that he too must be represented in Congress or the boardroom. If diversity is the measure, the born-again Christian who asks why there are not more evangelicals on the op-ed page or in front of the classroom has as compelling a grievance as anyone else.

A believer in cultural diversity will be confronted with political conservatism that cannot be challenged. However they are defined, either cultural diversity or political liberalism can prevail but not both. The problem is especially apparent in the case of the minority group that in turn mistreats the internal minority within its own ranks, all the more so if outsiders attempt to intervene: the community of color that insists on female genital mutilation or that invokes a cultural defense for domestic violence; or the non-Western religious adherents that abhor gays and lesbians or that shun the disabled.

Diversity presents us the challenge of saying what we mean so we can mean what we say. Mere diversity is not enough. It is its substance that matters.

Integration: The Long Hard Road to the Right Destination

Paul L. Wachtel

Leonard Steinhorn and Barbara Diggs-Brown perform a valuable service in reminding us of how the reality of daily life in America contradicts some of our society's cherished illusions. But in referring to integration as an illusion there is also a problematic ambiguity that has a potential to impede the very struggle whose continuing uphill nature they illuminate. There is a huge difference between viewing as illusory the idea that integration has very largely been achieved and viewing as illusory that integration is an attainable—or desirable—ideal.

In many sectors of the African American community today, and among progressives of all races and ethnic groups, the very ideal of integration is being seriously questioned, in part, because integration is viewed as entailing submission to white norms and standards. Certainly this view is understandable. There is clearly arrogance and ethnocentrism aplenty in the attitudes of white America toward all of its minorities and toward African Americans in particular. An integration or assimilation predicated on the idea that white suburban culture is the apex of human achievement most certainly should be challenged. But there is a troubling return of what amounts to the idea of "separate-but-equal" in much contemporary progressive critique of the goals of integration or assimilation. In my view, while the effort at integration has indeed been less than a resounding success, abandonment of the *very goal* of integration would be a strategic disaster.

In demonstrating that our continuing failure to achieve genuine integration can be traced to circumstances already in place before either liberals' or conservatives' "usual suspects" for explaining that failure had emerged, Steinhorn and Diggs-Brown actually illuminate why the dream of an integrated society is still worth pursuing. What becomes very clear from their analysis is that the disappointment many now feel about the fruits of the integra-

tionist effort corresponds to an unrealistic optimism at the outset of those efforts. As Steinhorn and Diggs-Brown state in a perceptive and noteworthy phrase,
"the infrastructure of a separated America" was already in place when the civil
rights movement hit its stride. The housing and transportation patterns established by suburbanization and the abandonment of our inner cities—phenomena that, as Steinhorn and Diggs-Brown point out, preceded passage of the
landmark 1960s civil rights legislation—do present enormous structural obstacles to achieving true integration and equality (as they do to maintaining the
quality of our environment). Appreciation of this brute fact makes it clear that
the task the movement faced was in some ways even more monumental than
was appreciated at the time. It thus suggests that the gains that have been achieved
are even more impressive than they otherwise might appear.

To be sure, Steinhorn and Diggs-Brown's observations also point to the long-
standing racism that led to this pattern of housing, which was by no means
motivated simply by a desire to live near trees. But no one in the movement
disputes that racism lay at the core of our society's divisions; that was what the
movement was designed to overcome. The real question is whether the degree
of racism has in any way moderated in the last thirty years. Here, while I can
understand and respect the view that the changes have been superficial and
even illusory, I draw different conclusions. It is true that the new norms, in
which attitudes once readily expressed in public are now unacceptable, are honored much more in word than in deed (and in public words more than in private). But they *are* new norms. Changes in the basic rules of acceptable public
discourse are not insignificant occurrences.

What I think Steinhorn and Diggs-Brown (along with many other writers
and activists) may underestimate is the central importance of conflict in psychological life. As a psychologist, I am accustomed to seeing in people's behavior
the kinds of contradictions that Steinhorn and Diggs-Brown point to. When
close attention is paid, it is clear that all of us, in almost all aspects of our lives,
show such contradictions. And interestingly, psychologists, as much as social
and political activists, often make the mistake of depicting one half of the conflict as the person's "real" attitude and the other as a deceptive or self-deceiving
facade. This works very poorly in psychotherapy, and it does not work much
better in the social sphere. White America does very largely profess one set of
ideals and apparently lives by quite another. That contradiction must indeed be
highlighted and illuminated. But it is a terrible mistake to conclude from this
correct observation that the commitment to racial equality expressed by many
whites is simply false or illusory. Dismissing the majority who hold political
and economic power as simply hypocrites or racists is a path that leads to certain failure and to the perpetuation of the very injustices we yearn to transcend.
Rather, the task is to speak to those inclinations in the conflicted white major-

ity—however submerged or limited to mere verbiage they may be at present—that reflect a genuine wish for a more just society.

The infrastructure of inequality to which Steinhorn and Diggs-Brown refer is still very much in place, and is part of a still larger set of structural obstacles to real integration. Their impact cannot be underestimated. But it is the very pervasiveness and power of that infrastructure that calls for persistence in pursuing the goal of integration. A separate Black economy is scarcely a realistic option. At the very least, integrating African Americans fully into the economic life of our society is an urgent necessity. Where there is greater controversy is in the realm of culture and personal association.

Many African Americans have abandoned the ideal of integration on this level largely for two somewhat related reasons. First, integration (to the extent it has been achieved) has often meant hurtful interactions. African Americans often feel slighted, overlooked, perceived through the filter of stereotypes. Many have concluded that they would just as soon spend as little time as possible with whites when the workday is over. Second—and here objections to the goal of integration are based on assumptions it is particularly important to reexamine—integration is seen as a process in which African Americans must give up their own culture to assimilate into what is essentially "white" culture. But the view that American culture is "white" culture ironically concedes too much to racist assumptions regarding what America is about. Yes, power and wealth are disproportionately white; but the vibrant culture of American society has been very powerfully shaped by the contributions of African Americans and other groups either presently or formerly accorded marginal status. The culture into which African Americans would assimilate is a culture on which their own imprint is already strongly evident.

The Supreme Court got it right in 1954 when it concluded that, in the context of our nation's terrible history with regard to race, separate can never really be equal. It would be a tragic error if the victims of that history were now to conclude that separate is the way to go.

The Politics of Perception

Ty dePass

Is the glass of progress toward racial justice half full . . . or half empty?

I use this apparently harmless cliché to examine the most persistent, perplexing, and perfidious aspect of our national fixation on the color line: the ease with which *race*, a complex social phenomenon, can be reduced to a trifling difference of opinion or perspective.

The glass is at least half empty for Leonard Steinhorn and Barbara Diggs-Brown. They argue persuasively that racism is alive and thriving in the institutions, customs, and consciousness of U.S. society. Steinhorn and Diggs-Brown present a mountain of statistical, observational, and anecdotal evidence in a scathing indictment of many cherished American myths. Their data confirm the chilling reality of the Kerner Riot Commission's 1968 prediction that the "nation is moving toward two societies, one black, one white . . . separate and unequal." Concluding that the dream of integration was an illusory quest doomed from the outset, the authors paint a particularly gloomy picture of prospects for achieving racial parity—never mind harmony—entering the twenty-first century. Such is the strength and weakness of their analysis.

Despite going to great lengths to describe these phenomena, the authors nevertheless missed their essence. We agree that the categories of "black" and "white" are both socially constructed and deeply etched into the national psyche. From its very beginning, the history, laws, and legal institutions of this nation were indispensable in the construction of racial identities and their corresponding arrangements of wealth, status, and political power. However, Steinhorn and Diggs-Brown fall prey to "white folks will be white folks" racial nihilism. In their exploration of the dark side of being "an American," the investigators uncritically accept the central tenet: that racial conflict is an inherent, objective, and therefore immutable feature of human society.

On the other hand, Steinhorn and Diggs-Brown suggest that the only viable alternative to continued racial confrontation is *racial co-existence*. Overestimating the significance of the reported liberalization in white attitudes toward intermarriage with Latinos and Asians (notably, not blacks), the authors suggest that a protracted process of social assimilation will facilitate this limited racial detente. It remains unclear whether the category Latinos includes the darker-skinned Caribbean peoples of Cuba, Puerto Rico, and the Dominican Republic. Moreover, this argument would be more convincing if substantiated by a corresponding increase in white tolerance for non-Anglo cultural practices and languages other than English. The recent spate of citizens' ballot initiatives espousing social conservative causes is not a particularly encouraging sign.

A new political orthodoxy overstates the gains of some minority groups, heralding the arrival of a color-blind society. The elimination of overtly discriminatory laws and our apparent willingness to embrace certain black and

Latino athletes and entertainers are proofs that we, as a nation, have overcome. Evidence of continuing injustice—like videotapes of police brutality in Los Angeles or a grisly lynching in rural Texas—are dismissed as regrettable, but isolated, "aberrations." Critics of Steinhorn and Diggs-Brown note that, relative to conditions of the past, recent indicators of economic, political, and social advancement by communities of color prove that the glass must be at least half full. Thankfully, these racial optimists reject the more outrageous claims of the popular death-of-racism narrative advanced by the Thernstroms and others. Sadly, they are just as swift to trumpet each episode of apparent racial progress (no matter how ephemeral) in a desperate, if well-intentioned, attempt to squeeze every drop of hope into that dusty glass. Steinhorn and Diggs-Brown rightly chide advocates of affirmative action, school desegregation, and similar race-conscious remedies for being dishonest in dodging the fact that authentic racial justice will require that "whites" also bear the burden of social change.

Yet even the most optimistic readily admit that the dream remains largely deferred—that an American nightmare is always a menacing presence. The merciless hail of gunfire that consumed the dreams of Amadou Diallo in February 1999 brings the nightmare into vivid focus. Diallo, a West African immigrant living in the South Bronx, an unwitting victim of his skin color and place of residence, gunned down on his front porch by four white police officers of the elite New York Police Department (NYPD) street crimes unit. At the unprecedented trial that followed, experts on police procedure assured jurors empanelled in Albany, New York (150 miles distant from the shooting scene) that the random stops and searches conducted by plainclothes street cowboys were appropriate for that neighborhood; that approaching a figure "lurking" in the hallway of an apartment building with guns drawn was appropriate for that neighborhood; that "fear for their safety" upon confronting a black man with a "dark object" in his hand was appropriate for that neighborhood; that the fear causing them to fire forty-one bullets into the narrow entryway of Diallo's apartment building was appropriate . . . for that neighborhood. An unarguably inept and ineffectual prosecution allowed the defense to cast the offending officers as the victims. Accordingly, finding no clear evidence of murderous intent or "racial motivation," the jury exonerated the white officers. In the end, the not guilty verdict not only reduced Diallo's death to another unfortunate statistic of ghetto violence, it declared open season on any black man in possession of a wallet. Two weeks later, Patrick Dorismond, another unarmed black New Yorker, was killed by NYPD undercover officers in Brooklyn.

So, is the glass half full or half empty?

The obvious answer is both—and neither. For anyone who has truly thirsted, the answer hinges on who's pouring.

Response to
"Is Integration Possible?" Symposium

Leonard Steinhorn

Perhaps it should be no surprise that the *Poverty & Race* discussion of *By the Color of Our Skin: The Illusion of Integration and The Reality of Race* mirrors many of the themes, issues, and shibboleths that dominate our national dialogue on race today. After reading the commentaries, what gives me hope is that some critics are probing thoughtfully and creatively about why integration has failed and what can be done to restore a culture of equality in America. What disappoints me, however, is how other critics, in the name of "new thinking," fall back upon tired clichés, easy ideology, and conventional wisdom as a substitute for a critical look at our society today. As for those who wrote polemics laced with the predictable language of the revolutionary class—using words like imperialist, racial dictatorship, political prisoners, psychological warfare—I merely wish them well as they take their gritty struggle into the salons of academia.

Of all the issues raised in *Poverty & Race*, the most provocative and thoughtful address the relationship between integration and desegregation, a core theme in the book. What my coauthor and I say in the book is that America is desegregating—albeit slowly and haltingly—but we are not integrating. We then suggest that America's failure to move toward integration during this time of progress bodes ill for the future of integration and indicates very deep cultural roadblocks to the Promised Land.

Though no one really takes issue with our analysis of the state of integration in America today, a few writers—among them Herbert Gans, William Taylor, and Don DeMarco—suggest that the obstacles to future integration may be less cultural than I believe them to be. What they argue, trenchantly so, is that integration may be failing not because history has set us on a course of racial separation but because our national desegregation effort has not been as vigorous, widespread, and deeply rooted as it needs to be. As Gans puts it, until blacks gain greater social, economic, and political equality with whites, "white homeowners may continue to treat current middle-class blacks as surrogates for the poor ones that might move in right behind them. This is one reason why white flight continues." Gans and the others argue that the best way to achieve integration is to ramp up desegregation efforts in America—to provide not merely increased opportunities, but guarantees that institutional bigotry will not undermine these opportunities.

I have deep respect for this perspective and wish I could agree. Implicit in it is a very American element of can-do optimism, a view that race relations is fixable through policy and national will. Unfortunately, I remain unconvinced. As we describe in the book, America's unique racial dowry and cultural history have grown too big for political solutions and even structural changes. Just look at the ongoing racial chasm at most colleges and universities, places that aggressively enforce equality and equal opportunity. Or look at it on the very personal level, how even accomplished black families living in predominantly white neighborhoods must still hide their family photos and mementos if they want to sell their homes to whites. Like it or not, culture always seems to trump the most effective policy.

This is not to say, of course, that policy is unimportant—it is, indispensably so, and we cannot sustain desegregation and move toward equality without it. But we should simply have no illusions that better desegregation policy will lead to integration. My coauthor and I write in our book that "desegregation is a necessary precondition for integration." But we also write "it is entirely possible to desegregate without integrating." That is the most likely scenario in America's future, regardless of how thoroughly we desegregate.

The most predictable and unoriginal critique of our book comes from those who argue that we need to move beyond the black/white paradigm toward a multicultural vision of the future. What makes this view even more humdrum is that its proponents are so deeply convinced they are on to something new. These commentators hail multiculturalism as "breaking new ground" and claim that the black/white divide is old and no longer makes sense in a nation of new immigrants. They trot out the usual statistics that minorities are increasing in numbers and whites are decreasing—and suggest that these apparent new realities demand radical and creative new approaches.

But like a soap bubble, this argument has lots of glimmer but little behind it. Most important, it focuses solely on a snapshot of today and completely ignores American history, which is no surprise since history is often an irritant to those with an ideological or political agenda. Anyone conscientious enough to learn about our past will see how immigrants throughout American history have assimilated into the majority, usually over a generation or two. It may be news to some, but the majority of a century ago looks very different from the majority today—a majority that now includes the children, grandchildren, and great-grandchildren of all those early twentieth-century immigrants and minorities whom nativists once said were "swarthy" and unmeltable. Much like the Betty Crocker image, the American majority has adjusted and changed to accommodate our changing ethnic population.

There is no reason to think the same dynamic is not taking place today. Assimilation is not easy, and immigrants have always faced rejection and worse, but recent studies—for example, of Latino immigrant attitudes and lifestyles—show clear patterns of assimilation not very different from the process immigrants undertook a century ago. If history is any lesson—and it is the best one we have—today's immigrants will face considerable hardship but ultimately will assimilate into the majority, and in the process they will change the majority, just as Jews and Italians and Poles did throughout the last century.

However, both history and current trends also show the exception to the rule: blacks will remain on the outside, noses pressed to the glass looking in. America has never let blacks integrate the way it lets immigrants assimilate. It is a process that repeats itself every time new immigrants arrive. First, we talk about a broad multicultural umbrella of minorities that includes both immigrants and blacks. Over a generation or two the immigrants begin to assimilate; a new majority is then created that excludes only blacks. Assuming white is a shorthand way of saying majority, the black/white paradigm remains our core national dilemma. It may be old, but it is central to our history and is as current as ever.

It is also worth noting some of the sloppy or ideological groupthink in some of the critiques on the assimilation issue. One author quotes a description of assimilation as "the nonchoice between being either different and inferior or the same and invisible, between eternal alien and assimilated mascot." It sounds trendy and nice, and it carries quite a sneer about an idea that many on the left demean and ridicule. But just as with any groupthink, it has little to do with people's lives. Does that quote apply to Irish? to Jews? to Italians? to Poles? to Russians? to Greeks? to Armenians? to Cubans? To any of the immigrant groups whose families have undergone the assimilation process? Do those who deride assimilation really believe that today's immigrants, if given the choice, would not want to follow the footsteps of the immigrants who came before them?

No one should minimize or trivialize the immense hardships many Latinos and Asians experience today. But they are not unlike the hardships that immigrants experienced a century ago. Assimilation is a process that does not happen overnight. We must look to history to put today's conventional wisdom in its proper perspective.

The final *Poverty & Race* commentary worth noting is the romantic view that race is less important than class, that somehow class-based policies will take the rough edges off racial conflict and tension. The class approach sounds very enticing. It appeals to popular leftist images of solidarity and common ground, and on first blush offers a politically savvy way of promoting progressive social goals without generating racial resentment.

But once again experience and history are hard taskmasters with little tolerance for ideological or wishful thinking. Take the idea of class-based affirmative action. If affirmative action were based on class, then presumably it would be targeted at the lower end of the job market. But what would happen when mid-level and managerial jobs need to be filled? The old boy network would take over, which means white people would generally recommend their neighbors, friends, fellow parishioners, Rotary Club colleagues, and other whites. Without race-based affirmative action, blacks once again would be left out—indeed left out of an important part of the economy, the decision-making part. With all due respect to the Marxists among us, America has done a remarkable job of erasing or at least blurring class distinctions among whites. But no matter how much black Americans achieve, the color line remains impermeable and strong.

As for those who promote a class-based approach for political reasons because they believe it would take race out of the equation, our current experience with affirmative action should serve as a cautionary note. Affirmative action today covers women and minorities, a large group that, like class, could create common ground. But while most white Americans support affirmative action for women—their spouses, daughters, sisters, neighbors, and friends—their blood begins to boil when it applies to blacks. Again, culture triumphs over reason.

No single book or idea or journal of commentary will solve our nation's racial stalemate, but it is heartening to read the many insightful observations in the two *Poverty & Race* issues devoted to *By the Color of Our Skin*. Some observations are quite elegantly stated, such as that idea that we must make a "common understanding about the benefits of integration" a national priority, or the notion that integration requires more than black effort, that white and middle-class Americans must be full partners, or the exhortation that we must seize on the opportunity provided by whites who may not want integrated lives but claim they do. Although the path to a more racially just society will have to be built brick by brick, and the final destination remains unclear, one thing is clear: we cannot give up trying to make this a better world.

History Quiz: Answers

1. b. False. Robinson was the first in the twentieth century. Blacks played Major League baseball in the nineteenth century. A protest by the president of the Chicago White Sox led to the removal of the last, about 1889.

2. b. False. Abraham Lincoln said this, while debating Stephen A. Douglas in 1858.

3. b. False. White intruders repeatedly burned Indian corn fields, chopped down orchards, and forced them to take to the woods and become nomadic.

4. Escaped African slaves of a failed Spanish colony in what is now South Carolina; 1526.

5. About 100,000,000, according to historian William H. McNeill, in *Plagues and Peoples* (1976).

6. 90 to 96 percent.

7. d. Woodrow Wilson.

8. c. He died alone and penniless.

Part 2

Poverty

Part 2

Poetry

Poverty seems to be as endemic to our society as is racism; and like racism, the majority of society deludes itself about its prevalence and the damage it inflicts, not only on its victims but on our nation's stated commitment to justice and democracy. To the extent that poverty is racialized, those inner-city (and, increasingly, inner-suburban) ghettos are simply out of sight and out of mind for middle- and upper-class Americans, of all races. One of the benefits of the Civil Rights Movement, affirmative action, and other positive steps over the past few decades has been the enormous growth of a Black, as well as Latino and Asian, middle class. And as these families understandably seek to improve their material conditions of life, they leave behind—both geographically and to a large extent politically and socially—the truly poor, who are isolated in what sociologists increasingly are recognizing as "hypersegregated" neighborhoods. Those trapped there are massively cut off from their larger surroundings and are bereft of decent educational and employment opportunities. The more recent phenomenon of gated communities is both a real and symbolic step toward isolating those with wealth and power from those at society's bottom.

The seven articles in this section deal in part with specific subpopulations of the poor: the welfare-dependent, low-income and minority women and children, Native Americans, and those living in rural areas, especially small farmers. While these are distinct groups, whose poverty has some special causes, the totality of the problem is huge, and the fact that America, with all its riches and economic boom times, allows these conditions to persist is as damning a statement about our values and the meaning of democracy as is our persistent institutionalized racism. While the special situation of the racialized poor must be identified, that should not prevent us from equally recognizing the extent of poverty among whites. There is need for universal solutions, as well as a need to approach the special barriers to eliminating the poverty that racial minorities face.

Economic Growth and Poverty: Lessons from the 1980s and 1990s

Jared Bernstein

Over the course of the 1990s business cycle, the U.S. economy racked up some pretty impressive statistics. Unemployment in 2000 fell to a thirty-year low, and the tightening labor market finally led to wage gains for many groups of workers whose income had stagnated or declined for decades. Productivity growth—a measure of how efficiently the economy is generating its output—sped up for the first time in years, handily paying for the aforementioned wage gains. Even the intractable problem of growing inequality slowed considerably in the latter half of the 1990s (it continued to grow over the decade, but half as fast as during the 1980s).

The poverty rate, however, was virtually the same in 1998 as it was in 1989.

Actually, it was one-tenth of a percent lower in 1998—12.7 percent of the population was poor in 1998 versus 12.8 percent in 1989: statistically indistinguishable. And since the population grew since 1989, more people were poor in the latter year (34.5 million versus 31.5 million).

How did this come to pass? Has the recent wave of prosperity washed over the poor? Are low-income families immune to the benefits of the so-called "new economy"? And if so, then what is so new about it?

Before addressing these larger issues, some facts are needed for context. First, a word about how we measure poverty. Each year, the Census Bureau collects a representative sample of data on family incomes, adds in the value of cash transfers (such as welfare benefits), and compares this amount to the poverty thresholds, which are adjusted for family size. In 1998, the threshold for a family of four with two children was $16,530.

The current thresholds were derived in the early 1960s based on data from the mid-1950s, and most experts agree that they are far out of date. They reflect neither the true resources available to many low-income families (for example, the cash value of food stamps), nor the higher thresholds that would prevail if the original measures were updated. Recent analysis by the U.S. Census Bureau shows that an updated method would lead to poverty rates on average about 3.5 percentage points higher in the 1990s. The trends over time, however, of the official and alternative rates are similar, and because of the pervasive use of the official rate, I will focus on it throughout. But it is well within our means to do a better job measuring poverty, and we should do so.

In much of what follows, I stress trends in the poverty rate (i.e., how it has evolved over time) since this is the best way to address the above set of questions. For 1998, the most recent year for which data are currently available, 12.7 percent of the population was poor by the official definition, as noted. Poverty rates for minorities are higher, since their income levels are lower, on average. The rate for African Americans was 26.1 percent, for Hispanics it was 25.6 percent. The child poverty rate was 18.9 percent, and the black child poverty rate was 36.7 percent. Child poverty rates in the United States are typically at least twice as those in many comparably advanced economies.

Some Key Trends

In order to examine the connection between economic growth and poverty trends, we must begin by looking more closely at some key trends over the last few decades. As the 1980s wound down, economists noticed that poverty rates had been pretty "sticky" over the decade. That is, they did not respond to economic growth as they had in the past. Of course, poverty continued to be cyclical, rising in economic downturns and falling in recoveries, but, while the rate rose as high as 15.2 percent as a result of the early 1980s recession, it never fell back as far as would have been expected, ending the decade a point higher in 1989 than in 1979 (12.8 percent versus 11.7 percent).

The beginning of the 1990s looked like more of the same. Despite the relatively shallow nature of the early 1990s recession, poverty rates rose to 15.1 percent, about as high as in the earlier, much deeper recession of the early 1980s. Thus, in terms of their response to overall growth, it appeared that poverty rates were less likely to fall, and more likely to rise, for a given amount of overall growth: the worst of both worlds!

Numerous factors were behind this unfortunate dynamic. The most important was the striking increase in inequality that took place over these years. Whether we look at wages, incomes, or wealth, the indicators show that the gap between the top, middle, and the bottom expanded to historic highs over these years. Low-income persons were disproportionately affected and actually lost ground in real terms. For example, between 1979 and 1989, the average income of the bottom 20 percent of families fell 6 percent in real terms, while that of the top 20 percent grew 20 percent. In a situation like that, aggregate indicators, such as GDP growth or productivity, tell us very little about who is getting ahead. In fact, the pie was growing, but the poor were getting ever smaller slices.

Also, we know now that the labor market never really tightened up in the 1980s and early 1990s relative to later years. The overall unemployment rate was 7.1 percent in the 1979–1989 period, well above both the averages of prior business cycles, and, most importantly for this analysis, the 5.7 percent average that prevailed over the 1989–1999 period. It was not until things really heated up in the mid-1990s that more of the rising tide finally began to reach some of the smaller vessels.

One of the most common explanations for poverty's failure to respond to growth is the growing share of family types more vulnerable to poverty, specifically mother-only families. It is important to examine this claim closely, because if it is true that this is a major explanation, then all the economic growth in world will not help much. But, while it seems like simple accounting—more single-mom families equal more poverty—a look at the relevant trends challenges a simple demographic story ("trends" is the key word—any explanation of changes over time must address not simply the level of poverty but the trend). When female-headed families were forming most rapidly, in the 1970s, their poverty rates were actually falling. Over the 1980s, their growth as a share of the population fell to one-third the 1970s rate, but their poverty rates grew. Over the 1990s, their poverty rates fell again, while their share continued to grow. (One relevant counterargument here is that if faster growth led to fewer single-parent families, then poverty would fall as a result.)

Thus, it is not so simple. While at any given point in time, more single-parent families lead to a higher poverty rate, there is no evidence that this factor has become more important over time. In fact, a more thorough decomposition shows that it has become considerably less important. In the 1970s, this shift raised poverty rates by 2 percentage points. In the 1990s, the effect was one-half of 1 percent.

What Explains the Gap Between Growth and Poverty? Clues from the 1990s

The latter half of the 1990s was a better economic period for the majority of American families, including the poor. Poverty rates fell from 15.1 percent in 1993 to 12.7 percent in 1998. For African Americans, the decline was much steeper, from 33.1 percent to 26.1 percent. We expect poverty rates to fall over a recovery, but these declines are greater than those that occurred over the 1980s.

Of course, this positive trend cannot diminish the deeply disturbing fact that over one-quarter of the black population in this country is poor, with incomes far below the level needed to meet their most basic needs (the same goes for Hispanics, whose poverty rate, as noted, was 25.6 percent in 1998). But the question at hand is: what useful lessons can we learn about the economy of the late 1990s? After all, we will never lower these levels if we fail to understand what drives the trends. As we will see, the past few years offer some important lessons about how our nation can reduce poverty.

For the first time in thirty years, as the 1990s came to a close, the labor market was once again operating at or close to full employment. This does not mean everyone who wanted a job had one. It does, however, mean that, on average, the ranks of the unemployed were much smaller (as a share of the workforce) than in the past. It also meant that labor demand was stronger than it had been in decades, finally giving a lift to the millions of workers left behind in previous upturns. Again, the level of joblessness was still much higher for minority workers than whites—the rule of thumb that the black unemployment rate is more than twice that of whites has not been revoked. But just as minority poverty rates fell the most in the latter half of the 1990s, so the labor market indicators improved the most for many minority workers.

But how did this affect the poor, who purportedly do not work very much? In fact, in tandem with welfare reform, it led to a dramatic increase in their success in the labor market. It is true that the hours spent by poor families in the labor force are much lower than those spent by the non-poor. But the trends are again very clear.

In both 1979 and 1989, the share of poor families who did not work at all was 41 percent. By 1998, that share had fallen to 34 percent. After growing 4 percent over the 1980s, the average hours worked by poor families grew 11 percent over the 1990s, to 1,112 annual hours. Among poor white families, average hours were unchanged in the 1990s: they worked about 1,145 hours in both 1989 and 1998. But the annual hours worked by poor African American families grew 21 percent, from 723 to 825. For poor single-parent families with children, average hours increased by 40 percent, from 577 to 808, an increase that partially reflects the welfare-to-work component of welfare reform. Poor families still work much less than non-poor families, but they are working much more than they have in the past.

These increases, coming off of such low bases, should not be expected to send poverty rates down to zero, but we would hope that they made a big difference in the poverty rates of poor families. Yet, while poverty rates for most families fell in the 1990s, the gains could be characterized as disappointing. For mother-only families, the group whose hours increased the most in percentage terms, poverty fell from 42.9 percent to 38.7 percent, in the 1989–1998 period. Black family poverty fell from 27.9 percent to 23.2 percent; Hispanic poverty from 23.4 percent to 22.7 percent. These gains all point in the right direction, and reinforce the point that the trends of the 1990s have made a big difference. But we might have hoped that "the best economy in thirty years," in tandem with the poor's increased work effort, would have knocked the rates down further.

The reasons these hopes were not realized has to do with the relatively few hours worked by the poor, their low wages, and the loss of cash benefits. Regarding the first point, it is often stressed that the poor do not work very much, and the above annual hours support this assertion. But why do the poor not work more? First, about half are children or elderly. When we take out the disabled and those going to school, and look just at those in their prime labor market years, we find that over two-thirds worked at some point during the year. But a very small share, relative to the non-poor with the same characteristics, worked full-time, year round.

If we are committed to a labor market strategy for lowering poverty, we need to learn more about why this is the case. For example, research on welfare-to-work often finds that reliable and safe child care is a significant barrier for single mothers. [See "The Outcomes of Welfare Reform for Women," pp. 102–106.]

However, even if the poor were to double their annual hours spent in the labor force—an extremely tall order—their market wages (the pre-tax wage) would leave them below the poverty line. The average family wage—family earnings divided by family hours—for poor families headed by someone aged twenty-five to fifty-four was about $6.30 in 1998 for families. (The average family hours statistics cited above include families with zero hours. These family wage calculations exclude these families.) Their average annual hours that year were 1,273. If this were a family of four, and they doubled their hours, they would still be poor, at least before adding in the Earned Income Tax Credit (EITC) —a wage subsidy for low-income workers—and food stamps, which would lift them above the poverty line.

But another trend is the decline in cash transfers to poor families that occurred over the late 1990s. Some of this was legislated, as in welfare re-form, but some of it, particularly the decline in the food stamp rolls, appears to be due in part to unauthorized administrative tightening of eligibility. Thankfully, the EITC was considerably expanded in the 1990s, and this has proven to be an important antipoverty tool.

What Lessons Can Be Drawn From Poverty in the 1990s?

The lessons of the above are not hard to identify. If we as a nation agree that work in the paid labor market is our primary antipoverty strategy, then the path is fairly clear. We have to identify and address the barriers that keep poor families from working more hours. To the extent that these have to do with economic constraints, such as lack of access to affordable child care of an acceptable quality, we must subsidize their use. At the same time, we need to implement policies to raise both the pre- and post-tax wages of the working poor. On the pre-tax side, the best plan is to make sure we stay at full employment. One of the key lessons of the 1990s is that this is the best way to create enough pressure in the labor market to raise the wages of those left behind when there is too much slack in the labor market, as was the case in the 1980s and early 1990s. Full employment is not an accident of fate; it results in large part from actions by the Federal Reserve, which, in the latter years of the 1990s, finally allowed the unemployment rate to fall. The mini-mum wage can be increased—in real terms, it still remains over 20 percent below the levels of the late 1970s. Of course, providing education and train-ing is a key longer-term strategy to raise the earnings the poor can command in the job market. On the post-tax side, expanding the EITC is a popular plan with considerable political support. Finally, we need to make sure poor families get the benefits to which they still are entitled, and add more benefits that are tied to work, such as child care subsidies.

Some of these ideas mean increased public expenditures (some, like full employment and the minimum wage, do not). But that is the inevitable outcome of a work-based strategy in an economy with such a large and flourishing low-wage labor market. It is simple: If we insist that the able-bodied poor work, and the low-wage labor market does not generate the wages needed to avoid poverty, even with full-time work, then we have two choices. We either make a very bad deal with the poor: you work, but you and your children continue to live in privation; or, we apply public policy in the spirit of a good-faith agreement: you work, and we as a society will make sure you have enough income to meet your needs. In my view and, I sincerely believe, in the view of most Americans, only the good deal is acceptable.

A more detailed treatment, with data through 1999, can be found in The State of Working America, 2000–01 *(Ithaca: ILS Press, 2001), coauthored with Lawrence Mishel and John Schmitt.*

Welfare Reform and Racial/Ethnic Minorities: The Questions to Ask

Steve Savner

As implementation of state programs funded under Temporary Assistance for Needy Families (TANF) block grants, the program that replaced Aid to Families with Dependent Children (AFDC) grants, has unfolded during the last years of the 1990s, the most noteworthy stories have been the dramatic decline in the number of families receiving cash assistance; the extent to which funds that would otherwise have been used to pay cash assistance have been freed up for other purposes; and the extent to which former welfare recipients have joined the ranks of the working poor. Relatively little attention has been paid to the impact of TANF implementation on racial and ethnic minorities. The evidence that does exist indicates somewhat differential impacts for minorities and whites, and in several studies potentially discriminatory treatment of minorities. While the significance and causes of these differences is not totally clear, the available information suggests that research explicitly focused on these issues, and increased attention by elected officials, administrators, and advocates, is very much needed.

Initially, one of the chief concerns of critics of the 1996 welfare reform legislation was the imposition of a lifetime sixty-month limit on federally funded assistance. Research carried out by the Urban Institute immediately prior to enactment of the 1996 welfare law—the Personal Responsibility and Work Opportunity Reconciliation Act—indicated that both blacks and Hispanics tended to have longer stays on welfare and therefore might be more seriously affected by time limits. The data suggested that about 27 percent of white (and others not black or Hispanic) recipients might be expected to remain on welfare for sixty months, while for blacks the figure was 41 percent, and for Hispanics 51 percent. Other characteristics associated with disproportionately long stays on welfare were: limited education and work experience, beginning to receive benefits when younger than 24, never having been married, and having three or more children. These various barriers to employment correlated with race and ethnicity and explained much of the predicted differences between whites and minorities. The dramatic and unexpected cash assistance caseload declines most states have experienced are largely due to work-first policies, a strong economy, policy changes designed to make paid work more rewarding, and other policy changes, such as sanctions but not, as of 2000, time limits. However, demographic information about those who have left welfare for all reasons during the late 1990s appears to be consistent with the earlier predictions about the effects of time limits.

Early TANF Experience

The number of families receiving cash assistance in state TANF programs fell by roughly 44 percent between August 1996 and September 1999, from 4,415,000 to 2,453,000 families, according to U.S. Department of Health and Human Services reports. While the number of families receiving assistance has fallen dramatically in all racial and ethnic subgroups, the predominant racial and ethnic subgroups (whites, blacks, and Hispanics) have fared differently. The white percentage of the caseload fell about 8 percent from Fiscal Year (FY) 96 to FY 98, while the black percentage rose by almost 5 percent and the Hispanic percentage rose by a little over 7 percent. Simply put, it appears that whites are leaving the caseloads more rapidly (and/or entering more slowly) than blacks and Hispanics.

These data are consistent with two longer-term caseload trends: the percentage of whites in the caseload has been falling since the mid-1980s and the percentage of Hispanics has been rising since the early 1980s. There has been no clear trend in the black portion of the caseload during this period. Among the states, there is substantial variation regarding trends in racial and ethnic composition of cash assistance caseloads. A number of possible explanations exist for these variations, including several concerning the labor market: limited job prospects for minorities living in economically stagnant central city areas, more limited skills and work experience among minorities, and employer discrimination.

Examination of studies designed to track the income and employment status of families that left the cash assistance caseload during the late 1990s yields a starker contrast between these subgroups. One national study of former welfare recipients shows that whites are more likely to have left welfare compared to Hispanics and nonwhite, non-Hispanics, and that Hispanics are less likely to have left than whites or nonwhite, non-Hispanics. Generally, those who have left have more education, and are less likely to face other employment barriers, such as limited work experience, health limitations, etc.

A study of families exiting welfare in Wisconsin in 1995–1996 reported that 61 percent of the white families receiving assistance left the caseload, compared to 36 percent of the black families. In an Arizona study of families exiting welfare in last quarter of 1996, researchers found that while blacks made up 34 percent of open cases, they were only 8.5 percent of all families that left the caseload during that quarter. The picture for Hispanic respondents is much less clear-cut, with studies from some states showing them leaving the caseload in disproportionately large numbers, while studies from other states reveal opposite results.

Studies in Arizona, Georgia, and Cuyahoga County, Ohio, show that shortly after leaving welfare, the percentages of blacks who are employed exceed the percentages of whites who are employed, and results from Arizona, Cuyahoga County, and Wisconsin reveal that blacks have somewhat higher quarterly earnings than whites. However, studies in those same areas also showed that a much higher percentage of blacks returned to welfare within one year of leaving, compared to whites who left. The data for Hispanics vary considerably on all of these measures from one state study to another.

These studies suggest a pattern in which black recipients are less likely to leave welfare than whites, are more likely to be employed shortly after leaving and at somewhat higher wages, but are also more likely to return to welfare within the first year after exiting. Many questions and possible explanations for these findings exist. Why are blacks leaving more slowly than whites? If whites leave in greater proportions but are employed less, what other sources of income are they relying on to get off welfare and stay off longer? And what are the prospective policy implications of these data?

Differential Treatment

Data from Illinois, Florida, and Virginia raise more troubling implications of differential treatment of recipients within local welfare systems based on racial or ethnic origin. An analysis of Illinois data by the *Chicago Reporter* concerning why welfare cases were closed between July 1997 and June 1999 revealed significant differences in the reasons for case closings between whites and minorities. A total of 340, 958 cases closed in this period, of which 102,423 were whites and 238,535 were minorities. Fifty-four percent of minority cases, but only 39 percent of white cases, closed because the recipient failed to comply with program rules. Though earned income made 40 percent of white families ineligible for support, earned income made only 27 percent of minority families ineligible.

Similar data are reported in a study of recipients in rural Florida who left welfare between October 1996 and December 1998, carried out by the Florida Inter-University Welfare Reform Collaborative. The study sample of 115 former recipients responded to questions about why they left welfare as follows: 53 percent of whites, as compared to 32 percent of blacks, found a job; 8 percent of whites and 22 percent of blacks were disqualified for noncompliance with program rules; 6 percent of whites and 17 percent of blacks chose to reject welfare status. These two studies raise important and troubling questions about whether blacks and Hispanics are being treated differently than whites.

Finally, a Virginia Tech study undertaken in two northern Virginia rural counties focused on the interactions between welfare caseworkers and recipients. In this study, thirty-nine recipients (twenty-two black and seventeen white) were interviewed in early 1996 about their interactions with welfare department caseworkers: how frequently caseworkers notified them about job openings, the extent to which caseworkers emphasized further education, caseworker assistance in locating child care, caseworker assistance with transportation, and whether respondents believed that black and white clients were treated fairly by caseworkers.

Except with regard to help with child care, respondents' views on these issues varied significantly by race. Fifty-nine percent of whites, but only 36 percent of blacks, indicated that their caseworkers were often or sometimes helpful in providing information about potential jobs. Forty-one percent of whites indicated that caseworkers encouraged them to go to school, particularly if they had not received a high school diploma. None of the blacks indicated that a caseworker had encouraged them to go to school. One white respondent stated: "They encouraged me to get my GED. I've been in school since October, working on the GED. I hope to graduate in the spring. My worker kept telling me, 'You're smarter than you think.' She really convinced me that I could do it." A black respondent stated: "They talk to you any kind of way. They say: 'Go get a job.' I told them that I only had two parts left on my GED and I wanted to finish, they said: 'That's not what this program is about.'"

About two-thirds of all respondents in this Virginia study indicated they had transportation barriers, and all respondents indicated that the welfare agency provided vouchers to pay for gasoline to those who needed them. However, 47 percent of whites stated that caseworkers indicated they would provide additional forms of transportation assistance, while none of the blacks reported receiving such offers of help. For example, one white respondent indicated: "I own my car but I need a brake job. I contacted DSS (Department of Social Services) about my car. She told me she will try to come up with some money to get it fixed." A black respondent stated: "DSS gives me money for gas. I have a car and a job, but it needs about $300 worth of work, so I can't use it. I asked DSS if they had any funds for car repairs, but she said I should try to use gas vouchers to take a cab or ride with a friend until I save up enough money to get my car fixed." Finally, nearly half (45 percent) of blacks—and even 18 percent of whites—indicated that black clients were not treated fairly by DSS.

While this study looked at a very small sample of recipients, it highlights the importance of a range of discretionary actions by caseworkers concerning the availability of services that may significantly affect the well-being of families receiving assistance and the ability of adults in those families to prepare for and succeed in employment. It also shows the potential for differential treatment based on race or ethnicity in the interactions between recipients and caseworkers.

Research Questions

Taken as a whole, this body of research raises many questions about the effect of changes in welfare policy on members of racial and ethnic minorities, and their treatment by welfare agencies. It is somewhat surprising that, given the very substantial amount of research already under way on welfare reform, so little focuses explicitly on differential racial and ethnic impacts.

The longer-term results of the 1996 welfare reform legislation will not be revealed until the first few years of the new century. Based on the scattered evidence already available, buttressed by what we know of the structural nature of poverty and racism in the United States, some less than positive findings for the minority poor can be anticipated.

The specific issues we need to focus on, and on which additional data collection and research is crucial, with respect to minorities are:

- whether training, transportation, and child care are available and adequate to enable the transition to stable employment
- the prevalence and impact of racially discriminatory actions and attitudes on the part of those who staff welfare systems
- what kinds of jobs those leaving the rolls have knowledge of and access to, and what kinds of jobs they actually get, in terms of pay rate, benefits, training/mobility, and stability
- whether people leaving the rolls are escaping poverty
- the extent to which racially discriminatory practices in the job market, as well as in related areas, continue to limit the potential of minorities

Research on these issues, together with thoughtful policy responses to research findings, will be critical elements of efforts to ensure that the new generation of welfare programs does not perpetuate poverty and racially disparate outcomes.

The Outcomes of Welfare Reform for Women

Barbara Gault and Annisah Um'rani

More than 90 percent of welfare recipient household heads are women, yet few policymakers recognize that discussions of welfare reform are by nature discussions of women's issues. Sex-based inequalities, such as occupational segregation, unequal pay, insufficient family supports for workers, and elevated exposure to physical abuse and sexual harassment, take a particularly hard toll on low-income and minority women. Debates on welfare policies and cost-benefit analyses of social supports for welfare recipients must take these realities into account.

The outcomes of welfare reform for women are mixed. New welfare policies have led to higher rates of work for current and former welfare recipients, but the jobs that women obtain are unstable, pay poor wages, and lack growth potential and benefits. At the same time, federal restrictions on job training diminish women's human capital development opportunities and reduce their potential to achieve long-term economic well-being. Welfare caseloads have dropped and employment rates have increased, but evidence suggests that hardship has increased for a significant proportion of women who leave welfare. While states have more funds and freedom to provide support services, most have failed to utilize available funds to make meaningful social investments in a timely fashion. African American and Latina women, as well as women from other underrepresented groups, are faring particularly poorly following welfare reform.

Poor Quality Jobs

Former welfare recipients typically find jobs with low wages and few benefits. Analyses by the Urban Institute, based on 1997 survey data, found that 61 percent of welfare recipients were employed after leaving welfare, and 21 percent of current welfare recipients were working. Those who left welfare were earning a median wage of $6.61 per hour, and fewer than a quarter received employer-provided health benefits. Another study found that current and former welfare recipients were very unlikely to receive even the most basic employer-provided benefits. Between 41 and 59 percent of welfare recipients did not have paid sick leave, and 26 to 41 percent did not receive even the most basic paid vacation time. Between 20 and 32 percent collected neither benefit. State-level welfare leaver studies indicate that most women obtain jobs in retail sales, fast food, or other service occupations.

Increased Poverty and Hardship

According to an analysis of Current Population Survey data, the poorest women became poorer following welfare reform. The Center on Budget and Policy Priorities found that while single mothers in the lowest earnings quintile experienced significant increases in earnings from 1993 to 1995, from 1995 to 1997 they experienced a 10.7 percent decrease in earnings and a 6.7 percent decrease in disposable income. These results suggest that the economic growth and declines in recipiency rates following the Personal Responsibility and Work Opportunity Reconciliation Act (PRWORA) may not bring greater well-being to the most disadvantaged welfare recipients.

Several studies suggest that Black and Latina women have fared particularly poorly following welfare reform, though little research has focused specifically on their experiences. Overall, Black and Latina women are more vulnerable to poverty than White women. While the overall poverty rate among single mothers in 1998 was 30 percent, 41 percent of Black, and 44 percent of Hispanic single mothers lived in poverty. In May 2000, the unemployment rate for the entire U.S. population was 4.1 percent, while the rate was 8.0 percent for African Americans and 5.8 percent for Hispanics. Educational disadvantages among minority women likely play a strong role in the higher poverty and unemployment rates experienced by this population.

Research suggests that Hispanic women have more difficulty finding jobs and may experience greater hardship than other welfare recipients. An analysis of the National Survey of America's Families found that adults remaining on welfare are more likely to be Hispanic and less likely to be White, compared to those who leave welfare. A 1999 survey conducted at soup kitchens and other emergency service locations found that Latinos are less likely than other welfare recipients to hold a non-workfare job (17 percent of Latinos versus 24 percent of Blacks and 24 percent of Whites).

Welfare reform has reduced some women's access to basic living necessities. In the 1997 National Survey of America's Families, approximately 34 percent of current and former welfare recipients said they were having difficulty providing their families with enough food. Those who left welfare were significantly more likely to report difficulty getting food and paying rent than other low-income women. Some food-related hardship may be explained by the rapid decline in food stamp use, even among former welfare recipients who are still eligible for the benefits, likely due to confusion among recipients about eligibility requirements.

Lack of Job Training and Educational Opportunities

Welfare reform legislation related to education has had a chilling effect on states' ability to provide meaningful job training. Restrictions in the law seem antithetical to consistent evidence demonstrating the relationship between job training, education, and long-term economic well-being. Federal welfare regulations permit no more than 30 percent of the caseload to count vocational education toward the first twenty hours of work activity. Vocational education can count as a work activity for a maximum of twelve months. GED training, basic education, and college education may be counted as work only if women are engaged in some other work activity for twenty hours a week, making it necessary for many women to drop out of school.

Following implementation of the welfare reform law, the U.S. General Accounting Office reported immediate drops in the proportion of welfare recipients receiving job training. Declines in welfare recipients' college enrollment have exceeded caseload declines. In addition, research indicates that welfare recipients who work outside of school are much more likely to drop out.

Lack of Child Care and Other Supports

Child care expenses and lack of available child care continue to place giant financial and logistical burdens on welfare recipients, despite an influx of child care dollars through the Child Care and Development Block Grant. The NOW Legal Defense and Education Fund found that 55 percent of welfare recipients surveyed in New York City reported that they had received no help from case managers in securing child care. A 1999 review of welfare leaver studies by the Center for Law and Social Policy found that fewer than 50 percent of families studied were receiving child care subsidies. Given consistent findings that low-income mothers spend a far larger portion of their incomes on child care compared to better-off families, it is clear that a large proportion of women's child care needs are still going unmet. Similarly, while thirty-two states have adopted the Family Violence Option and have policies and procedures in place to address domestic violence among welfare recipients, dozens of states are currently reported to have inadequate domestic violence screening procedures.

Access to Jobs

Forty-four percent of Temporary Assistance to Needy Families recipients in the 1997 National Survey of America's Families reported two or more obstacles to work, including lack of transportation. Studies in Massachusetts and Atlanta found that less than half of entry-level positions were accessible by public transportation, and in Michigan, over 50 percent of available entry-level positions were located in the suburbs. The relatively high level of unemployment among African Americans may be due in part to a lack of jobs in urban areas where African Americans are primarily concentrated. Hence, African American welfare recipients may experience lack of transportation as a barrier to ongoing employment more frequently than other portions of the welfare population.

Immigrants and Welfare Reform

Immigrants are particularly susceptible to poverty and hardship because PRWORA limited their ability to receive public assistance, and language barriers limit their access to services. A study of Mexican and Vietnamese welfare recipients in California by Equal Rights Advocates (ERA) found that immigrant women are more likely to live in overcrowded homes: Mexican welfare recipients in California reported an average household size of 6.3, about twice the average household size of Californian welfare recipients. Many of the jobs immigrant women found were low-wage, temporary positions with no benefits, which contributed to their poverty status.

Although federal rules allow legal immigrants to receive non-cash benefits, such as food stamps, Medicaid, housing assistance, and child care subsidies without risk of deportation, misinformation and language barriers likely prevent immigrants from receiving the benefits to which they are entitled. A 1999 ERA study found that immigrant women receive few services through CalWORKs, California's post-PRWORA welfare system. Many respondents were confused about the program requirements and were unaware of the time limits, the exemptions from work requirements, and/or the family cap. Limited English skills and limited education present a significant barrier to the respondents: 86 percent of the Vietnamese women and 46 percent of the Mexican women had a poor understanding of English. Only about 30 percent of Vietnamese women and 9 percent of Mexican women had completed high school.

Conclusion

While welfare reform has created new openings for programmatic innovation, in many cases women have reached their welfare time limits or have been sanctioned before needed support services were in place. Efforts are needed to create incentives for states to encourage meaningful human capital development for women. Advocates should push for new policies to encourage training for higher paying jobs with career paths and benefits, and policies that will stop the welfare clock when sufficient supports are lacking. Policymakers can look to successful programs, such as the Minnesota Family Independence Program, for replication in other states. New welfare policies are necessary to address particular needs of women of color that often follow years of cumulative disadvantage.

America's Fifth Child: It's Time To End Child Poverty in America

Marian Wright Edelman

What kind of people do we seek to be in the twenty-first century? What kind of people do we want our children to be? What kinds of moral, personal, community, political, and policy choices are we prepared to make to realize a more just and compassionate and less violent society and world—one where no child is left behind?

Imagine a very wealthy family blessed with five children. Four of their children have enough to eat and comfortable, warm rooms in which to sleep. One of their children does not. She is often hungry and lives in a cold room. On some nights, she has to sleep on the streets or in a temporary shelter and even be taken away from her neglectful family and placed in foster care with strangers.

Imagine this family giving four of their children nourishing meals three times a day, snacks to fuel boundless child energy, but sending the fifth child from the table and to school hungry with only one or two meals and never dessert the other children enjoy.

Imagine this very wealthy family making sure four of their children get all their shots, regular checkups before they get sick, and immediate health care when illness strikes, but ignoring the fifth child, who is plagued by chronic infections and respiratory diseases like asthma.

Imagine this family sending four of their children to good, stimulating preschools and music and swimming lessons, and sending the fifth child to unsafe daycare with untrained caregivers responsible for too many children, or leaving her with an occasionally accommodating relative or neighbor, or all alone.

Imagine the family reading every night to four of their children, who have books in their rooms, and leaving the other child not read to, not talked and sung to, or propped before a television screen which feeds him violence and sex-charged messages, ads for material things, and intellectual pablum.

Imagine this family sending four of their children to good schools in safe neighborhoods with enough books and computers and laboratories and science equipment and well-prepared teachers, and sending the fifth child to crumbling school buildings with peeling ceilings and leaks and asbestos in the paint and old, old books and not enough of them, and teachers untrained in the subjects they teach.

Imagine four of the family's children excited about learning, looking forward to finishing high school, going on to college and getting a job, and the fifth child falling farther behind grade level, unable to read, wanting to drop out of school, and at risk of getting pregnant or into trouble.

Imagine four of the children engaged in sports and music and arts enrichment after-school and summer camps, and the fifth child meeting his friends on the street or going home alone because mom and dad are working or have escaped—in drugs and alcohol—parenting responsibilities they feel unable to meet, and hanging out alone or with peers all summer.

This is our American family today where one in five of our children lives in poverty. It is not a stable or healthy family or a sufficiently compassionate one.

Amidst unprecedented prosperity, huge federal and state budget surpluses, hundreds of billions of tobacco settlement monies, eight years of continuous and unprecedented economic growth, and a presidential boast that the state of the union has never been better, 13.5 million children are poor in the wealthiest nation on earth. A child is more likely to be poor now than in any year between 1966 and 1980, and the gap between rich and poor is the greatest ever. Worse, in 1998, 5.8 million children lived in *extreme* poverty, with incomes below *half* the poverty line—$6,500 a year, or less than $6 a person a day in a family of three. Behind presidential and gubernatorial political spin about the success of ending welfare as we know it, rampant child hunger, homelessness, insecurity, and suffering persist.

Dramatic drops of families from welfare rolls have not seen commensurate drops in child poverty. In fact, decreasing food stamp and Medicaid rolls in the wake of welfare changes since 1996 have increased child hunger and pushed many poor families into deeper poverty. A Department of Agriculture study reports an increase of 3.7 million children in households without enough food between 1997 and 1998.

How long will we stand mute and indifferent in a 9 trillion dollar economy as poverty, poor health and housing, poor education, and family and community disintegration rob millions of our children's lives and futures; gnaw at their bellies; chill their bodies and spirits to the bone; scratch away their resilience; snatch away their families and sense of security; and make some of them wish they had never been born? When has the time ever been riper to end immoral child poverty, hunger, and homelessness, and to make America a safe and compassionate home for all our children?

Now that it is the nation's official public policy that all poor mothers must work after a set time limit, with no income safety net for children, what steps will local, state, and federal governments and private sector leaders take to ensure work at wages that lift families out of poverty? Seventy-four percent of poor children today live in working families who cannot make enough to escape poverty. Yet many states are sitting on billions of unspent welfare and child health dollars designed to help parents and children grab a lifeline of hope from poverty. Why is our nation not making sure work pays a decent wage and preparing parents left behind to get the education, training, and skills they need to stand on their feet? What will happen to children (who did not choose their parents) when their parents cannot feed, clothe, and care for them? And how do we make sure that state and local bureaucracies make it easier rather than harder for parents who are playing by the rules, working every day, struggling to make ends meet, and caring for children to receive the child care and health care and other assistance they need and the law provides to help them stay in the work force and become self-sufficient?

Contrary to popular stereotypes, America's fifth child is much more likely to live in a working family than to be on welfare, is more likely to be White than Black or Latino, and is more likely to live in a rural or suburban area than in an inner city. Three out of five poor children are White (8.4 million) although more than one-third of Black (4.2 million) and Hispanic (3.8 million) children are poor.

America's fifth child is twice as likely to be born without adequate prenatal care, at low birth weight, and to die before reaching her first birthday.

America's fifth child is more than twice as likely to be abused or neglected and three times as likely to live in substandard housing as non-poor children.

America's fifth child will not grow or develop as fast as other children physically, mentally, or educationally; is twice as likely to repeat a grade or drop out of school before graduation, and is more likely to require special education, end up on welfare, or in trouble than non-poor children.

America's fifth child begins school already thousands of words behind his middle-class peers because he is not read to, does not have books in the home, is not talked to, and is not provided a good preschool or Head Start experience.

America's fifth child suffers more than her share of asthma attacks and respiratory ailments and lead poisoning without getting treated; often cannot sleep at night from too many people and too much noise in overcrowded apartments or shelters, and is frequently tired and sleepy in school.

America's fifth child is worn down fighting a chronic multi-front war against sickness, family breakdown, family and neighborhood violence, drugs, fear and shame, struggling to get attention at home and at school, to keep spirits up, and to hang onto a tenuous sense of being somebody worthwhile going somewhere better.

America's fifth child is less likely to have a father at home, the consistent affection of two parents, the stability of a married family, a steady family income or significant extended family resources, and is more likely to be arrested, be convicted if arrested, be tried as an adult, and be sentenced to prison.

America's fifth child desperately wants but often finds it hard to trust adults, the world, and is almost always afraid—afraid of being hungry; of having no place to sleep; of having a mother, father, sister, brother, aunt, uncle, grandmother disappear or be killed; of being bitten in bed by a rat or crawled on by roaches or being accosted by a mean gang member or drug peddler in the streets; of being too hot in the summer and too cold in the winter; of being disrespected and ignored; of being lonely; and afraid of not existing in a world that is passing him by.

America's fifth child is usually a fifth wheel in schools, in religious congregations, in many community organizations, and in politics—ignored by too many school officials and teachers, faith leaders, providers, the media, and presidents and senators and representatives and governors and powerful budget and appropriation committee chairs catering to rich and powerful influences who vote, lobby, make campaign contributions, command the media and an unfair share of government attention and resources.

America's fifth child is almost twice as likely to be poor as adults who can vote and organize. If the safety net for American children were as effective as it is for our low-income elderly, three out of four poor children today would not be poor.

America's fifth child would fare better as a citizen of another nation. If America's poverty prevention safety net for children was as effective as the safety net is in France, two out of three poor children would escape poverty. If she lived in any of twenty-three other industrialized nations, she would be guaranteed health insurance, an income safety net, and the chance for a parent to stay at home with pay after childbirth.

An Action Agenda to Leave No Child Behind and to Ensure Every Child a Healthy Start, a Head Start, a Fair Start, a Safe Start, and a Moral Start in Life

At a time of great economic prosperity, a projected $1.9 trillion federal budget surplus over the next decade, and billions of state surplus and tobacco settlement dollars in a post-Cold War era, now is the time to end immoral and preventable child poverty, hunger, homelessness, and sickness in the richest nation on earth. Now is the time to stand up and show our children we truly value them. Now is the time to build a more just and compassionate and less violent society—one where no child is left behind. Together, the nation, states, communities, employers, parents, and citizens must:

I. Ensure Every Child a Healthy Start

There are 11.9 million uninsured children in America; nearly 90 percent of them live in working families. Seven million are currently eligible for health care under the Children's Health Insurance Program (CHIP) and Medicaid. Nearly 5 million are not covered under any program. We must:

- mount a massive and urgent campaign to reach and enroll every one of the 7 million children now eligible for CHIP and Medicaid
- simplify and unify application and eligibility procedures to make it easier for children to get health care
- expand health coverage to uninsured children and their parents

- encourage employers to expand coverage for employees and their children and stop dropping dependent coverage
- urge every community network—religious, healthcare, parents, senior citizens, education, grassroots, youths, and corporations—to join in a massive and persistent public awareness and enrollment campaign until every child is provided appropriate health care

II. Ensure Every Child a Head Start

Only 50 percent of children eligible for Head Start and only 10 percent of children eligible for federal childcare assistance receive it. Five million school-age children are home alone after school and are at risk of tobacco, alcohol and drug use, teen pregnancy, and violence. Quality preschool, child care, after-school and summer programs, and school systems are essential to getting all children ready to learn and achieve and keeping them safe when parents are in the work force.

- Head Start should be increased to serve all eligible children by 2002, and be expanded to full-day, full-year and to more children under three years old.
- The Child Care and Development Block Grant should be expanded to reach at least half of all eligible children by 2002.
- Congress should support a new Early Learning Initiative for very young children and significantly increase investments in 21st Century Community Learning Centers and other quality after-school and summer programs.
- Every state should provide a quality comprehensive pre-kindergarten program for all families who wish to participate and invest more state dollars in quality child care and Head Start programs.
- Every business should offer affordable, quality child care, flex-time, and paid parental leave options to help employees balance work and family responsibilities.
- Federal and state family and medical leave laws should be expanded and strengthened to include paid leave.
- Every child should be expected and helped to achieve in quality, equitable school systems.

III. Ensure Every Child a Fair Start

Our nation must commit to doing whatever is necessary to end child poverty in America by 2005. Children should get a fair share of the federal and state budget surpluses, tobacco settlement monies, and be guaranteed the same income and health security as senior citizens. We must:

- ensure work at a decent wage and education and training for parents to improve their job options and earnings
- expand the Earned Income Tax Credit, particularly for families with three or more children, increase the Dependent Care Tax Credit and the Child Tax Credit for lower- and middle-income working and stay-at-home parents, and make both credits refundable
- make sure that every poor family with children currently eligible for nutrition, health, housing, child care, and other aid receives assistance. States should immediately use rather than hoard dollars intended to help parents work and become more self-sufficient, decrease their bureaucracies, and create a culture of service among their employees
- strengthen child support enforcement

IV. Ensure Every Child a Safe Start

Over 80,000 American children have been killed by guns since 1979—a greater casualty rate than we suffered in battle casualties in the Vietnam War. American children under age fifteen are twelve times more likely to die from guns than children in twenty-five other industrialized nations combined. A child is reported abused or neglected every twelve seconds. Children are exposed to relentless glorification of violence on movie, television, and Internet screens.

- All gun purchasers and owners should be required to register and obtain a license.
- All non-hunting firearms, including junk guns and assault weapons, should be banned.
- Manufacturers and other adults should be held liable for guns that get into the hands of criminals and children.
- Parents should be educated about the dangers of owning a gun and required to store the gun locked and unloaded if they do own one.
- Cultural leaders, movie, television, and Internet producers, advertisers, and toy manufacturers should stop glorifying and marketing gratuitous violence, which incites some children and youths to violence and desensitizes others to the consequences of violence.
- Nonviolence training, conflict resolution, peer mediation, and other activities to prevent all forms of family violence should be instilled in our homes, congregations, schools, and every sphere of national life.

V. Ensure Every Child a Moral Start

It is time for American adults to stop our moral hypocrisy and to live the values we want our children to learn. If we want them to stop being violent, then we should stop being violent. If we want them to be honest, then we should be honest. Parents, preachers, teachers, and all public officials must conduct themselves in a manner that they would want their own child or any child to emulate. Private morality and public morality must go hand-in-hand. Our children need consistent love, time, attention, discipline, family stability, and limits at home and in school, and they need to see that adults in their nation, private sector, and communities value and care for them—not as consumers and future customers to be exploited or as a non-voting group to be ignored—but as the heirs of America's institutions and values. It is time for all adults to accept their responsibility to be good protectors of and mentors for the next generation.

Excerpted from Foreword to The State of America's Children Yearbook 2000. *Washington, DC: Children's Defense Fund, 2000.*

Wealth, Success, and Poverty in Indian Country

D. Bambi Kraus

When I was growing up, my Tlingit mother often told me something her father had told her. "Before we were civilized, we wore fur and leather. Then, they (Europeans) put rags on our backs." What was clear to me as a child was that the outsiders who came to the Tlingit people of southeast Alaska were not passive interlopers, and that they had changed our lives forever in ways that we could never have imagined.

According to the 1990 Census, the poverty rate for American Indians was the highest among the country's five racial and ethnic groups—31 percent of American Indians were living in poverty in 1989, compared to 13 percent of all Americans. Poverty rates for all racial and ethnic groups declined during the 1960s and early 1970s, but improved little over the next twenty years.

Social and economic indicators in Indian country are far below what most Americans consider to be acceptable living standards. The 1998 White House Council of Economic Advisors report, *Changing America*, pointed out that "American Indians are among the most disadvantaged Americans according to many available indicators, such as poverty rate and median income, although comparable data for this group are sparse due to their small representation in the population." Further, it is generally accepted that American Indians and Alaska Natives living on reservation lands were seriously underreported in the 1990 Census. One conclusion that can be drawn is that the true scale and scope of conditions on Indian reservations is not known. From the information that is available, a bleak picture is portrayed.

Most Americans are unaware of the special status of American Indian and Alaska Native Nations and the trust responsibility between the federal government and Indian Tribes. Natives are not merely a race of people in America; they are members of nations whose continuing sovereign status is recognized in the U.S. Constitution, federal statutes, and numerous federal court decisions. There are over 560 separate and unique tribal governments in the United States responsible for governing their tribal members and managing their own lands. No other population has a government-to-government relationship with the federal government defined by the Constitution, treaties, executive orders, court decisions, and acts of Congress; no other group of people in the United States has the responsibility to govern millions of acres of land. The 1990 Census counted an estimated 2 million Native people, roughly half of whom live on reservations, although this, too, is rapidly changing.

The Pine Ridge Indian Reservation (of the Oglala Lakota Oyate) and the Navajo Indian Reservation (of the Navajo Nation) are examples of both statistical confusion and undercounting, as well as the sheer enormity of the challenges facing the people who live on or near these reservations. Both reservations are large. The Navajo Indian Reservation is the largest in the country by far; its tribal lands total about 18.5 million acres (over 25,000 square miles), slightly bigger than West Virginia, almost the same size as South Carolina, and larger than ten states. The Pine Ridge Indian Reservation is over 1.7 million acres, considerably larger than Delaware.

Statistical Disparities

Although the U.S. government justifies its poor and limited statistics and Census figures by pointing to the small numbers of Native people among the U.S. population, most Native people do not see the problem as "small representation." Rather, they view the lack of reliable data as an example of neglect. The federal government has failed to properly document the extreme social and economic circumstances found on most Indian reservations and to disseminate this information to all Americans.

The following statistics demonstrate and compare: (1) the lack of consistent data for Indian country; (2) the extremely poor conditions on two Indian reservations; (3) conditions on the Navajo Reservation compared to those statewide in Arizona and New Mexico, and on the Pine Ridge Reservation compared to statewide conditions in South Dakota; and (4) conditions for Indian people compared to all residents in two cities located near the Navajo Reservation (Gallup, New Mexico) and Pine Ridge Reservation (Rapid City, South Dakota). Finally, disparities between Indian country and the country as a whole are demonstrated by listing rates for all Americans, as reported by the 1990 Census.

Population

The Bureau of Indian Affairs (BIA) determined in 1995 that the Indian population on and adjacent to the Navajo Reservation was 225,668; for the Pine Ridge Reservation, the figure was 38,426. However, the 1990 Census reported the total population on the Navajo Reservation as only 148,451 (the markedly lower figure could not be explained simply by exclusion of the relatively small population in the area adjacent to the Reservation); for the Pine Ridge Reservation, the figure was 12,215.

Unemployment

According to the Navajo Nation Division of Economic Development, unemployment on the Navajo Reservation was 43.3 percent in 1998. As reported in the 1990 Census, unemployment on the Navajo Reservation was 27.9 percent; in Arizona, the rate was 7.1 percent, and in New Mexico it was 7.9 percent. In Gallup, New Mexico, the unemployment rate for Indians was 12.0 percent; for all Gallup residents, it was 5.8 percent.

The annual survey done by the Oglala Sioux Tribe and the Bureau of Indian Affairs reported that unemployment on the Pine Ridge Reservation in 1998 was 73 percent; in 1995, the BIA reported Pine Ridge Reservation unemployment at 46 percent, while the 1990 Census reported a 28.9 percent rate. The unemployment rate for all South Dakota residents was 4.1 percent. In Rapid City, South Dakota, the unemployment rate was 21.7 percent; for all Rapid City residents, it was 5.2 percent. By comparison, the 1990 Census reported that the unemployment rate for all Americans was 6.2 percent.

Per Capita Income

The 1998 per capita income for the Navajo Reservation was $5,759, according to the Navajo Nation Division of Economic Development. The 1990

Census reported per capita income on the Navajo Reservation as $4,124. Per capita income for all of Arizona was $13,461; for New Mexico, it was $11,246. Per capita income for Indian residents in Gallup was $6,251; for all Gallup residents, it was $10,559. The 1990 Census reported the per capita income for all Americans as $14,420.

Defining Wealth and Success

Any measure of personal wealth in the year 2000, regardless of culture, race, or ethnicity, should include such basic human necessities as a home to live in, running water, electricity, telephone service, and plumbing. For far too many Native people in America, these basic amenities are simply not available. For example, 52 percent of Navajos lack complete plumbing facilities; over 81 percent do not have telephone service; and 54 percent of homes on the Navajo reservation are heated by wood (1990 Census). These examples indicate that Indian people, either on reservations or living in cities nearby their reservations, are not achieving even approximate equality with the economic status of their neighbors.

How do we define wealth in a country with such disparate living conditions in a way that makes sense to a variety of lifestyles and cultures? Measures of wealth and poverty in America are dynamic and have been defined most recently by dollars rather than by the cultural values of the people who have lived in this country or immigrated here. In earlier days, the Tlingit of southeast Alaska measured their wealth by accumulating possessions. Valuable assets included foodstuffs, clothing, and everyday objects that demonstrated your status in your village. In Tlingit tradition, individual wealth was measured not only by possessions, but also by how those possessions were shared with others.

Dire and depressed living conditions on Indian reservations are a legacy of Native people's 200-year-old history with the American government. There is no reason to assume that circumstances for Indian people will significantly change in the near future. Most tribal governments face the challenge of reversing failed federal policies of the past, in addition to planning for the future of their children, without the committed help and resources of the federal government or the cooperation of states.

The myth that Indian gaming will solve most of these infrastructure issues is just that. Indian gaming is the first—and only—economic development tool that has ever worked on reservations. But the long-term future of Indian gaming is uncertain and faces continued challenges from state governments, anti-gaming advocates, and equivocal support from the federal government (both Congress and the Executive). How can the United States consider itself a success while most first Americans battle hunger, poverty, and deeply institutionalized injustices? What will happen to Indian country with the next economic downturn?

Even though individual Tribes and the federal government differ in their statistical portraits of the same land and people, both still starkly show the need in Indian country for a large-scale review and effort to bring Native people closer to the realm of success and wealth in America. Having a roof overhead, food to eat, and the ability to continue practicing ancient ceremonies and traditions in traditional homelands is an indicator of health and personal wealth for many Native people.

We must question the definition of wealth and success in our country. My grandfather caught and hunted food for himself and family, built his commercial fishing boat, and built his own and other families' homes. He told his children and grandchildren the stories that embodied the culture's values and showed the places that were important to Tlingit people. He was proud that his children went to college in the lower forty-eight states, but even prouder that they would one day return to the village of Kake, Alaska, and work to make it a better place for all residents and not just for one individual. This is one value that is lost on most Americans in their drive to achieve wealth.

Race and Poverty in the Rural South

Margaret Walsh and Cynthia M. Duncan

Rural America calls to mind images of dramatic mountain views or peaceful green landscapes, small town living where people look out for one another. Tourists driving in the hills of northern Vermont or West Virginia notice rusty trailers not far from quaint colonial homes and think that it must be a better place to be poor because at least these areas are less crowded, friendlier spaces compared to the nearest city. However, the rural poor, especially in depressed regions, experience the same problems as the urban poor. People have a hard time finding jobs that can support a household. Work is often low-paying, part-time, or part-year, and wages do not cover families' expenses. Housing conditions are substandard. Schools may be as chaotic and ineffective as the worst inner-city schools. Community life in rural areas revolves around family and church, but in persistently poor regions there are rigid divisions between the haves and have-nots. Economic and political power is concentrated among a small white elite who discourage participation and do not invest in community-wide institutions. The poor are socially isolated and cut off from the mainstream.

Nine million people are poor in rural America, of whom 3 million live in persistently poor areas. Thirty-five percent of rural blacks and 33 percent of rural Hispanics live in poverty, as do half of all rural black and Hispanic children. The rural South and West are the poorest regions in the United States, and counties with high percentages of African Americans have disproportionately high poverty rates. Most of the counties in Mississippi have poverty rates above 20 percent, and some are more than 40 percent poor. In some, 80 percent of black residents are poor, and per capita income for whites may be five times that for blacks. African Americans are more likely to live in substandard, crowded, and run-down housing compared to whites, and, with high rates of single-parent households, African American women and children are especially disadvantaged.

Several decades ago, many rural areas welcomed industrial development when manufacturing plants moved out of urban centers and into communities where people needed work and were willing to accept lower wages. However, restructuring has taken its toll in the last decade. In the 1990s, the number of manufacturing jobs in rural areas grew by only 5 percent. Other dependable goods-producing sectors in rural areas are also diminishing. Between 1990 and 1997, the percentage of farming jobs in rural counties declined by almost 7 percent, mining jobs decreased by 21 percent. The booming technology fields have not reached out to rural America. Instead, the percentage of jobs in the service sector has increased by 26 percent and low-paying retail employment has grown by 21 percent. Service sector jobs comprise 53 percent of all jobs in rural areas. In 1997, average worker earnings for retail employment were $13,764, compared to $32,207 for manufacturing employment. The majority of the rural poor are in working families. In fact, up to 70 percent of the rural poor live in families with at least one employed person. But while more of the poor in rural areas work, their wages are low and their jobs are often seasonal or part-time.

To understand persistent rural poverty, we need to look beyond work and wages to consider who is working and who is not, and to assess the racial and class dynamics in these communities. Educational attainment and family structure matter greatly, of course, and those with low education or in single-parent households are invariably poor. In chronically poor rural areas, broader long-term inequalities perpetuate poverty. Rigid class and race divisions combine with corrupt, elite-controlled local politics to block the poor from opportunities to participate in the workforce and in civil society. Lingering racism and segregation by race and class mean that inclusive public programs that might provide equal opportunity do not exist. Those with limited resources have only family to fall back on when times are hard.

The brief case study that follows examines the link between race and family poverty in two persistently poor rural Mississippi Delta communities we call Dahlia, whose 1990 population was around 20,000. Thirty percent of households are female-headed, and 35 percent of births are to teens, 91 percent of those out of wedlock. Forty-two percent of families are poor and 62 percent had incomes less than half the U.S. median in 1990. The case study draws on 160 interviews conducted with African Americans and whites from all social classes in the early 1990s.

Work, Education, and Family in the Delta

The 6,000 working men and women in Dahlia have jobs in stores, government offices, and schools, on large plantation-style farms, in sewing factories and electrical assembly factories, in catfish plants, and, more recently, in casinos in neighboring counties. African American men and women have a difficult time finding work in a place still rigidly divided by race and class. Only about half of working-age black men have jobs, compared to two-thirds of whites; only one-third of black women are employed, while half of white women have jobs. Blacks who left school early or have a high school diploma work in fields and factories, while the few who have a college degree are likely to work in schools and public offices. Many black women still work as domestics. Jobs in the fields are seasonal, and during the winter months farm workers draw unemployment checks and subsist on Food Stamps. Jobs in sewing factories fluctuate as well, as managers lay off and hire to make production accommodate the demands of their retail customers. A plant with 300 employees may dismiss as many as 50 when orders are low in the spring, and then those workers too go on unemployment and public assistance.

In poor rural communities like Dahlia, black men and women do not have access to full-time jobs with wages that can support a family. Jobs are allocated according to reputation. One worker reported, "These farmers could say, 'Well, he's worth hiring, and they'll take you." Many white employers think of black men only as part-time workers: "My employees are colored men. I don't work anything but black because my business is part-time. I can't afford to pay somebody a monthly salary year round because we have a seasonal business. The whites are going to need more work that I'm not going to be able to give them."

African American men in particular have been excluded from the mainstream. Those seeking work say factory managers may worry that black men will cause trouble, and prefer women, whom they see as "docile." One black man said, "If you do have a job, and you're outspoken, you can be blackballed, and that's what happened to me." Young black men experience racial discrimination in hiring and firing, and many refuse to acquiesce to the poor working conditions their own parents and grandparents accepted from wealthy local employers. As one man describes the class discrimination they also experience: "If you colored and you got money, white people, they will talk to you. If you ain't got no money, all they want to hear is 'Yes, sir' and 'No, sir.' "

Job segregation by race affects women as well. For example, black women can be cooks in the local restaurants, but not waitresses. Even those who finish high school have difficulty finding steady work that will support their families, although those few who go on to college can find work with higher wages and some job security, even in Dahlia. There is one black woman working at each bank, and college-educated black women work in the schools and the welfare offices. But opportunities are limited, and young women from poor families are likely to have children young, drop out of school, and combine child-rearing duties with public assistance and part-time work in the fields chopping weeds, in the catfish plant cutting off fish heads, or in the sewing plant.

Although educational attainment in this region is increasing, by 1990 only 46 percent of people in Dahlia had finished high school, compared to 75 percent in the nation as a whole; 9 percent were college graduates, compared to 20 percent nationally. Eighty percent of the 91 low-income men and women interviewed in Dahlia had dropped out of school, girls often because they were pregnant, boys often because they got in trouble and tired of school authority. Mississippi consistently ranks at the bottom of national statistics on student educational outcomes. Many African Americans say the plantation boss men discourage blacks from finishing school. Whites, too, say there are farmers who see blacks reading as a threat and thus do not want them educated.

Local schools are segregated into public institutions (almost exclusively black) and private academies attended by whites. Dahlia's public schools have been on probationary status for years. Long neglected by all-white administrators intent on keeping costs down and programs to a minimum, they do not have the resources to provide students with adequate transferable skills, nor are they consistently held accountable for poor performance. Students, teachers, and administrators describe disorder: "It's a free for all"; and: "It was too wild, like the kids, they all be fighting and stuff, fighting during school, carrying knives around school and all like that."

The official family poverty rate in Dahlia in 1990 was 42 percent, but a much higher percentage is visibly poor and struggling. Approximately one out of five people receives public assistance and one out of three collects monthly Social Security payments. Family members rely on each other to raise, support, and feed children, and to care for aging parents. Several generations may live in a single household. Families are large, as grown children continue to share their grandparents' or parents' dwelling long after leaving school. Teenage girls may move in with their boyfriends and set up house for a time, perhaps raising children together, but they often return home when things go awry. Marriage is not the norm for poor young adults in Dahlia. Without job security, men and women are unsure about the future commitments they can make to each other. Sometimes news of better opportunities elsewhere from relatives who have moved away entices men to leave the mothers of their children.

Women view most men they know as unreliable marriage partners because they are unemployed and idle. As one woman reported, the women look for "someone who's gonna help me financially, help me with me and my kids, someone who'll treat me right, who won't be fussing and arguing all the time. You know, caring." Instead, they often find themselves in situations like this: "He started off real good but lately he done got lazy. I don't ask him for anything and he don't offer anything." Under these conditions, stable long-term male-female relationships are hard to maintain.

Many of the women interviewed described growing up fast with limited choices and many responsibilities. For example, one twenty-four-year-old woman had her first child at the age of fourteen and had five more, with three different fathers, before the age of twenty-one. Her own mother was twelve when she was born, and her grandmother, who ran a café and worked most evenings, raised her. Although she liked high school, especially cheerleading and playing the flute, she dropped out in ninth grade to take care of her two children. Despite an offer to baby-sit from her grandmother, who wanted the young woman to graduate, she was too overwhelmed by young motherhood and decided she should be at home herself. To earn money, she began working at a local fish plant, but was discouraged by the low pay and backbreaking work.

None of the men in this woman's life were suitable marriage candidates. If she was going to get ahead, she felt she needed to work on her own skills and returned to school. She talked to her caseworker and signed up for an educational program in the region, and is preparing to take the first portion of her GED exam. She plans to go to a community college nearby to earn a counseling degree and stay near her children. These expectations may be unrealistic. Although it has been difficult, this woman says she is pleased that she had her children while she was young and physically strong, and she imagines a long life ahead: "I always wanted a big family as far as having kids . . . Now by the time I get through with college, get me a settled-in job, my kids will be old enough and when they are out of my house I'll still be young enough to enjoy life."

Stable work and stable families are intertwined in the Delta, just as they are in other places. Unmarried women raising children try to piece together a living with income from their own jobs, help from their children's fathers, welfare, and family assistance. Although women may want to meet men to marry, the men they date lead lives that make it difficult for them to be reliable and provide for children. In relationships that started as short-term romantic attachments, discussions of marriage are usually postponed into the far future, and then mention of it fades away as problems arise. By then, a new boyfriend may be coming around and helping to support the household and children. Many women see their children as their own responsibility, although they pull together a variety of people and sources of support as the children grow up. Being "on their own" is not their ideal situation. They are unlikely to earn adequate income working by themselves. They also miss companionship of a partner. But in most cases the women and men we interviewed did not have access to the resources—skills, good jobs, income growth—that would lead them to the stability needed for a serious relationship or marriage.

Conclusion

Poverty in rural communities like Dahlia is not simply the result of young people "messing up," as they put it, dropping out of school and having babies young before they have stable relationships and work. Upward mobility and community change are thwarted by rigid stratification based on race and class. Whites live a separate "good life," looking after their own families, churches, and schools. Political and other civic participation by African Americans is actively discouraged by whites, and class and racial divisions create distrust on both sides. As described by one white person, investment in public goods is deliberately eschewed: "There is a standing rule that whites do not want to have anything public because the blacks might come." Community institutions do not serve poor families. Those who escape poverty are the fortunate few who have made heroic leaps, thanks to extraordinary sacrifice and encouragement by some caring family member or mentor.

In rural places where there is less poverty and inequality, young adults see options, and postpone childbearing and marriage to learn and pursue a job that might be interesting or lead to a career. When they do start families, they are more hopeful and less burdened. These are also places where community institutions work. A large blue-collar middle class supports an inclusive public sphere, and the poor are not isolated from the non-poor. People cooperate and invest in a rich civic culture characterized by trust, wide participation, and community-wide activities and programs. There the poor have a fighting chance to achieve upward mobility.

While various means-tested public assistance programs make life for Dahlia's poor less harsh than it would be otherwise, they do not combat the chronic poverty among blacks that has plagued the region since the 1800s. Investment in what Mickey Kaus, in *The End of Inequality*, calls the "egalitarian public sphere of life" is necessary to make a true difference. Real commitment to public education, with federal accountability, could turn schools around. Universal programs to provide family support, health care, and training, rather than means-tested subsidies, would help these working poor families without stigmatizing them. Most importantly, these efforts would begin to transform the civic culture and infrastructure in ways that end social isolation and integrate the poor into the community where they can have true equal opportunity.

This paper draws on Duncan's Worlds Apart: Why Poverty Persists in Rural America *(New Haven: Yale University Press, 1999), which provides a fuller account of differences between chronically poor divided communities and one with greater equality and opportunity, as well as work in progress on work and family stability by both authors. For a description of a rural community with lower levels of family poverty and more inclusive institutions, see Walsh's* Mothers' Helpers: The Resources of Female-Headed Households in a Working Class Community *(Ph.D. dissertation, University of New Hampshire, 1997).*

Poverty, Racial Discrimination, and the Family Farm

Stephen Carpenter

Food and fiber are raised on some 2 million farms in the United States. The vast majority of American farming operations are family farms. Squeezed by unwise government policies and an ever-enlarging industrial agriculture, tens of thousands of family farmers are forced from the land each year. Despite the continued growth of industrialized corporate agriculture, the vast majority—

perhaps 95 percent or more—of the farms in the country are operated by a family, are of a modest size, and rely primarily on family rather than paid labor. Over 60 percent of all farmers hire no wage labor at all. (By contrast, less than 2 percent of all farms account for half of all agricultural labor hired.) Those family farmers—of all races—remaining on the land often live in poverty.

It is easy to get the impression that virtually all of these farmers are white. A conservative estimate holds that at present only about 6 percent of the country's farms are operated by people of color, or, as the U.S. Department of Agriculture (USDA) defines it, people who are "other than white (black, Asian, American Indian, or other races) or of Hispanic origin." But in many parts of the country nonwhite farmers account for 10 to 20 percent of the farmers.

Family Farmer Poverty

Farmers generally are twice as likely as the rest of the population to live in poverty. The bulk of poor farmers are in the Midwest and South, although there are also significant numbers in both the West and Northeast. Nearly every state has areas where poverty among farmers has been widespread for a number of generations.

Poverty among farmers can sometimes seem invisible. When the Harvard School of Public Health's Physician Task Force on Hunger in America found "hunger counties" throughout the agricultural Midwest and South, the general reaction seemed to be one of surprise. This may be true for a few reasons. First, like rural poverty generally, geographic isolation can hide farmer poverty. Few people witness the actual living conditions of farm families. Second, the very large economic differences among farmers —income inequality is far more extreme among farmers than in the nation as a whole—are often blurred by the "we're all just folks" ideology of many farm communities, in which conspicuous consumption is frowned upon and those struggling economically hide financial difficulties. Third, some low-income farmers seem well off because they have significant assets—farmland, tractors, and the like—and a fairly large gross income. A closer look, however, often reveals that the farmer has little or no equity and a small net income.

Farm poverty is also not much noticed because the mainstream agricultural organizations, the media, and the USDA affirmatively choose to ignore it. A reader of *Farm Journal,* probably the most influential agricultural magazine, would almost certainly never read that a significant portion of the country's farmers live in poverty. Statistics regarding farm poverty quoted in this article come buried in the appendices of obscure USDA Agricultural Research Service studies.

Poor Farmers Feed America

When poverty among farmers is discussed at all, apologists for economic inequality in agriculture sometimes suggest that since poor and struggling farmers have small operations, these farmers are really marginal to the agricultural
economy as a whole. Further, since a large percentage of low-income farmers
are forced to work off the farm to make ends meet, they are sometimes described as merely "hobby" farmers. Two facts undermine these arguments.
First, while farmers living in poverty tend to operate farms smaller than average, it is not the case that low-income farms are merely marginal operations
that produce little. In fact, more than 20 percent of all agricultural production in the country comes from a farm where the household operating the
farm lives in poverty. Second, while many poor farmers have off-farm income, the farm families living in poverty work on average over forty hours
per week on the farm—in addition to off-farm work. Off-farm income therefore works to supplement farm income, not replace it.

Family Farmer Dispossession and Its Social Cost

More than 30,000 farms are lost each year in the United States. This pace of
dispossession has not noticeably slowed since the height of public attention
to the "farm crisis" in the mid-1980s. Agricultural economists expect the
loss of family farms to accelerate in the next decade.

For a farm family, dispossession means the end of employment and, without realistic prospects for similar work, often long-term poverty. Beyond
this, it means the loss of a home, a place in the community and, in many
cases, a family heritage.

Family farming is also crucial for the economic and social survival of
many rural communities. More than 500 rural counties are dependent on
farming as a central basis of their economy. One rule of thumb holds that for
every five to seven farms that go out of business, one business in town also
folds. While such indirect effects are difficult to measure in purely economic
terms, the downward "multiplier effect" of fewer farms is certainly significant. Inevitably, the loss of family farms leaves a community with lower
overall income and an increase in poverty.

The decline of family farming also undermines a community's social vi-
tality. An absolute decline in the number of farmers cripples churches, community groups, public schools, hospitals, social services, and ultimately the
prospects for a viable community-wide social life.

Because farming communities already have relatively high levels of economic distress, and the potential for new forms of development is severely

limited, the decline may be nearly irreversible. In sum, the ongoing farm crisis is really a rural crisis in which the underpinnings of whole communities are threatened.

Finally, the demise of family farming is also an environmental issue. As one would intuitively suspect, evidence suggests that farms using the most environmentally sound practices are modest in size. Certainly, the very largest livestock operations (hog and chicken "factories") are an ecological catastrophe.

How Race and Ethnicity Matter in Family Farming

The typical nonwhite farmer was reared on a farm and has worked his or her present farm for about two decades. In this and many other respects, farmers of color share a similar set of circumstances with white farmers. In several crucial ways, however, life is much more difficult for nonwhite farmers. Smaller farms and discrimination result in an average household income that is one-third lower for nonwhite farmers than white farmers; rates of poverty are about 20 percent higher for nonwhite farmers.

The fate of African American farmers is instructive. Black farmers tend to own smaller farms, making them especially vulnerable to economic downturns. They also find it more difficult than whites to secure mortgage loans, obtain government assistance, and reap the benefits of federal farm programs.

Dispossession is an especially acute problem for African American farmers. The failure of Reconstruction to create the conditions for a sustainable yeoman agriculture after the Civil War left African American farmers largely trapped in a sharecropping economy that resembled slavery. Still, many blacks managed to acquire land; by the 1920s more than 200,000 African American farmers owned land, and in total nearly 1 million black families farmed. However, during a single generation, from 1954 to 1987, farms with African American operators, including tenant farmers, declined by 95 percent, and between 1950 and 1974 the number of African American owners dropped 80 percent. As a USDA demographer observes, this has been "one of the most remarkable social and economic transformations in the history of our country." The decline of black farming continues today. The nation stands at the verge of losing, perhaps permanently, significant farmland ownership by African Americans.

Agricultural Policy and Farm Programs

A full explanation of the origin of the predicament of family farms would be lengthy and complicated. Certainly, technological innovations and changes in the larger economy have contributed. The full extent of the problems, however, has hardly been inevitable. In many ways, large and small, federal farm policy has contributed to the decline of family farming. Although farm programs in general are sometimes defended as promoting family farming, they, and a number of other government efforts—in research and extension services, as well as direct subsidies and tax policies—historically have tended to encourage the concentration of agriculture in the hands of fewer and fewer farmers.

The 1996 Farm Bill—technically known as the Federal Agriculture Improvement and Reform Act—sets farm programs for the subsequent seven years. Under the FAIR Act, farm program payments to farmers are scheduled to decline somewhat through the year 2002 and then, supposedly, end. Congress chose not to focus these payments on family farms. As has historically been the case with farm programs, large operations will receive a disproportionate share of the payments. Even when Congress has designated that funds should be limited to medium- and small-sized farms, the USDA tends to interpret the statute in ways that funnel resources to larger operations. Additional farm program spending allocated after 1996 has followed the same general pattern.

The Demise of Family Farming is Not Inevitable: Priorities for Policy

Although the siege of family farmers continues, changes in government policy could take steps toward equaling the playing field for all farmers:

- *Target Farm Programs to Family Farmers*
  As noted above, federal farm programs go disproportionately to larger operations. It is also true, however, that roughly one-third of all farmers living in poverty receive USDA program payments of some kind. Thus, although a relatively small percentage of the payments go to farmers living in poverty, for poor farming families the payments can be extremely important. Payments should be targeted for family farmers.
- *Preserve Family Farm Credit Programs*
  Credit problems are central to the concerns of family farmers. Virtually every farmer uses short-term operating credit to purchase inputs—such as seed, fertilizer, feed, and the like—and then pays the debt from farm proceeds. Most farms also have at least some real estate debt. Access to credit is therefore a serious problem for low-income farmers, especially nonwhite farmers. The USDA's Farm Service Agency (FSA) is designed to serve as the lender of last resort for family farmers. FSA therefore serves as the lender to tens of thousands of smaller, lower-income, and higher-risk farmers. Perhaps more than any other single program in the

federal government, FSA's farm lending targets struggling family farmers. Lending programs directed to family farmers, particularly nonwhite farmers, should be preserved and enhanced.

- *Treat Discrimination at USDA Seriously*

Discrimination by USDA has played, and continues to play, an important role in limiting the opportunities of the country's minority farmers. In fact, discrimination in modern agricultural programs has been aggressive and systematic. USDA's public responses to evidence of discrimination have become predictable. Widespread discrimination has been identified repeatedly over the years, perhaps most effectively in a series of U.S. Civil Rights Commission reports.

In 1999, the Farmers' Legal Action Group (FLAG), with PRRAC support, undertook a research project concerning the role the USDA has played in the dramatic decline in African American farming in America. Through field research and historical and legal research, FLAG interviewed farmers and reviewed articles, books, and government reports. This research shed light on the history of USDA's discrimination against African-American farmers, and analyzed the law that governs discrimination in USDA credit programs (primarily the Equal Credit Opportunity Act and the regulations governing the USDA credit programs).

FLAG learned that many of African American farmers' problems with discrimination by USDA can be grouped into the following categories: (1) inability to get basic technical assistance from USDA; (2) problems in getting a loan (including USDA discouraging written applications for credit; USDA making decisions about applications for credit late, or not at all; USDA underfunding loan requests; USDA charging high interest rates when they could and should have given lower interest rates; and USDA denying loans); (3) USDA failing to release its security interest in the farmers' income stream (when farmers pledge their crops, for example, to USDA as security for a loan, the farmer cannot use any income from those crops without USDA's permission); (4) problems in loan servicing (USDA's mechanism for adjusting payment obligations); (5) problems regarding administrative appeals; and, (6) problems regarding USDA's calculation of the farmer's cash flow (ability to repay debt).

FLAG also learned that USDA had a long history of discriminatory treatment of African American farmers, and that much of what the farmers complained about was not only unfair, it was also illegal.

In the face of such information, USDA officials admit there has been discrimination in the past and promise to do better. In the fall of 1996, for example, a high USDA official was quoted as saying that discrimination is still a problem with USDA programs, but that USDA would improve in the future. A similar admission and promise was made before Congress by USDA officials nearly a decade before.

In addition, in 1999 the government entered into a consent decree in *Pigford v. Glickman* and *Brewington v. Glickman*, a nationwide class action brought by African American farmers alleging race discrimination in USDA programs. The settlement provided a system of reviewing over 20,000 damage claims and provides for injunctive relief for each class member who prevails on a claim. The settlement is expected to result in payments of hundreds of millions of dollars. The consent decree can be found at www.dcd.uscourts.gov.

The central problem is that discrimination by USDA against farmers has never been a priority for the Department. Discrimination complaint procedures, for example, have been weak, ineffectual, and poorly funded. There are signs that the Department is interested in looking at discrimination and creating an effective and aggressive discrimination complaint procedure. For instance, USDA chose to adopt FLAG's civil rights investigators' handbook, created through their research project, as an official document of the Department. If efforts to address discrimination are not successful, however, one day soon there will be few farmers of color left to use the procedures that are developed.

- *Pursue the Connection Between Family Farming and Sustainable Agriculture*
  Traceable in some respects to the once tiny organic farm movement, sustainable agriculture is on the verge of gaining mainstream acceptability. The definition of sustainable agriculture is hotly contested, but most proponents agree that it involves the use of fewer chemical fertilizers, pesticides, and drug treatments for livestock. In practical terms, this tends to mean: using more crop rotations to fight the effects of weeds and insects; fertilizing the soil from on-farm sources such as small groups of unconfined livestock and nitrogen-fixing legumes; using biological practices and integrated pest management; and using careful conservation techniques. Arguably, sustainable farming is the best way to preserve family farming and rural communities. Unfortunately, farm programs have tended to penalize farmers using sustainable practices. Research, extension, and other USDA programs should focus on developing and promoting sustainable practices.

While there is increasing familiarity with the working conditions of migrant agricultural laborers and with conditions in meatpacking and other food processing plants, to this inventory of exploitation in the making of the nation's food and fiber must be added the difficulties faced by family farms.

Part 3

Education

Education is the key to opportunity—employment, contacts (or, as the current "in" phrase has it, social capital), diverse experience, career and behavior models, growth, enjoyment, wisdom. But there is no institution in the United States where race is more determinative of the racially disparate treatment a child will receive than our public schools. The litany of disparities by race includes the physical plant of schools, textbooks and equipment, teacher quality, teacher and student stability, expenditures, class size, etc., etc. What was so hopeful starting in the mid-1950s when the Supreme Court ruled racially segregated schools unconstitutional has turned into a nightmare: resegregation is rampant, the courts are totally resistant to allowing pro-integration steps by local school boards, and the education received by minority children overall is shockingly poor, as measured by almost all criteria (drop-out rates, graduation rates, etc.) and tests (good and bad ones, racially discriminatory and racially neutral ones).

The articles in this section describe this massive and growing education gap, and what should be done to close it; present a variety of views on how important (or unimportant) racial integration is in the school setting; and discuss the latest emphasis in the education area: the standards movement and its impact on minority students. The idea of making public education a lifelong opportunity is introduced as well.

The Growing Education Gap

Kati Haycock

If we had the will, we could close forever the achievement gap that has plagued this country for too long. In the 1970s and 1980s, we made tremendous progress in narrowing the gap that separates low-income students and minority students from others. We did this with only a little information and an awful lot of fervor.

Today, the reverse is true. We know a great deal more, but the progress, with few exceptions, has stopped. New research and lessons learned in pioneering communities point the way. But too few of us have been willing to act on that knowledge.

It is long past time to move forward.

America's achievement gap is both unnecessary and dangerous. It is unnecessary because low-income students and minority students *will* achieve at the highest levels *if* the adults responsible for their schooling are willing to ensure that these students are taught at the highest levels. The gap is dangerous because this country can ill afford the costs—human, economic, and civic—associated with failing to provide all of our young people with the skills and knowledge they and our nation need to compete and thrive in the new century.

What do we need to do to close the gap? First and most important is to assure that all students—but especially poor and minority students—are taught by effective and well-prepared teachers, teachers who know their subjects and how to teach them.

New research makes it abundantly clear that teachers make a very big difference in student achievement. Effective teachers can help students make enormous gains; ineffective teachers can do great and lasting damage to students. Poor children and children of color are far less likely than other children to be taught by qualified teachers. Indeed, no matter how you measure teacher qualifications—licensed versus unlicensed, in- versus out-of-field, performance on teacher licensure exams, or even actual effectiveness in producing learning gains—low-income and minority youngsters come up on the short end.

There are also significant differences in what is taught to different groups of students. We need to change our practice of placing only some of our children in challenging curricula. Students from poor families are much less likely to be placed in rigorous college preparatory classes and much more likely to be placed in watered-down "general" or "vocational" courses. Similarly, African American and Latino students are less likely than White students to be placed in courses that build high-level thinking skills, including geometry, algebra II, and chemistry. Even when the courses bear the same name, the standards are lower.

The final thing we need to change is the long-standing practice of just plain expecting less from some students than we do of others. Most states are trying to do this now with new standards for all children. But when we visit classrooms, it is very clear that teachers are not implementing the new standards. In high-poverty urban middle schools, for example, we typically find children getting more coloring assignments than writing and mathematics assignments. Even at the high school level, we see an awful lot of coloring assignments. For example, "Read *To Kill a Mockingbird,* and when you're done, color a poster on it." When our staff asks why not write an essay on it, the teachers will typically say something like, "With *these kids,* it's literally a criminal act to assign them an essay of more than three paragraphs in length."

The truth is that we expect so little of poor children that we are routinely giving them A's for work that would earn a C- or a D+ in the suburbs.

These inequities contribute to significant differences in the educational success of different students. On the whole, African American and Latino students experience the least success. They graduate from high school, enter college and graduate from college at rates below other students. While about twenty-five of every hundred White young Americans obtain at least a bachelor's degree, among African Americans only twelve do so, and among Latinos, only ten do so.

The good news is that *we can change practices that damage low-income and minority students*. And when we do, we see results very quickly.

Look, for example, at El Paso, Texas. In 1992, the educational and community leaders in this very poor border city gathered together to talk about education. They looked closely at the data on what happened to their young people—from kindergarten through college—and decided that they needed to do things very differently. They started by setting very high standards for what they wanted their students to know and be able to do, then they focused on two things: getting all students into rigorous courses, and helping teachers develop the knowledge and skills they need to get students to high levels of achievement. Look at their results just five years later:

School Ratings

Based on the Texas accountability system, which rates schools as either low performing, recognized, or exemplary:

- In 1992, there were fifteen "low performing" schools in El Paso. By 1997, there were none.
- In 1992, there were only two "recognized" schools in El Paso. By 1997, there were 60.
- And in 1992, there were no "exemplary" schools in El Paso. By 1997, there were 16.

Course-Taking

In 1992, only 59 percent of the Latino students in El Paso were enrolled in algebra. By 1995, 94 percent of Latino students were taking algebra.

Math Achievement

The percentage of students passing the Texas Assessment for Academic Success (TAAS) in math has risen steadily for all groups of students, simultaneously raising achievement levels for all groups and closing the achievement gap that separates these groups of students. In school year 1992–1993, only 32 percent African American, 36 percent Latino, and 63 percent White students passed TAAS. By school year 1997–1998, 75 percent African American, 79 percent Latino, and 91 percent White students passed.

Reading Achievement

Similarly, the percentage of students passing the TAAS in reading has risen steadily for all groups while simultaneously closing the gap. In school year 1992–1993, only 57 percent African American, 54 percent Latino, and 81 percent White students passed TAAS. By school year 1997–1998, 86 percent African American, 83 percent Latino, and 95 percent White students passed.

The low academic achievement of low-income students and minority students—and even the mediocre achievement of other American students—is neither preordained nor intractable. This is an achievement crisis of our own making. We must and we can do better. There are a growing number of states, school districts, schools, and colleges proving this every day, and they are doing it not with magic, but with common sense, political will, and hard work.

—— **Symposium** ——

Is Racial Integration Essential to Achieving Quality Education for Low-Income Minority Students? In the Short Term? In the Long Term?

A Case Could Be Made on Either Side

Phyllis Hart and Joyce Germaine Watts

"Integrated" or "racially isolated" public schools? Given the evidence, a case for equity could be made on either side. After almost thirty years in urban public education, we have to respond to this question by spotlighting what has shown to be as critical as material resources: teacher beliefs and expectations about student ability.

We live in a society with deeply held beliefs about ability and intelligence, and an educational system that is organized to sort and separate those who are perceived as talented and smart from those who are perceived as lacking those qualities. Institutional belief systems play out both in "racially isolated" and "integrated" school settings.

What is it that happens in a "racially isolated" school setting where students attend school in their home communities? At the risk of stereotyping, our experience shows that these schools have higher numbers of inexperienced teachers, many of whom are underprepared in pedagogy and content knowledge in their subject field. In many of these "racially isolated" school settings there is a culture of low expectations and remediation. From primary grades on, students are labeled and tracked. At the secondary level, too few college preparatory classes are offered, and few students have access to information about opportunities for higher education. These schools remain separate and unequal.

The obvious alternative would seem to be an "integrated" school, where ample resources are available and the test scores are higher, right? Well, not likely.

What are students finding at the end of the bus ride? Something that the plaintiffs in *Brown v. Board of Education* could never have foreseen. Because these students come from less desirable schools and are presumed to be less capable, regardless of their real potential, they often are "resegregated" into the same kinds of remedial curriculum that characterize their home schools. In elementary school, they are more likely to be placed in groups for "slow learners." When they reach high school, they are frequently programmed into the low-level track, with courses usually taught by the least prepared teachers. Obviously, these students are still not viewed as "college material" and do not get access to college prep courses or information about higher education. Educators defend the placement of these students in slow tracks according to what they consider "objective criteria." However, actual practice is to the contrary.

Since math is the gatekeeper subject, we asked teachers and counselors in many "integrated" schools why there were so few students of color in algebra, the first stepping-stone toward college. They explained that students are placed through a fair system of using standardized math test scores, and those who scored above the sixtieth percentile were enrolled in algebra. However, when disaggregated by race, the data revealed that even when African American and Latino students score at or above the *top* twenty-fifth percentile, only 51 percent and 42 percent, respectively, are programmed into algebra, compared to 100 percent Asians and 87.5 percent of Whites.

The struggle for racial integration of schools meant fighting for access and equity to have quality education nationwide, regardless of setting. In essence, this was an attempt to level the playing field. However, without addressing the beliefs held about African American, Latino, Native American, and low-income students, this does little to change the educational outcomes. The real question is how do we get all schools, whether "integrated" or "racially isolated," to hold high expectations for all students? There are success stories in both settings, but these occur only when educators and communities decide that educational equity must be central to a reform agenda and that a system that groups, sorts, and tracks students on "perceived" ability serves no one well.

There is no magic bullet of reform. We have to ask ourselves, as the renowned educator, Dr. Asa Hilliard, asks: Do we have the *will* to see every child in this society educated? If so, then we must invest in making the necessary changes to fundamentally overhaul our schools from a culture of low expectations and remediation to one of high expectations and a belief that all children, especially those who have been underserved historically, need and deserve the highest quality education.

Forced Racial Integration
Has Produced Poor Results

Lyman Ho

For the past thirty years, racial integration has been used as an essential tool to provide equitable access to facilities, teachers, and educational budgets for low-income minority students. Very often, federal judges oversaw implementation of this access by local boards and administration staff. Chief Federal Judge Richard Matsch released the Denver Public Schools District from federal supervision on September 18, 1995. From Denver's experience, low-income minority students have benefited in terms of access to better facilities, better teachers, and a more equitable share of the district budget, but have not achieved the goal of a quality education.

As damning as this conclusion may appear, forced racial integration remains an incomplete social policy that after a quarter-century of massive public funding has produced particularly poor results, as demonstrated in high drop-out rates, low graduation rates, and consistently large gaps in test scores between African American/Hispanic students and Anglo/Asian American students. The results of this failed social policy, coupled with trends toward fiscal and social conservatism, have contributed to increasing racial separatism. Similarly, Denver's movement toward neighborhood schools is a theme that excites many white families frightened from the district by court-ordered busing, while scaring many minority families too familiar with the inequities that forced the district into the federal lawsuit in the 1960s. The district, committed to returning to neighborhood schools, has reacted convulsively, alternating between passing a resolution against inferior as well as superior school facilities, reopening closed schools in low-income minority neighborhoods, relocating popular magnet schools to white middle-class neighborhoods, and hiring a new superintendent to lead the district into the new millennium, then firing him nine months later because he was a leader and not a manager.

If a quality education for low-income minority students is the goal, Afro or African-centric charter schools, back-to-basics magnet schools, and small neighborhood schools are simply the school design *du jour*. Separationist ideals are not new and do not automatically lead to a bad education, any more than racial integration automatically implies a quality education. Examples of extreme separationist school designs currently out of vogue include male military academies and finishing schools for girls. A quality education, particularly for low-income minority students, is a direct result from successful schools, notwithstanding design or operating philosophy.

Successful schools include well-trained staff, engaged communities, and a focus on learning. The successful schools share with the student the assumption of responsibility in the classroom, share with the parent the value of education, and share with the community the high expectations in a school's role within society. Essential ingredients to a quality education include parents and students engaged in the process of learning, school districts focused on providing basic and clear standards, and staff devoted to the challenge of teaching children.

Racial integration and quality education are not necessarily dependent on each other or mutually exclusive from each other. Forcing one to accomplish the other has not produced the intended results, nor has it lessened friction between interested factions or tribes. It is time for those interested in quality education to focus on education, to produce literate children who are ready for school each morning and are prepared to learn the skills necessary to survive and succeed in life, build businesses, and strengthen families. When the merit of a quality education rises above the considerations of personal finances and ethnicity, the education of all children will benefit.

Upgrade Education in Schools Serving Poor and Minority Children

Kati Haycock

"Is racial integration essential to achieving quality education for low-income minority students?"

Twenty years ago, I was dead certain that the answer to this question was a resounding "No"! Black kids and brown kids absolutely did not need white kids sitting next to them in order to achieve at high levels. Rather than obsessing about who was sitting next to whom—an increasingly useless preoccupation given the pitifully small numbers of whites left in urban school districts like Oakland, where I lived—it seemed to me that we ought to be concentrating on ensuring that students in predominantly minority schools were educated at the highest levels.

That, in fact, is what I have spent most of the last fifteen years doing: working to upgrade the education provided by schools serving poor and minority children, first in California and then in urban centers across the country. I figured that while Gary Orfield and others like him were worrying about how to get a better mix of students, people like me could work on improving schools no matter *whom* they served.

I still believe today what I believed back then: students with lots of pigment do not need students with less pigment in order to achieve at the highest levels. I believe it because I have seen it over and over again. When students are *taught* to high levels, when they are *challenged* to use their minds, they absolutely will achieve.

But I am haunted by three as yet unanswered questions:

- Will the American people ever care enough about schools filled with poor black and brown children to invest in them the resources necessary to get these young people to high levels of achievement . . . or will these investments occur only when these schools contain more affluent white children?
- Will rank-and-file teachers—minority and white—ever abandon their low expectations and watered-down curriculum for poor minority children . . . or must teaching be forced upward by the presence of more affluent white children?
- Will graduates of racially isolated schools—no matter how well educated—ever be able to come together across racial lines to create a cul-

ture where race is no longer a hindrance . . . or must such a society be seeded in our classrooms?

In my bleaker moments—when I despair in the dark of night about the pace of change or about how difficult it is to secure change not just in a few schools but in a whole system—these doubts crowd their way in and demand equal time. At those moments, I wonder whether Gary has not been right all along.

But then there are the good days—the days when our work is going very well; when more poor and minority students in our cities are writing at high levels, passing courses like algebra and geometry, and moving on to college; and when we feel like nothing can stop us. On those days, which, fortunately, are in the majority, I do not spend a lot of time agonizing about these questions. I figure Gary can do that.

Integration Is Not Cultural Assimilation

john a. powell

"My schooling gave me no training as the oppressor, as an unfairly advantaged person, or a person in a damaged culture. . . . At school, we were not taught about slavery in any depth; we were not taught to see slaveholders as damaged people. Slaves were seen as the only group at risk of being dehumanized. My schooling followed the pattern which Elizabeth Minnich has pointed out: whites are taught to think of their lives as morally neutral, normative, and average, and also ideal, so that when we work to benefit others, this is seen as work that will allow 'them' to be more like 'us.'"
—Peggy McIntosh, "White Privilege: Male Privilege"

The roles of segregation and integration have been central to understanding and maintaining or destabilizing white privilege. Much of the discussion about integration and segregation has been fought out with poignant focus on schools and education. This is understandable, in that schools play a central role in the formation of the American citizenry. Common schools are the crucible of American identity. They are the place where our children spend a tremendous portion of their lives, where their values and identities are shaped. In my discussion about integration and segregation, however, I will start, not with schools or even housing, but by rethinking what we mean by integration and segregation, and how our misunderstanding of these limits our imagination and practice with respect to racial issues in this country. What I am suggesting, then, is that our collective conceptual error has important implications for the movement toward a racially just society, a racial democracy. Recognition of this error should play an important role in our thinking about integration and segregation in the educational context.

The Assimilationist Trap

Today, there is re-questioning of the relative benefits of integration and segregation. Despite this questioning, much of the discussion around these issues remains largely unreflective. The debate about the relative merits of integration and segregation has a long, rich history in the black community. The pros and cons of each approach were thoughtfully and often sharply debated by W.E.B. DuBois and Booker T. Washington at the turn of the last century. Washington posited that blacks should rely on themselves for self-help, whereas DuBois thought the most talented blacks should learn from whites, and then bring these attributes back to the black community. Much of today's discussions draws on some of the ideas raised by DuBois and Washington without the benefit of the depth of thought they used to support their conclusions.

In order to deepen the discussion, it is important to give pause and reflect on what integration and segregation mean in contemporary terms and what the implications for these two strategies are in the twenty-first century. Part of the difficulty is that scholars and others have not been clear about what we mean by the words integration and segregation. Indeed, I would suggest that in recent times the debate has not focused on integration and segregation, but assimilation and segregation. The attack on integration, then, has largely not been an attack on integration but an attack on assimilation.

Assimilation is problematic because it is a product of racial hierarchy. Although there have been many distinct versions of assimilation and segregation, both of these concepts have been framed primarily by the dominant white society and operate under the implicit assumption that there is something wrong with the racial "other." The less extreme assimilationist would *fix* the racial other by acculturating him or her to the dominant culture. The more extreme assimilationist position is that the racial other must intermarry into the dominant race and cease to be. In either scenario, the voice of the minority is either ignored or eliminated.

The white segregationist shares this belief in white racial hierarchy. The segregationist also believes there is something defective about the racial other. But unlike the assimilationist, the run-of-the-mill segregationist takes the position that the racial other must prove that he or she has been fixed or modified before segregation can end. A more extreme segregationist view is that the racial others cannot be fixed, and affiliation with any of them will diminish and contaminate whites. The idea that one drop of African blood contaminates white blood is closely associated with this view. Both assimilationists and segregationists are disturbed by the otherness of the racial other. The extreme segregationist is also concerned about the other as well as otherness.

One may protest that this is the position only of the dominant society. What about racial minority groups that want to segregate themselves from the dominant society? While theoretically one can imagine that a racial minority might, for positive reasons, want to segregate itself despite openness from the dominant society, this is simply not the history of racial politics in the United States. Indeed, when Washington called for self-segregation, it was in part because he accepted the position that blacks were unfit and must prove themselves to whites before segregation could end. The reality is that many African Americans have adopted segregation as an accommodation and protection from white racism. While this is understandable from a self-survival point of view, the problem is that it does not destabilize white hierarchy, and it also has very little practical benefit. When one looks at middle-class blacks who choose to live in black neighborhoods, among the prevalent reasons cited is the desire to have space to retreat from white racism and the frustration of dealing with whites in the workplace. This does not mean that there are not positive things about the black community or black culture. This is another variation of the assimilationist position. What I am suggesting is that when one examines the roots of segregation, either self-imposed or imposed by the dominant society, white racism is central to understanding it.

Social interaction is constitutive of the individual and the collective identity of the community. Assimilation envisions the absorption of minorities into the mainstream. Real integration is measured, however, by the transformation of institutions, communities, and individuals. Real integration involves fundamental change among whites and people of color, as people and communities. Segregation is not just the exclusion of people, but also the limitation of their opportunities and economic resources. It creates and maintains a culture of racial hierarchy and subjugation. Integration, as a solution to segregation, has broader meaning: it refers to community-wide efforts to create a more inclusive society, where individuals and groups have opportunities to participate equally in their communities. Inclusion gives us tools to build democratic communities, the ability to approach complex issues from a multitude of perspectives. Integration, then, transforms racial hierarchy. Rather than creating a benefactor-beneficiary distinction along lines of race and class, true integration makes it possible for all groups to benefit from each other's resources. Homogeneous education fails to prepare students of all races for a multicultural society. Integrated education necessarily implies a curriculum that respects and values cultural difference, while building a community of equals.

Although I cannot do justice to this issue in a short article, it is important to consider the situation of Native Americans. There is a strong feeling among American Indians that if they integrate, they will lose their culture and be overwhelmed by the dominant society. The discussion about segregation and assimilation in many ways is not germane for Native Americans. First of all, the issue of segregation and assimilation is a discussion that takes place within a nation. The debate for Native Americans is about how to build or maintain a nation within a nation. Native Americans have not been pushing to be part of this nation, but rather to preserve their own nation. If they cannot maintain their nation, it is likely that these other issues will become more important. In addition, when one asserts that Native Americans or other groups that are not allowed to segregate may lose their culture and identity, one is essentially making a claim that if not allowed to segregate, a group may be forced to assimilate. Given the two alternatives, maybe segregation is more desirable.

But this is not the issue that blacks face in large numbers. While it may be possible for a few African Americans to assimilate, that is not possible for large numbers. Blacks in the United States are "unassimilable"—what one writer calls "the designated other." This leads us to segregation or something else.

Before considering something else, I want to assert that segregation is morally, pragmatically, and ontologically flawed. It is morally flawed because it cannot be reconciled in our society with the fundamental value of equal respect and dignity of all people. It is pragmatically flawed in that it can never produce equal life chances for whites and "others." It is ontologically flawed in that it damages and distorts the identity of all members of the racist society where segregation is practiced.

Problems Caused By Segregation

Segregation prevents access to wealth accumulation by residents of isolated, poor communities of color, thereby establishing barriers to market participation. Lack of educational opportunities, poor job accessibility, and declining housing values in isolated, low-income communities are symptoms of the problem. Further, racial and economic segregation damages the whole metropolitan region, including both the urban cores and the suburbs. Segregation geographically polarizes metropolitan communities along lines of race, income, and opportunity, and separates urban centers from the surrounding suburbs. The experience of attending desegregated schools is likely to increase participation in desegregated environments in later life. When students attend integrated schools, they are more likely to attend desegregated colleges, live in integrated neighborhoods, work in integrated environments, have friends of another race, and send their children to integrated schools. Conversely, students from segregated schools are more likely to avoid interactions with other races and generally conduct their lives in segregated settings. As Peggy McIntosh points out in her article, "White Privilege: Male Privilege," her schooling as a white attending an all-white school led to strained interactions in the workplace as an adult. Once she entered an integrated workspace, she realized she would not be able to get along if she asked her nonwhite coworkers to adapt to her worldview. One thing is clear to me: that racial neutrality or "color blindness" is more likely to maintain the status quo than destabilize it.

Toward Incorporation

Traditionally, desegregation in education has meant either removing formal barriers or simply placing students in physical proximity to one another. These remedies are limited. Segregation is not just the exclusion of people, but also the limitation of their opportunities and economic resources. Properly conceived, integration is transformative for everyone involved. Integration embraces a multicultural concept of social interaction. Much of the focus on the benefits of integration has been on how integration will benefit blacks and other "others." What has been missing is an understanding of how integration, as well as segregation, affects us all. If we are to be successful at integration, we move much closer to David Goldberg's notion of incorporation. He asserts that: "Incorporation, then, does not involve extension of established values and protections over the formerly excluded group. . . . [T]he body politic becomes a medium for transformative incorporation, a political arena of contestation, rather than a base from which exclusions can be more or less silently extended, managed, and manipulated." Incorporation allows the views and experiences of both the dominant group and minority groups to meet, informing and transforming each other. With incorporation, no experience is the exclusive one. In this respect, incorporation clearly differs from assimilation and desegregation models. The ultimate goal of integration is this transformative incorporation Goldberg describes.

Building a Participatory Democracy

If we accept this reconstituted way of viewing integration, it provides a positive strategy for how to start thinking about integration in relationship to schools, as well as a critical perspective on how integration in the past has failed. Most of the efforts of the past and even today are half-hearted, leaving students de facto segregated or token, assimilated. Too often the assumption is that if we can fix the other by having them go to schools with whites, without addressing the underlying assumption of white privilege, including cultural privilege, we have successfully integrated. In assessing integration efforts, we too often look at the racial composition of a school, and not at what happens in the school. But if we look at integration in the way suggested above, it requires that we look at what goes on in school as well as outside of school. It requires that we link housing, school, employment, and cultural opportunities. Linking housing and education policies, rather than focusing solely on integrating schools, directs attention to the importance and benefits of racial integration in multiple settings. By contrast, the approach of desegregating schools in isolation from other important institutions disregards the significance of building and strengthening communities. A qualitative analysis of the social effect of integration makes clear that achieving broad integration remains a central goal in, and a necessary step toward, making a fully participatory democracy a reality. The social value of integration embodies the founding ideals of this country. Making it possible for everyone to participate actively in our democracy should be a fundamental goal woven into the fabric of the nation's public policies. Another necessary element of participation is for residents to feel connected to the community as valued members of the polity. Segregated society has continued to exclude community members, even when formal rights to participate exist. The school setting provides both academic and social tools for participating in society. The less formal environment of our neighborhoods and social circles provides equally important tools for everyday life. Integration of both schools and housing demonstrates for all of us how the practice of living and learning together can inform our understanding of the world.

The Legacy of *Brown*

More than forty years ago, the Supreme Court, in *Brown v. Board of Education*, recognized the unique harm experienced by black students forced to attend racially segregated schools. The court declared the circumstances unacceptable. Today, after a half-hearted effort at best, most American schools remain segregated. While the explicitly segregationist policies of the *Brown* era seldom exist today, a subtler network of social and institutional barriers persist, working to maintain segregation in our schools and communities. Desegregated schools may be the only institutions in which African Americans and Latinos students have access to the abundance of college and employment contacts that whites and wealthy students take for granted. William Julius Wilson and other social scientists have noted that the greatest barrier to social and economic mobility for inner-city blacks is their isolation from the opportunities and networks of the mostly white and middle-class society. School desegregation has a profound impact on blacks' ability to acquire knowledge that would enhance their academic and occupational success via social contacts and integrated institutions. Integration can be a tough concept to embrace when one considers that it cannot claim many examples. Integration has been attacked by both ends of the political spectrum. In 1995, in his concurring opinion in *Missouri v. Jenkins*, Justice Clarence Thomas noted that "[I]t never ceases to amaze me that the courts are so willing to assume that anything that is predominantly black must be inferior." Several Afrocentrists recall early attempts at integration that resulted in assimilation. The implications of assimilation have appropriately been criticized by a number of scholars.

The Link Between Housing and Education

The spatial isolation of minority poor students concentrates the education disadvantages inherent in poverty. Racial segregation, moreover, denies all students the benefits of an integrated education. For parents fortunate enough to be able to choose where they live, their selection is often determined by the quality of public education for their children. America's metropolitan areas increasingly have become characterized by a poor minority core, with a white, middle-class suburban ring. More often than not, the public schools considered best are in the middle-class and upper-middle class neighborhoods. Negative perceptions about urban schools contribute to the unwillingness of white families to move to urban neighborhoods. Part of the reason urban schools have a poor reputation is, of course, because they are segregated by race and class. The two most commonly expressed concerns about integration are "white flight" and mandatory busing, both of which can weaken communities, resulting in the drive of many school districts to return to neighborhood schools. The return to neighborhood schools, which many policymakers are now calling for, may, in fact, maintain or increase the racial segregation of communities that are isolated by race and class. Integrating schools while simultaneously creating greater housing opportunities makes true integration the goal, while it recognizes the social and economic barriers to integration. Building more integrated communities seems possible and desirable when people of different racial and economic groups begin to recognize that, without ignoring their differences, they share many goals and concerns. When housing and school policies work together, integrated communities maintain a stable, yet diverse, population.

Peggy McIntosh's 1988 article, "White Privilege: Male Privilege," is Working Paper #189 from the Wellesley College Center for Research on Women, Wellesley, MA 02481, 781/283–2500.

All Students Are Not Equal

Sheryl Denbo and Byron Williams

Current reform initiatives are insisting that all students benefit from school improvement, thereby making it more difficult to pose the goals of educational excellence and educational equity as conflicting or contradictory. A view of the "equity problem" as one that is created by students, something that children of color bring with them into the school, is no longer sustainable. This view is slowly yielding to one that sees an "equity problem" as something that children of color encounter in the schools they attend.

Thus, the question we must pose is not what children of color must do to achieve to high standards, but how all of the stakeholders can facilitate that achievement. We here pose the question of how the larger community, Euro-Americans, African Americans, Asian Americans, and Latino Americans, can work together to assure that our democratic rhetoric of "all children achieving to high standards" becomes a reality.

First and foremost, we must find the political will to ensure that all schools receive equitable funding. Local funding of schools maintains economic disparities between urban, high minority concentration schools and their suburban counterparts, and has created separate and unequal systems of education. A disproportionate number of children of color live in poverty and attend schools that suffer from severe funding disparities. Schools face shrinking budgets and fading economic support for public education, which limits their capacity to invest in reform. Since the poorest children attend the poorest schools, often with the least experienced teachers, poverty has become the best predictor of low educational achievement. Funding disparities mean that poor minority students get relatively little benefit from the research, techniques, programs, and practices that have proven highly effective in improving learning opportunities. Reduced class size; increased attention to individual learning style; team teaching and planning; peer coaching among teachers, for example, all require financial resources. A lack of educational resources, such as libraries, science labs, computers, recreation space, and equipment reduces the quality of education. Investment in high-quality in-service professional staff development is cost-effective, but costly. It is most unfortunate that contemporary American schools provide those children with the greatest needs the most limited access to resources.

Second, schools must be pressured, both from within the school and from the outside community, to end discriminatory practices. Stereotypes and prejudice are masking discriminatory practices and preventing communities from working collaboratively. Prejudice can make differences in expectations and opportunities by race, national origin, or gender seem "natural." The disproportionate expulsion of minority boys may seem unremarkable if society's disproportionate imprisonment of men of color seems inevitable. Schools' expectations of students in general tend to parallel and reflect societal expectations. Curricular tracking, ability grouping, application of discipline policies, and supportive versus non-supportive counseling frequently divide along racial lines. African American and Latino students are disproportionately suspended and expelled. Curricular offerings in the poorest, most segregated schools are limited, in comparison to the offerings in more affluent schools. Instructional content, goals, and practices that emphasize rote learning and repetitive drills are narrowing the learning opportunities of low-income children. Special needs programs further isolate students from challenging curricula. Tracking often results in hostility and suspicion, separating "mainstream" teachers, students, and parents from teachers, students, and parents of children tracked in low-ability programs or urban schools, reinforcing between and within school "ghettoization." Students reacting to group isolation may, in turn, face increased problems of discipline and even violence. Mistrust of schools and inter-group hostility prevent school boards, school administrators, teachers, parents, and community groups from working effectively together to improve student achievement.

Finally, we must both reform our schools of education so that they address issues of cultural diversity, and reschedule our school calendars to allow sufficient time for professional development and collaboration. The professional teaching force is 90 percent white, predominantly female, and monolingual. Students are increasingly diverse. Systemic reform formulations foresee the restructuring of schools in which teachers bear a significant share of the responsibility, both for creating high-quality educational opportunities and for ensuring that those opportunities are equitably available to all of their students.

Given the kind of teacher training programs that presently exist, it is not surprising that new teachers report little desire to teach in urban, poor, or diverse schools. Many view student diversity as a problem and agree with the statement that some children cannot learn. If we are to expect teachers to confront today's challenges, they must receive the necessary resources and tools to meet them. The ability of the teaching profession to provide low-income students and students of color with the learning environments and opportunities they need will depend, to a large extent, on effective pre-service and in-service training. This training must be designed to improve cross-cultural understanding, instructional practices, classroom management skills, assessment practices, and other skills.

Conclusion

To make the rhetoric that all children can learn to high standards a reality, we must face the fact that all children are not equal. They come from communities and homes with unequal resources into schools with unequal resources. Children of color experience prejudice and discrimination and are more likely than their white counterparts to be tracked into less challenging academic programs.

If our schools are going to help create a level playing field, the schools that serve low-income students need the additional resources necessary to address the serious issues outlined above. Schools of education that train teachers must train these teachers to understand and utilize the rich diversity of culture children bring to the classroom. Increasingly, teachers view student diversity as a problem rather than an opportunity.

Unfortunately, the children most in need are most likely to be taught by teachers who are the least qualified and do not understand their culture. They are most likely to attend schools or participate in programs that have the fewest resources and/or provide the least challenging educational environments.

A country that fails to capitalize on the rich diversity of its own human resources is a country in severe trouble. America cannot and will not prosper if it fails to adequately educate its low-income and culturally diverse students, who are quickly becoming America's New Majority. It is everyone's responsibility to find the political will and resources to end discrimination in our schools and provide each and every child with high-quality educational opportunities.

When the "Is Integration Possible?" symposium appeared in Poverty & Race, *it was reprinted and distributed via the excellent Black Radical Congress listserv (www.blackradicalcongress.org). The following letter (see page 151) came to us via the listserv. We reprint it here with the writer's permission, although we have not been able to secure any biographical information about Dr. Failla.*

Separation, Then Integration

Marcelitte Failla

Integration is possible once children of color are educated early on by teachers of color who are aware of their history/herstory and who have a genuine self-love and self-awareness.

They should create separate schools up to possibly fourth or fifth grade initially so as to instill in the children a good sense of self which can trickle up to their parents.

Children should not be taught early on by European-American teachers because of the subtle brain-washing Europeans in America have of our children, however wonderful the teacher may be. This may include low expectations, a sweet, but destructive, form of pity, to having deep-set (but gratefully still trying to fight) feelings that they (Europeans) are superior to people of color.

I was fortunate to be able to home school my children for some time, and I notice the difference even in my children's expression, physically and intellectually.

—— **Symposium** ——

The Standards Movement in Education: Will Poor and Minority Students Benefit?

The Standards Movement: Another Warning

John Cawthorne

"If there is anything that we wish to change in the child, we should first examine it and see whether it is not something that could better change in ourselves."

—Carl G. Jung

Standards, by themselves, will not change the educational experiences of poor children, especially those in urban areas. I want to explore in more detail three areas policymakers must address if the standards movement is to alter radically the educational landscape. They are: using test results, tracking, and professional development.

Using Test Results

The standards movement will be another frustrating reform effort unless we change how we use test results. Currently, most results, regardless of the test or the institution mandating it, are used to label and sort. The media constantly label our students and schools as failures. The American Federation of Teachers recently released *What Students Abroad Are Expected to Know About Mathematics*. This report concludes that "one reason students in other countries perform better than ours is because they are held to higher expectations." It claims that American students do poorly because there are no consequences attached to the tests they take. This report, and others like it, implies that students will not work hard unless there are serious repercussions for failure. The proponents would use test results to deny students admission to higher-level courses, to college, and to work.

This stance contradicts what we know about how best to motivate students and places the blame on students instead of on systems that have failed them. When we use tests only to assess whether or not students reached our "high expectations," we are doing them, and ourselves, a disservice. There are other ways to use test results. We could utilize such data to ask ourselves, "What is wrong with the adults who control our schools? What are their weaknesses as teachers and administrators? Do they know the content but not good pedagogy? Do they know pedagogy but not mathematics? Do adults organize schools in ways that help students learn most effectively? Do adults use test results to design more effective instructional strategies?"

In 1989, the Boston public schools planned to use standardized test results as one criterion for high school graduation. When officials learned that over 50 percent would be denied a diploma, the policy was quickly scrapped. The message was not about students failing school, but of schools failing students. When we use test results to deny opportunities, we run the great risk of endangering students whose test results reflect poor teaching and administering. Urban and poor students whose schools have inadequate resources, including teachers who are not capable of teaching mathematics, for example, would be "punished" for the misfortune of geography, not because they did not work hard.

Tracking

Tracking, the practice of grouping students by "ability," has become acceptable practice in our schools. The "top" group gets the best teachers, the most challenging curriculum, and the experiences needed to succeed. The "middle" and "low" groups get what is left over. This hardly democratic practice results in students having vastly different school experiences and correspondingly different achievement results.

If we demand that all children achieve at high standards, we must stop tracking students. The notion of "ability" grouping, especially when resources are allocated unevenly, is inconsistent with the desire that all achieve at high levels. To hold children accountable for achieving at high levels while placing them in low-level courses is a cruel hoax!

Professional Development

According to the National Commission on Teaching and America's Future, "What teachers know and can do makes the crucial difference in what children learn. . . . Policies can improve schools only if the people in them are armed with the knowledge, skills, and supports they need. Student learning . . . will improve only when we focus our efforts on improving teaching."

The standards movement creates new expectations for educators, and unless we take the time to prepare teachers to meet them, the "experiment" is doomed to fail. As students with more diverse learning needs enroll and remain in schools, teachers will have to learn how to work with those they would have discarded and hidden only a few years ago. They have to learn how to teach *all* children. It is just as barbaric to hold teachers to new norms without providing them the opportunity to acquire new skills, as it is to hold children accountable while denying them sufficient opportunity.

Teachers, however, need more than new instructional techniques; they need to know more! For example, over 30 percent of all mathematics teachers do not have even a minor in this field. We cannot attain "world class standards" without "world class teachers." We must all work to realize the Commission's goal of providing "a caring and qualified teacher for every child . . ."

The standards movement offers this nation a tremendous opportunity to educate all children well. If it is to succeed, we must change drastically the way we organize our schools, who teaches in them, and what they are capable of teaching.

In the final analysis, the standards movement's success depends on the willingness and ability of adults to heed Jung's advice and explore how we must change. Perhaps the first and most powerful "standards" should be applied to adults and those with power and privilege.

The Standards Movement in Education: A Part of Systemic Reform

Peter Negroni

If we believe that setting standards will solve the ineffectiveness of American education for poor and minority students, we are doomed to failure. Standards reflecting curriculum-learning outcomes provide the goal, the "star" that must be reached. The journey to reaching that star for all cannot be the traditional curriculum, instructional strategies, and factory system production schedules that have dominated our education system. Although some can still excel in this system, today's and tomorrow's global economy requires higher thinking skills, problem-solving, team approaches to fulfilling tasks, and invention of solutions to new needs and circumstances.

The journey toward the goal is influenced by time. The navigators may be slow and direct by ship or fast and direct by airplane. In either case, determination and desire to reach the goal are essential. It does not matter ultimately if there are detours or delays. The system must be flexible in allowing for detours and delays, in providing alternative routes to the same destination.

The journey is influenced by appropriate funding. Students who face multiple issues—poverty, learning disabilities, second language learning—need different and, often, more costly interventions. There is a difference in results if one assumes the journey on a raft or a cabin cruiser. Money makes the difference. National, state, and local governments must make education the priority in allocating funds.

The journey is influenced by the leadership, the implementers, and support personnel. Money must be spent wisely. There must be a connection between what we do and how successful children are in the learning process. Leaders must identify the needs of the "voyagers"; they must have a variety of strategies to ensure success for all. Teachers need to know their students, to know how children learn, and what impedes and what accelerates student learning. All involved in teaching must be continual learners, must work in a collaborative model, and must extend themselves beyond the traditional school hours.

The journey can be successful for all, minority or majority students, males or females, rich or poor, when we recognize that our work is to develop ourselves continually so that we can develop our students' skills. Standards must place the responsibility of learning on teachers and principals; those who teach the children to reach the standards must be capable of accomplishing the standards themselves. Therefore, colleges and universities must prepare top teacher candidates; communities must compensate educators in a competitive market; and government must provide appropriate funding for education to ensure that the best educators are hired and retained, and to support instruction with instructional materials and modern facilities that support the educational programs.

And so, I view the movement toward standards as an essential *beginning* to ensure quality education for all. The means involve ongoing professional development, alternative teaching strategies, innovative programs, flexible schedules, updated and modern facilities, quality staff, and accountability for the design of the educational program. The end is approachable; the star must always be before us to direct and to affirm the direction.

Standards or Standardization?

William Ayers

The "standards movement"—the reform *du jour* of the educational establishment and its camp-following gurus—is at its heart a fraud. It is demagoguery at its most depraved: the leaders feign knowledge and concern about the crisis, all the while drawing energy and attention away from the substantive demands of that crisis and toward a manufactured ill. Campaigning vigorously against their invented problem, they attempt to drown out more promising and progressive voices. Their shrill and insistent message—simple and believable in its own right—slowly and subtly shifts responsibility away from the powerful, making scapegoats of the victims of power. The bandwagon is decorated and overflowing, the drumbeat deafening, but it is all illusion: the "standards movement" is not a popular upheaval for positive or fundamental change—it is a deceptive crusade in the service of the status quo.

High academic standards (as well as social and community standards) are essential to good schools, of course. Such standards, in part, can demonstrate a commitment to high expectations for all students. A watery curriculum, vague or meaningless goals, expectations of failure—these are a few of the ingredients of academic ruin. Other elements include the inequitable distribution of educational resources, the capacity of a range of self-interested bureaucracies to work their will against the common good, and a profound disconnect between schools and the communities they are supposed to serve. Any hopeful strategy to improve our schools must address these underlying causes of crisis as well.

The "standards movement" is flailing at shadows. All schools in Illinois, for example, follow the same guidelines—these standards apply to successful schools as well as collapsing ones. While we could argue about this or that specific item, the fact is that standards are in place and have been for decades. Why, then, do some schools succeed brilliantly while others stumble and fall? More than standards must be at stake.

The school crisis is neither natural nor uniform, but particular and selective—it is a crisis of the poor, of the cities, of Latino and African American communities. All the structures of privilege and oppression apparent in the larger society are mirrored in our schools: Chicago public school students, for example, are overwhelmingly children of color—65 percent are African American, 25 percent are Latino—and children of the poor—68 percent qualify for federal lunch programs. More than half of the poorest children in Illinois (and over two-thirds of the bilingual children) attend Chicago schools. Yet Chicago schools must struggle to educate children with considerably fewer human and material resources than neighboring districts.

Illinois in effect has created two parallel systems—one privileged, adequate, successful, and largely white, the other disadvantaged in countless ways, disabled, starving, failing, and African American. When former Governor James Thompson called Chicago schools "a black hole" as he rejected appeals for more equitable support, he brought out all the racial justifications and tensions inherent in that situation. And when Lieutenant Governor Robert Kustra called Chicago schools "a rat hole," he was merely following suit.

In 1998–1999 ten thousand kids repeated eighth grade in Chicago in the name of standards. It is impossible to argue that they should have been passed along routinely—that has been the cynical response for years. But holding that huge group back without seriously addressing the ways school has failed them—that is, without changing the structures and cultures of those schools— is to punish those kids for the failures of all of us. Further, the standard turns out to be a standardized test and nothing more—a measure designed so that half of those who take it must fail it.

The purpose of education in a democracy is to break down barriers, to overcome obstacles, to open doors, minds, and possibilities. Education is empowering and enabling; it points to strength, to critical capacity, to thoughtfulness, and expanding capabilities. It aims at something deeper and richer than simply imbibing and accepting existing codes and conventions, acceding to whatever common sense society posits. The larger goal of education is to assist people in seeing the world through their own eyes, interpreting and analyzing through their own experiences and reflective thinking, feeling themselves capable of representing, manifesting, or even, if they choose, transforming all that is before them. Education, then, is linked to freedom, to the ability to see and also to alter, to understand, and also to reinvent, to know and also to change the world as we find it. Can we imagine this at the core of all schools, even poor city schools?

If city school systems are to be retooled, streamlined, and made workable, and city schools are to become palaces of learning for all children (why not? why does it sound so provocatively extravagant?), then we must fight for a comprehensive program of change: Educational resources must be distributed fairly. Justice—the notion that all children deserve a decent life, and that the greatest need deserves the greatest support—must be our guide. Equity, not sameness.

School people must find common cause with students and parents. We must remake schools by drawing on strengths and capacities in communities rather than exclusively on deficiencies and difficulties. We must focus on problems as shared and social, and solutions as collective and manageable. We must talk of solidarity rather than "services," people as self-activated problem-solvers rather than passive and pacified "clients."

School is a public space where the American hope for democracy, participation, and transformation collides with the historic reality of privilege and oppression, the hierarchies of race and class. The "standards movement"—geared to simple, punitive, one-size-fits-all solutions—is not worthy of our support.

Without Good Assessment, Standards Will Fail

Monty Neill

In the discussion about standards in education, the various authors have correctly observed that high-quality standards can be valuable for improving education for all students. They are equally correct in warning that the standards movement may fail due to inadequate support for education (lack of funding, prepared teachers, decent schools and books), the misuse of standards and testing (tracking and grade retention), or low-quality standards (more facts but not thinking, Eurocentrism).

To a great extent, the effectiveness of standards also will depend on the quality of the assessments states and districts use to measure student progress. The parts of the standards schools will focus on the most—the *real* standards —will be those parts that are measured by a test or other assessment tool. Thus, schools that rely on narrow tests will likely neglect significant components of the standards.

Students should learn to analyze, synthesize, evaluate, create, and apply knowledge—to think—in each subject, and they should be assessed to see if they have learned to do so. By these lights, people in most states should not be confident that the real standards would be high quality. In 1997, Fair Test released a detailed study, *Testing Our Children*, which concludes that most states have very low-level testing programs. Only seven states have adequate programs, and most of those are not really good enough. (The evaluation was based on the National Forum on Assessment's *Principles and Indicators for Student Assessment Systems*, which 80 civil rights and education organizations have signed.) Meanwhile, most districts rely on norm-referenced, multiple-choice tests that completely fail to assess the ability to think and use knowledge.

Since schools and districts often teach to the test, many students will not be taught to the broader standards, but to the narrow, low-level version in the tests. Children of color and those from low-income families are far more likely to be taught a low-level curriculum by drill-and-kill methods focused on standardized tests. Outside of Kentucky, the South relies most heavily on multiple-choice tests, and big cities use such tests more than other areas.

Standardized testing also tends to impose a standardized curriculum. If that means all students are helped to a high-quality education, fine. But it is likely instead to negate the great diversity of our nation in order to impose a one-size-fits-all schooling. The *Principles* call for assessment practices that "allow students multiple ways to demonstrate their learning" and "recognize and incorporate the variety of cultural backgrounds of students who are assessed . . . [and] the variety of different student learning styles." Almost all large-scale assessments fail to meet these principles and therefore do not help schools to meet the learning needs of all their students.

Assessment reform is not a panacea and will not by itself fix the deep problems of U.S. education. But education reform without assessment reform will not succeed. Most of the needed changes in assessment will have to take place in the classroom, which in turn will require substantial professional development. These, in turn, should be part of comprehensive changes aimed at making each school a supportive community of learners. To encourage these changes, to ensure that assessment really does support important learning, state and district assessment must also change fundamentally.

The promise of standards is that they will be used to improve education for all students. Unless states are willing to create much better assessments (among other necessary improvements), that promise will once again be broken. Rich kids will still learn to use knowledge to think and solve problems, while poor kids will learn to pass basic skills tests, thereby reproducing our society's class and race inequities.

The following is an edited version of an article, "High-Stakes Testing: Opportunities and Risks for Students of Color, English-Language Learners, and Students with Disabilities," that first appeared in M. Pines, ed. The Continuing Challenge: Moving the Youth Agenda Forward. *Policy Issues Monograph 00–02, Sar Levitan Center for Social Policy Studies, Johns Hopkins University. In its original form, the article presents additional research findings and documentation of all claims. The full article is available at http:// www.cast.org/ncac/policy2.*

High-Stakes Testing: Potential Consequences for Students of Color, English-Language Learners, and Students with Disabilities

Jay P. Heubert

The stated objective of the "standards" movement in American public education is to hold all schools, teachers, and students to high standards of teaching and learning. Accountability can take many forms, one of which is tests that have high stakes for individual students. They are "high-stakes" tests because they are used in making decisions about which students will be promoted or retained in grade and which will receive high school diplomas. While many agree that high-stakes testing will especially affect minority students, English-language learners, and students with disabilities, there are disputes over whether the consequences will be beneficial or harmful.

Graduation and Promotion Testing

Graduation testing has gone through several stages of development in the United States and varies considerably from state to state. In the 1970s and 1980s, a number of states adopted requirements under which students had to pass "minimum competency tests" as a condition of getting high school diplomas, even if the students had satisfied all other requirements for graduation. In the late 1980s and 1990s—responding in part to *A Nation At Risk*, a report that warned of "a rising tide of mediocrity" in American public education, and to the rise of today's "standards" movement—some states replaced minimum competency tests with graduation exams measuring knowledge and skills at the tenth-grade level or higher. At present, about twenty-three states—up from eighteen in 1998—require students to pass graduation tests, and the number is expected to increase to twenty-nine by 2003. Of the twenty-three, fourteen now set graduation-test standards at the tenth grade level or higher.

Further, in response to concerns about "social promotion," a growing number of states—thirteen, about twice as many as the year before—now require students to pass standardized tests as a condition of grade-to-grade promotion. Moreover, many school districts, particularly in urban areas, have also adopted promotion-test policies. Thus, large numbers of the nation's minority students and English-language learners are now subject to these state or local promotion-test programs.

Moreover, under current federal law, students with disabilities and English-language learners—whom many states and school districts have traditionally exempted from large-scale assessments—must now be included in state and local testing programs, with accommodation and alternative assessment where necessary. To promote *system* accountability, states and school districts must not only assess such students but also publish disaggregated data on their performance. Significantly, federal law takes no position on whether states and districts should use test results to determine whether individual students will receive high school diplomas or be promoted to the next grade.

Effects of High-Stakes Testing

Proponents of standards-based reform and high-stakes testing point out that blacks, Latinos, English-language learners, students with disabilities, and poor children are among those who most often receive low-quality instruction, and who therefore have the most to gain from any movement that attempts to hold all schools, teachers, and students to high standards of teaching and learning. Meanwhile, critics of high-stakes testing fear that such children will be disproportionately retained in grade or denied high school diplomas because their schools do not expose them to the knowledge and skills students need to pass the tests. There is support for both positions, but the story is complex and the evidence incomplete.

Even on graduation tests that measure basic skills, for example, minority students and students with disabilities usually fail at higher rates than other students, especially in the years after such tests are first introduced. For example, in the 1970s, when minimum competency tests gained popularity, 20 percent of black students, compared with 2 percent of white students—a discrepancy of ten to one—initially failed Florida's graduation tests and were denied high school diplomas. And while many students with disabilities were excluded from state graduation-test programs, those who did participate failed at rates over 50 percent.

For a variety of reasons, failure rates typically decline among all groups in the years after a new graduation test is introduced. This was true of the early minimum competency tests; after a few years, for example, black failure rates were far lower than 20 percent, and failure rates for students with disabilities also declined. This also appears to be true for graduation tests adopted more recently. Texas, for example, which has a graduation test set at the seventh or eighth grade level, reports that pass rates of blacks and Latinos roughly doubled between 1994 and 1998, and that the gap in failure rates between whites, blacks, and Latinos narrowed considerably during that time. Even so, 1998 data from the Texas graduation tests show continuing disparities of three to one: cumulative failure rates of 17.6 percent for black students, 17.4 percent for Hispanic students, and 6.7 percent for white students.

Data for students with disabilities are harder to find, but they show a similar pattern. On one hand, there is evidence that many students with disabilities do pass state tests in higher numbers over time: New York reports, for example, that the number of students with disabilities who passed the state's English Regents exam in 1998–1999 was nearly twice as high as the number who *took* the exam two years earlier. On the other hand, 1998 data from fourteen states show gaps that remain quite high: Students with disabilities consistently fail state graduation tests at rates 35 to 40 percentage points higher than those for non-disabled students.

An important, largely unanswered question concerns the extent to which improved pass rates on graduation tests actually reflect improved teaching and learning on the part of teachers and students. Such improvements are plainly one explanation and the most desirable one. During the 1980s, however, when many states reported sharply improved pass rates on graduation tests, scores on the National Assessment of Educational Progress (NAEP)—a highly regarded nationally administered examination—showed little or no gain in student learning. Indeed, evidence that minimum competency tests were not producing improved student performance on the NAEP is one reason why the current standards movement emphasizes higher standards, and why some states have been raising graduation-test standards. More recent fourth- and eighth-grade NAEP scores suggest improvements in student mathematics performance—especially for minority students and low-SES students—during the period 1990–1996, particularly in some states (including Texas and North Carolina) that invested heavily in smaller class sizes, preschool programs, and better resources for teachers. Gains reported on state tests continued to exceed the improvements measured by NAEP, however, and it is unclear to what extent improved fourth and eighth grade NAEP scores are due to high-stakes graduation testing rather than to the other educational interventions mentioned just above.

What factors other than improved achievement may explain increased pass rates on state tests? First, test scores often increase, especially during the years after a test is first introduced, because teachers increasingly "teach to the test," that is, focus on subject matter and formats that appear on the test, and students become familiar with that test's format. Second, some states may reduce initially high failure rates by making the state graduation tests easier or by setting lower cutoff scores that students must achieve to pass. Third, if low-achieving students are not part of the test-taking population, then the pass rates of those who remain will be higher—even if the achievement of those who actually take the test has not improved.

Thus, reported pass rates should be viewed in the context of such factors as (a) dropout rates; (b) whether states count among dropouts (or include in test results) students who choose—or are encouraged—to leave school to pursue general equivalency diplomas; (c) exemption of students with disabilities or English-language learners from the test-taking population; and (d) improper testing accommodations that may artificially inflate some students' scores.

Not surprisingly, there is also a spirited debate about whether graduation testing causes increased dropout rates. On one hand, it appears that many low-achievers start to disengage from school well before graduation tests loom. On the other hand, there are reputable scholars who argue—credibly—that fear of failing a graduation test increases the likelihood that low-achievers will leave school. (Such fears presumably are greater in states where graduation-test standards are high.) Also, the current climate of accountability places new pressures on schools to increase student pass rates, which can lead to increased and/or understated dropout rates. Unfortunately, this critical issue is complicated by a lack of uniformity among the states in defining and counting dropouts.

Given these complexities, it is difficult to draw firm, general conclusions

—even regarding minimum competency tests—about the effects of graduation testing on minority students, students with disabilities, and English-language learners.

In any event, the consequences of basic skills graduation tests are becoming less relevant in the face of two important developments. One such development, already noted, is that more states are raising the bar: setting higher standards on state graduation exams. The most ambitious states are adopting graduation tests that reflect "world-class" standards, such as those embodied in NAEP.

Based on national NAEP data, about 38 percent of all students would fail tests that reflect such standards if the tests were administered today. For minority students and English-language learners, moreover, there is clear evidence that failure rates on tests embodying "world-class" standards would be extremely high—about 80 percent—at least initially. These predictions are consistent with recent data from Massachusetts, where students have begun taking graduation tests that reflect "world-class" standards. For students with disabilities, it is also reasonable to assume that initial failure rates on such tests would also be very high: in the 75 to 80 percent range.

Equally important, the proliferation of large-scale promotion testing, which is most pronounced in large, urban school districts, has led to sharply higher rates of retention in grade, especially for black students, Latino students, and English-language learners. In New York City, Chicago, and other cities, hundreds of thousands of students, the vast majority black, Latino, and/or English-language learners, have failed promotion tests and been retained in grade, and it is reasonable to expect that students with disabilities would also be retained in large numbers.

The single strongest predictor of whether students will drop out of school is whether they have been retained in grade. The rapid growth of promotion testing, particularly in our large cities, is therefore likely to create an increasingly large class of students—disproportionately comprised of blacks, Latinos, English-language learners, students with disabilities, and low-SES students—who are at increased risk of dropout by virtue of having been retained in grade one or more times. Those retained in grade even once are much likelier to drop out later than are students not retained, and the effects are even greater for students retained more than once.

Promotion testing is thus likely to reduce, perhaps significantly, the numbers of students who remain in school long enough to take graduation tests, and to increase the numbers of students who suffer the serious consequences of dropping out. The effects of retention, moreover, may not be felt until years later, by which time it is often too late. These potential consequences warrant more attention than they have received thus far.

Promotion and graduation testing may also have unintended consequences for teachers. High-stakes testing is intended to raise teacher motivation and effectiveness, and there is evidence that with appropriate professional development, support, resources, and time teaching effectiveness can improve significantly. There is also evidence, however, that the negative publicity associated with poor test scores can lead experienced teachers to leave urban schools for the suburbs. Plainly, efforts to improve low-performing urban schools—and to educate all children effectively—will be undermined if those schools lose strong teachers.

Policies that lead to improved teaching and learning are likely to benefit minority students, English-language learners, and students with disabilities even more than they do other students. New York State Education Commissioner Richard Mills, for example, has defended stringent graduation test requirements partly because he hopes they will bring an end to low-track classes, in which students—most of them black, Latino, and/or English-language learners—typically receive poor quality, low-level instruction from less-qualified teachers. There is very strong evidence that placement in typical low-track classes is educationally harmful for students, and that students in low-track classes would learn more if they were placed in more demanding classes. Disability rights groups likewise hope that state standards and tests will drive teachers to upgrade the individualized education programs (IEPs) of students with disabilities, so that IEPs reflect more of the knowledge and skills that non-disabled students are expected to acquire—and here, too, there is evidence that higher expectations and improved instruction lead to improved achievement.

Advocates for minority children and low-SES children hope that high standards will provide the political and legal leverage needed to improve resources and school effectiveness so that all children receive the high-quality instruction they need to be able to meet demanding academic standards. Moreover, some proponents of high-stakes testing argue that fear of negative consequences— retention or diploma denial for students, negative publicity, and (in rare instances) adverse personnel action for educators—can be a positive force, which serves to increase the motivation to teach and learn effectively.

Standards of Appropriate Test Use: Widely Accepted, Often Ignored

Whether graduation testing helps or hurts low achievers depends largely on whether such tests are used to promote high-quality education for all children—the stated objective of standards-based reform—or to penalize students for not having knowledge and skills they have not been taught in school.

If high-stakes tests are used properly—a very big "if"—they can help leverage improved instruction.

Norms of appropriate test use have been articulated by the testing profession, the National Research Council (NRC), and the American Educational Research Association (AERA). For example, the December 1999 *Standards for Educational and Psychological Testing* (by the AERA, the American Psychological Association, and the National Council on Measurement in Education) asserts that promotion and graduation tests should cover only the "content and skills that students have had an opportunity to learn." The Congressionally mandated NRC study, *High Stakes: Testing for Tracking, Promotion, and Graduation*, reached a similar conclusion in 1999: "Tests should be used for high-stakes decisions . . . only after schools have implemented changes in teaching and curriculum that ensure that students have been taught the knowledge and skills on which they will be tested." So did the AERA, in a July 2000 *Policy Statement Concerning High Stakes Testing*.

Unfortunately, there often are discrepancies between what high-stakes tests measure and what students have been taught. Results of a recent ten-state study suggest that there is surprisingly little overlap between a state's standards and what teachers in the state say they are actually teaching students. The actual overlap ranged from a low of 5 percent to a high of 46 percent, depending on the subject, grade level, and state. Such discrepancies are likely to be high for minority students, English-language learners, and students with disabilities, if only because such students often lack access to high-quality instruction.

Similarly, as noted above, increasing numbers of states and school districts automatically deny promotion or high school diplomas to students who fail state tests, regardless of how well the students have performed on other measures of achievement, such as course grades. The NRC study emphasizes that educators should buttress test score information with "other relevant information about the student's knowledge and skills, such as grades, teacher recommendations, and extenuating circumstances" when making high-stakes decisions about individual students. This is consistent with the *Standards for Educational and Psychological Testing*, which states that "in elementary or secondary education, a decision or characterization that will have a major impact on a test taker should not automatically be made on the basis of a single test score. Other relevant information . . . should be taken into account if it will enhance the overall validity of the decision." Similarly, the July 2000 AERA *Policy Statement* provides that "[d]ecisions that affect individual students' life chances or educational opportunities should not be made on the basis of test scores alone. . . ."

Why is it so important to use multiple measures in making important decisions about individuals? The answer is that any single measure is inevitably imprecise and limited in the information it provides. Proponents of high-stakes testing sometimes point out the problems associated with exclusive reliance on student grades in making promotion and graduation decisions: there has been considerable grade inflation during the last three decades, and there is considerable variation among teachers, schools, and school districts in what particular grades mean. Their points are well taken.

At the same time, large-scale tests are also limited in what they measure. It is well known, for example, that standardized tests do not measure student motivation over time, as important as motivation is to later success. Moreover, even the best standardized tests are far less precise than most people realize. Given the imprecision of grades and test scores, judgments based on combinations of both are more accurate and reliable than those based on either by itself.

To complicate matters, there is at present no satisfactory mechanism for ensuring that test developers, states, and school districts respect even widely accepted norms of appropriate, nondiscriminatory test use. The two existing mechanisms—professional discipline through the organizations that develop test-use standards and legal enforcement through courts and administrative agencies—have complementary shortcomings. The professional associations that define appropriate test use have detailed standards, but they lack mechanisms for monitoring or enforcing compliance with those standards. For courts and federal civil rights agencies, the reverse is true: they have complaint procedures and enforcement power, but lack specific, legally enforceable standards on the appropriate use of high-stakes tests. Recognizing the problem, the U.S. Department of Education's Office for Civil Rights has produced a draft resource guide that, while not legally binding, aims to promote appropriate use of high-stakes tests.

In conclusion, the standards movement and high-stakes testing present both opportunities and risks to students of color, English-language learners, and students with disabilities. These students are among those who stand to benefit most if states and school districts insist that all schools and teachers provide high-quality instruction to all students. Such students are also at great risk, however, especially in states that administer high-stakes promotion and graduation tests before having made the improvements in instruction that will enable all students to meet the standards. As noted above, if graduation tests embodying "world-class" standards were implemented today—when far too many students do not receive "world-class" instruction—students of color, English-language learners, and students with disabilities would be denied high-school diplomas at rates of 75 to 80 percent, rates that are plainly unacceptable, for those students and for our entire society.

The key, then, is for students to have an opportunity to acquire the relevant knowledge and skills before individuals suffer high-stakes consequences, such as retention in grade or denial of a regular high school diploma. On this point, there is agreement among the authors of *Standards for Educational and Psychological Testing*, the Congressionally mandated NRC study, and the July 2000 AERA *Policy Statement*. This has important implications for all low-achieving students, and special consequences for some. For students with disabilities, it will be necessary to revisit IEPs to make sure that all students subject to high-stakes tests are taught the relevant knowledge and skills. English-language learners should get the opportunity to acquire high levels of English proficiency as well as the other knowledge and skills that high-stakes tests measure.

Unfortunately, there are some test developers, states, and school districts that do not appear to be observing these and other norms of appropriate test use. Is this problem due to insufficient knowledge about norms of appropriate test use, or are states under political pressure to disregard such norms as a national debate over educational accountability rages? Will states also face political pressure to back away from tests that lead to very large numbers of students being retained in grade or denied regular high school diplomas? The prospect of high failure rates has already produced a backlash against high-stakes testing programs in some states. Lawsuits are beginning, if only because there exists no viable alternative by which to ensure appropriate use of graduation and promotion tests.

All these questions call for additional research. There also remains a need for significantly improved data on the effects of high-stakes testing on student achievement and dropout rates, for students generally, and for such important groups as students of color, English-language learners, and students with disabilities.

The stakes are high indeed.

The Education Vision: A Third Tier

S.M. Miller

We need to move beyond our pseudo-meritocracy (or, if we want to be charitable, quasi-meritocracy) to public responsibility to invest in everyone, to discover, develop, and realize the potential of *all* Americans at any age. The underlying theme would be that what people have done educationally and occupationally at age sixteen, thirty, forty, or later does not definitively demarcate their possibilities. This profound change moves us from the misleading metaphor of a sorting race in which we all jump off from a common starting line to an ongoing concern with the lifetime development of everyone—no discarded people.

This radical shift requires, among other steps, building an accessible, effective learning and training system that is available throughout one's lifetime. In France, this way of thinking is termed "permanent education," and here was once called "recurrent education." In the French public system, workers had paid time off from the job to pursue education-training studies. In the United States, the United Steelworkers of America had contracts that enabled workers to have periodic paid "sabbaticals" of several months duration.

What exists now in the United States is an unconnected, limited, underfinanced, and shakily financed *non-system* or *anti-system* of training initiatives, with high staff turnover, often dubious quality, and wide local variation in availability, a system that lacks a continuous concern for past and present students.

A new "Third Tier" is needed in education and training (Third Tier, because it is beyond the two tiers of public and private education systems for children and youth). It would supplant or connect the present hodgepodge of employment training programs and community colleges. It would not depend on what employers are willing to do in training their employees. With unstable work situations and careers, employers are reluctant to invest in upgrading employees, especially low-skilled workers. If education is the new hope of American economic competitiveness, then it should be a national responsibility to provide all people with real chances of development.

The narrow vocationalizing of education and training should be transcended. Citizenship education, including enhanced literacy, information about our society and the larger world, the deepening of capacities to reason and analyze, all should be part of the new Third Tier. At a time when our worlds are changing rapidly, why should "education" in this broader sense be restricted to the young, and narrow vocational training be the main possibility for older persons?

The charge, then, is not only to move the "educationally excluded," those children whom present-day schools under-educate, into somewhat improved schools, but to recast education as a lifetime development experience. The Third Tier would improve education and job possibilities especially for African Americans, Hispanics, Asian Americans, as well as many whites. That will not happen by simply modifying current school situations. Transformation is needed.

Part 4

Democratic Participation

The persistence of racism and poverty in America is a massive blot on our claims to be the world's leading democracy. It is a vicious cycle: Poor and minority citizens vote less and participate less because (aside from some practical constraints) they understand all too well that their votes and participation count for little. And when they don't participate, they lose their opportunity to influence the political system, and politicians feel little need to court their vote.

There are some obvious and simple steps that would increase participation and strengthen democracy, which the following articles offer. Most have to do with changing the rules with regard to voting systems and campaign finance. Steps in the former direction would dramatically increase representation of and by poor and minority citizens in legislative bodies (that there is not, as of 2000, a single African American member of the U.S. Senate is an astounding statistic) and with respect to the outcome of voter propositions and initiatives. Reforms of the latter type would serve to even the playing field (always an attractive image to most Americans, at least in concept) with regard to the role of the wealthy both in buying elections and, increasingly, buying legislative seats for themselves (a bored hi-tech investor or investment house executive, with $30 or $40 million of his own money—for some, an easy expenditure—can turn himself quickly into a Senator or Congressman). The needed reforms are obvious: how to get there is the rub. Sitting legislators are not likely to vote to change the rules of the game by which they benefit, and the courts have been notably unhelpful. Voter initiatives and good-old community organizing, get-out-the-vote work, and registering eligible voters are how these reforms will come about.

Why Not Democracy?

David Kairys

Perhaps the greatest public relations coup of recent decades was the instantaneous conversion of the 1994 electoral campaigns—almost universally condemned as unprincipled and repulsive—into a "mandate" and "landslide" for Republicans swept into office by slim margins.

The most that can fairly be said of the election results is that less than 20 percent of those eligible to vote favored the Republican "Contract with America" program (and many of those were anti-Clinton votes), almost the same number went the other way, and most people stayed home.

President Clinton's 1992 victory was treated similarly. Like most winning presidents, he received more than a dismal 20 percent, but not by much. Even President Reagan's 1980 "landslide" consisted of his getting only 27 percent of the eligible voters. And participation in these and all recent elections is disproportionately white and higher-income. In the November 1992 elections, 37.2 percent of persons 18 and over with incomes under $10,000 voted, compared with 80.0 percent of those with incomes over $50,000. By race, 63.6 percent of voting age whites voted, 54.0 percent of Blacks, 28.9 percent of Hispanic origin (of any race).

A mantle of legitimacy is regularly bestowed on anyone who wins, no matter how they win, or how minuscule their margins of victory or the proportions of the electorate who voted. Our electoral process doesn't yield mandates, only exaggerated legitimacy, frustrated citizens, and precarious winners.

Bestowing legitimacy and power on winners with sometimes small pluralities contradicts basic democratic precepts, particularly when so few of our people vote. An old Latin word—quorum—embodies a traditional American idea about the legitimacy of political processes. If you don't have a quorum, usually set at half the eligible voters, there can be no valid or binding vote. That's the rule for nearly every board of directors, neighborhood group, and Cub Scout troop. It means you can't chase away most of the voters and then claim victory.

Progressive voices are often silent or silenced these days, but the silence on this issue—the fundamental crisis of democracy in America—is puzzling. There is a widespread sense that things aren't working right and that the political system is part of the problem rather than the solution. Most Americans, across the political spectrum, perceive themselves and their views and interests as excluded from public discourse and political decision-making.

The deep anger and alienation from the political process presents an opportunity for progressives to continue perhaps our most sustained and successful struggle since the beginning of the republic: the extension and redefinition of democracy to include all our people.

This alienation and anger is often expressed in terms of hostility to those who have, or seem to have, power, particularly "politicians"—a label that now connotes disgrace. It is also evident in the cynicism and basic lack of respect or common decency shown to candidates and officeholders. This has been nurtured and exploited by the media, but they have struck a chord with the public. Politics has become a spectator sport in which strategy and tactics are more important than principle, and the capacity to endure humiliation is more important than insight or integrity.

Needed Reforms

A long overdue revitalization of democracy should focus on four major issues: meaningful campaign finance reform, as the current system amounts to sanitized and legalized bribery (see "Race, Poverty, and the 'Wealth Primary'" pp. 183–190, and "Not the Rich, More Than the Poor," pp. 193–199); proportional representation (see "New Means for Political Empowerment," pp. 176–183); parliamentary democracy; and barriers to voting and third-party campaigns.

The United States is almost alone among Western democracies, and democracies throughout the world, in rejecting the parliamentary system in favor of a winner-take-all, fixed-term presidential election that is divorced from elections of legislators. The formal name for this is "checks and balances," but it is at the core of what we now call and condemn as "gridlock" and the "two-party monopoly." The winner wins all, and the losers get no ongoing power or influence in the Presidency or Congress. This encourages compromise before elections—the watered down, mushy positions and the low level of political debate to which we have become accustomed—and the tendency of winners after elections to ignore the range of voter views rather than engage in dialogue or compromise. Votes for candidates who do not win are in this sense "wasted," and votes for third-party candidates can seem senseless, since they reduce the total vote for the major-party candidate closest to the voter's views.

Contrast this to parliamentary systems: A range of parties and candidates put forward their various positions before elections and compromise afterwards to form a majority coalition that selects the chief executive (usually called prime minister). Each party maintains ongoing power and influence in the legislature in proportion to its vote, and if at any time a majority no longer supports the ruling coalition, there is a new election. Voters have every reason to participate even if their favorite candidate is unlikely to win. These systems regularly draw three-quarters to over 90 percent of the voters to the polls. (A "Representation Index" published by the Center for Voting and Democracy—calculated by multiplying voter turnout by the percentage of votes cast for winning candidates—showed that in the 1994 House of Representatives election Florida brought up the rear with a 12.4 rating, while South Dakota was the highest, with 35.0. By contrast, Germany had a 76.3 and South Africa was close to 90 in their 1994 elections.)

In parliamentary systems, or systems that directly elect a president, each person's vote carries the same weight and effect, and the winning head of state emerges with the support of a majority. In our winner-take-all, plurality system, citizens in each state vote for the candidates they favor but actually choose "electors" whose "votes" are tallied in the Electoral College. In almost every state, all the electoral votes for each state go to the candidate who won the most votes in that state. The winner doesn't even have to get a majority: A plurality is sufficient.

Consider what happened in Colorado in the 1992 election. The vote was

40 percent for Bill Clinton, 36 percent for George Bush, and 23 percent for Ross Perot–but Clinton got all of Colorado's electoral votes. The votes for Bush and Perot–nearly 60 percent of the total–were negated. Nationwide, Clinton got only 43 percent of the popular vote; Bush got 37 percent, and Perot 19. In most democracies, Perot would have entered a coalition with either Bush or Clinton, which would have taken office with majority support.

The framers of the Constitution designed the Electoral College system to thwart popular discontent, which–they feared most–might take the form of laws that would undercut the privileges of wealth and property. The people tended to get upset about matters such as the widespread seizures of family farms during economic downturns, and there was substantial opposition to slavery on moral, religious, and economic grounds. The distribution of electoral votes disproportionately favored small and southern states. The constitutional formula for each state's electoral votes adds the number of senators, two for each state, to the number of House members. And three-fifths of the slaves were included for purposes of counting the population and distributing House seats (but not voting). Almost all of the presidents chosen by this system for the first quarter century were southern slaveholders.

The simplest reform of the Electoral College is direct election with instant runoff voting in situations in which no candidate has a majority. Citizens vote for their first and second choices; the lowest vote-getter is eliminated in a series of rounds until one candidate receives a majority, using voters' second choices after their first choices are eliminated. A more ambitiously democratic reform could use the Electoral College framework to introduce proportionality and majority coalitions without disturbing the U.S. tradition of a fixed-term presidency or its independence from Congress. Electors could be selected proportionately, and they and their parties could form a majority coalition. Countries that use such systems are not faced with lesser-of-evils voting, make every vote count, and have leaders who govern with majority support. Their people also tend to vote.

Finally, we should eliminate the barriers to voting and to ballot access by third parties. A party or individual shouldn't have to be as rich as Ross Perot to get on the ballot, and third-party candidates should be included in candidate debates. We are the only major democracy that requires voters to register and regularly strikes them off lists of eligible voters if they haven't voted recently. Most everywhere else, if you are a citizen and you show up on election day, you vote.

These systemic features should be the focus of the widespread popular discontent with the electoral process, but conservative Republicans, who routinely oppose even minor democratic reforms such as the motor-voter bill, have diverted our attention to the issue of term limits. Without the re-

A Democracy Agenda

- eliminate PACs and private funding of elections, and strictly limit payments of any kind to public officials
- provide all qualified candidates limited public funding and limited, free media time in equal amounts
- proportional representation at the federal, state, and local levels
- investigate a longer-term conversion to a parliamentary system
- a quorum requirement set at one half of all people eligible to vote, without which a new election would be required
- eliminate voter registration requirements
- eliminate barriers to third-parties' ballot access, and include them in candidate debates
- access to the media for people of ordinary means
- uniform, national voting procedures and equipment
- elimination or reform of the Electoral College system
- instant run-off voting for elections in which no candidate receives a majority
- end disenfranchisement of former prisoners and residents of the District of Columbia
- full enforcement of the Voting Rights Act

forms emphasized here, term limits would most likely increase, not decrease, the proportion of our legislators who are wealthy and the speed of the revolving door between government and special interests, only deepening the reality and the public's sense that the system is closed and fixed. Nothing in the term-limited process encourages new directions, new leadership, or enhanced popular participation in the political process.

The problem is not with the notion of a life or career of public service. We need more of that—particularly the brand of public service that includes the insight and courage to look beyond appeals to fear and narrow self-interest. And public service should be available to people of ordinary means. But term limits are, at best, a gimmicky diversion.

What we must confront is the fear of democracy at the core of the system devised by the framers of the Constitution and the fundamental obstacle their approach poses to meaningful democracy in the twenty-first century. The constitutional convention was attended by representatives chosen by state legislatures to resolve interstate commercial rivalries that were impeding trade. The framers, who transformed their gathering into a constitutional convention on their own, were among the elite of each state, and they met in secret behind closed doors. Their fear that the people, if really empowered, would undercut the privileges of wealth and create chaos dominated the proceedings.

An Issue for Progressives

The reluctance or hesitance of progressives to embrace the democracy issue, which is a frequent response when these ideas are presented to them, is hard to understand. There is a tendency to see political democracy in an exclusively instrumental fashion. Perhaps at a deeper level, there may be some distrust of the people, which we often discuss as a problem unique to conservatives. Mass democracy surely involves risks; perhaps some of the reluctance is based on a sense that currently oppressed groups might have even more to fear from broadened participation. However, a revitalization of American democracy would increase the proportion of the vote that comes from groups currently excluded or discounted in mainstream politics and would promote dialogue and compromise.

Most fundamentally, there simply will not be progressive reform—or significant attention paid to progressive concerns—unless politicians feel responsibility to and pressure from the people in the midsection and at the bottom of the economic ladder, who are not major campaign contributors or consistent voters. Further, the appeal to democracy raises the question of control by an elite—the question of class—in a way that can be heard even in the current political environment, and may be extended to other issues.

As we search our old files and our souls for progressive visions and program ideas, shouldn't meaningful participation in a fair, democratic process, and in a political dialogue to which people of ordinary means have access, be seen as a fundamental need of the people? It is a necessary prerequisite for progressive change and for a basic sense of national purpose, cohesion, and connection in a large, diverse society such as ours.

New Means for Political Empowerment:
Proportional Voting

Douglas J. Amy, Fred McBride, and Robert Richie

In May 2000, the citizens of Amarillo, Texas, filled four seats on its school board by cumulative voting. No black or Latino candidate had been elected to Amarillo's seven-member school board in more than two decades, despite Latinos and African Americans making up more than 20 percent of the city's population and an even larger share of the student population. Instituted to settle a voting rights lawsuit, cumulative voting had an immediate impact: a black candidate and Latino candidate won seats with strong support in their communities; voter turnout increased four times over the most recent school board election; and all parties in the voting rights settlement expressed satisfaction with the new system.

That a generally conservative city like Amarillo would adopt cumulative voting is only one example of how proportional and semi-proportional voting systems in recent years have moved from being "controversial" to credible alternatives for political empowerment. On their own merits and as a strategic response to Supreme Court rulings that hinder creation of district boundaries to provide for increased representation of racial minorities, these voting methods—specifically, choice voting, cumulative voting, and limited voting [see box]—are increasingly recognized as a means to increase minority representation in local, state, and even federal elections.

Proportional representation (PR) creates new avenues of political power for people of color and the poor, two groups traditionally denied fair access to power in this country. Despite making up a quarter of the U.S. population, African Americans and Latinos (as of 2000) hold less than 10 percent of the country's elected offices and not a single governorship or U.S. Senate seat. Imagine for a moment how different it would be if the Senate had twenty-five African Americans and Latinos instead of none. They would make up an important voting bloc, and their very presence on committees and as colleagues on the Senate floor would be a powerful reminder of the political concerns of people of color. No longer would it be easy to put these issues on the back-burner, as so often happens today.

Adopting PR to elect the U.S. Senate would require constitutional change, but all other legislative bodies in the United States—including the House of Representatives—could be elected by PR without touching the Constitution. What prevents such fantasies of fair representation from more often becoming a reality is our continued adherence to an election principle—winner-take-all—that is inherently unjust and undemocratic. Winner-take-all elections, whether in single-member districts or for at-large positions, require winning candidates to attract a majority or substantial plurality of the vote. By definition, candidates representing political minorities have great difficulty amassing this large a share of votes, and so stand little chance of being elected. Thus, under our current system, racial minorities and the poor have the right to vote, but are often denied the equally fundamental right to representation. This systematic disempowerment of minorities and the poor is an inevitable result of winner-take-all systems.

Proportional representation is designed to remedy these electoral injustices. It ensures that any grouping of like-minded people—minorities and majorities—gets a fair share of power and representation in our legislative bodies, whereas our current winner-take-all principle can award 100 percent of the representation to a 50.1 percent majority. If black voters comprise 20 percent of the vote in a racially polarized county, they can elect at least one of the five seats—rather than be shut out, as they would be in a traditional at-large election or in a single-member district plan that dispersed their vote across several districts.

Versions of proportional representation are used in most well-established democracies. In 1999, there were thirty-six democracies with a high Freedom House human rights rating and a population over 2 million. Of these, only two—the United States and Canada—used exclusively winner-take-all elections for national elections; most used proportional representation for their most powerful legislative body. In 1999, South Africa held its second elections using proportional representation; once again, voter turnout and voter respect for the outcome were high, all racial and political groupings elected a fair share of seats, and women won more than twice the share of seats held by women in the U.S. Congress.

Various proportional and semi-proportional systems exist in both partisan and nonpartisan forms. More than 200 localities in the United States use one of three nonpartisan systems: cumulative voting, limited voting, or choice voting. The many forms of PR embody the same goals: (1) assuring that all eligible voters have an effective vote; (2) assuring that as many voters as possible have someone to represent them in policy-making bodies; (3) enabling both majorities and minorities to have fair representation, and (4) creating legislatures that truly represent the wide diversity of political opinions and interests in the electorate. Not all PR elections achieve these goals, particularly for very small groupings of voters, but they have a proven record of achieving these goals more effectively than winner-take-all systems.

  Proportional representation allows for the emergence of a pluralistic multi-party system that could include parties speaking strongly for racial and ethnic minorities and people of all incomes and across the political spectrum. If PR were adopted in the United States, the electoral prospects of lower-income Americans likely would be improved by the first successful organization of leftist or labor parties, as exist in virtually all Western democracies with PR. Under winner-take-all rules, it is essentially futile to organize such parties. A third party stands little chance of electoral victory and in fact has the perverse impact of helping the party its supporters most oppose by splitting the vote of the established party it would otherwise support.

In a PR system, a labor party or other low-income party could create a viable electoral presence without splitting the vote. Knowing that each new vote could help gain more seats, a low-income party would have more incentive to inform, cultivate, and mobilize its supporters. By creating a viable electoral presence, the party would give low-income Americans a powerful, urgently needed reason to vote. Data from the U.S. Census show a direct correlation between voter turnout and income that is becoming only more pronounced. In the 1996 presidential race, under the current system, voter turnout was only 44 percent among the 17 million American citizens earning less than $15,000 a year, in stark contrast to the 76 percent turnout among the 23 million citizens earning more than $75,000. Under PR, the poor would have much greater incentive to vote because they would know that their votes would actually elect someone to represent their interests.

Proportional Voting in Practice

- Texas provides a good example of the increasing use of proportional voting systems. In addition to Amarillo, more than fifty Texas jurisdictions adopted cumulative voting in the 1990s; in 1995, Texas Governor George W. Bush signed legislation that allows school districts to adopt cumulative voting and limited voting.
- Cumulative voting and limited voting have been used in nearly two dozen Alabama localities for a decade in the wake of a sweeping win in a voting rights case. Studies of these Alabama elections demonstrate that they have boosted turnout and increased black representation as much as or more than would have occurred if single-member districts had been used. In Chilton County, black candidate Bobby Agee in 1988 led the field in the first elections using cumulative voting for a seven-seat county commission, even though blacks were barely 10 percent of the population and he was heavily outspent. Most of his supporters, overwhelmingly black, took advantage of their opportunity to allocate all seven of their votes for him rather than spread their votes among other candidates. The first black commissioner in Chilton County's history, Agee has twice been reelected and has served as chair of the commission.
- Choice voting has been used for decades to elect the city council in Cambridge, Massachusetts, and the local school boards in New York City. These bodies have reflected the diversity of the cities far better than other elected bodies in the same cities. This was also typically true when choice voting was used to elect city councils in New York City, Cincinnati, and other major cities before its Cold War-era repeal.
- Starting in 1995 with Congresswoman Cynthia McKinney's Voters' Choice Act, bills to allow states to use proportional systems for U.S. House elections were introduced in every session. North Carolina Con-

gressman Melvin Watt's 1999 States' Choice of Voting Systems Act drew bipartisan support and was the subject of a hearing; those testifying in favor of the bill and proportional systems included the Department of Justice and Republican Congressman Tom Campbell.

- Nearly 100 jurisdictions have adopted proportional systems to settle voting rights challenges, and federal judges several times have sought to impose them directly as remedies in voting rights cases. Very familiar with redistricting as a result of having presided over a challenge to Illinois's congressional districts in which majority-minority districts were upheld, Federal Judge David Coar in 1998 ordered the city of Chicago Heights to adopt cumulative voting to elect its city council and park board. Cumulative voting has a rich history in Illinois, being specifically permitted in state law, used currently in Peoria, and used for more than a century to elect the state's House of Representatives, during which time representatives like Harold Washington and Carol Moseley-Braun were elected.
- The U.S. Department of Justice (DOJ) has taken important positions involving proportional systems. The DOJ has pre-cleared use of cumulative voting and limited voting in numerous states covered by Section Five of the Voting Rights Act; as of 2000, every jurisdiction seeking to convert from a winner-take-all system to one of these systems ultimately was permitted to do so. In 1999, the DOJ wrote an amicus brief for the Chicago Heights case, backing Judge Coar's order of cumulative voting. Also in 1999, the DOJ denied pre-clearance to New York City after the legislature voted to replace choice voting (a fully proportional voting system) with limited voting (a less proportional system) for electing the city's local school boards; choice voting had elected a significantly higher percentage of racial minorities to school boards than had been elected to other legislative bodies in the city.
- Significant organizations support education about proportional voting methods. In 1998, a National Black Caucus of State Legislators task force found strong interest among black legislators in learning more about proportional and semi-proportional systems, particularly in how they might assist redistricting negotiations. The League of United Latin American Citizens, National Association for the Advancement of Colored People (NAACP), and the Mexican American Legal Defense and Educational Fund joined with local plaintiffs to win the adoption of cumulative voting in Amarillo, the largest city now using cumulative voting; the NAACP has asked the Center for Voting and Democracy to help educate its chapters about proportional systems. The National Conference of Black Political Scientists endorsed proportional systems in 1999. In 2000, the Southern Center for Studies in Public Policy pursued

Proportional Voting Systems

- *Limited Voting:* In limited voting, voters either cast fewer votes than the number of seats or political parties nominate fewer candidates than there are seats. The greater the difference between the number of seats and the number for which one can vote, the greater the opportunities for minority representation. Versions of limited voting are used in Washington, DC, Philadelphia, Hartford, and numerous other local jurisdictions. It has been adopted to resolve at least thirty voting rights cases in Alabama and North Carolina since 1987.
  Example: In a race to elect five candidates, voters might be limited to two votes. Winning candidates are determined by a simple plurality: the five candidates with the most votes.
- *Cumulative Voting:* In cumulative voting, voters cast as many votes as there are seats to be elected. But unlike winner-take-all systems, voters are not restricted to giving only one vote to a candidate. Instead, they can cast multiple votes for one or more candidates. Cumulative voting was used to elect the Illinois state legislature from 1870 to 1980. In recent years it has been used to resolve voting rights cases for city council and county commission elections in Alabama, Illinois, and New Mexico and for school board elections in Alabama, South Dakota, and Texas.
  Example: In a race to elect five candidates, voters can cast one vote for five candidates, five votes for one candidate, or any combination in between. The five highest vote-getters win.
- *Choice Voting:* Also known as "single transferable vote" and "preference voting," choice voting is the most common candidate-based proportional system used in other nations. Each voter has one vote, but can rank candidates in order of choice (1, 2, 3, etc.). Candidates win by reaching a "victory threshold" roughly equal to the number of votes divided by the number of seats. If a candidate has too little first-choice support to win, votes for that candidate are transferred to those voters' next choices. This transfer of votes facilitates coalition-building and allows a candidate to run without fear of being a "spoiler" splitting the vote. Choice voting has been used for city council and school board elections in Cambridge, MA, since 1941 and is used for New York City local school board elections. Ireland and Australia use choice voting for national elections. The city council in Cambridge (where blacks are 13 percent of the population) has had black representatives since the 1950s. Choice voting in other cities, including for five elections to the New York City Council from 1937 to 1945, also resulted in fair racial, ethnic, and partisan representation.
  Example: In a race to elect five candidates, voters can rank in order of choice as many candidates as they wish. Candidates win by gaining the support of about one-fifth of the voters. A ballot counts toward the election of that voter's top-ranked candidate who needs that vote to win.

ambitious educational outreach to black elected officials and historically black colleges and universities, while the Southern Regional Council produced a booklet on Alabama's history with proportional systems.
National and state affiliates of U.S. PIRG, Common Cause, the National Organization for Women, and the League of Women Voters
adopted positions in favor of proportional representation.

An Alternative to Majority-Minority Districts

This rising interest in proportional representation obviously is not occurring
in a vacuum. Voting Rights Act provisions on redistricting divided and pre-
occupied the Supreme Court more than any other issue in the 1990s. The
court heard arguments in cases involving voting rights and redistricting every year in the wake of its 1993 *Shaw v. Reno* ruling, often producing bitterly
contested five to four decisions that had the general—if poorly defined—
impact of limiting states' use of race in drawing legislative district lines.

Proportional representation can increase representation of people of color
without requiring the creation of "majority-minority districts"—districts where
a racial minority is the majority. Drawing such districts has been the most
effective solution to minority underrepresentation, but can have important
drawbacks.

For example, majority-minority districts require the continuation of some
degree of housing segregation that concentrates minority populations within
easily drawn boundaries. Another problem is that minority-dominated districts still deny representation to many voters—even if candidates they might
like can win in some districts, many people will be left as "filler people" in a
district in which they are the minority. A third difficulty is that the process of
concentrating predominantly Democratic racial minorities into one district
can create surrounding districts that are more Republican, resulting in the
election of more conservatives who are less likely to support the interests of
minorities. Majority-minority districts are fairer than the old white-domi-
nated districts, but not always as good as proportional representation.

Apart from legal battles over *Shaw* and philosophical concerns, civil rights
attorneys have discovered, in states like Texas, Alabama, and North Carolina, that alternative systems can simply be a good fit with local conditions.
Perhaps a minority community is more geographically dispersed than necessary for a single-member district plan. Perhaps a jurisdiction may want to
avoid redistricting every decade. Perhaps there is frustration that most voters
in a minority community are still left out of a chance to elect a candidate of
choice even with a district plan that provides for enhanced minority representation. Perhaps in a multiracial community, a citywide proportional plan

is the easiest way for different racial minorities to elect representation.

Local government is an obvious place for stressing the utility of a proportional plan, as the mathematics of what it takes to win representation are quite straightforward. But higher election levels such as state legislatures also now are being considered. As for Congress, it would take a version of Representative Watt's legislation to give states the sensible option to consider some degree of proportional voting in seeking to fairly represent our increasingly complex diversity.

The goal of proportional systems is simple: providing means to allow fair and realistic opportunities for citizens to elect individuals of their own choosing. While no cure-all, they are necessary steps toward creation of a more inclusive, responsive political system, and will finally give badly needed representation to poor and minority Americans who have been systematically denied access to power by our flawed winner-take-all election rules.

Race, Poverty, and the "Wealth Primary"

Jamin B. Raskin

"It has become a quasi-corporate process. . . . The big contributors [become] the major shareholders. The rest of the population is left just to vote, to affirm the management."

> —Senator Dianne Feinstein's political consultant,
> Joe Scott, as quoted in the *Wall Street Journal.*

"Enclosed please find my check in the amount of $50,000."

> —The acceptance card to an invitation from Michael
> and Arianna Huffington to a fund-raising dinner for
> National Empowerment Television with Newt Gingrich.

Everyone knows that the poll tax discriminated against African Americans and poor people in the South. Thus, when the Supreme Court in 1966 invalidated Virginia's $1.50 poll tax, it was an important moment in the history of struggle against both plutocracy and white supremacy. Likening wealth-based voting exclusions to racial disenfranchisement, Justice William Douglas held that "a State violates the Equal Protection Clause . . . whenever it makes the affluence of the voter or payment of any fee an electoral standard."

Similarly, the imposition by states of hefty filing fees for political candidates effected a class-based political exclusion. In striking down candidate fees in Texas ranging from $150 to $6,300, Chief Justice Warren Burger in 1972 had to recognize that "the very size of the fees" gave Texas elections "a patently exclusionary character," as many "potential office seekers lacking both personal wealth and affluent backers are in every practical sense precluded from seeking the nomination of their chosen party, and no matter how enthusiastic their popular support." The consequent shrinking of electoral choices "falls more heavily on the less affluent segment of the community, whose favorites are likely to be unable to pay the large costs . . ."

Today, wealth-based political domination has returned with a vengeance. And yet, because the new plutocracy charges the wealthy thousands of dollars to participate, rather than charging the poor a buck-fifty, people are missing the obvious. Today's "wealth primary" is every bit as exclusionary to poorer candidates and voters as the regime of the high-filing fee and the poll tax. In 1996, forces vying for state power spent a breathtaking $2.6 billion, and you can bet that money didn't come from the poor. U.S. Senate seats were taken by candidates who spent, on average, more than $4 million, and the average House seat went to a candidate who spent more than $650,000. Better than 90 percent of House seats, as usual, were retained by incumbents, who use the combination of the partisan gerrymander, franking (free postage), and PAC contributions to squeeze out competition. Incumbent or not, the big spender won in nine out of ten races, and a record number of millionaires (over 100) now serve in Congress. Thus, the citizen without wealth or access to it has as much chance of winning the Lotto as a seat in Congress. We have essentially reestablished wealth and property qualifications for political leadership.

Donors Replace Voters

Most voters are bypassed in the mad search for dollars from the donor class. Less than one percent of the people give the vast majority of all money to candidates for Congress, and 95 percent of the people give no money at all. Certain upscale zip codes around Wall Street, Washington, and Hollywood yield more in campaign contributions than do the dozen poorest states combined. The effective mechanism of political exclusion today is year-round fundraising and spending, the daily Millionaire Man march through Washington: the $1,000–a-plate black-tie dinner, the slumber parties in the Lincoln Bedroom; the ceaseless mobilization of hundreds of millions of dollars from affluent citizens and corporate PACs; the rampant trade of private checks for public legislation; the infusion of hundreds of millions of corporate dollars in soft money to the Democratic and Republican Parties; the hundreds of millions of dollars in incumbent perks (paid press secretaries and speech writers, franking privileges, etc.); and then, above all, the systematic domination of governmental process and outcomes by moneyed interests. Former Senate Majority Leader George Mitchell put it nicely in his last days in that post when he corrected someone asking him how money was affecting our political system: "Money *is* the system," he said.

In cash-driven politics, there is no need to charge the poor to vote because they will rarely find anyone they want to vote for anyway. Like a high filing fee but much more effective, the wealth primary screens out candidates (and parties) who do not have personal wealth or political affinity with those who do. It has not taken long for the poor to figure out the system on their own and to stop voting. In 1994, when Newt Gingrich rose to power, the working and non-working poor, who make up nearly 38 percent of the country, comprised only 10 percent of the voting electorate. Widespread voter apathy, rather than being some kind of massive personality disorder, may be a perfectly rational response to the closed system of money politics that leaves the interests of the non-wealthy in the dust. In 1992, of 4 million eligible African Americans age eighteen through twenty-four, only 638,000 showed up at the polls.

The policy consequences are obvious. Government has become the instrument of wealth maximization for the powerful and social control over the rabble below. Congress bailed out politically active S&Ls with a half-trillion dollars of taxpayer money; keeps billions flowing to the Pentagon because the corporations that profit are PAC-carrying members of the electoral-industrial complex; and passes imbalanced free trade agreements while most Americans register their disapproval. Meanwhile, Congress has turned our meager social safety net into a tight rope, and pushed hundreds of thousands of other people's children out into mid-air to practice trapeze. Stupid kids—they should have formed a PAC.

The Strange Silence of the Progressive Community

It is worth asking why the social change and human service communities that find themselves losing in the face of America's money politics do not organize to attack the system as an exclusionary process that enlarges social inequality. I want to suggest four main reasons.

- Many progressive groups are playing the money game themselves. Labor unions, for example, fill the coffers of Democratic candidates with tens of millions of dollars every election. One can hardly blame them for trying to even the score and buy the same access their business counterparts enjoy.

But, in failing to champion reform of the system, unions not only freeze the status quo but refuse to accept the obvious: the labor movement will never be able to outbid corporate America and buy itself a Congress. In 1995–1996, business PACs and business forces outspent labor unions seven to one, a ratio that has been steady over time. Wouldn't union dues be better spent organizing unorganized workers? Unions finally seem to be waking up to the vicious cycle of the wealth primary.

Women's and minority groups have played the same game. Emily's List, which has done a great job collecting cash from around the country and sending it to women candidates in close races, has lost sight of the big picture in its active opposition to campaign finance reform. There are eighty-seven male and thirteen women senators as of 2001. Wouldn't women candidates, who lack access to circles of mostly male corporate benefactors, do a lot better in a system of public financing in which all candidates were put on an equal footing? Emily's List is mistaking the nobility of its own rescue mission for a handful of women candidates with the virtue of the entire system, which systematically disadvantages women. Meanwhile, many of the women who do get elected, like millionaire Senator Diane Feinstein, quickly get assimilated to the politics of the authoritarian corporate-welfare state.

Many African-American and Hispanic members of Congress, disproportionately dependent on PAC contributions and out-of-state money, have also opposed changing the system. Their districts are poor and, as incumbents, they want to be able to roam freely to pick up special-interest cash in order to build their warchests. The satisfaction of incumbents with America's money politics is no secret, but we should demand more from the minority caucuses.

Big-money politics is a killer for most progressive minority candidates who go head-to-head against whites. The Chicago Urban League reported in September 1996 that the high spender won in twenty-nine out of thirty-six of the most recent contested aldermanic elections in that city, and the high spender was almost always white. White candidates spent on average $101,300, while Hispanics spent on average $51,100 and African-American candidates spent $37,000. According to the study, the candidate's race is "the most important determinant of how much money a candidate will be able to raise."

This pattern has been repeated nationally. In 1994, only two black candidates—Alan Wheat in Missouri and Ron Sims in Washington—even tried to run against whites for the U.S. Senate, and both were overwhelmed by the white candidate's money. In his second match-up against Jesse Helms in 1996, Harvey Gantt was again outspent by Helms by a margin of two to one and could not survive the onslaught of tobacco, big-business, and right-wing money. A federal district court in Texas in the 1970s struck down multi-member State House districts, ruling that the "cost of conducting electoral campaigns in countywide races" was "so excessive that this factor alone has inhibited the recruitment and nomination or election of Mexican-American candidates for the Texas House of Representatives."

In sum, the wealth primary is a dressed-up version of the "white primary," which the Supreme Court abolished in a series of cases in the 1940s and 1950s. In *Terry v. Adams* (1953), the Court held that the Texas Jaybirds, a large private political club made up of white voters, was unlawfully excluding African Americans from its pre-primary endorsement process. According to Justice Hugo Black, government cannot allow private groups to exclude disfavored citizens from "an integral part" of "the elective process that determines who shall rule and govern . . ." Justice Felix Frankfurter described the Jaybird primary as "the instrument of those few . . . who are politically active—the officials of the local Democratic Party and, we may assume, the elected officials." These officials pretended to be loyal to the voting process, but in fact participated in "a wholly successful effort to withdraw significance from" the original election process.

To be sure, the existence today of numerous majority-black and Hispanic districts, brought into being by the Voting Rights Act amendments of 1982, has mitigated the racial effects of the wealth primary by, in essence, creating a separate playing field for minority congressional candidates. But the antidemocratic effects of money power are no less offensive in majority-minority districts where incumbents can spend their opponents into oblivion. At any rate, the Supreme Court's ongoing demolition of such districts is thrusting minorities into districts where white rivals begin with much greater personal wealth and much stronger fundraising capacity. True, incumbents like Cynthia McKinney will be able to win in some of these districts, but as McKinney honestly points out (see "I Am a Product of the Voting Rights Act!" pp. 199–202), it was her original "majority-black district" that "gave voters the opportunity to elect someone like me who had only $38,000 to spend against a well-funded establishment candidate in the Democratic primary four years ago. Representing that majority-minority district for three and a half years enabled me to develop a track record . . . and the local and national contacts necessary to raise the nearly $1 million I spent to win in the new district." When majority-black districts are reduced in number, where will the Cynthia McKinneys of the future find the hundreds of thousands of dollars needed to compete?

It is time for a new strategy for minority empowerment that advocates equal access to the right to run for office. Perhaps it is time to recreate Freedom Democratic Parties to bring the poor back into politics.

Of course, insider elites in labor, women, and minority communities can play big-money politics to their personal advantage. Think of union presidents, Barbara Streisand and Pamela Harriman, Willie Brown in Sacramento, or Ron Brown and John Huang at the DNC and the Commerce Department. But the overall effect of this strategy is profoundly damaging to their constituencies. Money politics creates a crisis of moral leadership. In 1996, for example, shortly after President Clinton signed the welfare bill, the Democrats gathered in convention in Chicago to celebrate Dick Morris's triangulation strategy. Not a single union leader, feminist, or minority official present pointed out the shocking juxtaposition of Democrats joining Republicans to further impoverish a million kids and then spend a long weekend munching jumbo shrimp and Swedish meatballs-on-a-toothpick with armies of corporate lobbyists and millionaire benefactors in sky suites.

- Many progressives secretly doubt whether money power actually makes any difference in politics and assume that Republican control of Congress faithfully reflects the will of the people.

Many progressives don't realize how critical money is to the current conservative cast of our politics, including the Republican capture of Congress in 1994. With Newt Gingrich jawboning the corporate class for money, campaign expenditures by Republican challengers rose an amazing 66 percent over 1992, providing enough money for thirty-four of them to knock off Democratic incumbents. These thirty-four spent an average of $625,000 apiece. As political scientist Thomas Ferguson wrote, "A sea of money that had long been flowing reliably to Congressional Democrats and the party that controlled the White House abruptly reversed direction and began gushing in torrents to Republican challengers."

Moreover, public opinion does not develop in a vacuum, but rather ends up reflecting the same power consensus that corporate America buys on Capitol Hill. Every year, candidates give hundreds of millions of dollars to corporate broadcasters to buy thirty-second campaign ads to saturate the public. These ads, relentlessly negative in tone, usually try to align the candidate with the voting public's carefully cultivated fear of aliens, criminals, poor people, and minorities. But the cash-driven manipulation of public consciousness does not end with the election. The multi-million dollar publicity campaign that killed a national health plan shows us how public opinion can be shaped by the same money that sways politicians. In short, "public opinion," far from driving public policy, is more often the product of the same corporate money power that defines "realism" in elite circles.

- Liberals have characterized campaign finance reform as an issue of "ethics" rather than a democratic imperative. The leading campaign reform group, Common Cause, places campaign reform in the context of a host of issues relating to the personal ethics of elected officials—a real problem, but one that pales next to the far more important issue of who will, in effect, control government. The issue is not just one of clean hands versus dirty hands, but whether we will have government by the affluent or by all the people.

- Finally, even when progressives have organized to challenge political money power— such as ACORN's very popular initiatives to cap campaign contributions at $100 in states and cities—they have run smack into the Supreme Court's 1976 *Buckley v. Valeo* decision. That case brought private political money under the protection of the First Amendment, essentially constitutionalizing a free market in campaign contributions. Many people simply have given up on changing the system.

Buckley has become the *Plessy v. Ferguson* of politics, fostering a polity segregated by money. Under the majesty of the Supreme Court's elitist gloss on the First Amendment, the rich and poor now experience separate political realities but are deemed equals before the law. Every citizen has the right to be rich and contribute tens of thousands of dollars a year to campaigns or to spend to the heavens to finance his own candidacy. Every citizen also has the right not to be rich and to give nothing to campaigns, to watch the scandal-packed wealth primary on TV, and to cast a vote for candidates preselected by PACs and money elites. *Buckley's* "separate but equal" electoral regime empowers the wealthy to be the nation's citizen-owners but leaves everyone else as passive consumers of ads from the cash-soaked political consultant industry.

Signs of Change?

Despite all of the legal and political reasons for the suppression of campaign finance as a class and race issue, there are signs that change is coming. Public outrage is at an all-time high, and the natural alternative for people who want more democracy in America is finally emerging: public financing of elections. The smashing success of Maine's 1996 public-financing initiative and similar measures since in Massachusetts, Vermont, and Arizona have given impetus to a push at the national level. A new group called Public Campaign, headed by Ellen Miller, formerly of the Center for Responsive Politics, is waging a national campaign to press for a Clean Money Option, a system of publicly financed congressional campaigns to run parallel to private campaigns. Federal candidates who collect a certain number of $5 qualifying contributions and agree to raise no other money would receive media vouchers and public funding for their campaigns. Broadcast licenses would be conditioned on corporations surrendering time for political speech in the weeks before an election. Attempts by privately-financed candidates to spend public candidates into oblivion would trigger release of matching funds to the public candidates in escalator fashion.

Because it is voluntary, the new regime would be perfectly constitutional, even under the pinched understandings of *Buckley*, and the system would end up looking like the electoral equivalent of our education system, where we have public and private schools operating side-by-side. It obviously wouldn't be ideal, and corporate money would still shout, but today it's as if all we have are private schools. Public values are under siege in the electoral process.

Of course, the effort to develop a public system runs counter to the pervasive traducing by corporate America of all things public, as well as national cynicism about politicians as a group. But the success of "clean money" initiatives in Maine, Vermont, Massachusetts, and Missouri suggests that a majority of Americans would back public financing of campaigns if given the choice. It would then be up to progressives to summon up the political creativity to thrust new kinds of activists and leaders into elective politics.

It's time to reduce corporate control over our political parties and candidates, liberate elected officials from the tyranny of money power, and create the possibility for working-class people to run for office and win. It would be an important first step in trying to take back our politics for the people.

—— Commentaries ——

Operating Most Effectively Under the Current System

Ellen Malcolm

Jamin Raskin and I agree that the best prescription for the current campaign finance system is public financing. Though I believe that federal campaigns will ultimately be funded publicly, that isn't going to happen soon. The Republican majority in Congress is adamantly opposed to most campaign finance reform, especially public financing; Senate Majority Leader Trent Lott is often quoted as calling public financing "food stamps for politicians."

The challenge for EMILY's List and other groups working on behalf of nontraditional candidates is to be effective in the current system or in a future "reformed" system that is not publicly financed.

Raskin correctly points out the critical problem for women and minority candidates is that they rarely receive support from traditional political funders. Any partial reform that does not replace private contributions with public funds will always be dominated by special interest money. After all, economic interests have tremendous incentive and ability to participate in the election system.

The key to electing women and minorities is to encourage the participation of small contributors, the foundation of nontraditional candidates' campaigns. EMILY's List has done that by creating a donor network.

Our members pay $100 to join EMILY's List and agree to contribute $100 or more to two candidates during a two-year election cycle. We send our members profiles of pro-choice Democratic women who are running viable campaigns for House, Senate, and governor. The members decide whom to support and write checks directly to the candidates. EMILY's List gathers the contributions and sends them on to the campaigns.

A case study of how our small donor network can be effective can be seen in the 1992 campaign of Eva Clayton in North Carolina's 1st congressional district. Clayton was a county commissioner running in a newly created, majority African-American district that took up twenty-seven counties in the northeastern part of the state. Her own county had a population of 9,000. The frontrunner was the son of the congressman who had held the seat for thirty-five years. Clayton had the experience and a grassroots network. What she didn't have was support from the traditional political donors in North Carolina or Washington, DC.

EMILY's List recommended Clayton to our members and raised more than $30,000 from contributors across the country, most of whom would never have heard of her candidacy. She won her primary and beat the congressman's son in a runoff. She was elected president of the 1992 Democratic congressional class, the first woman and first African American ever to hold that position.

Since real, fundamental reform does not seem to be a current option, we must hope that partial reform will work. However, we have compelling evidence that partial reform does not work at all for women.

EMILY's List was formed in 1985, a decade after the last major Common Cause-backed reform had gone into effect. In ten years that reform had not helped women. In fact, the number of Democratic women in the House had actually declined from fourteen to twelve, and not one Democratic woman had been elected to the Senate in her own right.

In the last eight elections, EMILY's List has helped to elect fifty-two Democratic women to the House and ten Democratic women to the Senate. We have raised more than $5 million for the elections of women of color, helping to elect eighteen women of color to the House and the first African-American woman, Carol Moseley-Braun, ever elected to the U.S. Senate.

EMILY's List is reform that opens the system for women. Until we can get a fundamental change through public financing, we will fight long and hard to protect the donor network option that brings small contributors into the system, making it possible for nontraditional candidates to win.

"We've Closed Down"

Hollywood Women's Political Committee

As of April 1997, The Hollywood Women's Political Committee (HWPC) is permanently closing its doors and will no longer participate as a PAC in the raising of funds for political candidates. We will no longer collaborate with a system that promotes the buying and selling of political office.

For the first time in seventy years, less than 50 percent of eligible voters elected our president and members of Congress in 1996. Two billion was raised and spent to run political campaigns. Only one-quarter of 1 percent of this campaign money came from contributions of $200 or less. One percent of contributors gave the vast majority of this campaign money; 95 percent of the people of the United States gave nothing.

What does all of this mean to us? It means that less than 5 percent of America controls campaign funding and the influence this control brings. It means that hardly anyone without a personal fortune or connections to great wealth can be elected to public office. It means that the best and the brightest among us who do not have personal wealth or meaningful access to it will likely never become dedicated public servants, the visionary leaders we so desperately need. It means the continued alienation of the vast majority of Americans who believe that without money and the influence it purchases their voices will never be heard, their needs never met. It means these disenfranchised Americans believe their vote will change nothing in a ransomed political system, and so they do not vote. It means that when less than 50 percent of eligible voters go to the polls we no longer have a representative democracy. It means that our federal and state representatives spend more time raising money than legislating. It means that when corporate PACs outspend labor and organization PACs by seven to one, money has become the system, a closed system, a society of the very rich and the very poor where economic, ethnic, and racial tensions abound.

We must work against the assumption that this is the only way our government can run. As we disarm from the political fundraising race, we do so calling for comprehensive campaign finance reform that includes lower contributions, expenditure limits, halting the influx of "soft money," setting limits on personal expenditures, reducing television and radio costs, and ultimately, the establishment of a full and fair public financing system. We challenge Congress to do what is right for the country, not only what is necessary to be reelected.

Since 1983, the HWPC has been working toward campaign finance reform and is the only PAC ever to testify before Congress to advocate doing away with PACs. Today we are proud of our past success, and our passion for and commitment to our ideals is as strong as ever. We will, as concerned political women, continue to fight for our vision of America, but we can no longer do so in a way that has become part of the problem.

"Not the Rich, More Than the Poor": Poverty, Race, and Campaign Finance Reform

John C. Bonifaz

The American experiment with democracy is failing. In this new Gilded Age, wealth is increasingly concentrated in fewer hands, and the gap between the rich and poor has grown ever wider. For the 13 percent of this nation living in poverty and for the millions of the working poor, the current political process is bankrupt. It does not provide any meaningful opportunity for the voices of ordinary citizens to be heard. The very forces that control and directly benefit from the U.S. economy also control and directly benefit from today's campaign finance system, and in doing so, disproportionately influence our public elections.

No experiment with democracy can survive under these conditions. Instead, it becomes a plutocracy, which *Webster's Unabridged Dictionary* defines as: "1. the rule or power of wealth or the wealthy; 2. a government or state in which the wealthy class rules; 3. a class or group ruling, or exercising power or influence, by virtue of its wealth."

We can change the direction. To do this, we must not only highlight the standard arguments of the danger of corruption posed by our money-dominated political system. We must also return to the bedrock principle of democracy: political equality for all. The power of the democratic vision lies in that simple promise. As James Madison wrote in *The Federalist Papers No. 57*:

> Who are to be the electors of the federal representatives? Not the rich, more than the poor; not the learned, more than the ignorant; not the haughty heirs of distinguished names, more than the humble sons of obscure and unpropitious fortune. The electors are to be the great body of the people of the United States . . .

This article focuses on the campaign finance system's impact on the political voice of the poor of this nation. Too often in the campaign finance debate, this question is largely ignored. Yet, if the promise of political equality is to mean anything, it must, first and foremost, have meaning for the most powerless of our society. The political process cannot serve as an avenue for changing economic conditions for the poor when the playing field is uneven. In a true democracy, the poor and the rich must stand on equal ground.

The Poll Tax As History

Despite James Madison's eloquent words more than two centuries ago, this nation has a long tradition of property and wealth conditioning political participation. The history of the poll tax presents the proper context for assessing today's system of privately financed public election campaigns.

Over three decades ago, in addressing the poll tax barrier for the third time, the U.S. Supreme Court finally articulated the principle that wealth discrimination in the political process is prohibited, in state as well as federal elections. In 1966, Annie Harper, a poor Virginia voter, made history. She and other poor voters brought a constitutional challenge to Virginia's $1.50 poll tax to the Supreme Court—and won. The nation's highest court, in *Harper v. Virginia Board of Elections*, struck down the poll tax on equal protection grounds. "A State violates the Equal Protection Clause of the Fourteenth Amendment to the U.S. Constitution," the Court ruled, "whenever it makes the affluence of the voter or payment of any fee an electoral standard. Voter qualifications have no relation to wealth. . . ." The poll tax, a fee charged to citizens throughout the South as a requirement for exercising their right to vote, was no longer consistent with the U.S. Constitution. And of course, the barrier the poll tax created to democratic participation, while aimed at both poor whites and poor African Americans, disproportionately disenfranchised African Americans.

In issuing this ruling, which came two years after the Twenty-Fourth Amendment to the U.S. Constitution banned poll taxes in federal elections, the Supreme Court reversed its two prior decisions upholding the poll tax. In 1937 (*Breedlove v. Suttles*) and in 1951 (*Butler v. Thompson*), poor voters had challenged the poll tax on equal protection grounds. In both cases, the Court found constitutional justification for requiring citizens to pay a fee in order to vote. But Justice William O. Douglas, speaking for the Court in the 1966 *Harper* case, stated:

> [T]he Equal Protection Clause is not shackled to the political theory of a particular era. In determining what lines are unconstitutionally discriminatory, we have never been confined to historic notions of equality, any more than we have restricted due process to a fixed catalogue of what was at a given time deemed to be the limits of fundamental rights. Notions of what constitutes equal treatment for purposes of the Equal Protection Clause *do* change. [emphasis in original]

The Campaign Finance Barrier

The campaign finance system of today has replaced the poll tax of the past as the newest wealth barrier to equal and meaningful participation in the political process. Like the earlier poll tax, the current campaign finance system "makes the affluence of the voter . . . an electoral standard." The system operates like a "wealth primary," effectively pre-selecting the candidates who will be viable and who, almost invariably, will go on to win election. Voters lacking access to wealth are too often left simply to ratify the decisions made by that exclusionary process.

Consider these facts: In the 1998 elections, 92 percent of U.S. House of Representative winners and 88 percent of U.S. Senate winners first won the wealth primary—outraising and outspending their opponents—and then went on to win election. The vast majority of campaign money comes from a tiny and wealthy segment of our society. Less than 1 percent of the population contributes more than 80 percent of all money in federal elections in amounts of $200 or more. Wealthy individuals and monied interests increasingly control our elections, drowning out the voices of ordinary citizens.

While the campaign finance system discriminates against the vast majority of Americans who cannot amass and contribute large sums of money for the candidates of their choice, it reserves its harshest impact for the poor. Annie Harper did not have $1.50 in order to vote in Virginia's state elections. A candidate running for the U.S. House of Representatives today must have, on average, half a million dollars in order to win. A U.S. Senate candidate must have $4.6 million. A presidential run? Check back soon for the latest record. For the Annie Harpers of today, equal and meaningful participation in the political process remains only a dream. The wealth barrier is higher than ever.

When we consider the intersection of campaign finance and race, we find that the system's disenfranchisement of the poor disproportionately harms communities of color. While the poverty rate for white Americans nationally is 11 percent, the poverty rates for both for African Americans and Hispanics are more than double that, each at 27 percent. It is not surprising, then, that this wealth barrier maintains its strongest presence in communities of color.

A 1998 study by Public Campaign ("The Color of Money: Campaign Contributions and Race"), a Washington, DC-based organization supporting full public financing of elections, found that the nation's top 100 communities in terms of campaign contributions are 80 percent white and that each of these communities gave an average of $1.4 million. In contrast, the 100 communities with the highest concentration of people of color each gave an average of $7,000. Similarly, a 1997 national survey of major congressional campaign contributors (giving $200 or more) revealed that 95 percent of such donors are white and 81 percent have annual incomes of $100,000 or more, with the top 20 percent in the $500,000 plus income category. As Nelson Rivers, the NAACP's National Field Director, says: "We're impacted negatively in a disproportionate way. Since African Americans have decidedly less income, less disposable money than other people in the country, we're at a disadvantage when money is the deciding factor in whether you can participate."

And what about our politics? Where are the voices, where are the policies focused on eliminating poverty and the sharpening division between the haves and the have-nots in this, the richest nation in the world? Who is speaking for the Other America? A 1998 study by Second Harvest, a national network of food banks, revealed that, in the midst of this so-called economic boom, more people are visiting soup kitchens, shelters, and food pantries across the country, seeking relief from hunger. The October 1998 *Forbes Magazine* reported that the net worth of the 400 wealthiest Americans increased by $114 billion over the previous year. As United for a Fair Economy (UFE), a national nonprofit focusing public attention on economic inequality here at home, points out in its important book, *Shifting Fortunes*: "Less than half that increase—$48.4 billion—would have been enough to bring all poor Americans up to the official poverty line."

Government policy with respect to the minimum wage provides a classic example of the lockout facing the poor in this system of privately financed public election campaigns. Business interests, which dominate the campaign financing process, consistently oppose increasing the minimum wage to a livable wage. As a result, as UFE says, "[T]he minimum wage has become a poverty wage. It was 19 percent lower in 1998 at $5.15 than it was in 1979, when it was worth $6.39, adjusted for inflation. The minimum wage used to bring a family of three, with a full-time worker, above the official poverty line. Now it doesn't bring a full-time worker with one child above the poverty line."

Meanwhile, the pay America's corporate executives receive has skyrocketed. According to *Business Week's* annual survey of executive salaries, CEOs now make 419 times the pay of factory workers. UFE calculates that if the minimum wage increased as fast as CEO pay since 1960, it would be over $57 an hour today.

Now, more than ever, another voice is needed in the public debate of our national priorities. But it cannot be heard—not under the current campaign finance regime.

The Movement for Full Public Financing of Our Public Elections

When the campaign finance system is viewed in the context of the poll tax history, the solution becomes all the more apparent. The solution for addressing the poll tax barrier was abolition. No response short of that would have been acceptable. The state of Virginia could not, for example, simply have lowered its poll tax from $1.50 to 75 cents and have survived constitutional scrutiny. Its only option, in accordance with the U.S. Constitution, was to eliminate the fee.

Abolition is the appropriate response to the campaign finance barrier. Abolition here means full public financing of our elections. In a democracy, public elections should be publicly financed. No one would reasonably suggest that we should revert to the days of privately financed election ballots or that we should begin to auction our election precincts to the highest bidder. Why, then, do we allow private wealthy interests to finance our public elec-

---

Organizations Working on Democratic Participation

- Ballot Access News, P.O. Box 470296, San Francisco, CA 94147; 415/ 922–9779; ban@igc.org; www.ballot-access.org
- The Center for Responsive Politics, 1101 14th St. NW, #1030,Washington, DC 20005; 202/857–0044; info@crp.org; www.opensecrets.org
- Center for Voting and Democracy, 6930 Carroll Ave., #901 Takoma Park, MD 20912; 301/270–4616; cvdusa@aol.com; www.fairvote.org
- Center on Budget and Policy Priorities, 820 First St. NE, #510, Washington, DC 20002; 202/408–1080; www.cbpp.org
- Children's Defense Fund, 25 E St. NW, Washington, DC 20001; 202/ 628–8787; cdfinfo@childrensdefense.org; www.childrensdefense.org
- Committee for the Study of the American Electorate, 421 New Jersey Ave. SE, Washington, DC 20003; 202/546–3221; www.gspm.org/csae
- Common Cause, 1250 Connecticut Ave. NW, #600, Washington, D.C. 20036; 202/833–1200; www.commoncause.org
- National Institute on Money in State Politics, 648 N. Jackson, #1, Helena, MT 59601; 406/449–2480; institute@statemoney.org; www.followthemoney.org
- National Voting Rights Institute, One Bromfield St., 3rd. flr., Boston, MA 02108; 617/441–8200; nvri@nvri.org; www.nvri.org
- Public Campaign, 1320 19th St. NW, # M-1, Washington, DC 20036; 202/293–0222; info@publicampaign.org; www.publicampaign.org
- Public Citizen, 1600 20th St. NW, Washington, DC 20009; 202/588–1000; www.citizen.org
- United for a Fair Economy, 37 Temple Pl., 2nd Flr., Boston, MA 02111; 617/423–2148; info@ufe.net.org; www.ufenet.org

---

tion campaigns? If we are truly to own our electoral process, then we must own its financing structure.

Six years after its landmark ruling in the *Harper* case, the Supreme Court struck down a system of high candidate filing fees for primary elections in the state of Texas (*Bullock v. Carter*). "We would ignore reality," the court stated, "were we not to find that this system falls with unequal weight on voters, as well as candidates, according to their economic status." Texas had argued that the filing fees were necessary to pay for the cost of conducting the primary elections. If the fees were struck down, the state said, "the voters, as taxpayers, will ultimately be burdened with the expense of the primaries."

The Supreme Court did not yield. Primary elections, the court emphasized, are part of the democratic process.

> . . . [I]t is far too late to make out a case that the party primary is such a lesser part of the democratic process that its cost must be shifted away from the taxpayers generally. The financial burden for general elections is

Democratic Participation Readings

Basco, Sharon. "The Color of Money: Georgia's Civil Rights Leaders Are Taking The 'Wealth Primary' To Court." *The Nation* 269 (February 1, 1999).
———. "Incomes/Outcomes: Campaign Finance as a Civil Rights Issue." *Southern Changes* (1998).
Bonifaz, John, Gregory G. Luke, and Brenda Wright. "Challenging *Buckley v. Valeo*: A Legal Strategy." *University of Akron Law Review* (Fall 1999).
Bonifaz, John, and Jamin Raskin. "Equal Protection and the Wealth Primary." *Yale Law and Policy Review* 273 (1993): 11.
———. "The Constitutional Imperative and Practical Superiority of Democratically Financed Elections." *Columbia Law Review* 1160 (1994): 94.
Cole, David. "First Amendment Anti-Trust: The End of Laissez-Faire in Campaign Finance." *Yale Law and Policy Review* 236 (1991): 9.
Collins, Chuck, Betsy Leondar-Wright, and Holly Sklar. *Shifting Fortunes: The Perils of the Growing American Wealth Gap.* Boston: United for a Fair Economy, 1999.
Donnelly, David, Janice Fine, and Ellen Miller. *Money and Politics: Financing Our Elections Democratically.* Boston: Beacon Press, 1999.
Fairfield, Roy P., ed. *The Federalist papers: A collection of essays written in support of the Constitution of the United States, from the original text of Alexander Hamilton, James Madison, John Jay.* Garden City, NY: Anchor Books, 1961.
Herbert, Bob. "The Donor Class." *The New York Times* (July 19, 1998).
Public Campaign. "The Color of Money: Campaign Contributions and Race" Washington, DC, September, 1998.
Stern, Philip M. *Still The Best Congress Money Can Buy.* Lanham, MD: Distributed to the trade by National Book Network, 1992.
Wright, J. Skelly. "Politics and the Constitution: Is Money Speech?" *Yale Law Journal* 1001 (1976): 85.
———. "Money and the Pollution of Politics: Is the First Amendment an Obstacle to Political Equality?" *Columbia Law Review* 609 (1982): 82.

carried by all taxpayers. . . . It seems appropriate that a primary system designed to give the voters some influence at the nominating stage should spread the cost among all the voters in an attempt to distribute the influence without regard to wealth.

"Viewing the myriad governmental functions supported from general revenues," the Court continued, "it is difficult to single out any of a higher order than the conduct of elections at all levels to bring forth those persons desired by their fellow citizens to govern."

Like the party primary process, the campaign financing process has become an integral part of our elections. As with the *Bullock* case, the solution here must be to "distribute the influence" to all voters, regardless of their economic status. A new campaign finance system, in which candidates forgo private funds and receive equal amounts of public financing for their campaigns, would end the wealth primary and open up the candidate selection process to all voters. The cost, at $5 to $10 per taxpayer, would be far less than the billions of dollars in legislative favors to campaign contributors—in the form of corporate subsidies and payoffs—for which taxpayers now foot the bill.

In the past several years, a grassroots movement for full public financing of elections has emerged to respond to the campaign finance barrier. As a result of activist campaigns, voters in Arizona, Maine, and Massachusetts have passed, by ballot initiative, nearly full or full public financing systems for their state elections. In Vermont, grassroots organizers pressured the state legislature to enact a similar law for its gubernatorial and lieutenant governor races. Activist coalitions in more than thirty states, led by Public Campaign, which is pushing the, "Clean Money Campaign Reform" model, are working for additional victories in the years to come.

All of these systems are voluntary so as to comport with the Supreme Court's 1976 ruling in *Buckley v. Valeo*, which equated money with speech in the political process and which struck down mandatory congressional campaign spending limits. Ultimately, however, *Buckley* must be revisited and reversed. If candidates want to opt out of public funding, that is their prerogative. *But no one has the right to drown out other people's speech.* Mandatory spending limits are necessary to ensure that those who participate in a public financing system are on equal ground with those who do not.

Longtime civil rights leader Roger Wilkins spoke of the link between the poll tax of another era and today's campaign finance system in his keynote speech before a February 1999 national conference on "Campaign Finance as a Civil Rights Issue," at Howard Law School:

> [E]verybody knew that the poll tax was a civil rights issue. Everybody could see that because it was obviously an instrument for the exclusion of lots of people. But it was also an instrument for preserving the power of those who had long held power. . . .
>
> To the poor and the uneducated, the current system looks like exactly what it is, a tightly wrapped plutocracy which breeds the idea: "They are rich. That's not for me. I can't get in, so what's the use?" That is the attitude that destroys democratic participation just as surely as the poll tax ever did.

The moral and legal promise of political equality cannot coexist with the current campaign financing structure. If this nation is to uphold its expressed commitment to a democratic vision, then this barrier, like ones before it, must come down.

I Am a Product of The Voting Rights Act!

Cynthia A. McKinney

A lot of people, particularly conservatives, interpreted my 1996 reelection to Congress as proof positive that majority-minority districts of the kind fostered by the Voting Rights Act are no longer necessary to ensure fair representation of minorities on Capitol Hill. The attorney who successfully dismantled my old majority-black district in Georgia has stated publicly that he intends to use my victory as a weapon to dismantle even more such districts at the state and county level.

Well, it's true that I won with 59 percent of the vote (better than Newt Gingrich and most of the Georgia delegation did) to become the first and only black woman in the South to win from a 65 percent majority-white district. But the fact is that I won because of the majority-minority district that I used to represent, not in spite of it. That majority-black district gave voters the opportunity to elect someone like me who had only $38,000 to spend against a well-funded establishment candidate in the Democratic primary four years earlier. Representing that majority-minority district for three-and-a-half years enabled me to develop a track record, name recognition, and the local and national contacts necessary to raise the nearly $1 million I spent to win in the new 4th district.

The old 11th district was a highly integrated one (60 percent black and 40 percent white) that gave me a chance to depolarize race relations in rural Georgia, prove myself as a member of Congress, and expose both black and white voters to activist representation from a black elected official. Hence, my victory says more about the power of incumbency than anything else. Proof of this lies in the fact that all of Georgia's incumbents were reelected in 1996.

The new court-drawn district I ran in spread out black voters into Republican districts, making GOP incumbents highly vulnerable to Democratic challengers. But even with the shuffling of literally hundreds of thousands of black voters into Republican districts—and a political climate most favorable to Democrats—not a single Republican incumbent was defeated in the state of Georgia in 1996.

This must have come as a huge disappointment to Georgia's Democratic Party bosses, who worked long and hard to dismantle my district and Representative Sanford Bishop's majority-black district in the hopes of using those black voters as spare parts for their aging Dixiecrat political machine. They woke up November 6 to find that the delegation still consisted of eight Republicans and three Democrats.

Georgia's majority-black districts were squarely blamed for the loss of Democrats in 1994, even though those districts were in place before the 1992 elections. But the real reason Georgia Democrats lost in 1994 was not because of majority-black districts, but because too many Democrats were running on Republican platforms. Now that the majority-minority districts are all but gone, who will the state party blame this time?

The real test of whether majority-minority districts are still necessary will come from the minority candidates who vie for the seat after me. It may very well be the case that attitudes in the South have changed for the better. But one thing is certain: Representing the old 11th district allowed me to run and win in the new 4th district without having to change my views, my gold tennis shoes, or my braids, or having to auction off my principles to the highest bidder.

While commentators were describing me as "too liberal" to win in my new district and predicting my defeat, the voters were looking at my record and listening to my defense of working- and middle-class families. But without the ability to represent the old 11th district and develop a political profile, I would have been largely unknown to voters in the new 4th district, and unlikely to win election.

So as these same commentators spin my victory as proof that majority-minority districts should be dismantled, I say, think again. Don't use my victory to gut the Voting Rights Act, because I am a product of the Voting Rights Act!

Part 5

Environmental Justice

Environmental justice is a health issue, of course, and an issue of political power: toxic waste sites, incinerators, uranium enrichment plants, and similar highly undesirable land uses go where there is the least resistance and least cost to private industry (and at times to governments). The four case studies reprinted here, from very different locales and involving a variety of unwanted uses, show the power of information, organizing, good legal work, media work, lobbying, and research in protecting minority communities and populations. The arguments favoring environmental justice work are outlined as well.

Race, Poverty, and Sustainable Communities

Carl Anthony

The movement for sustainable communities could give an important boost to the struggle for racial and economic justice in the United States. But without incorporating the quest for racial and economic justice, and significant leadership from communities of color and their allies, this movement may at best be irrelevant to the fight against racism. At worst, it could be more of a liability than an asset. Fortunately, a new cadre of social justice activists and thinkers is emerging seeking to address the challenges of sustainable development. They are pursuing new strategies to link grassroots struggles of disenfranchised communities in neighborhoods and workplaces to the politics of sustainability at the metropolitan regional level.

The sustainability movement is a series of loosely organized efforts to address local and international environmental problems and reduce the negative impacts of human consumption and waste on the natural world. Advocates hope to strengthen community-based efforts to tackle sustainability issues. Supporters say they are also committed to eliminating poverty, especially in the Third World. Across the United States, this movement is allied with recently emerging efforts called "smart growth," which seek metropolitan solutions to intractable urban problems.

The first elements of the sustainability movement grew out of a series of international conferences beginning in 1972, sponsored by the United Nations. Global concern for the environment reached a fever pitch during the

1980s and led to conflicts between environmental groups from industrial nations, and governments and nongovernmental organizations based in the Third World. Third World nations saw the antigrowth environmental agenda as just another way to prevent them from attaining their goals of economic development. Seeking to resolve this conflict, the UN set up the World Commission on Environment and Development, which published its report, *Our Common Future,* in 1987. The report defined sustainable development as a pattern of development that "meets the needs of the present without compromising the ability of future generations to meet their own needs."

"African Americans have a long history of solidarity with the global community and with peoples who have struggled with justice and fairness," notes Clarence Lusane in his important book, *Race in the Global Era.* "In the period ahead, new opportunities and challenges to global participation abound," he writes. Global perspectives on environment and development, however, often overlook the impacts of poverty within industrial nations. The struggle for racial and economic justice in the U.S. requires strengthening community-based organizations while dismantling residential apartheid, generating good jobs, and combating growing wage inequality among workers. To achieve these outcomes, scholars and practitioners are seeking employment, education, and family support systems, and new strategies for metropolitan regional cooperation within the United States.

Poverty and Environmental Concerns

During the last two decades, grassroots struggles for environmental justice have begun to focus public attention on connections between poverty and the environment in the United States. As a concept, environmental justice affirms the use value of life in all its manifestations, against the interests of wealth, power, and technology—a very appealing perspective. To date, however, most of these struggles have been oppositional. The movement to link conservation with appropriate patterns of development could strengthen environmental justice efforts to building new allies, further transforming both the environmental and social justice debates, and bringing substantial new resources to impoverished communities.

At a domestic regional level, advocates of sustainable communities are fighting to stop suburban sprawl. Opposition to uncoordinated development on the metropolitan fringe is spreading like wildfire and has emerged as a major political force across the country. Much of what has been written about sprawl, however, has been framed from the perspectives of environmentalists and white suburban residents. Typically, environmental groups see sprawl as poorly planned real estate development destroying wildlife habitat, plants, animals, and natural ecosystems. In recent years throughout the nation, suburban citizen groups, fed up with Walmarts, ugly housing developments, traffic jams, and air pollution, have placed over 200 successful growth management initiatives on the ballot. Elected officials grappling with sales and property taxes are alarmed by the negative impact of sprawl on public revenues. A new breed of architects and urban designers sees the potential for new patterns of metropolitan form. This trend is sparking an alliance between environmentalists and developers for better urban design, more compact, pedestrian-friendly, transit-oriented development, and metropolitan regional coordination, including reinvestment in the inner city—a new development pragmatism dubbed "Smart Growth."

But another new breed of environmental justice advocates, while sympathetic to these concerns, comes at the issue of sprawl from a different perspective. They understand that institutional racism has shaped metropolitan growth patterns, and that any effective solution must come to terms with race. They are willing to explore new relationships with advocates of sustainable development. Manuel Pastor, Director of Latin American studies at the University of California-Santa Cruz, points out: "Linking to regional economic dynamism may be a powerful antidote to what have been ineffective strategies to attract investment to poor areas. After all, wealthy suburbs are not only jobs-rich—they are connection-rich for individuals from inner-city locales."

To be sure, there are limitations to efforts at building alliances between advocates of racial justice and the movement for sustainable communities. After a decade of efforts to generate racial diversity within the environmental movement, the leaders and political base of these organizations are still overwhelmingly white.

There is also a cultural disconnect between advocates of sustainability and organizations struggling in neighborhoods and workplaces to achieve racial and economic justice. While the sustainability movement shares with social justice advocates a deep suspicion of free-market capitalism as a solution to the major challenges of our time, advocates of social and racial justice are forced to be less utopian and far more pragmatic about jobs and economic opportunity.

Advocates of sustainable development rely heavily on technological innovation, such as waste reduction and recycling, energy efficiency and renewables, transportation planning, and traffic management as solutions for community problems—as if building healthy communities were primarily a plumbing problem. They also suggest changing individual lifestyles, such as learning to raise one's own food, walking rather than riding in automobiles, and throwing away credit cards.

Important as these proposals are, they may appear quixotic, perhaps even insulting, in the everyday world of the urban poor, ironically forced to take such measures in the absence of alternatives. As Rutgers University professor Robert Lake has noted, "A vista of shuttered factories, deserted shopping malls, deteriorating infrastructure, depopulated cities, and abandoned toxic waste dumps does not welcome discussion of limits, carrying capacity, ecological footprints, or environmental constraints."

Despite lip-service to supporting cultural diversity and eliminating poverty, strategies to accomplish such objectives are usually missing from the environmental movement's otherwise voluminous outpouring of research and publications.

A more problematic prospect is that an alliance between business and environmental interests may provide the rationale for public policies that override and set back the quest for racial and economic justice. A regional analysis of gentrification and community stability undertaken in the San Francisco Bay Area by the Urban Habitat Program, for example, shows that implementation of urban growth boundaries protecting open space and wildlife habitat on the suburban fringe may well drive up land values in the inner cities. Without countervailing measures, such a policy will force displacement of communities of color now residing in central urban areas.

As a case in point, Oakland's Mayor Jerry Brown, responding to encouragement to make the city more livable, has initiated a campaign to bring 10,000 new residents into downtown by the year 2003. From a conventional environmental perspective, this effort is cause for celebration. The infill strategy will cut down on suburban sprawl, by making higher-density market-rate housing available to populations who would normally seek out housing opportunities in suburban locations. The plan will make efficient use of existing infrastructure, promoting 24-hour use of a pedestrian-friendly downtown. Thus, it will help reduce traffic congestion, squandering of energy, pollution of air and water, and the loss of biodiversity on the suburban fringe. Businesses will benefit from the mayor's leadership. Telecommunications, software/multimedia biotechnology and food processing firms are being offered a ten-year tax holiday to relocate to the city in order to be near where employees will work. Big name developers are vying for free land to build in Oakland's downtown.

The future of 6,000 current residents of Oakland's downtown—mostly poor people of color—is also at stake. With careful planning, they could also benefit from new development downtown. Unfortunately, however, new investment in the area, driven by regional pressures, will raise land values and rents. This could bring gentrification and displacement into neighborhoods like West Oakland, Chinatown, and Lake Merritt. No planning is currently being done by the city to meet the needs of these residents.

A New Metropolitan Agenda

Racial, economic, and environmental justice advocates around the country are beginning to grapple with such challenges and opportunities of sustainable development at the metropolitan scale. They are seeking ways to link grassroots struggles of disenfranchised communities in neighborhoods and workplaces to the politics of what has been called the "new metropolitan agenda."

Four new trends are opening up metropolitan politics as a terrain of struggle for advocates of racial and economic justice. The first is a nationwide confrontation between powerful suburban constituencies and developers on the issue of sprawl. This clash, driven by suburban efforts to protect property values, status, and amenities, and to reduce the inconvenience of traffic congestion, converges with a larger environmental agenda to protect and conserve land, air, water quality, energy, and biodiversity. Second, corporate interests need greater collaboration with local jurisdictions in order to promote economic development and competitiveness in a rapidly changing global marketplace. Third is the growing awareness that suburban communities are not monolithic. In his study of twenty-nine metropolitan regions throughout the United States, Myron Orfield has persuasively argued that the economic interests of older suburban communities are more aligned with core cities than with the outer suburbs. These insights open the possibility of greater collaboration between communities of color and the white working class. Finally, internal racial diversity within communities of color and greater stratification along class and geographic lines suggest that the political model of inner cities versus suburbs no longer matches reality.

The central question is: will smart growth policies curb suburban sprawl at the expense of inner-city communities of color, or can social activists and their allies fashion a version of sustainable communities at the metropolitan scale to realize new visions of racial and economic justice?

Race and Poverty Data as a Tool in the Struggle for Environmental Justice

Kary L. Moss

A common theme in the four case studies presented here is the importance of information about the communities themselves, which should be used as a tool in the struggle to organize effective opposition against corporations whose bottom line is their shareholders, and not the communities in which they site pollution sources, or the environment.

An important case that culminated in a consent judgment, signed in January 1996 by Judge Valdamar Washington of Genesee County (Michigan) Circuit Court, placed severe controls on a new incinerator designed to burn wood from demolished structures. The plant, built by the Genesee Power Company, had been sited in a predominantly African-American residential neighborhood in Flint. The lawsuit (*NAACP-Flint Chapter et al. v. Engler et al.*, No. 95–38228–CZ [Circuit Court, Genesee County, filed 7/22/95]), filed by two community groups—United for Action and the NAACP-Flint Chapter—and several African-American women, challenged the state of Michigan's decision to grant a construction permit to the power company and allow that facility to emit over two tons of lead per year upon a community already suffering from elevated levels of lead exposure.

The Maurice and Jane Sugar Law Center for Economic and Social Justice, a Detroit-based national civil rights organization representing the plaintiffs, charged the state of Michigan and the Michigan Department of Environmental Quality (MDEQ) with violating the equal protection clause of the Michigan Constitution and the state's human rights law. Additionally, the lawsuit charged the MDEQ, Genesee Township, and Genesee Power Company with violating the Michigan Environmental Protection Act, which recognizes claims for harm to the environment.

Background

The Environmental Justice Movement has become one of the most compelling and exciting grassroots movements in recent history. It has gathered strength and momentum from a variety of sources:

- several widely publicized national studies demonstrating that communities of color bear disproportionate burdens of environmental harm and that the benefits of environmental protection have been inequitably distributed in these communities;
- local successes engineered by grassroots organizations, such as those efforts by the farmworkers, especially in the early pesticide campaigns of the 1960s and 1970s;
- President Clinton's Executive Order 12898, ordering federal agencies to develop strategies to address the problem of environmental racism;
- a number of conferences organized over the last several years around the country, bringing together grassroots activists, academics, and lawyers; and

- the willingness of several foundations to provide financial support for work in this area by nonprofit organizations.

On occasion, the efforts undertaken by an organized community have been enough to defeat a proposed new pollution source, generate changes in or stop an existing source. However, at times local communities have had to resort to legal action as well, especially once an application for a construction or operation permit begins to wind its way through the largely mystified bureaucratic processes of all state regulatory agencies, as well as the federal Environmental Protection Agency.

The legal fight is rarely easy and historically has suffered from several obstacles. Two in particular emanate from the limited nature of the law itself: First, lawyers seeking to argue that the imposition of a pollution source on a particular community constitutes race discrimination have tended to rely solely upon the Fourteenth Amendment of the federal Constitution. Lawsuits based upon this theory have been largely unsuccessful because a plaintiff must demonstrate that a government body has "intended" to discriminate, which is extremely difficult to prove.

A second obstacle results from the tendency of legal groups to raise only environmental, and not civil rights, claims in court. The problem with use of environmental laws is that they tend in effect to be written by those in the industry. Thus, the questions presented to courts tend to accept many dangerous assumptions. For example, use of these laws requires plaintiffs to prove that the risk of harm is "bad enough" or show that a particular facility exceeds relevant ambient air or water standards. Such questions presume that some harm is acceptable, that each site can be evaluated by a regulatory body without regard to cumulative impacts and that private corporations have no responsibility to protect and promote the public health so long as a state has determined that operations of a particular corporation fall within the requirements of various laws and regulations. The effect is to marginalize the affected communities and leave critical questions out of the debate.

A related obstacle is the necessity for large amounts of money to finance environmental litigation. Assuming that a low-income community can even find an environmental lawyer willing to donate her or his services pro bono, proving a case using traditional environmental laws is extremely expensive. Low-income communities are therefore poorly positioned to protect their interests. For example, if a community argues that various governmental or private actions violate permit limitations, dumping laws, and record-keeping and reporting requirements established under state and federal laws, it must then hire experts who can testify about the risk of harm, effectiveness of pollution controls, etc. Few communities, especially at the stage of the pre-permit hearing process, can afford to gather such information.

As activists and lawyers have taken up the struggle for environmental justice, a new opportunity has presented itself to expand the discussion and empower communities themselves. Lawyers have begun looking to other civil rights laws to advance their claims. Both Title VI of the 1964 Civil Rights Act, which prohibits discrimination on the basis of race by recipients of federal funds, and the equal protection clauses in several (but not all) state constitutions provide a more favorable standard of proof. In order to make a case using these laws, a plaintiff does not have to show "discriminatory animus," but rather only that a particular decision, or pattern of decisions, has a "disparate impact" upon a protected group of people. In this context, race and poverty data, which are relatively accessible, provide a source of power to community organizations and lawyers.

In the Flint case, we argued that the state's decision to grant a permit to Genesee Power to build the incinerator violated the disparate impact test of the Michigan Constitution's civil rights clause. Since little legal authority existed regarding a similar factual situation as the one involving the demolition wood incinerator, we relied on several types of cases: those involving challenges to local zoning schemes that had the effect of excluding low- and moderate-income families; those involving challenges to municipal policies, such as limiting use of parks to residents, but which had a disparate impact on communities of color; and those finding that a state's system of financing public education which caused wealth-based disparities in the quality of public education violated the state's constitutional equal protection guarantees.

These cases, in general, require a plaintiff to demonstrate that people of color are disadvantaged at a "substantially higher" rate than whites; that the state's permitting practice results in a racial pattern significantly different from that of the applicable pool, such as the statewide population of African Americans; and that it burdens a "substantially disproportionate" number of blacks.

In support of this theory, we offered statistical proof of the disparate impact of MDEQ's permitting practice. We used simple Census data to show that a substantial disparity exists in the racial composition of the population surrounding the demolition wood incinerator site, as compared to that existing in the county and state. Specifically, the population within a one-mile radius surrounding the incinerator is 55.8 percent African American; by contrast, African Americans comprise 19.6 percent of those living in Genesee County and 13.9 percent of Michigan's population.

We also showed that there was a substantial disparity in the racial composition of the population surrounding each of the four municipal solid waste incinerator sites located throughout Michigan. The MDEQ had granted permits in areas that have substantially higher concentrations of African Americans than the respective countywide populations. For example, 43 percent of the population living within a one-mile radius of each of these incinerator sites is African American, compared with the 14 percent statewide.

Another type of useful, and not very expensive, information was a risk assessment study, performed by Dr. Stuart Batterman of the University of Michigan's School of Public Health, demonstrating that African Americans living in Flint constituted the population that would be most impacted by operation of this incinerator.

Other easily obtained health data we used included public reports, studies from scientific journals, and privately commissioned studies. General health information about the population itself brings real people with real problems into a courtroom or public decision-making body. In the Flint case, the population surrounding the incinerator suffered from more severe health problems than those living elsewhere in the county. A county health department study and a recent report commissioned by the governor also indicated that there already existed elevated levels of lead exposure in the area near the incinerator.

Health information specific to children was also important. For example, children under six are especially vulnerable to lead's negative effects, because the blood-brain barrier of the neurological system is still developing. Children absorb more lead in proportion to their weight than do adults—50 percent as compared to 10 to 20 percent for adults. The governor's report also indicated that 49.2 percent of children ages six months to five years living in the Flint metropolitan area already have elevated blood lead levels.

Similarly, health information specific to race/ethnicity and poverty is important, since it has been widely reported that race/ethnicity is the only variable that significantly predicts blood lead levels in all age-specific models. A much higher percentage of African American (23 percent) than white (8 percent) children living in cities similar in size to Flint (i.e., central cities with a population less than 1 million) have blood lead levels exceeding 10 mg/dl. Additionally, the poverty rate for African-American children ages five and under living within one mile of the proposed incinerator was 77 percent. This is the population most at risk from lead poisoning: the Michigan Environmental Science Board Lead Panel concludes that lower socio-economic urban preschool children (less than six years old) living in older (pre-1980s) homes are the most vulnerable to lead exposure.

Finally, other essential information included the cumulative risk of adding another polluting site. Flint has numerous unregulated junk yards that burn trash and tires, bulk storage gas tanks, an asphalt company, and cement factory that contribute to noise and air pollution, and a fenced-off holding pond containing sludge and other liquid waste northwest of the industrial park that may have negative effects on the local groundwater. The Flint River, considered the second most polluted river in Michigan, runs close to the area, so the water table is relatively high, and two streams run through the park near the river passing close to residential sites.

Presentation of this evidence at trial (before the defense had even put on its own case) alone prompted the state court judge to push the parties into settlement discussions. Thus, collection of data is one of the most critical tasks any community group or lawyer can undertake when trying to keep a new source of pollution out of a neighborhood.

Prospects for the Future

After settlement with the power plant, the case proceeded against the state. The trial court ruled that the MDEQ policy failed to protect the health, safety, and welfare of Michigan citizens. In a fifty-page decision, the trial court found that the MDEQ's failure to consider multiple pathways of lead exposure and consideration of the urban environment and existing sources of pollution violated the state constitution by failing to protect the health, safety, and welfare of its citizens.

As a remedy, the court required the state to assess the cumulative impact of proposed facilities in combination with the pollution existing in an area through all exposure pathways, and ordered the state to provide a meaningful opportunity for public participation. The MDEQ appealed, and the injunction has been stayed by the Michigan Court of Appeals.

The difficulty inherent in innovating legal challenges of this type underscores the importance of community-based advocacy undertaken with the support of health and environmental professionals. Nonetheless, the author believes that a great deal was accomplished through the litigation process. First, the court placed significant limitations on the amount of demolition wood that could be burned. Second, the community had an avenue in which to advocate for itself in a way not allowed during the permitting process itself. Third, it allowed the community to build relationships with academicians and health/environmental specialists which are beneficial for future advocacy. Finally, it generated several years of publicity that increased the level of scrutiny levied on local decision-makers.

In the absence of litigation, data of this type often are inaccessible to communities at the critical early stages because many community organizations lack access to computers, public health professionals, risk assessment analysts, etc., and because these groups are not familiar with the types of data that can be useful and important. Thus, one key challenge facing those working in the Environmental Justice Movement is how to improve community access to information.

A second challenge is how to link the various environmental struggles occurring in communities throughout the country. Almost every instance of struggle involves common questions, the most fundamental of which is how to address the growing conflict between corporate self-interest and the good of the people. Debating this question provides an opportunity to develop powerful responses to the ascendancy of the Right and the new wave of deregulation of finance capital and manufacturing industries. Facing this question is one of the most important steps that can be taken in the environmental movement, and one which can make the environmental movement the leading edge for policies that place people over profits.

Analysis of Racially Disparate Impacts in the Siting of Environmental Hazards

Thomas J. Henderson, David S. Bailey, and Selena Mendy Singleton

This article focuses on one aspect of a broad challenge by Citizens Against Nuclear Trash (CANT), a grassroots coalition in Louisiana, to the proposed construction, between two small African American communities—Forest Grove and Center Springs—of the first privately owned uranium-enrichment plant in the United States.

CANT engaged Nathalie Walker of the Sierra Club Legal Defense Fund and Diane Curran and Ann Spielberg, of Harmon, Curran, Gallagher, and Spielberg, to challenge the license application by Louisiana Energy Services (LES) to the Nuclear Regulatory Commission on a variety of technical and environmental grounds, including the adequacy of the National Environmental Policy Act (NEPA) Environmental Impact Statement (EIS) prepared by LES. The Lawyers' Committee for Civil Rights Under Law later joined the case to assist in developing the environmental justice claims.

Disparate Impact

In siting decisions, "disparate impact" means that the proposed facility more heavily burdens an identifiable community of color, and thus has a racially discriminatory result. Establishing disparate impact is essential to any challenge based on discrimination.

LES purportedly employed a sophisticated and carefully documented selection process that ranked potential sites against "essential" and "desired" site location factors, beginning at the national level and incrementally narrowing choices until selection of a final site. Their initial criteria were essentially technical—such as shipping distances, meteorological requirements, and geological and geographical limitations—and narrowed the national regions to certain states. However, as the focus of the site selection process narrowed, the criteria became inherently more vague and subjective, including factors such as "local support," "active and cohesive community," "manufacturing mentality," or "opinion leader unity." Evaluation of the use LES made of these subjective criteria revealed that they were applied in a discriminatory manner. For example, they were applied to the majority-white town of Homer, five miles distant from the site, and not to the 97 percent African-American communities of Forest Grove and Center Springs immediately adjoining the site.

Through discovery, CANT obtained the records underlying the site selection process, which revealed not the meticulous process touted by LES, but largely unorganized and incomplete documentation, missing and inaccurate calculations and site scores, and sites—including the Forest Grove/Center Springs site—added late in the process. This evidence demonstrated that the process was anything but objective and methodical and, instead, was easily subject to manipulation. Further, in depositions, LES officials and consultants claimed they were unaware of the racial composition of communities associated with the various potential sites and, thus, racial impact had no place in their evaluation process. This testimony represented an admission that the LES process, by its own design, ignored any evidence of disparate impact on African-American communities. This evidence cemented CANT's claim that the EIS utterly failed to identify or evaluate the disparate racial impact, required by President Clinton's Executive Order 12898 on Environmental Justice.

In analyzing the racial impact of the selection process, population data were gathered for each area under consideration by LES, starting with the nationwide selection of northern Louisiana, down to the specific sites from which the final site was selected (where Census block data were available on the racial makeup and income level of the population adjacent to each site considered).

The results were dramatic. Beginning with the selection of northern Louisiana as the best national site area, LES chose the state with the second lowest income level and second highest African-American population (30.8 percent) in the nation. As LES further narrowed its selections, analysis showed that the aggregate average percentage of African-American population within a one-mile radius of each of the 78 sites in northern Louisiana was 28.4 percent. When LES reduced the list to 37 sites within nine communities, the aggregate percentage of African Americans rose to 36.8 percent. When LES then further limited its focus to six sites in Claiborne Parish, the aggregate average percent African-American population rose again, to 64.7 percent. The final site selected had the highest African-American population of all 78 considered—97.1 percent.

The disparate impact analysis with respect to the final site was premised not only on the stark racial impact of the selection process, but also took account of the nature, extent, and reach of the predictable effects of the proposed facility—burdens as well as benefits—and the impact of those effects on the African-American and white communities. LES had identified benefits and burdens, but the EIS failed to analyze their impact, at all in some cases, and never on populations by racial composition. For example, LES identified as burdens the risk of nuclear accidents, contamination of surface and ground water, ground water supply, noise, traffic, depressed real estate values, and crime. When the impact of these effects on racial population groups was analyzed, it was clear that the African-American population in the immediate vicinity of the planned facility was disproportionately impacted.

Conversely, analysis of the racial impact of the proposed benefits of the facility—construction and operation jobs, increased real estate values, and the economic growth associated with development—demonstrated that they would disproportionately be enjoyed by the more remote white communities with higher levels of income, education, and training.

Expert Testimony

This information was integrated into the expert testimony of Dr. Robert Bullard of Clark-Atlanta University's Environmental Justice Research Center. In pre-filed testimony, Dr. Bullard described the disparate impact evidence in the context of three elements of environmental equity—procedural, geographic, and social. He described procedural equity as the extent to which governing rules, evaluation, and selection criteria are implemented consistently and in a non-discriminatory manner. Here, neither the criteria nor the selection process took race into account or included input from members of the African-American community. Such information is essential to assessing disparate impact and crucial to developing the NEPA "alternative analysis" required in the EIS, which provides basic information on the social, economic and other significant impacts of the proposed project. Thus, procedural equity was absent from the site selection process.

Characterizing geographic equity as the location and spatial configuration of communities and their proximity to environmentally harmful facilities and land uses, Dr. Bullard concluded that the geographic and spatial configuration of Forest Grove and Center Springs rendered these African-American communities more susceptible to environmental risks than other communities. Finally, Dr. Bullard indicated that social equity assesses the role of sociological factors on environmental decision-making. Such factors may include race, ethnicity, class, culture, lifestyles, political power, organization, or legal incorporation. Determining that the social costs were disproportionately borne by the African-American communities closest to the facility, Dr. Bullard concluded that social equity issues were not adequately addressed in the EIS.

Legal Claims

In addition to disparate impact analysis, pressing an environmental justice claim required developing a legal claim that recognized such analysis. Because no constitutional or civil rights claims were stated, a claim was developed using NEPA in conjunction with Executive Order 12898. Specifically, it was argued that NEPA's "significant impacts" and "informational" requirements demanded that LES prepare an EIS that properly recognized and evaluated environmental justice issues.

Although the Supreme Court had held that NEPA analysis is limited to the physical, as opposed to emotional or psychological, impacts of a project, the record in the CANT case clearly illustrated that disparate impacts can have real social and economic effects subject to NEPA's requirements. Furthermore, NEPA has an important "informational component"—a mandate to fully inform the decision-maker of the adverse impacts of the proposed project.

Further support for this argument was found in Executive Order 12898 and EPA's (then draft) Environmental Justice Policy. The logical way for many federal agencies to implement the Executive Order on Environmental Justice is through the EIS process, and failure to do so can violate NEPA. Where such adverse impacts further environmental injustice and disproportionate risk to racial minorities, and run contrary to the policy articulated in the Executive Order and civil rights statutes, such information is indeed relevant. Although the Executive Order does not create an independently actionable claim, its application is important to agency decision-making. The courts have encouraged agencies to apply Executive Orders in their decision-making process, stating that agencies that follow such Presidential directives do not act illegally, but rather in "laudable fashion."

Combining NEPA requirements with what is contained in the Executive Order creates an obligation that any EIS should include an evaluation of disparate racial impact and related environmental justice issues. Carefully analyzing and developing evidence of disparate racial impacts can create a record that demonstrates that an EIS fails to satisfy this aspect of NEPA.

Decision

On May 1, 1997, the Atomic Safety and Licensing Board of the U.S. Nuclear Regulatory Commission (NRC) issued a decision denying LES's request for a license. The Board held that Executive Order 12898, although it creates no new enforceable rights, provides an interpretation of NEPA that binds all executive agencies as well as independent regulatory agencies, such as NRC, that have voluntarily acceded to the Order. In light of the Order, NEPA requires an inquiry into both racially discriminatory intent and racially disparate impacts of siting decisions. Accordingly, the Board ordered the NRC staff to undertake a thorough inquiry into the racial motives of LES's siting decision and to expand its disparate impact analysis to encompass property value changes and road relocations.

LES appealed the Licensing Board's decision to a panel of NRC commissioners. On April 3, 1998, the NRC reversed the Board's order that NRC staff investigate possible intentional racial discrimination in the siting, but affirmed the Board's findings on the inadequacy of the EIS's disparate impact assessment. The NRC held that because the language of NEPA refers only to environmental and socioeconomic impacts, inquiries into motive are beyond its scope. However, the NRC held that Executive Order 12898 demands attention to racially disparate impacts when conducting the socioeconomic impact inquiry required under NEPA. The decision also required the NRC staff to investigate possible strategies to mitigate the facility's effect on property values.

On April 22, 1998, LES dropped its request for a permit for the Claiborne Parish facility, and in August of that year it announced it had sold its property and would not attempt to site anywhere in the region.

The Streets, the Courts, the Legislature, and the Press: Where Environmental Struggles Happen

Rachel Godsil

In November 1995, the East New York Community Committee Against the Incinerator celebrated a victory: the Committee had just defeated a wood-waste incinerator slated for a permit in the primarily African American and Latino community of Brooklyn's East New York area.

A few months later, another Brooklyn community coalition, the Community Alliance for the Environment (CAFE)—comprised of Latinos, Hasidic Jews, and African Americans from Williamsburg and Fort Greene—also celebrated a victory. CAFE had staved off a 5 million pound per day municipal waste incinerator proposed for the Brooklyn Navy Yard for over a decade. It had just received word that the City of New York agreed to its most recent demand: a Supplemental Environmental Impact Statement (SEIS) for the project to replace the Environmental Impact Statement (EIS) issued in 1985.

From the perspective of a civil rights lawyer in New York City in the late 1990s, the world looks bleak: judicial hostility; the resurgence of conservative politics at the city, state, and federal levels; and a powerful backlash against the civil rights gains of the past decades. But as a lawyer in the Environmental Justice Movement, a participant in the East New York struggle, and a latecomer to the Brooklyn Navy Yard battle, I cannot help but be cautiously optimistic.

East New York

In March 1995, the NY State Department of Environmental Conservation (DEC) declared that the Atlas-Bioenergy Corporation need not prepare an Environmental Impact Statement to build a wood-waste incinerator. East New York was not Atlas' first choice. The company first sought to build the incinerator—euphemistically called a waste wood gasification facility—in Southhampton, Long Island. But when the Southhampton town board declared its opposition, Atlas agreed not to seek a state permit, and instead focused on East New York. Atlas filed a permit application with the DEC and sought funding for the environmental review of the incinerator from the NY State Energy Research and Development Agency. In New York, before an agency may grant a permit for a project that may have an environmental impact, it must conduct an environmental review. The agency conducts an initial review to determine whether the project "may have a significant environmental impact," and if so, a full EIS must be prepared. The EIS grants an opportunity for public review and comment and requires consideration of the project's potential effect on community health and character, as well as a range of more blatant environmental effects.

When DEC filed a notice of complete application in March 1995 and declared that an EIS was unnecessary for the incinerator—sited for a small industrial plot in a largely residential community, within blocks of daycare centers, schools, public housing, senior centers, and single-family homes—

East New York residents finally received notice of the plan and began to organize. Residents learned that the incinerator would spew tons of toxic pollutants into the neighborhood's already polluted air.

The notice of complete application was rescinded when the New York Public Interest Research Group (NYPIRG) pointed out to the state that the permit application was not, in fact, complete. Community members and their elected officials, working with lawyers and organizers from the NAACP Legal Defense and Educational Fund (LDF), NY Lawyers for the Public Interest, and NYPIRG, pressured the City to take over the environmental review and require preparation of an EIS. The lawyers explained to the newly formed East New York Community Committee Against the Incinerator that the EIS process, which provides significant opportunity for community involvement, could result in delay sufficient to doom the project. It is also an excellent organizing opportunity, since public meetings and other public review and comment are required. As East New York activists organized weekly meetings of thirty to fifty people, the lawyers drew charts and passed out fact sheets and glossaries to make the EIS process accessible.

At one meeting, Committee Chair Charles Barron told the lawyers that a community resident had informed him of a city law prohibiting incinerators in apartment buildings and asked that we research whether the law might also apply to the proposed Atlas incinerator. With scant belief that the incinerator was illegal, but out of respect for Barron, we researched the City Administrative Code. To our welcome surprise, the code stated: "No person shall cause or permit the installation of refuse burning equipment." The only exceptions were for municipally-sponsored and medical waste incinerators. The Atlas incinerator was neither.

The committee sent a letter outlining the law—which had never been interpreted in a court—to the City Department of Environmental Protection and requested a meeting. There was no response. The committee upped its organizing. On July 15, a 105-degree day, the committee held a rally at the incinerator site with several hundred people, demanding that the city uphold its own law. A few weeks later, the committee held a Community Update for 200 residents, to which it demanded attendance from the Department Commissioner. She did not attend, but sent a representative and a letter, stating that the city had not decided whether the incinerator was illegal and that the Committee could air its concerns in the EIS process. The committee began to consider litigation to short-circuit the EIS process. The environmental impacts—dire though they would be—were secondary: the city code stated that the incinerator was illegal.

Litigation proved unnecessary. After more organizing, and pressuring the city with thousands of petition signatures, letters, press and political work, the city denied Atlas its permit, pursuant to the Administrative Code provision unearthed by the committee.

Brooklyn Navy Yard

A coalition among divergent communities—formalized with the birth of CAFE in 1992—has fought a battle against three different mayors to stop construction of a fifty-five-story (!) incinerator in the heart of the Williamsburg and Fort Greene sections of Brooklyn. After ten years of struggle, which produced considerable community expertise around city and state environmental review laws, CAFE and NYPIRG organized to demand a Supplemental Environmental Impact Statement from the City to replace a ten-year-old EIS.

In June 1995, ninety-six community and environmental organizations, ninety medical and technical professionals, and fifty-five elected officials requested a SEIS from the city. A thorough report by New York City Public Advocate Mark Green provided clear factual support for the legal claim that an SEIS was necessary. The public advocate's report documented significant new information about the incinerator's harmful impacts from toxic emissions, vulnerabilities in the affected communities from AIDS, increased asthma and tuberculosis, and the fact that new housing development and changed patterns of economic development have taken place in the nearby communities. This new information rendered the 1985 EIS useless. But, as in East New York, despite a clear legal necessity, the city balked.

CAFE and NYPIRG decided to litigate. In November 1995, the coalition, represented by lawyers from NYPIRG and the NAACP LDF, filed in state Supreme Court an expedited proceeding challenging the city's determination, citing city and state environmental review laws and the Americans with Disabilities Act, for failing to study the effects of the incinerator on people with HIV. While the litigation proceeded slowly, CAFE and NYPIRG continued to organize.

The City's Department of Sanitation, the project's sponsor, was completing its bi-annual Solid Waste Management Update, which required approval from the city council. CAFE and NY PIRG applied political pressure to city council members to require the city to agree to prepare the SEIS as part of the Solid Waste Management Update. Last February, the city agreed. Now, a new environmental review process will precede any attempt to build the incinerator. Larry Shapiro, then an attorney for NYPIRG, predicted in 1995 that after more than a decade, "the incinerator will never be built." As of 2000, his prediction is still accurate.

Charles Barron advises that for any struggle, "We need action on the social, legal, political, and information fronts: in other words, we have to fight them in the streets, the courts, the legislatures, and the press." The Brooklyn victories resulted from strategies on all four fronts.

The Social Front

It has become axiomatic—and rightly so—that environmental justice struggles are grassroots-led. Both the East New York and Brooklyn Navy Yard struggles benefited from brilliant leadership and committed community participation.

In East New York, a reputedly fractious community came together weekly in the East New York Community Committee Against the Incinerator. Committee members sent letters to politicians, attended community board meetings, aggressively sought to meet with the commissioner, demanded support from politicians, and held rallies and community updates with hundreds of participants. Charles Barron summed it up as follows: "The victory against the incinerator was a triumph of community people rising up to fight environmental racism and promote environmental justice."

In Williamsburg and Fort Greene, the often antagonistic Latino, Hasidic, and African-American communities "found common ground in the ground itself," as CAFE Co-chair Luis Garden Acosta has said. CAFE emerged in 1992 out of an environmental summit meeting that drew 1,200 residents. The fact that CAFE is a multiracial, multiethnic coalition of highly organized communities means that it can demand support from a wide variety of politicians beholden to different segments of the coalition.

The Legal and Political Fronts

Lawyers working with the communities in the Environmental Justice Movement have to be prepared to break down the traditional relationship in which the lawyer is the advisor and the client the advisee. Working hand-in-hand, the community and lawyer can find fresh approaches by combining the community's political expertise and knowledge with the lawyer's ability to interpret arcane rules and regulations to help find inroads for the community's political work. The close relationship between the lawyers and the Community Committee resulted in better legal work by the lawyers and a fruitful avenue for the community to apply political pressure.

In their most recent victory, CAFE and NYPIRG focused upon the state environmental review process and used it creatively. First, they sought full implementation by demanding the SEIS. When the city demurred, CAFE and NYPIRG filed suit—but continued to apply political pressure. By complementing the litigation strategy with political work and following the minutiae of city law—the requirement for the city council to approve the City's Solid Waste Management Update—CAFE and NYPIRG achieved a much quicker victory than even the expedited suit they had filed.

The Information Front

Many of us first became aware of the state's decision not to require an EIS for the Atlas incinerator in the *New York Daily News*. An attorney with Public Advocate Mark Green's office had noticed the state's decision to not require an EIS for the incinerator. Green's office issued a press release, along with NYPIRG, decrying the decision—which was picked up by *Daily News* reporter Annette Fuentes. Fuentes continued to follow the story, and the Community Committee worked hard to ensure that the extraordinary community effort under way was reported. Atlas-Bioenergy vice president Thomas Polsinelli acknowledged the power of the media in a *Village Voice* interview after the city denied his permit: "Polsinelli was clear about where the firm wants to place future furnaces: One at the offices of the *Village Voice*, four at the *Daily News*, and one at the *New York Times*."

The Future

In both communities, a fight against an outside threat has blossomed into a fight for community sustainability. The East New York Community Committee Against the Incinerator has reconstituted itself as the East New York United Front (ENYUF), which continues to meet and is tackling education issues, economic and community development, and violence in the community, as well as continuing to focus on environmental justice. CAFE also plans to expand its scope, focusing on the existing overabundance of environmental threats, as well as developing local leadership to ensure future existence and strength.

These Brooklyn victories are examples of the power of communities in the Environmental Justice Movement. They also establish steps that are necessary to victory: organized communities, creative uses of the legal and political processes, and a sound media strategy. Sadly, the experiences of other communities with equally brilliant leadership and community commitment and equally able technical assistance indicate that these steps may not always be sufficient. Without certain basic statutory structures—such as environmental review processes that allow for community participation—and some supportive elected officials, there are few inroads for community organizers. Similarly, the unavailability of technical assistants (organizers, lawyers, scientists) early in the process who are committed to the principles of environmental justice and supporting the community can impede a community's efforts. Hopefully, the strategies applied by communities in East New York, Williamsburg, and Fort Greene will prove useful to other communities engaged in environmental justice struggles—and inspiring to civil rights lawyers and activists thirsty for hope in this seemingly desolate time.

The Truth Won't Set You Free (But It Might Make the Evening News): The Use of Demographic Information in Struggles for Environmental Justice in California

Luke W. Cole

One of the great myths of white America is that the truth will set you free. What I mean by this is that simply being right, or having the truth on your side, does not mean you will win a particular struggle. The struggles of communities fighting dangerous and unwanted facilities across the country for the last two decades are not about who has the right facts, or the right science, or even the right law. They are about who has the political and economic power to make their voice heard.

This said, having the truth on your side nonetheless is both useful and important. This article focuses on one particular type of "truth," the use of demographic information in community-based struggles for environmental justice. Despite its many drawbacks, demographic information, when used properly, can be a powerful tool in local fights.

In our work at the Center on Race, Poverty & the Environment, we have used demographic information in a variety of studies to build local movements, educate policymakers and the public, and bolster legal claims. Here are some of the uses we've found for such data:

Community Education and Mobilization

Community groups can use demographic information and studies to anger and motivate their members or community. This important movement-building function occurs when demographic information helps a local community see what it may have considered merely an environmental problem in a new light, as a civil rights problem. A community's reaction to "They want to build a new plant at Third and Bayshore" might be very different from its reaction to that same information in the context of a demographic study showing: "San Francisco has two power plants, both in the Bayview-Hunters Point community. Now they want to build the third plant here, too. Thus, Bayview's residents, 70 percent of whom are African American, will bear 100 percent of the burden of producing San Francisco's energy."

Media Hook

Demographic studies are important educational tools beyond the local community. Media outlets are constantly looking for "scientific" information on different topics and will readily report demographic surveys, even in draft form. These articles or news pieces help a community group reach a much broader audience, thus helping identify potential allies or other similarly situated communities: many times, community leaders will get a phone call from a new supporter, who will say, "I just read about your fight in the paper and I want to help."

The demographic studies we have used are generally graphic illustrations of environmental racism, such as when we revealed that all three of California's Class I toxic waste dumps are in low-income, Latino farmworker communities or when we released a study documenting that billboards in San Francisco's African American community were three times more likely to feature alcohol advertisements than billboards in other neighborhoods. Such studies further public understanding of environmental racism.

Administrative Advocacy

In California, we have used demographic data in administrative advocacy before local, state, and federal agencies. These data have helped community groups provide a context for a local siting decision, such as when residents of Kettleman City discovered, and then pointed out to the local Board of Supervisors, that their town was the only majority Latino town in Kings County and also was the only town asked to host a toxic waste dump. As groups around California investigated the demographics of their own communities, they found a similar pattern: most of California's toxic waste treatment, storage, and disposal facilities are in or near communities of color. In its 1995 report, *Toxic Wastes and Race Revisited,* the United Church of Christ reported that, based on its demographic analyses, fifty-three of California's fifty-four toxic waste sites were in communities that had a greater proportion of people of color than the national average. Findings such as these—by both grassroots activists investigating their own communities and national environmental justice groups painting a big picture—have been a key in community groups' ongoing challenges to California's Department of Toxic Substances Control (DTSC), the state agency responsible for permitting toxic waste facilities. On behalf of a number of California grassroots environmental justice groups, our Center has filed six administrative complaints with the U.S. Environmental Protection Agency (EPA) under Title VI of the Civil Rights Act of 1964, which forbids discrimination by entities, such as DTSC, that receive federal funds. Administrative complaints have a great deal of potential power, as EPA's regulations forbid even discriminatory impact (in addition to intent)—and in California, such impact is easily demonstrated by demographic studies such as the United Church of Christ's.

Litigation Support

Finally, demographic information is useful in planning and bringing environmental justice lawsuits. Just as in administrative advocacy, demographic information that shows a pattern of siting dangerous facilities in communities of color is an essential foundation to lawsuits alleging violations of civil rights laws. Lawsuits under Title VI, or under Title VIII of the Civil Rights Act of 1968 (the Fair Housing Act), are a new but increasingly popular tool in the Environmental Justice Movement, and a number have been filed in California, challenging everything from rebuilding a freeway through the predominantly African American community of West Oakland to expansion of a toxic waste dump near Buttonwillow. Advocates should note that all evidence introduced in such hard-fought cases, including demographic studies, will be subject to exacting scrutiny by one's opponents and may also be the target of studies performed by the other side's hired-gun experts.

Things to Watch Out For

Inherent Limitations

In using Census data, one should be aware of some of their limitations in describing a particular community, region, or state. The Census Bureau does not count Latinos as a separate race, but allows that they can be of any race;

"Hispanic" is reported as a separate category. This can lead to an interesting situation: When the people of Kettleman City told Kings County officials that "Kettleman City is 95 percent Latino," a figure they based on the 1990 Census, the County responded: "Our figures show that Kettleman City is 67 percent white." Both were right.

Inaccurate Data

Some data sets are flawed, and it is important to know about this and take it into account in fashioning any study, or risk having one's study (rightly) attacked. One recent example is a flaw in EPA's powerful Landview program, which plots demographic information as well as a host of other information on the siting of toxic facilities. The location of the toxic facilities plotted on Landview is based on those facilities' self-reported latitude and longitude. If the location of the facility inadvertently is reported incorrectly by the facility itself (do you know the exact latitude and longitude of *your* office?), then that information is incorrectly entered into the Landview database. As the saying goes, garbage in, garbage out. When using Landview, we have had to double-check the actual location of facilities in the study area in question.

The Bottom Line

In sum, the experiences of the Center on Race, Poverty & the Environment show that demographic information can prove highly useful in local environmental justice struggles. Activists and advocates must remember, however, that like any other tactic in the struggle, demographic studies are only a means toward an end, not an end in themselves. The truth will not set us free, but it is an important ally in our struggle for environmental justice.

Key Research and Policy Issues Facing Environmental Justice

Bunyan Bryant

Environmental justice refers to those cultural norms, values, rules, regulations, behaviors, policies, and decisions that support sustainable communities, where people can interact with confidence that their environment is safe, nurturing, and productive. Environmental justice is served when people can realize their highest potential, without experiencing "isms." Environmental justice is supported by decent-paying and safe jobs, quality schools and recreation, decent housing and adequate health care, democratic decision-making, personal empowerment, and communities free of violence, drugs, and poverty. These are communities where both cultural and biological diversity are respected and highly revered and where distributive justice prevails.

The Environmental Justice Movement has generated a good deal of attention and debate. The arguments presented below are those I have encountered in various forms in conferences and in my work with community groups across the country. These arguments are by no means conclusive.

Argument One: Policy decisions should be based on a demonstration of a causal relationship, between a given chemical and a corresponding health effect.

Response: Causal relationships are most difficult to establish, even under the most ideal research conditions. The use of control groups using human beings to test the effect of certain toxic chemicals is unethical, thus rendering it extremely difficult to demonstrate causality. The best we can do in many instances is simply to demonstrate an association between certain chemicals and certain corresponding health effects. Given these uncertainties, an alternative view is to focus on pollution prevention.

Argument Two: Pollution control of harmful emissions by 90 percent is a reasonable policy to implement because it reduces emissions to acceptable risks and allows for reasonable profits.

Response: Not everyone agrees that pollution control of harmful emissions by 90 percent is safe, because some chemicals are persistent and fat-soluble. Synthetic chemicals, such as the pesticide DDT, radioactive materials, toxic mercury, and lead compounds, become more concentrated in fatty tissues of organisms at successively higher trophic levels in various food chains and food webs. These bioaccumulate or amplify themselves hundreds of thousands of times as they move up the food chain. By the time these chemicals reach the top of the food chain, they are highly concentrated and may present a public health problem. This is a key reason many environmental justice groups champion pollution prevention rather than pollution control.

Argument Three: Income is a greater explanatory variable than race in determining where pollution sources are located

Response: The results of sixteen urban, regional, and national studies demonstrate a consistent pattern: Where the distribution of pollution has been analyzed by both income and race (and where it has been possible to weigh the relative importance of each), race has been found, in most cases, to be more strongly related to the siting of polluting sources.

One response by industry is that their sitings are motivated not by race, but only by an attraction to low land values. However, it is possible to establish decisions motivated by race, so long as there is a pattern of locating LULUs (locally unwanted land uses) in communities of color more so than in poor white neighborhoods.

Argument Four: Census tract rather than zip code data is a more critical unit of analysis to test hypotheses regarding disparate impact.

Response: In recent years, an epistemological debate has been taking place about how to measure whether a particular practice has disproportionately harmed communities of color to a degree that far exceeds their percentage of the population. Many studies that attempt to show "disparate impact" have used either census tracts or zip codes as the unit of analysis. When census tracts are used, the relative weight of income often becomes a greater explanatory variable than race. When zip codes are used, we often get the opposite effect: the relative weight of race often becomes the greater explanatory variable. While some critics claim that census tracts are too small to yield meaningful results, other critics claim that zip codes are too large to yield meaningful results. There are compelling arguments on both sides. The question is: what is the appropriate unit of analysis to show disparate impact?

Argument Five: Too many environmental regulations hinder efficient business practices, causing loss of valuable time and profits.

Response: This assumption is not necessarily true. For example, although Germany and Japan have some of the most stringent environmental regulations in the world, their regulations have motivated industry to become more creative in developing pollution prevention and abatement technologies. Further, the development of technology helps move us toward an environmentally just society by creating safe, decent-paying jobs, and balances the national debt by exporting pollution prevention, abatement, and control technologies to Eastern Europe and developing countries. Finally, dismantling of environmental regulations often leaves people of color and low-income groups who live close to LULUs vulnerable and overexposed to toxic waste in the interest of corporate profits.

Argument Six: Government officials assume that community people are too irrational and that environmental problems are too complex for the public to understand. Therefore, policy decisions should be left to the experts.

Response: Community members can and must be intimately involved in shaping environmental policy. Few policies will work without the affected community having a vested interest in their success. In fact, studies have shown that the vast majority of community groups interact successfully with scientists (89 percent) and health professionals (73 percent). One scientist, Nicholas Freudenberg, found that these groups had a sophisticated understanding of the limits of scientific studies, issues of toxic waste and waste site remediation, and alternatives to area spraying of pesticides. He also found that these activist groups understood science more than policymakers realized.

Argument Seven: Positivism is a better way of knowing because it embraces a specific scientific methodology that reduces complex phenomena to hypotheses to be tested and quantified.

Response: It is often difficult for environmental justice to prevail when the locus of control is placed with the outside researcher. Positivism or traditional scientific methodology is not the only effective method of problem-solving. Positivism or traditional research is adversarial and contradictory: it often leaves laypeople confused about the certainty and solutions regarding exposure to environmental toxins.

Often scientists or policymakers cannot be certain about the singular or synergistic effects of chemicals on the health of people. This inability has created both anger and distrust of scientists and government officials and has led affected groups to question traditional science as the only legitimate and effective way of problem-solving.

Participatory research enables community people to become an integral part of the research process. Affected groups feel that environmental justice is better served if they themselves are involved in a participatory research process, where they at least share in the locus of control of the research process along with researchers and policymakers. They want to be involved in problem identification, questionnaire construction, data collection, and data analysis. Often the process of inclusion, decision-making, and respect for the affected populations may be more important and weigh heavier on satisfactory outcomes.

Argument Eight: Building incinerators or landfills will provide jobs and economic growth for local communities.

Response: Although new landfills and incinerators will provide jobs, the number of jobs they provide is relatively few. Technical jobs have a tendency to go to people outside the relevant community. Further, there exist serious potential health effects of exposing people to pollutants that arise from capacity expansion. The relevant question is not just simply job quantity but job quality.

In conclusion, we need to spend greater resources to clean up our pollution. If the effects of certain illnesses disappear, we then know that we have dealt with the general causes, even though we may never know the specific cause and effect outcomes. Second, we need to devote more research money to pollution prevention technologies. Third, we must ask ourselves the role population and consumption play in the unequal impacts of pollution on low-income communities and communities of color.

Part 6

Race, Poverty, and . . .

*A type of article PRRAC frequently commissions is designed to focus atten-
tion on the race/poverty dimensions of an issue that normally is not looked at
from that perspective. The template title we use for such pieces is "Race,
Poverty, and _____." In earlier years, such articles dealt with "The Deficit," "Disability," "Sustainable Communities," "Corporate Rule," "The 2000
Census," "Consumerism," and "The Internet."*

*This section contains articles on issues we have treated more recently:
"The Two-Tiered Financial Services System," "Transportation," "Corporate Welfare," "The Militarized Welfare State," "The Federal Reserve System," "Social Security," "Immigration," and "Globalization."*

Race, Poverty, and
the Two-Tiered
Financial Services System

Robert D. Manning

Those on the margins of the "economic miracle" of the late 1990s—the working poor, the very poor, the recently bankrupt, minorities, immigrants—encounter
a financial services system markedly different from what is offered to middle-
and upper-income, largely white consumers. This "second tier" system includes check cashing outlets, pawnshops, "low-end" credit cards, car title
loans (also known as car pawns), rent-to-own stores, "sub-prime" auto lenders, high-cost second mortgage companies, and "cash leasing" operations—
all of which charge usurious, but largely hidden, interest rates. In these murky
waters of fringe banking, corporate loan sharks feed on their hapless victims
with virtual impunity. Indeed, while middle-class demands for government
regulation are frequently heard following reports of billion dollar bank profits from ATM fees or "excessive" interest rates on 22.9 percent APR credit
cards, politicians have largely ignored the complaints of the working poor,
whose cost of credit typically exceeds 20 percent per month!

Deregulation of Financial Services: Where Did The Banks Go?

The deregulation of the U.S. banking industry, which began in earnest with
the "Reagan Revolution," achieved unparalleled success for its corporate

beneficiaries during the Clinton Administration: unprecedented industry concentration (mergers and acquisitions such as the BankAmerica-NationsBank
union); enormous bank profits (the highest in modern history); proliferation
of automated services (resulting in large-scale layoffs of low-wage workers
such as tellers); and the systematic dismantling of interstate banking restrictions (the 1927 McFadden Act) as well as Depression-era prohibitions (the
1933 Glass-Steagall Act) against the "cross-selling" of diverse financial services (wholesale versus retail banking). This latter shift is responsible for the
emergence of financial services conglomerates, such as Morgan Stanley Dean
Witter and Discover. Passage of the Financial Services Modernization Act in
October 1999 marked the end of traditional federal regulatory oversight of
the nation's banking system. Astoundingly, only a decade after the massive
public bail-out of the savings & loan industry following its deregulation in
1982, this legislation was hailed by its bipartisan political supporters as the
beginning of a new era of American banking. But to whose benefit?

For affluent urban neighborhoods and white suburban middle-class communities, financial deregulation has produced a proliferation of attractive bank
branches and financial products at moderate, albeit steadily rising, prices: today, three to four dollars ATM fees, twenty-nine dollar returned check fees, and
22.9 percent credit cards are common middle-class expenses. New upscale,
"child friendly," and coffee shop branches offer convenient and personalized
"relationship" banking with cordial account representatives and sophisticated
financial advisors. For the technologically proficient, huge investments in "virtual banking" have created user-friendly, online account systems primarily for
middle- and upper-income clients.

More instructively, approval of the 1998 Citicorp-Travelers merger—which
will produce the world's first trillion dollar financial services conglomerate
—is accelerating the marketing segmentation of consumer financial services.
That is, industry consolidation in the 1980s and early 1990s resulted in the
withdrawal of first-tier banks from low-income and minority (especially
urban) communities. A continuation of earlier geographic "redlining" policies, this trend has been accompanied by only minimal satisfaction of 1977
Community Reinvestment Act (CRA) requirements; banks want the deposits
of poor people but do not want to offer them moderate-cost loans. The most
recent Wall Street-financed "feeding frenzy" is spawning new consumer services conglomerates that are tailoring their marketing and investment policies toward ever higher-income households who use a wider range of financial
products and services.

For example, Citigroup's expanding array of consumer financial services
includes brokerage services (Solomon Smith Barney), mutual funds (Primerica
Financial), property/casualty insurance (Travelers Property Casualty), retire-

ment products (Travelers Life & Annuity), and real estate services (Citicorp Real Estate). Typically, the demand for these nonbanking products is relatively modest in lower-income, middle- and working-class neighborhoods. Hence, the new "full service" banks can be expected to embark on a secondary exodus from these communities in order to focus their resources on more affluent areas that utilize the full range of their consumer financial services. This is why the banking industry lobbies so aggressively to dismantle consumer privacy laws; intra-corporate sharing of consumer information is the cornerstone of the cross-marketing strategies of these evolving corporate behemoths. For instance, an auto loan application at a Citibank branch may result in solicitations from Travelers Life for insurance, Primerica Financial for mutual funds, or recently acquired Associated First Capital for "subprime" consumer loans.

As first-tier banks close their full-service branch locations in lower-income areas, they are being replaced with inferior substitutes, such as ATMs or limited-service supermarket offices. Together with sharply rising costs (high returned check fees and minimum checking account balances) that discourage participation by poor customers, it is not surprising that the number of households without bank accounts rose sharply during the first decade of deregulation: from 6.5 million (9 percent) in 1977 to 11.5 million (14.9 percent) in 1989. As of 2000, the most credible estimates are that 13 to 15 percent of U.S. households are "unbanked." However, it is the poorest of the poor who are the most disadvantaged by the "new era" of banking deregulation. For instance, in New York City's poverty-stricken South Bronx, Citigroup has only one consumer bank branch for approximately 500,000 residents.

Overall, only about 60 percent of families with less than $10,000 annual income are estimated to have banking accounts. And, according to a study of family wealth patterns in 1995, the highest consumer debt burdens are borne by these low-wage-earning households. For families with an annual income of less than $12,940 (lowest family income quintile), their mean consumer debt of $4,104 is an enormous 52.8 percent of their mean family income of $7,779. This compares with 27.9 percent consumer debt for the second quintile of family income ($12,940–$23,138), 22.6 percent for the third quintile ($23,139–$35,918), 20.3 percent for the fourth quintile ($35,919–$54,946), and 16.2 percent for the fifth quintile (over $54,946). Clearly, as evidenced by these consumer-debt-to-family-income ratios, the working poor are the most debt-dependent households in America. Therefore, the key issues concern where they get their consumer credit and how much it costs.

Corporate Loan Sharks: "Relationship Banking" for the Poor

Over the last decade, many myths concerning the undesirability of the working poor as consumer markets have been dispelled. These stereotypes of low-income households include: (1) they receive little corporate attention because of their modest disposable income; (2) they are served primarily by small "mom and pop" stores due to their limited growth potential; and (3) their irresponsible financial behavior justifies the punitive "stick" of high-cost credit. The latter view—a variant of the "Blame the Victim" syndrome—is a cultural legacy of the Puritan-influenced "morality of debt": usurious interest rates are socially justified as negative incentives to encourage more diligent work and frugal spending habits. Indeed, most customers of second-tier financial services are erroneously characterized as erratically employed, unmotivated, or welfare-dependent.

These enduring misconceptions have been revealed in the aftermath of the withdrawal of first-tier banks from poor and low-income communities. That is, the emergent vacuum of financial services has exacerbated the desperation of these residents and demonstrated their willingness to pay usurious interest rates. In the process, the employment dislocations caused by U.S. industrial restructuring; standard personal and social crises (divorce, illness, accidents, family emergencies); recurrent financial difficulties (auto repairs, health insurance problems); rapid growth of new immigrant communities (which lack relations with first-tier banks); dramatic rise in personal bankruptcies (6 million in the second half of the 1990s); enormous expansion of modern fringe banking outlets; and aggressive corporate marketing campaigns all have attracted millions of temporarily and persistently "broke" customers. And, as the social composition of fringe banking clients has become more diverse, so too has the array of new products and services—especially with the arrival of heavily indebted, middle-income households. In sum, the fringe banking sector has been swiftly transformed by the arrival of what Michael Hudson in his 1996 book termed the "Merchants of Misery."

Like the marketing of "relationship banking" in the first tier, the rapid expansion of the fringe banking sector has been fueled by the "merchandising of respect" to traditionally neglected customers and their neighborhoods, where, as Hudson put it, "The customer should feel like this is home, a place [to] feel comfortable and [where the staff] cares about you." In fact, the industry's market research has shown that potential customers are more pride- than price-sensitive, "craving good treatment even more than low prices." This has led to refurbishing the image and business practices of the second tier by "upscaling" showrooms, offering "state-of-the-art" models, emphasizing products with "premium" features, personalizing greetings to customers, introducing high-technology services, fostering long-term relationships with clients, and even sending cheap flower arrangements to funerals of local residents.

Pawnshops

The rapid expansion of second-tier financial services is illustrated by the enormous growth of its three main pillars. The first, pawnshops, has nearly tripled during this period of banking deregulation. From about 5,000 in 1985 to 7,760 in 1991 (across United States, but especially in the South), the number of pawnshops jumped to nearly 9,000 by the end of the recession in 1992. In 2000, distressed urban neighborhoods, and even new suburban strip malls, are littered with almost 14,000 pawn shops with names like National Pawnbrokers, EZPawn, First Cash, and Mr. Cash. Although about 30 percent of customers default on their "pawns," this financial loss (loans are typically 25 to 30 percent of appraised value of pawned items) is lauded as advantageous for clients. That is, failure to "redeem" a pawn (by not paying the monthly interest) is not reported to a credit bureau and thus does not adversely affect a client's credit history. Amazingly, many clients regard this as a desirable business practice. They have internalized the ideology of economic oppression: "you play, you pay"—even if the cards are stacked against you.

The largest chain of pawnshops, a subsidiary of Cash America Investments, illustrates the meteoric rise of the industry as well as the flow of second-tier profits to first-tier corporate balance sheets. Beginning with four Texas pawnshops in 1984, founder Jack Daugherty's ambitious vision featured an aggressive acquisition strategy that required a large infusion of investment capital. This was realized through a public stock offering in 1987 which made Cash America Pawn the first pawnshop company to be publicly traded on the New York Stock Exchange. At the time, its initial public offering was one of the most profitable of the pre-dot.com era as Cash America immediately became the industry leader. By 1991, it had grown to 178 pawnshops in 7 states. Four years later, Cash America had amassed a total of 365 stores, including operations in Europe; its first English pawnshops were acquired in 1992. Aided by its financial ties with Bank of America, Cash America has continued its expansion strategy, with 414 domestic and 50 foreign operating locations in 1999.

Pawnshops are the most popular source of collateralized credit, due to their confidentiality, quick access to small sums of money, and lack of negative reporting on one's personal credit history. Significantly, state regulations limit interest rates of pawned items to 5 percent per month (60 percent APR) in the District of Columbia while Virginia rates typically range from 10 to 15 percent per month and Maryland rates are as high as 20 percent per month.

Fieldwork in Virginia, the District of Columbia, and Maryland revealed a striking pattern of different interest rates according to the social class of a store's clientele. High-end or upper-middle class pawnshops offer monthly rates of 4 to 5 percent, negotiated on an individual basis. Loans can be made up to $50,000, and pawned items are typically designer jewelry, complete sliver sets, artwork (sometimes a real Picasso), and cars (BMWs, Mercedes). In unregulated areas, middle-income patrons are able to negotiate monthly rates of 10 to 15 percent (120 to 180 percent APR). Loans commonly range from $90 to $175.

In contrast, the poorest of the poor have no choice but to accept 20 percent per month to pawn Timex watches, Fender guitars, Magnavox televisions, power tools, bicycles, fishing equipment, and winter coats. Pawns are small and loans typically range from $25 to $75. Not incidentally, pawnshops have become active in the payday loan business (see below).

Significantly, mega-chain Cash America has eagerly explored expansion into other segments of fringe banking. It has established a separate subsidiary (Rent-A-Tire) that only offers new tires and wheels, increasing its outreach from four original stores to twenty-seven by 1999. More instructively, Cash American Investments, Inc. forged a joint venture with Wells Fargo Bank in 1999. Both companies are equal equity partners (45 percent) in Mr. Payroll, the first fully automated check cashing and financial services company. The Wells Fargo investment includes $21 million in equity capital and the assets of an existing network of 200 ATMs valued at $6 million.

Check Cashing Outlets

This latter business venture constitutes a technological "leap" into the second (albeit related) pillar of fringe banking services. The proliferation of check cashing outlets (CCOs) reflects both the rapid growth of the "self-banked" population and the magnitude of its financial transactions. The primary service provided by CCOs is cashing checks for a fee (typically 1 to 4 percent), and most offer ancillary services, such as money orders, "pay-day" loans, prepaid phone cards, lottery tickets, fax transmissions, notary services, mailbox and postal services, and copying machines. Between 1985 and 1987, the number of CCOs increased moderately—from about 2,000 to 2,151. Over the next five years, however, they more than doubled to almost 5,000 and then stabilized at about 5,500 in 1999. But this modest growth trend is not an indication that the market is nearing its saturation point. Rather, it reflects the expansion of pawnshops into this highly profitable segment of fringe banking services. Overall, industry reports estimate that CCO revenues will approach $2 billion by 2000.

The largest check-cashing company is ACE Cash Express. Established in 1968, its corporate literature describes it as a "significant provider of related retail financial services." Twenty-two years later, ACE celebrated its one-thousandth location: 854 company-owned stores and 146 franchises. Initially, ACE's impressive expansion pace had been propelled by its financial ties with American Express. More recently, however, it has partnered with other corporations in an effort to modernize its processing systems and offer new financial services. For example, in collaboration with Travelers Express Company, ACE now provides universal bill payment service for "walk-in" customers in all of its stores. This state-of-the-art system enables ACE to accept and process any retail bill that can be prepaid through an Internet payment system; it is the same as "home" banking on a PC via the Internet. ACE is also entering the new market of automated check cashing services which was pioneered by Cash America's Mr. Payroll. In late 1999, ACE introduced twenty-one advanced function ATMs in the Dallas-Ft. Worth area. The machines are very user-friendly, with touch screen menus that can verify personal information and disburse cash within a few seconds. And ACE has negotiated an exclusive agreement with ePOWER International to provide prepaid Internet service through its retail network. Consequently, those who cannot enter the high-tech financial corridors of first-tier banks can now enter through the "back door" of the second tier. But, as will be shown, the financial "toll" is very expensive.

Although modernizing its processing systems and offering high-tech services are important goals (its secondary objective is upgrading its corporate image), ACE has continued to diversify into traditional fringe banking services. For example, ACE is now allied with Instant Auto Insurance, an underwriter of "specialty" (high-risk) insurance. Customers can discuss policies over the phone with licensed insurance agents and then activate their new policies at an affiliated ACE store; as of 2000, this service is offered at 385 locations in 10 major markets. Not incidentally, diversification into other financial services has been constrained by ACE's limited access to corporate credit. With over 2 million monthly customers, the volume of cash transactions at ACE locations has reached staggering proportions. In 1999, ACE cashed $2.9 billion worth of checks and issued 14.5 million money orders totaling $1.9 billion. These enormous daily cash demands necessitate large lines of credit from first-tier banks at favorable rates. Indeed, without reliable access to a cash spigot, second-tier fringe banks would wither away from credit starvation. As a result, ACE has partnered with Goleta National Bank and now processes small consumer loans ($100–$500) and money orders (maximum: $500)—the most profitable services of CCOs.

Rent-to-Own

The final pillar of the fringe banking sector is the burgeoning "lease ownership" or "rent-to-own" industry. Located usually in low-rent storefronts or strip malls, its corporate landscape features names like Buddy's, Rent-Way, and Rent-A-Center. Flyers and direct-mail advertisements regularly flood the mailboxes of poor communities, much like the arrival of "pre-approved" credit card applications in middle-class neighborhoods. Although they extol the opportunity to "*Buy It! Charge It! Lease It!*," these pronouncements have a hollow ring, since few would shop there if they had cash or even credit card options. As "retail rejects," the rapidly growing "self-banked" understand that these high-pressure stores are their only opportunity to enjoy the fruits of the longest economic expansion in U.S. history. Like pawnshops, whose patrons often refer to them as the "poor man's bank," rent-to-own stores are often viewed by their clients as a "democratic" option for the poor because "Everyone is Pre-Approved . . . No Credit [is] Needed" and thus "no dream is denied." Of course, the cost of fulfilling these consumer dreams usually exceeds state usury statutes, which is the reason the financial terms are not clearly explained. Even so, the industry has experienced tremendous growth: from 2,000 stores in 1982 to nearly 7,000 in 1996. As of 2000, there are about 7,500 rent-to-own stores that serve over 3.3 million customers. In 1999, total revenues were estimated at $4.7 billion, up from $3.6 billion in 1991.

Rent-to-own stores have expanded to satisfy the consumption demands of the working poor, recently bankrupt, divorced, students, new immigrants, government assistance recipients, and those living in the informal economy. The most popular merchandise include stereos, TV/VCRs, sofas, dining sets, kitchen appliances, sofas, bedroom furniture, washer/dryers, and jewelry. Rent-to-own stores appeal to those seeking instant gratification, with unstable lifestyles, and participating in the cash-only economy. Weekly payments tend to obscure usurious interest rates; same-day delivery and return policies appeal to those experiencing recent lifestyle transitions; and high-pressure sales staff are trained to prey on low-income consumption desires.

Customers who "purchase" through a "lease ownership" plan do not accumulate any equity until the entire principal and all interest is paid in full. As a result, with APRs that commonly range from 180 to 360 percent, the poor pay excessively for their goods and rarely accumulate much equity for future emergency loans; pawnshops must verify that rent-to-own products have been paid off before they will approve a loan on an item identified as rent-to-own in origin. An example of rent-to-own economics, using fieldwork data from Rent-A-Center and Circuit City stores in suburban Maryland, both accessible by public transportation: A new 19-inch Magnavox TV lists for $195.99 at Circuit City and will cost $233.37 if financed with the company's own credit card (less if the customer uses a personal bank credit card) for seventy-eight weeks; at Rent-A-Center, the same model television set will cost $779.22 after it is finally paid off, seventy-eight weeks later.

The undisputed leader in the "lease ownership" industry is Rent-A-Center (RAC), which owns 26 percent of all rent-to-own stores. Like a minnow swallowing a whale, it controlled only twenty-seven stores in 1993 before embarking on its extraordinary expansion strategy. Beginning in May 1998, RAC purchased Central Rents and its 176 stores for $100 million in cash. This transaction was a mere preclude to its monumental acquisition three months later: Thorn Americas. For $900 million in cash plus assumption of Thorn's outstanding debts, RAC received the industry's prize network of 1,409 company-owned outlets and 65 franchise stores in 49 states and the District of Columbia; $260 million in preferred stock was issued to help finance the Thorn purchase (most through an affiliate of Bear Stearns, & Co).

As of 2000, RAC owns and operates over 2,300 stores in 50 states, Washington, DC, and Puerto Rico. In the just the first quarter of 1999, RAC reported spending $109.3 million on new rental merchandise. As an exemplar of buying cheap and selling dear, the financial success of RAC is primarily due to its relations with first-tier banks, which explains the enormous "spread" between the corporate cost of borrowing and the returns on lending to the poor. That is, RAC reports that its "average rate on outstanding borrowing was 7.9 percent" APR in 1999—on a total debt of nearly $1 billion—while the rent-to-own rate to its customers, as noted above, typically ranges from 180 to 360 percent APR. Also these usurious rates do not include multiple resale of individual items due to repossession. Overall, only about one-fourth of rent-to-own customers ever realize their dream of ownership, and three-fourths of all leased items are returned within four months.

The High Cost of Being Poor

The most distinguishing feature of second-tier financial services is their high cost. As shown in the accompanying table, based primarily on field-work in Metropolitan Washington, DC, the annual percentage interest rate (APR) of most unregulated financial services ranges from 180 to 360 percent, with the exception of "cash leasing" at 730 percent APR and some especially exploitative "payday loans" that range from 442 to 988 percent APR. Services include cashing payroll or government checks at 1 to 2 percent of the face value (essentially a two-to-three-day loan at an APR from 182 to 365 percent); "payday loans" from check cashing stores and pawn-shops for a maximum of $300 to $600 at 15 to 20 percent (312 to 391 percent APR), which are transacted as post-dated checks (two to three days to two weeks); and tax return loans (10 percent for an approximately 10- to 15-day loan or 240 to 360 percent APR).

Overall, the annual cost of fringe banking services (check cashing, money orders, utility payments) in the early 1990s has been estimated at $199 for those with take-home pay of $10,000, rising to $313 for $16,500 in take-home pay, and jumping to $444 for household take-home pay of $24,000. This cost has been rising due to the growing use of "payday" and "car title" loans. By comparison, the annual cost for a traditional checking account with less than a $300 minimum balance has nearly doubled, from about $60 per year in 1991 to over $100 today.

Although industry reports generally explain that patrons prefer using check cashing outlets, primarily due to convenience (location, extended hours), interviews reveal that it is the policies of first-tier banks that drive lower-income, working-class, and immigrant clients to more costly check cashing outlets and the dwindling numbers of small mom-and-pop stores. These policies include costly returned check fees and requirements for extensive documentation, such as utility bills, payroll check receipts, and driver's license or passport. Additionally, patrons express a distrust of first-tier financial institutions, concern over inadequate English skills (among immigrants), and fear that financial transactions will be tracked by government and corporate agencies. Although long lines at check cashing outlets can be time-consuming, customers report that the situation is no worse than first-tier banks and, more importantly, one avoids the condescension so often experienced at banks. Furthermore, automated check cashing systems are making the process more convenient. The sudden increase in hi-tech investment by CCOs is due to the tremendous profitability of payday loans, which are essentially post-dated checks that are cashed at a substantial premium; nationally, they average 15 to 18 percent for two weeks. According to a 1999 survey of twenty states conducted by the Consumer Federation of America and U.S. Public Interest Research Group, payday loans ranged from 260 to 988 percent; the average APR was 474 percent. As of 2000, only nineteen states prohibit payday lending through statutory interest rate ceilings and/or usury laws.

Car Title Loans

With names like Money Mart, Kwicash, and Last Chance Finance, car title loans have become increasingly common. Their popularity is due to the larger loan value and ease of appraising the value of the automobile. Customers simply provide their car title for collateral, which reduces space and inventory requirements, lowering the store's overhead costs. Loans are commonly used to stave off eviction, restore utility service, or avoid possible arrest due to child support arrears or delinquent taxes. In Florida, abusive lending and collection/repossession practices, as well as employment disruption due to loss of transportation, has produced a broad political coalition whose objective is to reform this "sub-prime" loan industry.

Cash Leasing

The most expensive credit offered by corporate loan sharks is the "cash lease" scam of companies like "Cash-2–U Leasing." In order to evade state usury laws, money is technically "leased" rather than loaned, at the cost of 30 percent per fifteen days. A maximum of $300 can be leased at any time. Clients must have an active checking account and verify ownership of at least three electronic items that can be pledged as collateral, such as a stereo, computer, or television. Advertising to low-income and economically distressed groups is aggressive, with particular attention to maxed-out, lower-income, working-class minorities and, more recently, to college students. Radio and print advertising target racial and ethnic minority communities, with the emphasis on "helping you out" during those "cash crunch periods," especially during the holiday gift-giving season. The APR is a whopping 730 percent.

Exploitative Credit Cards

A final trend concerns the direct marketing of highly exploitative credit cards. For those with bad credit histories, a collateralized "secured" credit card that requires processing and membership fees of over $100 for the privilege of borrowing your own money at 21.9 percent APR (secured through a savings account held in escrow by the credit card company) may be worth the price for beginning the tortuous process of rebuilding a "worthy" credit history. Others desperately seek a credit card as a "bank account of last resort." But an investigation of recent marketing to the poor reveals a new and extraordinarily costly type of credit card that imposes the purchase of unwanted educational materials and high membership fees with little available credit. This is illustrated by the outrageous terms of the United Credit National Bank Visa. Its direct mail solicitation declares, "ACE VISA-GUARANTEED ISSUE or we'll send you $100.00! (See inside for details.)" For those who bother to read the fine print, and it is very small, the terms of the contract are:

> [I]nitial credit line will be at least $400.00. By accepting this offer, you agree to subscribe to the American Credit Educator Financial and Credit Education Program. The ACE program costs $289.00 plus $11.95 for shipping and handling plus $19.00 Processing Fee—a small price to pay compared to the high cost of bad credit! The Annual Card Fee [is] $49.00. . . . For your convenience, we will charge these costs to your new ACE Affinity VISA card. [They] are considered Finance charges for Truth-In-Lending Act purposes.

Second-Tier Banks: Short-term and Annual Percentage Interest Rates [APR]

Check cashing	Pawnshop loan*	Car title loan**	Rent-to- own	Cash leasing	Payday loans
		Short-term			
1–2% per 2–3 days	5%–20% per month	22% per month	15–30% per month	30% per 15 days	11–21% per 2 weeks
		Annual			
182–365%	60% (regulated) 120–240% (unregulated)	264%	180–360%	730%	286–546%***

Sources: Author's field survey of metropolitan Washington, DC area.

Robert D. Manning and Liana Prieto. "I Have to Pawn to Pay For My Credit Cards: Post-Industrial Inequality and the Social Stratification of American Pawnshops." Unpublished manuscript, Department of Sociology, Georgetown University, 1999.

*The District of Columbia restricts pawnshop loans to a maximum of 5 percent per month (60 percent APR), although related fees can increase the total loan cost. In Virginia, monthly rates typically range from 10 percent to 15 percent (120–180 percent APR), and in Maryland from 15 percent to 20 percent (180–240 percent APR).

**Established by state and local usury laws. For example, Illinois does not have an interest rate ceiling for consumer loans, while New Jersey limits most consumer loans to a maximum of 30 percent APR. Florida, the nation's car loan capital, has legislatively mandated a 22 percent maximum monthly interest rate. In metropolitan Washington, DC, car title loans (auto pawns) are negotiated on an individual basis, depending upon the value of the car.

***In a 1999 national survey of 230 payday lenders in 20 states, conducted by Consumer Federation of America and Public Interest Research Group, APR ranged from 260 to 988 percent, and average APR was 474 percent. Nationally, only 19 states currently prohibit payday lending through statutory interest rate ceilings and/or usury laws.

Progressive Social Policy/Consumer Action Organizations

- ACORN, 739 8th St. SE, Washington, DC 20003; 202/547–2500; www.acorn.org
- Consumer Federation of America, 1424 16th St. NW, #604, Washington, DC 20036; 202/387–6121; www.consumerfed.org
- Consumers Union, 1666 Connecticut Ave. NW, #310, Washington, DC 20036; 202/462–6262; www.consumersunion.org
- National Community Reinvestment Coalition, 733 15th St. NW, #540, Washington, DC 20005; 202/628–8866; www.ncrc.org
- National Consumer Law Center, 18 Tremont St., #400, Boston, MA 02108; 617/523–8010; www.consumerlaw.org
- U.S. Public Interest Research Group, 218 D St. SE, Washington, DC 20003; 202/546–9707; www.pirg.org

Incredibly, an unsuspecting applicant could pay $369 for a net credit line of only $31 at a moderate 19.8 percent APR!

The Bottom Line

The social and economic integration of second-tier financial services underscores the spiraling cost of credit for the most economically disadvantaged. That is, inflated finance charges dramatically increase the cost of living in neighborhoods with large numbers of low-income and minority residents. Furthermore, the credit strategies of the working poor are becoming more complex than can be possibly understood by examining discrete segments of the fringe banking system. Imagine trying to estimate the cost of consumer credit where $200 television sets cost over $700 and then are pawned for $45 at a 20 percent monthly interest rate. To make matters worse, police and newspaper reports indicate that check-cashing patrons are increasingly vulnerable to robberies after leaving these stores; unlike the first-tier, second-tier banks rarely employ armed security staff. Consequently, as long as corporate loan sharks are not effectively regulated, the most economically disadvantaged will find themselves ensnared in enduring forms of debt peonage relationships.

Of course, the first-tier banks will feign ignorance and decry the high cost of conducting business with the poor. They may even have the audacity to trumpet their business practices as a valuable community service by "democratizing" access to consumer credit that otherwise would be denied to "needy" residents of disadvantaged communities. The reality, of course, is that Citigroup is making huge profits reselling sub-prime loans through its Solomon Smith Barney subsidiary. Others such as Wells Fargo Bank, Eagle National Bank, Banco Popular, and Goleta National Bank are making huge profits on payday loans and providing the lines of credit for check cashing outlets. Bank of America, through its relations with Cash America, and American Express, through its relations with ACE, profit handsomely through their direct and indirect ties. In addition, brokerage companies are making millions of dollars in commissions selling the stocks and bonds of second-tier banks, while mutual fund managers are eager to benefit from their appreciating fringe bank stock portfolio. In the process, the growing chasm between the rich and poor means that low-income households will continue to depend on money orders rather than personal checks and pawnshops rather than credit cards. It is these linkages between poverty, race, and corporate greed that underscore the largely ignored social costs imposed by the rampaging bulls of Wall Street.

Race, Poverty, and Transportation

Rich Stolz

For decades, minorities have fought against the discriminatory impact of transportation planning and practices in their communities.

Transportation equity was a critical element of the Civil Rights Movement from its beginning. In 1946, the Supreme Court ruled segregation in interstate bus travel unconstitutional. It was no accident that Rosa Parks chose as her protest the laws requiring Blacks to ride in the back of the bus in Montgomery, Alabama in 1955. Several years later, the Freedom Rides through the South provided powerful testament to the extraordinary courage of individuals acting together to change what is wrong about society.

Today, the movement continues, and the goal is basically the same: a publicly funded system, paid for by all, should benefit all equally. But as is often the case with issues that intersect race and poverty, easier said than done.

A Race and Transportation Roadmap

Transportation is a fundamental, yet often overlooked, element in the struggle for equality of opportunity. Access to reliable means of transportation impacts quality of life, financial security, and freedom of movement. Too often, poor and minority people find themselves unable to find or get to their jobs or the grocery store, to bring their children to childcare, or to accomplish all the other daily tasks many of us take for granted. These difficulties speak to symptoms of poverty and transportation inequity.

Assets and income of course have a lot to do with transportation access. Studies show that only 6 percent of welfare recipients own cars, and of course lack of transportation is a critical barrier to finding and keeping a job. Without access to their own vehicles, many poor and minority households must rely on public transportation or fragile arrangements with friends and neighbors.

Poor and minority households usually must devote a larger percentage of their income to transportation-related expenses. Adding insult to injury, in most parts of the country low-income households must put up with inadequate and often deteriorating public transportation systems.

Efforts to address these unfair burdens on low-income and minority households are constantly frustrated by archaic and unaccountable transportation planning practices that reflect the political strength of white and suburban residents and businesses and the road-building industries.

Organizations seeking to challenge "business as usual" are stymied by the fact that the federal government has no accurate, coordinated, or reliable system to track how its own transportation funds are spent. And people at the local or state level looking for this information generally encounter significant resistance or incomprehensible spreadsheets. Despite new federal laws in the last decade and some progress in a handful of locations across the nation, transportation planning practices still lack meaningful opportunities for public participation and fail to adequately address inequitable impacts on minorities.

Low-income and minority communities also bear the brunt of transportation infrastructure improvements that sweep through and destroy neighborhoods. The federal highway program of the 1950s and 1960s, like the urban renewal program, displaced tens of thousands of mainly low-income, minority households. Currently, for example, in Seattle, community activists are fighting to prevent a proposed light rail system from displacing minority-owned businesses. In most cases, activists are unable to prevent highways from cutting their communities in half, and more often than not the jobs created by these projects are inaccessible to the unemployed residents of these neighborhoods.

Exacerbating unfair distribution of burdens on minority communities are significant demographic and political changes over the last several decades. Increasingly, metropolitan regions are divided, on the one hand, between low-income minority enclaves, usually concentrated in central cities, or unstable older communities, and on the other hand, wealthier, politically powerful communities often located in suburbs. As jobs and wealth move further out into suburban communities, poor and minority households in and near central cities are increasingly isolated from economic opportunity. Transportation is a key potential element to bridge this distance.

The fruits of inequitable transportation planning practices and policies are pervasive unemployment in low-income communities, higher rates of asthma and other pollution-related problems among children of color, and compromised public safety. An outrageous 1995 incident was the death of Cynthia Wiggins in Buffalo, New York, killed when forced to cross a seven-lane highway in order to get from the bus stop to her job in a suburban mall because the mall barred city buses from driving into its parking lot (although suburban and tourist buses were permitted).

What Is Transportation Equity?

An equitable transportation system would:

- ensure opportunities for meaningful public involvement in the transportation planning process;

- be held to standards of public accountability and financial transparency;
- equally prioritize efforts to revitalize poor and minority communities in addition to expanding infrastructure;
- ensure that benefits and burdens from transportation projects (e.g., jobs, pollution, etc.) are equally distributed across all income levels;
- provide high-quality services to low-income minority communities.

Quite a bit still separates vision from reality. But community groups and some transportation planners are attempting to envision what such a system might look like. In the meantime, several tools are available to people working to improve transportation equity in their own communities:

Transportation Equity Act for the Twenty-First Century

In 1991, Congress enacted the Intermodal Surface Transportation Efficiency Act (ISTEA), which established a new focus on regional planning and community involvement in the nation's transportation system. These principles were carried over into the 1998 Transportation Equity Act for the 21st Century (TEA-21). Thanks to activism by community organizations, TEA-21 re-authorized processes that support regional planning and accountability, and added requirements meant to ensure public involvement and access to information in the transportation planning process.

Title VI of the 1964 Civil Rights Act

This provision prohibits discrimination by any program receiving federal assistance. Under Title VI, it is only necessary to demonstrate discriminatory effect rather than the more difficult threshold of discriminatory intent.

Executive Order 12898 on Environmental Justice

In 1994, President Clinton issued an executive order on environmental justice directing federal agencies to conduct their programs, policies, and activities that affect human health and the environment so as to ensure that people may participate in planning processes that impact their communities, and are not unfairly denied benefits or discriminated against on the basis of their race, color, or national origin. Authority for this order derives from Title VI.

In 1998, the Federal Highway Administration released an internal guidance on environmental justice, addressing the agency's intent to prevent disproportionately high and adverse impacts on minority and low-income communities.

Joint Transportation Guidance on Title VI Requirements

In 1999, the Federal Highway Administration and Federal Transit Administrations released further guidance with respect to implementation of Title VI requirements in metropolitan and statewide transportation planning. The guidance directs federal transportation agencies to scrutinize potential civil rights and environmental justice impacts in the metropolitan certification process.

Clean Air Act

In jurisdictions not in compliance with federal air quality guidelines, communities have additional leverage to try to influence transportation planning decisions. Failure to attain federal air quality standards could lead to diverting funding from pollution-causing projects to environmentally friendly investments.

Jobs Access and Reverse Commute Competitive Grant Program

As part of TEA-21, Congress created the Jobs Access Grant Program to supplement welfare-to-work transportation activities. Authorized for five years beginning with FY1999, and administered by the Federal Transit Administration, the program funds jobs access projects that provide transportation options to welfare recipients and other low-income people trying to get to jobs and job opportunities, as well as work-related support services like child care and job training.

A Growing Movement

Montgomery, Alabama: Montgomery Transportation Coalition

If Rosa Parks were in Montgomery today, she would be lucky to catch a bus, let alone ride in a front seat. Used primarily by low-income African Americans, Montgomery's transit system came under a nearly fatal attack in 1998. The mayor abandoned the city's fixed route bus system and implemented a new Demand And Response Transit (DART) system. Montgomery now has no bus stops, bus shelters, or bus routes. And until late 1999, the transit system was in danger of being scrapped entirely for lack of riders.

These changes took place amid growing racial geographic segregation and tension between white and Black members of the city council. The city described its actions publicly as fiscally necessary, even as Montgomery received large federal transportation subsidies to fund renovation of non-transit improvements. Poor Blacks felt the brunt of the change as they continued to struggle to get to work and other destinations.

Under new city leadership, and growing support for a reliable public transportation system, spurred by the Montgomery Transportation Coalition and its allies, a proposal for a return to fixed bus routes has been floated. Montgomery demonstrates how politically vulnerable basic services most people take for granted can be to racist politics.

Northwest Indiana: Interfaith Federation

In 1999, the Interfaith Federation of Northwest Indiana (a coalition of congregations in the central cities and suburbs of Gary, Hammond, and East Chicago) succeeded in persuading the federal government to hold the Northwest Indiana regional transportation planning agency accountable for that region's discriminatory transportation system. Every three years, metropolitan planning organizations (MPOs), which are responsible for devising plans for how federal funds should be spent regionally, must be examined by the federal government to ensure that their activities are in compliance with federal laws and regulations. If an MPO is decertified or found out of compliance, it may be forced to temporarily forfeit federal transportation funds for its region.

The Federation demonstrated that years of poor planning had placed disparate burdens on the region's minority and low-income population, subjecting it to pollution and harmful health impacts, lack of access to jobs and economic opportunity, and contributing to suburban sprawl and divestments from urban centers. The MPO was therefore "conditionally" certified, pending corrective actions. In fall 2000, the federal government found that the regional agency had made sufficient progress to meet the corrective actions required by the conditional certification, but will continue to monitor the MPO as it implements its environmental justice plan.

The Interfaith Federation is part of a broader network of congregation-based organizations supported by the Gamaliel Foundation. The Foundation has prioritized transportation equity as a means to address broader issues of regional inequity, segregation, and concentrated poverty.

Los Angeles: Labor/Community Strategy Center

For the better part of the last decade, the Los Angeles Bus Riders Union, the Labor/Community Strategy Center, and legal allies have fought a drawn-out battle with the Los Angeles Metropolitan Transportation Authority. The Center, aided by the NAACP Legal Defense and Educational Fund, demonstrated that the MTA's actions had discriminatory impact on poor minority bus riders, on the basis of Title VI and the Equal Protection Clause of the Fourteenth Amendment of the U.S. Constitution.

Los Angeles bus riders experienced worse services, less security, and benefited from fewer subsidies than rail riders. Almost 94 percent of the MTA's users are bus riders; 80 percent of them are people of color. The MTA spent only 30 percent of its resources on buses, but 70 percent on rail, which carries only 6 percent of its riders and serves a primarily white ridership. The MTA also spent significantly more money per rider on security to protect rail users than it did on bus users.

A court-ordered consent decree in 1996 required the MTA to address the needs of transit-dependent residents in future long-range plans, major capital projects, and annual budgets. It also required the MTA to invest $1 billion more in transit, including mandated bus purchases, to improve the regional transit system and reduce overcrowding.

Los Angeles: Alameda Corridor Jobs Coalition

In 1998, the Alameda Corridor Jobs Coalition (ACJC) secured a significant victory for minority and low-income people seeking work in transportation construction projects. The Alameda Corridor construction project, a railroad project, involves digging a twenty-mile long, thirty-foot deep, fifty-foot wide trench, lining it with concrete, and then building twenty-six highway overpasses over it. The tunnel is designed to speed movement of cargo from the region's ports to rail yards near downtown Los Angeles.

As is often the case, this major project will cut through and disrupt primarily low-income, minority communities. Several years earlier, the Century Freeway was built right next to two of the region's largest public housing developments. The people living there got all of the noise, dirt, and traffic, but none of the jobs. With this new project coming through, residents sought some return for the disruption.

ACJC successfully organized to win a major hiring agreement with the Alameda Corridor Transportation Authority. It guarantees that 30 percent of all hours worked by new hires will go to local community residents.

ACJC's victory speaks to ongoing struggles within the transportation industry to diversify its workforce to embrace women and minorities and women- and minority-owned businesses.

The Transportation Equity Network

In 1997, a national coalition of grassroots organizations, staffed by the Center for Community Change, came together to find common issues that it could insert into the Congressional debate on the reauthorization of ISTEA. This coalition, the Transportation Equity Network (TEN), successfully persuaded Congress to include in TEA-21 a requirement for public involvement

---

Additional Resources

Bullard, Robert D. and Glenn S. Johnson, eds. *Just Transportation: Disman-
tling Race and Class Barriers to Mobility.* Stony Creek, CT: New Society
Publishers, 1997.
"Getting to Work, An Organizer's Guide to Transportation Equity." Washing-
ton, DC: Center for Community Change, 1998. Available from the Center
for Community Change. $8. 202/342–0567.
"Helping Ourselves; How to Design and Implement Transportation Solutions
in Low-Income Communities." San Francisco: Bay Area Transportation
Choices Forum, 1999. Available from the Bay Area Transportation Choices
Forum. $8. 510/540–7220.
University of Toledo Urban Affairs Center. "Transportation Information Study:
Getting on Track." May 2000. Available at http://uac.rdp.utoledo.edu or call
419/530–3591

- The Center for Community Change. www.communitychange.org/trans-
portation
- The Environmental Justice Resource Center. www.ejrc.cau.edu
- Federal Highway Administration. www.fhwa.dot.gov
- Federal Transit Administration. www.fta.dot.gov
- The Gamaliel Foundation. www.gamaliel.org.
- The Labor/Community Strategy Center. www.igc.apc.org/lctr
- The Surface Transportation Policy Project. www.transact.org
- U.S. Department of Transportation. www.dot.gov

---

by transit-dependent constituencies; a statutory requirement for public involvement in the metropolitan planning certification process; and a requirement that
MPOs provide a public accounting for how federal funds are spent in their
regions. TEN also participated in the national coalition that helped win the federal Jobs Access and Reverse Commute competitive grant program.

The organizations involved in TEN include faith-based coalitions fighting for metropolitan equity among suburbs and central cities, statewide coalitions advocating for improved welfare-to-work programs, neighborhood
groups organizing to win jobs for low-income members, and membership
organizations trying to have a say in the transportation decisions that impact
their lives. TEN demonstrates that a broad-based constituency can be built
around race and transportation issues.

TEN and the Center for Community Change have also begun working
closely with new national and local allies. Environmental groups concerned
with air quality and containing suburban sprawl, civil rights organizations
concerned with disparate impacts of transportation investment, community
development groups interested in transportation-related strategies for com-

munity revitalization, and human needs organizations concerned with welfare reform all are coming together around transportation issues.

TEN is working to ensure that the regulations implementing its victories in TEA-21 are written in a manner that will meet the needs of local communities and organizations. Activists and their allies in the transportation planning world across the country are working to develop methods to use Geographic Information Systems (GIS) to illustrate, or map, how transportation investments are distributed across regions. Taking this a step further may allow communities to demonstrate visually the benefits and burdens of transportation projects on different populations. TEN advocates for federal regulations and policies that will make such analyses an industry standard.

The intersections among race, poverty, and transportation are complex. They involve federal law and local planning processes. They challenge governments to describe what is meant by compliance with civil rights laws and principles of environmental justice. They are given meaning by community activism and the experiences of everyday people.

Race, Poverty, and Corporate Welfare

Greg LeRoy

The last two decades have seen an explosion in the number and value of state and local "business incentives" enacted in the name of economic development. Often these subsidies are promoted as a way to alleviate poverty or reverse urban decline.

However, many such programs have become so deregulated that their original targeting intentions have been subverted. Some very disturbing evidence is now emerging that instead of reducing poverty or discrimination, taxpayer money that some call "corporate welfare" is actually subsidizing poverty and fueling racial inequality.

While the evidence is disturbing, news from the organizing front lines is heartening. Armed with breakthrough disclosure data and a trickle of foundation support, a small but determined network of nonprofit groups is aggressively rewriting the policy dialogue about development. Coalescing with many diverse movements, these groups are winning dozens of accountability precedents. Their breakthroughs suggest that "back to basics"—raising workers' living standards—is winning the day.

Development Subsidies: Mushrooming and Loose

A new book (Kenneth Thomas, *Competing for Capital: Europe and North America in a Global Era*, University of Chicago Press, 2000) estimates that states, cities, and counties spend $48.8 billion a year for economic development. Only an estimate is possible because very few states report development budgets that combine spending in both appropriations and the tax code. Even fewer have centralized records about local property tax abatements.

The spending trend is undeniably up. Twenty years ago, only twenty-one states granted corporate income-tax credits; today, thirty-seven do. Then, only nine states granted tax credits for research and development; today, thirty-six allow them. Only twenty states provided low-interest, tax-exempt bond financing; today, forty-four provide it.

It's not at all unusual now to find deals worth more than $100,000 per job; five of Good Jobs First's "Terrible Ten Candy Store Deals of 1998" exceeded that price—including one at *$8.8 million* per job!

If such spending benefited needy workers, perhaps it could be justified. But many such programs have become so deregulated as to moot anti-poverty intentions. For example, Louisiana, Arkansas, and Ohio now have a total of 2,360 enterprise zones. Turning an anti-blight program into a "gimme" cancels the original targeting intent.

Other subsidies undermine public services critical to equal opportunity. For example, the Louisiana Coalition for Tax Justice found that the state's industrial property tax exemptions for the 1980s cost schools $941 million. Louisiana has one of the nation's lowest high school graduation rates. (And almost three-fourths of the subsidized projects created no new jobs!)

Despite this boom in development spending, real wages for average working people have declined about 15 percent since the late 1970s, and the share of working poor has increased by 5 percent. How could so much be spent for such bad results? The answer: most development subsidies still lack basic safeguards, such as real targeting, wage floors, employer-paid health care, or full-time work requirements.

Job Subsidies and Equal Opportunity

There is also a small but disturbing body of evidence that development subsidies are being used by employers with discriminatory employment practices or by industries that are moving good jobs away from people of color.

For example, a 1984 analysis of industrial revenue bonds (IRBs— low-interest loans supported by tax-free bonds) by the Illinois Advisory Committee to the U.S. Commission on Civil Rights found an adverse effect on minority workers and entrepreneurs. They examined 104 IRBs in the Chicago area. In fully one-fifth of the deals, either the recipient company or the bank that bought the bonds had recently violated the federal fair employment rules of the Equal Employment Opportunity Commission.

The study also found that only three IRBs went to African American-owned firms, one to an Asian-owned firm, and none to Hispanic-owned firms. At one-third of the companies, Black workers were far underrepresented compared to the area's overall labor market. Two-thirds of the companies also had disproportionately small Hispanic employment, and more than half had disproportionately small female workforces.

The auto industry presents a troubling multi-state story. Since the mid-1980s, there have been massive auto investments in the United States by foreign car makers, especially Japanese firms, building more than 300 plants. Virtually all received multiple state and local development subsidies. This new "auto belt" is concentrated in Kentucky, Tennessee, southern Indiana and Ohio, South Carolina, and Alabama, far away from traditional metal-working cities, such as Detroit and Cleveland, with large minority workforces. A 1988 study by University of Michigan professors Robert Cole and Donald Deskins of three early assembly "transplants" (Honda, Nissan, and Mazda) and fifty-one Japanese parts plants or "subplants" found that African-American workers were significantly underrepresented at almost all of the fifty-four plants.

A few transplants have been charged with discriminatory practices, such as defining recruitment territories that excluded urban areas with minority populations. Cole and Deskins found that Blacks comprised 2.8 percent of Honda's Marysville, Ohio workforce, although they made up 10.5 percent of that area's available workforce.

The Woodstock Institute examined the geographic distribution of Small Business Administration loan guarantees in the Chicago area. It found that higher-income and outlying zip codes received more loans than lower-income and closer-in areas. Several studies have found that incentives such as IRBs, intended to benefit distressed areas, are used more often by prosperous jurisdictions.

Sprawl: A New Analytical Wedge

Although urban sprawl is often viewed as a suburban quality-of-life issue driven by environmentalists, there is a social equity wing of the smart growth debate focusing on race. That wing views the new "metropolitics" as a way for advocates of traditional equity causes, such as community reinvestment, affordable housing, and fair employment to frame their work as part of a regional solution.

A new study by Good Jobs First links development subsidies to sprawl and concludes that taxpayer-financed corporate migrations are harming people of color in the Twin Cities. The study, "Another Way Sprawl Happens," analyzes 29 companies with 1,600 jobs that relocated to a 300–acre industrial park in the distant suburb of Anoka, which gave the companies free land valued at more than $7.5 million.

The net result of the subsidized relocations was to move the jobs away from the region's largest concentrations of people of color, away from pockets of poverty, and away from households receiving public assistance. The migrations also had a devastating effect on transit accessibility. Before the relocations, more than 70 percent of the jobs were accessible by regularly scheduled transit. In the Anoka Park, they are no longer accessible.

This movement will especially harm inner-city workers, who are more likely to rely on public transportation. Only 40 percent of Black households in the Twin Cities region owned a vehicle in 1990. A report on the region found that 50 percent of the region's employment growth will occur in the outer-ring developing area where nearly half the projects are inaccessible by transit. Many studies have shown that decentralization of employment from central city to suburban locations has disproportionately harmed minority and low-income workers because they face barriers finding housing in the suburbs.

A few journalists have made the subsidy-sprawl link. A 1995 *Kansas City Star* series cited several prosperous suburbs giving tax breaks to companies leaving depressed core areas. The paper found the deals particularly galling because the tools being used by the wealthy suburbs were originally intended to help central cities. "Created to combat sprawl, tax breaks now subsidize it," the *Star* concluded. A 1999 *Milwaukee Journal Sentinel* series cited a mutual fund company in suburban Menomenee Falls which received a $3 million tax credit, justified because it is "close to Milwaukee County, which continues to have higher unemployment than the state average." A state senator commented: "[I]t's essentially a government subsidy to promote sprawl."

Disclosure and Accountability: Hope on the Horizon

As mentioned above, a small but growing network of grassroots groups is working to rewrite the policy dialogue about development. Building coalitions of organized labor, consumer, religious and civic groups, and living wage campaigns, these groups are literally redefining economic development.

The Minnesota Alliance for Progressive Action (MAPA) won the nation's first comprehensive subsidy disclosure law in 1995. It requires annual, company-specific reports on job creation and wages. The data enabled Good Jobs First to analyze 525 deals and identify 38 deals valued at $100,000 or more per job. Despite such high subsidies, 65 percent of the subsidized companies were paying wages so low that a family of three would still qualify for Medicaid and

25 percent would still qualify for Food Stamps. Armed with these findings, MAPA won major reforms, including mandatory wage standards.

The Maine Citizens Leadership Fund and the Maine Center for Economic Policy helped win disclosure in that state in 1997; the Cambridge-based Commonwealth Institute has analyzed the data. Among the key findings: 27 percent of the subsidized jobs pay wages below a living-wage benchmark tied to the federal poverty line, prompting a reform debate.

The Los Angeles Alliance for a New Economy, the nation's largest local subsidy-accountability project, analyzed that city's biggest redevelopment deals of the 1990s. It found that low-wage retail deals got 65 percent of the subsidies, and that 55 percent of those retail jobs paid less than $8 an hour, so little that a family of three would still qualify for public assistance.

Such pioneering efforts are moving the public debate. As Good Jobs First recently documented, at least thirty-seven states, twenty-five cities, and four counties now attach job quality standards, such as wage rules, health care requirements, and full-time hours to development subsidies—an elevenfold increase since 1994!

Race, Poverty, and the Militarized Welfare State

Bristow Hardin

George Bush expressed the views of many when he gushed in the afterglow of the Gulf War that "the U.S. military is the greatest equal opportunity employer around." And as sociologist Charles Moskos has observed, the armed forces is the only institution in American society where blacks routinely order whites around. But despite the notable benefits African Americans have received from the military services, these are proportionately fewer than those accruing to whites. Beyond that, the various related institutions of the U.S. military apparatus—veterans programs, the Department of Defense (DoD) and related government agencies, and private arms contractors—also have provided far more benefits to whites than blacks since World War II. The sum of these disparate benefits thus has directly fostered and perpetuated racial inequality and poverty. Data from the 1945–1985 period, when the impact of military spending on the nation's economic development, class structure, and political alliances was at its height, show this clearly.

The Militarized Welfare State (MWS)

Major benefits provided by the MWS include:

Veterans Programs

The G.I. Bill for World War II veterans constituted what is probably the largest and most generous social welfare program in the nation's history. Its provisions included up to a year of readjustment (unemployment) benefits; education and training benefits, with college aid sufficient to cover tuition, fees, room and board; guaranteed home, farm, or business loans; medical and dental care; pensions and compensation; low-cost life insurance; and vocational rehabilitation.

By 1950, over 12.5 million people had benefited from at least one of these programs. In each immediate postwar year, 1946 and 1947, over 1 million vets used G.I. Bill benefits to attend college, and they comprised seven-tenths of males in higher education institutions. By 1950, nearly 2 million had used a G.I. direct or guaranteed loan to buy a home or farm or to set up a business.

This support enabled millions to join the middle class, and many more to enhance or consolidate their middle-class positions. In terms of wealth creation alone, easy access to homeownership enabled these vets to reap the inflated housing market values of the subsequent years, providing savings and equity that in turn solidified their middle-class position and enabled them to pass these wealth-associated benefits on to their children and grandchildren.

Until the 1960s, veterans programs were the major, the best, and in some case the only federal programs providing welfare state benefits in key areas. Into the 1980s, ex-servicepeople and their dependents had access to comprehensive welfare state benefits that were often better than or unavailable to the rest of the population. Even after the significant expansions of Social Security and the establishment of programs such as Medicare, Medicaid, educational aid, etc., analysts noted that veterans programs were a "parallel" social welfare system but with more generous benefits and eligibility.

Moreover, in contrast to the operations of civilian welfare departments that generally sought to minimize the income and other benefits provided low-income people, analysts noted that the Veterans Administration's (VA) efforts in the means-tested pension program were "directed more toward ensuring veterans maximum benefits." Also, in contrast to the often punitive and demeaning practices of civilian welfare departments, veterans programs were "administered with due regard to the dignity of the recipients."

Civilian Employment

DoD, the Armed Services, the Arms Industry

It is a commonplace that military spending constitutes the major federal jobs program. Conservative estimates (including multiplier effects) are that from 1953, when the country's permanent global military apparatus was being established, through the rest of the 1950s, military spending generated 15 to 20 percent of U.S. jobs; in the 1960s, the range was between 13 percent and 17 percent. In each year during those decades, military spending supported at least 9.2 million and as many as 14.3 million jobs. Also, especially after the Korean War through the 1960s, these jobs typically provided security not just to individual workers, but rather to entire households.

These generally are well-paying jobs with critical employment-related benefits, e.g., health care, insurance, pension plans, access to quality housing. Such benefits have been significantly better than average.

Disparate Benefits for Different Racial Groups

Available data illustrate clearly that throughout the post-World War II era the benefits provided by each and every component of the MWS disproportionately accrued to whites.

Veterans Programs

Jim Crow and related overt exclusionary policies ensured that African Americans' proportion of World War II veterans (6.9 percent) was significantly less than their portion of the total population (about 10 percent). In the Korean War veterans population they were nearly as underrepresented. This underrepresentation alone caused African Americans to receive far fewer benefits than whites from the first G.I. Bills. African Americans' inability to capitalize on these and subsequent veterans programs was exacerbated by additional factors that were products of current or past discriminatory practices. Thus, not only were far fewer blacks than whites able to participate in these programs, but those blacks who could participate received fewer benefits than their white counterparts.

Studies revealed that whites were far more likely than blacks to obtain college aid, while blacks were more likely to obtain training and vocational rehabilitation services. While this would be expected, given blacks' lower average educational levels, these variances had critical short- and long-term consequences. Not only was aid for higher education more generous than that for training and vocational rehabilitation services, but higher education obviously generated much higher economic returns.

Similarly, by the early 1960s only 19 percent of blacks versus 30 percent of whites had obtained G.I. life insurance, and only 14 percent of blacks versus 35 percent of whites had gotten a VA home, farm, or business loan. These variances might be expected, given blacks' lower incomes and hence greater difficulty in making regular payments. Nonetheless, they reveal starkly that blacks were far less able than whites to provide security for their families in the event of their untimely death, and that they were far less able to obtain the loans that could prove instrumental in attaining or enhancing economic success and wealth.

African Americans were twice as likely as whites to take advantage of VA hospitalization services, however. This was a function of the respective groups' alternatives: whites' higher incomes enabled them to use other hospitals, where, with the exception of facilities in the inner cities or extreme rural areas, the quality of care was generally recognized as superior to that provided in veterans hospitals.

Civilian Employment

The federal government has been a major source of jobs for African Americans since World War II, especially since the 1960s. From 1965 to 1980, their portion of the federal civilian workforce increased from 13.5 percent to 17 percent. However, their portion of the workforce in the civilian agencies dealing with "current military" (CM) activities—DoD, NASA, and the Atomic Energy Commission/Department of Energy (responsible for nuclear weapons production)—was much lower, going from 11.2 percent in 1965 to 12.7 percent in 1980. They comprised a much higher portion of the VA workforce— around 25 percent in both years.

However, during the 1965 to 1980 period, African Americans' portion of other civilian agencies' workforces was significantly higher than in the CM departments. In 1980, their proportions of the Postal Service's and the General Services Administration's workforces were about two and three times greater, respectively. And blacks comprised 24.6 percent of the combined workforces of what might be called the "social democratic" agencies—the Departments of Labor, HUD, HEW/HHS, Education, and smaller related agencies (OEO/CSA, EEOC, and Civil Rights Commission).

Data show that there were significant differences in blacks' success in ascending the organizational hierarchies in the various sectors. They had far greater success securing positions in the upper echelons of the "social democratic" hierarchies than in the military departments, where they were relegated to the lower strata of both the white-collar and blue-collar categories. In 1980, for example, blacks' share of jobs in the upper white-collar grades in the "social democratic" sector was more than five times that in the CM sector, and their share of blue-collar supervisors jobs was over four times greater. African Americans' share of the jobs in upper white-collar grades in the "social democratic" sector was over three times that in the VA, while their share of jobs in the blue-collar supervisor category was 25 percent higher.

To appreciate the full impact of these disparities, note that since World War II the DoD and VA civilian workforces together have been larger than all other civilian agencies combined (excluding the Postal Service).

Private Arms Contractors

Past and continuing racism, combined with the location of the "Gunbelt" (the regions where arms production has been concentrated), severely limited African Americans' employment in the federally financed arms industry, the major sectors of which are the aerospace and electronics/communications industries. These relatively meager benefits are illustrated by 1966 and 1985 employment data. In 1966, blacks comprised only 4.3 percent of the total workforces of these industries. Although this increased to 8.2 percent by 1985, it was far less than their 12.1 percent weight in the total U.S. workforce. These limited returns from the nation's major public works program resulted from three principal factors.

First, the myriad limitations on blacks' educational opportunities constrained their ability to gain the training and credentials essential for the scientific-managerial jobs that are the leading occupational categories in the arms sector. In 1966, officials and managers, professionals, and technicians comprised 40 percent of the workforces in both the aerospace and electronics and communications industries; by 1985 that proportion had risen to at least 45 percent. Blacks were certain to obtain relatively meager employment benefits from this largesse since they comprised only 5.7 percent of these job categories in 1970 and 10.7 percent in 1985.

Second, educational constraints and the racist practices of craft unions blocked African Americans' entry into the craft and metal trades that are the arms industry's most economically rewarding blue-collar jobs. Most notably, the International Association of Machinists, the leading metals workers union and the union with the most members in the arms industries, was renowned for its discriminatory practices well into the 1970s. As a result of this and related factors, as late as 1970 blacks comprised only 5.6 percent of those classified as crafts workers.

Finally, as the Gunbelt developed, the African American population increased markedly in the very states whose share of military spending—and the economic stimulus and jobs it provided—was plummeting. Specifically, between 1940 and 1980 the black population increased markedly in the "rust belt" states of New York (+321 percent), New Jersey (+307 percent), Pennsylvania (+123 percent), Ohio (+217 percent), Michigan (+476 percent), and Illinois (+609 percent), states which had contained major centers of armaments production during World War II. As the postwar Gunbelt developed, these states' share of the DoD's prime contracts and military and civilian payrolls fell sharply. From 1951 to 1983, the share of DoD prime contract awards going to five of these states fell at least 56 percent and as much as 82 percent.

The deleterious effects private arms spending has had for African Americans are further highlighted by contrasting workforce data for the major arms industries (aerospace and electronics/communications) and the major rust belt industries (basic steel and autos). In contrast to their limited employment inroads into the arms industry, blacks made significant gains in the auto and steel industries, comprising 13.3 percent of their total workforces in 1966 and 14.9 percent in 1985. The returns from these hard-won gains were significantly limited, however, since the total number of jobs in these industries fell from 1.5 million to 1.2 million between 1966 and 1985, while the number of jobs in the arms industries increased from 1.6 million to 2.1 million.

The Armed Services

While the uniformed services are regarded by many as the major institution where blacks have made their greatest advances in American society (perhaps the most compelling indicator of this is that African Americans' rates of enlistment and re-enlistment in the uniformed services consistently have exceeded those of whites), this opportunity must be assessed in the context of the marked lack of viable employment opportunities available to blacks in civilian life. Because of this, blacks' high rates of entry and retention in the armed forces can be seen as a form of economic conscription. Moreover, the returns from their service seem significantly less than those accruing to whites.

Several points are worth noting. First, the percentage of blacks in the services was not proportional to their numbers in the population until the early 1970s. It peaked at 18.6 percent in 1981, after which the share of white enlistees increased because of the combination of bad economic conditions, improved compensation, and recruitment policy changes. Second, the proportion of blacks in the Army has always been higher than that in the other services, due to lower entrance standards (set to allow for the Army's higher casualty rates). Third, the percentage of black officers has consistently been lower than their numbers in the services would seem to warrant. In 1985, when the percent of black officers was at its highest, to that point, 18.9 percent of total personnel but only 6.4 percent of officers were black. Fourth, black officers and enlisted personnel alike have consistently been concentrated in the lower echelons. African Americans were 6.4 percent of all officers but only 2.6 percent of those in the upper grades in 1985. This portion had been unchanged since the late 1970s. Likewise, blacks comprised 21 percent of all enlisted personnel in 1985, but only 16.3 percent of those in upper grades (down from 17.2 percent in 1983). Studies from the late 1960s to the early 1980s revealed that blacks were not promoted as fast as whites, even controlling for Armed Forces Qualifying Test scores. Finally, black officers and enlisted personnel have been systematically concentrated in the least desirable occupational categories. (Again, this occurred even when controlling for AFQT scores.) This inhibits their opportunities for advancement, equips them with fewer skills that are valuable in the civilian labor market, and increases the likelihood they will be combat casualties.

Conclusion

The foregoing analysis demonstrates that African Americans have obtained far fewer benefits than whites from each and every component of the Militarized Welfare State. Thus, the postwar military apparatus and the MWS it funds have been major mechanisms through which racial inequality and poverty have been perpetuated since World War II.

The answer to the "so what?" question seems clear. That is, as many have long argued, a necessary but not sufficient condition for diminishing racial inequality and poverty is the dismantling of the military state. This is essential not just because military spending diverts resources from human needs, but because it directly reproduces the racial inequalities that are fundamental causes of poverty.

The answer to the "what is to be done?" question seems no less clear. Those working for social and economic justice must reexamine the reasoning and structures that have fragmented progressive forces into a variety of single-issue groups. Part of this reexamination must be a better understanding of how unnecessary military spending is fueled not merely by "national security" concerns (however they are defined) or a "military industrial complex," but rather a *racialized military welfare state* as well. Social and economic justice groups must develop strategies to overcome their compartmentalization so they can fight both single-issue and broad-based battles.

Race, Poverty, and the Federal Reserve System

Tom Schlesinger

As the Federal Reserve undertook a series of interest rate hikes between June 1999 and June 2000, investors and financial reporters weighed each pronouncement from the central bank's marble headquarters as warily as a bomb squad inspecting a mysterious package. But why should ordinary citizens pay attention to the actions of this esoteric institution? Four reasons stand out.

First and foremost, the Fed's power to adjust interest rates and the money supply wields enormous influence over employment patterns, debt burdens, and the distribution of income and wealth.

- When interest rates remain low and stable, businesses thrive, labor markets tighten, and individuals at the bottom of the job ladder find new opportunities for employment, training, and workplace leverage. During 1998 to 1999, this virtuous circle widely benefited have-not and have-some communities as the Fed adopted an expansive monetary policy and unemployment dropped to the lowest sustained levels in two generations.

  When the cost of business borrowing goes up, however, employers retrench and workers lose their jobs. Less-skilled, lower-income workers are always the first to feel the pinch during a monetary tightening. According to a Jerome Levy Institute study by economist Willem Thorbecke, minority unemployment increases twice as much as white unemployment in the wake of rising interest rates. If downsizing, underemployment, or job insecurity accelerates, workers lose leverage across the board.

  The Fed's last concerted campaign to slow the economy illustrates the point. Despite the absence of inflation, the central bank began a series of seven interest rate hikes in January 1994 that doubled short-term interest rates by early 1995. As a result, economic growth slowed to a snail's pace—a mere 0.6 percent—by the first quarter of 1995, and remained anemic for most of the year. For 1995 as a whole, the shortfall in national income relative to what would have been generated by a moderate growth rate of 3 percent amounted to $75 billion—$755 for every household in the country. Since each billion dollars of national income translates into 14,000 jobs, restrictive monetary policy probably cost Americans more than a million jobs in 1995.

• Higher interest rates compound household debt burdens and stifle consumer demand by jacking up the cost of mortgage, car, credit card, and student loan payments. When household debt expands at high real (inflation-adjusted) interest rates, as it did during the 1990s, income is redistributed from working households to wealthy creditors. The result: greater inequality.

Rate-sensitive households are especially vulnerable. Based on figures in the Federal Reserve's Survey of Consumer Finances for 1998, the median household in the $25,000–$50,000 income bracket with mortgage, installment, and credit card debt pays nearly $12 per month more for every one-quarter percent interest rate increase if it has a variable-rate mortgage and its consumer loan balances are also susceptible to rate adjustments. That means $569 per year in additional debt payments for every full percentage point rise in interest rates.

Second, the Fed's regulatory duties include enforcement of fair lending and community reinvestment statutes, which powerfully influence the availability of credit and the ownership opportunities arising from it. The Fed also has substantial authority—almost all of it unused—to curtail predatory lending practices like equity stripping and usurious interest rates that target poor, working-class, and minority communities. Recent legislation (the Gramm-Leach-Bliley Act) that encourages mergers between banks, insurers, and securities firms expands the Fed's direct regulatory reach far beyond the banking industry.

Third, the central bank maintains a little-known but extensive set of community development resources at its Washington headquarters (the Board of Governors) and twelve regional Federal Reserve Banks. This community affairs infrastructure is designed to support local development activities and dwarfs the corresponding divisions at other federal agencies that regulate depository institutions.

Fourth, the Federal Reserve has become the only game in town. As Congress and the Administration developed a bipartisan consensus to ratchet down the role of public spending and investment—and to use budget surpluses to retire Treasury debt—monetary policy has become the preeminent lever of federal influence over the country's economic direction. More than ever, the central bank effectively determines the governing choices of America's elected leaders.

In theory, these far-reaching powers equip the central bank to be a powerful engine of widespread prosperity and rising equality—a role it has embraced on some occasions, notably during the New Deal chairmanship of Marriner Eccles. In practice, of course, the Fed has usually embraced a narrower vision of the greater economic good—one defined by the wealth-preservation agenda of bankers and Wall Street.

The Fed's Unique Structure

Historically, the Fed's unusual structure and unique status have formed one of the biggest obstacles to people-friendly central banking. Unlike other federal banking agencies, the Fed is not part of the executive branch. And even though it's a creature of Congress, the central bank remains separate in most respects from the legislative branch as well.

For example, the Fed is the only civilian agency that writes its own budget and completely finances its own operations (mostly through earnings from its portfolio of government securities), without congressional oversight, authorization, or audits. It conducts its most important business behind closed doors, due to unique exemptions to the Government in the Sunshine and Freedom of Information Acts.

Moreover, the Fed contains a unique mix of public, private, federal, and regional features—including a power-sharing arrangement that gives policy-making authority both to Federal Reserve governors, who are nominated by the President and confirmed by the Senate, and Reserve Bank presidents, who are appointed by regional boards of directors, the majority of whose members are chosen by commercial banking firms.

This structure provides the central bank its famous insulation from partisan politics. But it also enables banks, securities firms, money management companies, and other segments of the financial industry to lobby the Fed quietly and continuously out of public view.

Over the years, reformers have persistently tried to increase the Fed's accountability and democratize its governance through legislation and litigation. But virtually all these attempts have failed—including those led by senior members of Congress and powerful business interests.

Reform Efforts From Below

Given this history of frustrated reform, it may be time to consider other approaches to changing the Fed. For example, some organizations are attempting to increase the number of Reserve Bank directors who represent labor and community groups (the law expressly provides for representation of these interests along with those of agriculture, commerce, and services).

In addition, some of the same organizations have undertaken efforts to boost Reserve Bank accountability to residents in their districts. In 1997, for example, an informal alliance of labor, community, and nonprofit organizations began an initiative focused on the Federal Reserve Bank of Richmond. The group's concerns fell into three areas:

- *governance:* diversifying the interests and perspectives represented on the boards of directors at the Richmond Bank and its branches
- *community development:* strengthening the Richmond Bank's role in community-based reinvestment and development activities
- *monetary policy:* encouraging the Richmond Bank to adopt a more worker- and community-friendly approach to macro-policy by expanding and diversifying its collection of regional economic data and its analysis of the distributional effects of interest-rate policy decisions

During 1997 and 1998, members of this informal alliance held three meetings with Richmond Fed President Alfred Broaddus, Jr. and other senior staff at the Bank. Participating organizations also sponsored day-long trips for President Broaddus, arranging for him to meet with leaders, staff, and members of grassroots groups, union locals, and other organizations. Two trips, sponsored by the Virginia Organizing Project, took Broaddus to Virginia's southside and eastern shore. Another, organized by the South Carolina AFL-CIO, took him on a tour of the Palmetto State. In addition, the informal alliance conducted a briefing for CRA compliance examiners at the Richmond Bank and helped the bank's community affairs office conduct workshops in Roanoke and Charlottesville.

As a result of these activities, the Richmond Fed decided to create a Community Development Advisory Council, which held its initial meeting in November 1998. Its members include three leaders from the informal group: South Carolina AFL-CIO President Donna DeWitt; architect Greta Harris, who directs Richmond's Local Initiatives Support Corporation; and Rep. Gilda Cobb-Hunter, who works at a domestic violence center and is the first African American since Reconstruction and the first woman ever to lead a party in the South Carolina General Assembly.

A few days of exposure to factory workers and other ordinary citizens in southside Virginia and South Carolina does not appear to have changed President Broaddus' hard-money world view. But to their credit, Broaddus and the Richmond Bank have not conceived their new advisory group as a perfunctory nod to narrow community development interests. Instead, the council is designed to incorporate a broad range of previously overlooked perspectives and information into the bank's regional economic surveys, research agenda, and monetary policy calculus.

Small steps like this won't turn the Fed on its ear and don't negate the need for systemic changes in Reserve Bank governance. But persistent, local, move-the-runner-over measures have been a missing ingredient in most previous Fed reform efforts. Without sustained political and intellectual ferment bubbling at the grassroots, even the best-conceived swing-for-the-fences legislation or litigation is unlikely to alter the Fed's governing structure in the future.

Race, Poverty, and Social Security

john a. powell

Since the presidency of Ronald Reagan, politicians have attacked and undermined this country's hard-won social safety net. This attack has been color- and class-conscious: they have slashed and burned programs for low-income Americans, especially people of color. Meanwhile, Social Security remains sacrosanct. There is heated debate over Social Security, but it focuses on how to finance it and distribute its benefits, not how to cut or eliminate it.

This sacred cow status may seem odd, because Old Age Insurance (OAI), the heart of Social Security, redistributes more wealth and costs far more than any other government benefit program. Perhaps this popularity is owing to the fact that OAI and Medicare are the only welfare programs that benefit people regardless of income: retired migrant farmworkers and retired Fortune 500 CEOs alike receive OAI benefits.

One key factor obscured in the national debate about how to reform this popular government program is race. The reason so many politicians and voters support Social Security—even as they dismantle other, much less expensive social programs—is surely related to the fact that most of its beneficiaries are white and middle-class.

Racial Exclusion

The Social Security Act, originally passed in 1935 in the middle of the Great Depression, was the nation's most serious foray into the area of social rights and the welfare state. Yet, from the outset the program was racially exclusionary.

At the time of the Act's passage, influential southern and western Congressmen opposed any program that would grant payments to black, Mexican, or Asian agricultural workers for fear of undermining the oppressive southern plantation economy or western agribusiness. To win the support of affluent whites, the Act also shut out domestic workers, most of whom were black women.

The exclusion of domestic, agricultural, and government workers—the other major sector of black employment—from OAI and Unemployment Insurance (UI) meant that many, maybe even a majority, of black, Latino, and Asian workers were ineligible.

Struggles for civil and labor rights have since corrected the Social Security system's most egregious forms of racial and gender inequity. Virtually all workers now pay into and are eligible for OAI and UI. Government workers have their own retirement systems; and medical insurance, missing from the Act, was added in the 1960s. Benefits to widows have been expanded and increased.

Continued Unfairness

Despite these improvements, the Social Security system still perpetuates racial, class, and gender disparities, though in somewhat disguised form.

First, Social Security taxes are regressive: a payroll tax of 12.7 percent is taken, regardless of whether a person makes the minimum wage and works for only one week of the year or makes $76,200—no Social Security taxes at all are paid on income above that level (as of 2000). Recent tax law changes have made matters worse by lowering income tax rates (which are progressive because the more you earn, the greater percentage of taxes you pay) and increasing Social Security taxes (which tax rate, as noted, is flat).

Once they retire, poorer folk also get smaller monthly payouts than the affluent. OAI benefits begin upon retirement no earlier than age 62, and the amount received is based on the total amount paid in by the recipient over his/her lifetime: the less you pay in, the less you receive. People of color have lower incomes than whites. They thus put fewer total dollars into the system and receive lower benefits. In 1997, the median income of Latino families was $28,142; for African-American families, it was $28,602; and for whites, it was $46,754. Similarly, women earn about 60 percent as much as men.

Finally, people of color receive OAI benefits for a significantly shorter amount of time than whites, because they retire older and die younger. The life expectancy for African-American males is only 65 years, compared to 73 for white men. A huge number of people of color die before ever receiving Social Security benefits, even though they pay taxes into the system throughout their lives.

Notwithstanding these inequities, Social Security represents the most important source of retirement income for most people of color. Because people of color have far fewer assets than whites and are much less likely to be covered by private pension programs, they tend to be more dependent on Social Security at retirement.

The Race of Age

Dramatic changes in our national demographics threaten the viability of the Social Security system. As baby boomers reach retirement, the U.S. population is rapidly aging. In 1960, there were nine active workers paying into the system for each beneficiary. By 1996, the ratio of workers to beneficiaries had plummeted to 5.33.

This trend, together with an increasing life expectancy and a declining birth rate, means that a larger number of longer-living retirees will be supported by a shrinking number of younger workers. Unless substantial changes are made in the way Social Security is structured, many project that the system will go broke by 2037.

Yet, with a booming economy and a huge budget surplus, politicians still insist on cutting taxes to corporations and the rich, and returning money to middle-class taxpayers instead of funding Social Security for the long run. Recently, George W. Bush proposed to transform the current guaranteed benefits program into individual stock accounts, a move which threatens to deprive millions of inexperienced investors of benefits and subject all recipients to tremendous stock market volatility.

The parties in the current debate, from left to right, completely skirt the important racial issues involved. The aging baby boomers are disproportionately white, while younger and new workers are increasingly people of color. This trend is reflected in school enrollment statistics. In 1996, students of color were 36 percent of the total K-12 enrollment nationally—an increase of 50 percent since 1976 and still rising rapidly.

When these students become young workers of color, they will pay into a system in which most of the beneficiaries are white.

Racial Time Bomb

Starting with the Great Depression, the U.S. government created a social compact, promising that the society would support the young in becoming productive citizens and workers, especially through quality public education. Those productive workers would in turn pay taxes to support the young and the retired elderly. No one segment would thereby be forced to bear more than its fair social share.

However, today, government is abandoning youth of color. Inner-city schools suffer from inadequate investment, and racist housing and zoning

RACE, POVERTY, AND... 273

practices continue the segregation and concentration of low-income students of color. Current tax policies have left low-income, largely minority communities to try to do the impossible—provide fiscal support to maintain their cities and take care of their young.

Taken together, these facts make it clear why the Social Security problem is a racialized time bomb. Youth of color are inadequately prepared to enter the workforce, condemning many of them to low-wage, dead-end service jobs—and to prison. In the not-too-distant future, this same poorly educated, underpaid population of color may be asked to accept an even higher rate of taxation to benefit elderly white baby boomers and to replace a crumbling infrastructure of school buildings, parks, sewers, bridges, and roads. And, as the boomers continue to age, they will have to invite these young workers into their nursing homes and gated communities to attend to their aging bodies and failing health.

The solution to these intergenerational and racial tensions is not to cut benefits to the elderly or to refuse to invest in our children. Corporations, which have enjoyed major tax cuts, and workers, especially those at higher income levels, must be made to assume their fair share of taxes. We must insist that existing budget surpluses be used to shore up Social Security and to finance infrastructure and educational improvements, especially in the inner cities. And we must demand that Social Security benefits, upon which retirees of color are so dependent, continue to be guaranteed.

Failure to live up to the social compact because of a shortsighted racial gaze will hurl us into a perilous future.

Race, Poverty, and Immigration

Arnoldo García

"A specter haunts the world and it is the specter of migration," declared Michael Hardt and Antonio Negri in *Empire*, their analysis on the state of global capitalism, stressing by analogy the potential of immigrants as agents of social change. Our struggles for economic and racial justice have no alternative other than to include immigrant rights.

Migration reflects the deep transformations and restructuring of national economies and civil society. The displacement of entire communities and segments of social classes is unprecedented in human history: one in every fifty persons worldwide is an economic migrant or political refugee. Migration sunders home communities and creates demographic revolution in receiving ones. However, migration has been a natural, if not a defining, aspect of human history and development.

In the Americas, since the arrival of Europeans in 1492, the migration of peoples has been repeatedly forced: from the enslavement and violent displacement of Indians from their lands, first into laborers for systems of private property and economic development for individual profit; to the trans-Atlantic African slave trade and importation of "free" labor from Europe; and the "modern" transnational labor mobility, including agricultural workers and computer engineers. They all have one thing in common: people are forcibly displaced and restructured into diverse communities to meet the labor needs of capital.

The specter of immigrants is a fundamental issue that all U.S. movements for social justice and equality must grapple with in order to develop a new, inclusive, anti-racist, internationalist, progressive agenda. Our movements need to progress from targeting and even scapegoating immigrants as obstacles to, or weakening, civil rights. They must see immigrants as central to the leadership and goals of extending and strengthening democracy and attaining social and economic justice in the United States.

Immigration in the United States is simultaneously a system of coerced labor pool creation, propelling new forms of racial stratification, and a cornerstone of the new international economy that has created greater subordination of the South countries by the North. According to the Census Bureau, six out of every ten Asian Pacific Islanders and four out of ten Latinos in the U.S. are foreign-born. In 1999, there were about 2 million foreign-born Blacks, 8 percent of all foreign-born. Some 85 percent of immigrants are considered "people of color." Recent increasing immigration into the South, where the majority of African Americans reside, means that the demographic impacts already experienced in California and Texas, where half of all immigrants live, could significantly alter the U.S. political landscape. While the potential for Black-immigrant polarization exists in the South, it is up to the leadership of progressives and people of color from all communities to creatively hone common ground for a different political outcome.

In the post-Cold War setting, migration has become a condition of unprecedented growth as well as a global security issue, giving rise to xenophobia without borders. In the United States, immigrants are scapegoated for a variety of social ills, including environmental degradation, sprawl, unemployment, poverty, and even for the cultural decay of the country.

Set against the backdrop of an increasingly politically conservative climate, these intertwined processes pose historic challenges for communities of color still struggling for social and racial justice. The demand and fight for immigrant rights is not primarily about "legalization" or labor protections—although these are very important and must be fought for. It is not about getting rights at the expense of the rights of U.S. citizens or people of color. Immigrant rights are about transforming how our country develops, about how political power and representation are achieved and shared, and, above all, how all humans, regardless of immigration status, have the same rights to person, community, place, and culture.

The issues of migration and immigrants have forced open a debate and, in some quarters, a dialogue about who we are as communities of color, as workers, as citizens, and how our country should interact with the rest of the world. Ultimately, the issue of immigrant rights raises the question of how we define civil rights as a global issue, too.

Against this backdrop, we are faced with some key issues. First, the demands for equality and civil rights in the context of "free" trade and globalization have to include a burgeoning sector of U.S. society that is nonwhite, nonblack, and perceived to be noncitizen. U.S. immigration policies affect civil and labor rights at home and abroad, disrupting our communities without consultation. These demands must propose alternatives to U.S. foreign investment and development policies that are displacing millions across borders.

Second, the main U.S. political and economic arenas have been steadily constricting the space for progressive and antiracist politics since the Reagan Administration. Antiquated class frameworks and racial analyses rooted in previous eras of racial and class struggles still hold sway, hindering the political vision and organizational initiatives of the traditional Civil Rights Movement.

Three broad, intertwined political trends have created this situation: The cutbacks in and privatization of public services; the rolling back of and institutionalization of attacks on social, political, civil, and human rights—including the severe curtailing of labor and environmental protections—resulting in the expansion of property rights and the market; and third, the deregulation and/or reregulation of investments, capital, goods, industries, services, and labor across national borders and economic regions, subordinating labor mobility to globalization or capitalist restructuring.

This threefold political program, rising in the early 1960s, took full power with the ascendancy of Ronald Reagan, and has become the framework for the majority of social and fiscal policies that are facing all communities of color, immigrants, labor, and the working poor. For example, Proposition 187 (approved by California voters in 1994 but constitutionally checked from implementation), which would have denied health, social, and educational services to immigrants, is a corollary of U.S. immigration and trade policies. Although formally directed at immigrants, Prop. 187 was a plebiscite on the rights of citizens to public services and was essentially a "free trade" policy, aimed at privatizing access to education, health, and social services. The combination of welfare reform and the 1996 Illegal Immigration Reform and Immigrant Responsibility Act essentially installed Prop. 187 nationally.

The lines between the rights of immigrants—especially between legal and undocumented immigrants—and low-income people of color now are increasingly blurred. This is one of the results of the national debate on the costs and burdens of immigration and who pays. Now the scapegoating of immigrants, by many citizen and legal resident people of color, for the mounting cutbacks of services and curtailment of rights is the natural order of business. This in spite of the fact that immigrants and people of color occupy similar socioeconomic space: in 1997–1998, the poverty rate for Latinos was 27.1 percent; for African Americans, 26.1 percent; and for Asian Pacific Islanders, 12.5 percent.

"Immigrant" has become a full-fledged member of the racial lexicon of our country, usually referring only to Latinos and Asians, although immigrants hail from Canada, Europe, Africa, and places in between. This is not surprising; passage of the Immigration Act of 1965, ending racial quotas, stressed family reunification and job skills, changing the demographics of immigration in the United States. During the 1950s, more than half of all immigrants were from European countries; by the 1970s, that proportion had declined to less than 20 percent. Some 9 million immigrants came from Asian and Latin American countries. Since 1965, the Latino population increased 141 percent, Asian Pacific Americans by 385 percent.

A 1990 General Accounting Office study found that the employer sanctions provisions of the 1986 Immigration Reform and Control Act (IRCA) were creating new forms of racism when those seeking employment, primarily Latino and Asian legal residents and U.S. citizens who "looked or sounded like" immigrants, were unlawfully asked for documentation or denied work.

How does immigration impact people of color? Studies both pro- and anti-immigrant have contradictory findings about the economic impact of immigrants, especially on African Americans and other people of color; some studies believe the impact is more severe on other, less recent immigrants. But however real or imaginary the burden of immigration, immigrants are being scapegoated by people of color and whites directly and indirectly. Stephen Steinberg, in his 1995 book, *Turning Back: The Retreat from Racial Justice in American Thought and Policy*, asserts: "The economic fortunes of African Americans have always been linked to immigration." Steinberg argues that, historically, African-American economic and social progress have coincided with ebbs in immigration. Immigrants take jobs that otherwise would have gone to African Americans, and immigration policy is a form of disinvestment in U.S. workers that has especially severe consequences for African Americans and other marginalized communities.

In a different vein, William Julius Wilson, in his 1999 book, *The Bridge Over the Racial Divide: Rising Inequality and Coalition Politics*, shows how immigration is one of several factors contributing to the growing racial inequalities. Immigrants are mainly concentrated in several states (California, Texas, New York, Florida, Illinois, New Jersey), and while inequality deepened in these states, it also rose in other areas where there are few immigrants. However, Steinberg correctly demands, "[W]hy is policy not directed at addressing the scandalously high rates of black unemployment?" and points out a glaring contradiction: "Although immigration has produced a more racially diverse population, paradoxically this new diversity has reinforced the pre-existing structure of occupational apartheid."

If the economic lot of African Americans is bound up with immigration, as Steinberg argues, then the political demands of people of color must include immigrant rights. Otherwise, how do we dismantle the racial stratification of labor? By excluding and ultimately deporting immigrants, especially the undocumented and legal residents who have broken U.S. laws, so that opportunities are opened to people of color who occupy the same social and economic segment? Or do we include all immigrants, regardless of status and occupation, as part of the fight to expand the franchise so that all members of communities of color, including immigrants, have equal rights and protections and self-representation?

In summary, the immigrant rights struggle faces several monumental challenges to build a cross-class and multiracial/multinational coalition that advocates for equality, civil rights, and labor protections of all communities, regardless of immigration status. These include addressing:

- *Racial arguments against immigration and immigrant rights.* Under this scenario, immigrants are perceived to worsen the conditions and opportunities of legal resident and citizen people of color, especially African Americans. This argument lets whites off the hook and ignores the pattern of economic development, where jobs, services, housing, and investment have fled the urban centers into the suburbs and overseas. Furthermore, it pits the rights of people of color against marginalized communities which are perceived to have no rights under U.S. law. Nobel Laureate novelist Toni Morrison, addressing the complexity that immigration adds to the black-white paradigm, states, "Although U.S. history is awash in labor battles, political fights, and property wars among all religious and ethnic groups, their struggles are persistently framed as struggles between recent arrivals and blacks."

- *Cultural arguments against immigration and immigrant communities.* Anti-immigrant forces allege that immigrants pollute and mongrelize "American" culture. This argument disdains the multicultural/multiracial/multinational nature of the United States, exaggerates the role of whites, and diminishes the contributions of African Americans, Indians, Asians, and Latinos to the development of our country and its significance to forging a political agenda that integrates citizens and non-citizens on the basis of equality. María Jiménez, director of American Friends Service Committee's Immigration Law Enforcement Monitoring Project, asserts in this regard, "[I]t is important for various cultures to interact and engage in political projects together because these become laboratories for breaking down barriers and finding strategic unity. . . . The disparate experiences of immigrant and refugee communities must be integrated to craft a long-term strategy based on this analysis."

- *Labor arguments against immigration and the rights of immigrant workers.* Immigrant workers are characterized as low-skilled, unorganizable, and driving down wages of U.S. workers. This argument ignores the public subsidies and benefits given to corporations and certain sectors of industry that depend on immigrant labor. Also, special anti-immigrant labor laws and enforcement—especially employer sanctions and the use of the Border Patrol, a special anti-immigrant labor police force— are in effect, which make immigrants more vulnerable to exploitative wage and labor conditions, isolating them from their natural allies in communities of color and the social justice and labor movements. While immigrants are perceived to have few or no rights, they—especially the undocumented—are seen as undermining labor and other social rights, depriving citizens of jobs, especially low-income and people of color communities. In truth, working-class immigrants, documented and undocumented, are revitalizing the labor movement. Immigrants are made to appear invisible, and their role and contributions beyond the economy are ignored and/or minimized. For example, Mae M. Ngai writes, in *Audacious Democracy: Labor, Intellectuals, and the Social Reconstruction of America*, edited by Steven Fraser and Joshua B. Freeman, "Historically and today, Asian immigrants have carried the twin burdens of race and foreign birth, both barriers to being considered 'American workers' in the fullest meaning of that concept." According to racist and anti-immigrant logic, American, i.e. white, workers unquestioningly have full rights and powers; immigrants, i.e. people of color, do not. Only by recognizing that immigrants are part of and not the cause of the racial stratification of labor and its accompanying wealth and income

come gaps can our historical demands for civil and labor rights and social justice address migration with dignity and integrity.

We are again at the ending and beginning of a new cycle of development, where labor needs in a booming economy demand a reordering of rights and responsibilities. The AFL-CIO in February 2000, recognizing the revitalizing force of immigrants to union organizing, changed its long-held positions and called for repeal of employer sanctions and demanded amnesty for all undocumented workers. In addition to racial stratification, immigration status creates a two-tiered workforce that undermines labor organizing. This deepens the impoverishment of immigrant workers, denying them living wages, job security, and benefits. The last legalization under IRCA granted some 3 million undocumented residents legal status. This time, however, the demand for amnesty must be accompanied by the demand for full rights for the undocumented. Short of this, amnesty or legalization will only lead to creation of a new form of apartheid, where immigrant workers will increasingly be subject to indentured servitude. Take away the "immigrant" classification and you have another worker of color, exploited, many times marginalized, but one with dignity and capacity to transform the nation and the people in a multicultural, socially just direction.

Immigrant rights are key to racial and social justice. Misunderstood and under-appreciated, the fight for immigrant rights is also a fight against racism and reframes the demand for racial equality in the United States.

Race, Poverty, and Globalization

john a. powell and S.P. Udayakumar

The world economy is in a state of what is commonly viewed as unprecedented growth. But with this growth has come dangerous and destructive economic disparity. On the one hand, we see the "impressive" economy in the Northern Hemisphere, particularly in the United States, where Silicon Valley, a region of 2.3 million people, has produced tens of thousands of millionaires, with sixty-four new ones every day. There are regular reports of historically low unemployment rates, labor shortages, and a booming economy.

On the other hand, many people of color, particularly those in the Southern Hemisphere, do not have enough food to eat, resulting in malnutrition and disease. They face growing inflation while their governments, which used to subsidize some aspects of their marginal living, are urged to stop subsidies for food and adopt a more market-oriented economics. Many workers in these economies are trapped in poor working conditions with low pay. Women are often expected to do back-breaking farm and domestic work with few rights or benefits. Yet many of the fiscal policies pushed on to developing countries and adopted in northern countries exacerbate the problem of the most marginal while celebrating the wealth of the rich.

In the North as well, people of color often find themselves being left farther and farther behind. Even as some U.S. states and the nation as a whole report budget surpluses, we seem unable or unwilling to provide adequate housing for the growing number of working-class and homeless families, to repair the physical structures of schools that house low-income students of color, or to provide social services or medical attention for those most in need.

Sweatshops that employ people of color working as virtual slave laborers are tolerated—even encouraged—as part of the new world trade. The public spaces people of color and marginal groups are most dependent on—public hospitals, schools, or parks—as well as the social welfare system, are constantly attacked as inconsistent with the needs of capital and the market. Indeed, we are encouraged to remake public space to mimic private space with a market, anti-democratic orientation, where we are consumers, not citizens.

How are these disparate conditions related to globalism, and why are people of color under the most severe threat from this process? Certainly, other people are also under a threat from this globalization process, and some would assert that democracy and capitalism itself may be undone by this process if it is not checked. To answer that question and better understand why minorities and other marginal populations are most at risk, it is first necessary to better understand what globalism is, particularly the type of globalism that dominates today's markets.

What Is Globalism?

In the most general sense, globalism refers to the process in which goods and services, including capital, move more freely within and among nations. As globalism advances, national boundaries become more and more porous, and to some extent, less relevant.

Since many of our early industries, such as steel, were location-sensitive, there was a natural limitation to globalization. To be sure, some things remain location-sensitive, but mobility is the trend. It is assumed that liberalizing laws and structures, so that goods and services can become more globally focused, will produce more wealth, and indeed this seems to be true. Using this general understanding of globalism and globalization, it would be accurate to say this process has been developing and growing for well over a hundred years.

But there have been many changes in the globalization process in the last two decades that distinguishes it from earlier incarnations. The major thing being traded in today's global market is information and capital itself, rather than commodities or other products. Technological change allows capital to move almost instantaneously. Earlier, products and capital were more rooted to a place. But today, many of the things traded and produced in the global market, such as knowledge and computer technology, are extremely mobile or rootless.

The United States has emerged as the only world superpower. This has allowed our country tremendous influence in setting the terms for global trade. The style of globalism pushed by the United States has favored the free movement and protection of capital, while being at best indifferent and at worse hostile to more place-dependent labor. It is the dual relationship of mobile capital and fixed, unorganized, and unprotected labor that has created the conditions for capital to dominate. While the United States has been aggressive in protecting capital both at home and abroad, it has encouraged the weakening of organized labor and removing protections for workers.

While both Japan and Europe have aggressively pushed for globalism, each has been more willing to protect labor, the environment, and certain markets—at least within their own borders. It is the United States that has consistently been the most radical on liberalizing capital and protecting it as it moves across boundaries, and the most hostile to protecting labor and fragile markets. The United States has used the globalism it advocates as justification for keeping job security, pay, and benefits relatively low. Workers are told that pushing hard for benefits will cause capital to leave to another location in the country or the world where workers are willing to work for less with fewer benefits.

The United States and the international organizations over which it has substantial influence, such as the International Monetary Fund, have demanded protection of capital and encouraged or tolerated the suppression of labor and the environment in the weaker southern countries. Capital is actively directed to markets with low wages, where workers are sometimes abused and labor organizations suppressed. The wealth this globalism creates is being forcefully subsidized by vulnerable workers and the environment, especially in the Southern Hemisphere. This logic is then used to weaken the position of labor in the North, as we are required to compete with unorganized, suppressed labor in the South.

While sweatshops and slave labor may attract capital investments, what about the futures of black welfare mothers in Detroit or the Aborigines in Australia, who need government assistance to take advantage of, say, the educational system? How or why does U.S.-style globalism affect their needs? U.S.-style globalism seeks to suppress social welfare systems and support for public expenditures that do not directly benefit the expansion of capital. The social welfare system and other public services, such as schools, social services in the North, and food subsidies in the South, are supported through taxes, and taxes reduce short-term benefits to capital.

In the North, it is women and minorities who are most dependent on the public sector. These racial and gender correlations make it all the easier to attack the legitimacy of taxing for this purpose. Taxes are seen as undesirable because they reduce profits and interfere with the market. But the public space, and the welfare system, can only be supported by the public in the form of taxes. Whether we are talking about education or other public services, we are encouraged to believe that they should be as limited as possible and made to mimic the market. Those who cannot thrive in the market environment without help, especially if they are people of color, are seen as freeloaders and illegitimate. In many ways, much of the public space in the United States becomes associated with people of color.

Goodbye, Democratic Vision?

Public purposes and civic goods—to the extent that they are even recognized —are no longer to be achieved through public institutions, but are to be privatized. The democratic vision associated with public functions is to be abandoned or seriously curtailed in favor of the ideal of efficiency. There is an abiding belief that democracy must be limited because it interferes with the private decisions of market experts, thereby reducing wealth and capital. And anything that is perceived as interfering with the growth of capitalism —be it the social welfare system, labor unions, civil rights, or government programs—is being curtailed while government policies and structures that protect capital, including the military, are enhanced.

Although proponents of this style of globalism purport to support democracy, it is only in a role subservient to capital. In the United States, we are softly encouraged to vote, while being constantly reminded that in these global matters that shape our everyday life, we have no say. We are told that no city, state, or nation can or should try to influence this powerful, but uncontrollable process. We are reminded that one can regulate capital, but any attempt to do so will hurt the economy.

The deregulation of capital is made to appear both good and natural. Our attention is drawn away from the fact that there are powerful organizations supported by the U.S. government's leadership that protect and facilitate the flow of capital. These institutions include the World Bank, International Development Association, International Finance Corporation, International Monetary Fund, World Trade Organization, etc.

Unfortunately, there are no organizations of equal stature to protect the interests of workers, racial minorities, the environment, or women and children. There are, of course, several treaties and international instruments dealing with some of these issues, such as the Convention on International Trade in Endangered Species, Convention on the Elimination of All Forms of Discrimination against Women, Declaration on the Rights of Persons Belonging to National or Ethnic, Religious, or Linguistic Minorities.

These are nearly impotent, however, compared with the institutions with far-reaching and substantial goals of protecting capital. When citizens try to raise such issues, it is simply asserted that making working conditions or the environment part of trade agreements would unduly interfere with free trade. American-style globalism has not just transformed the flow of capital, it has transformed the role of government and the meaning of citizenship.

People are now brought together as consumers, but kept apart as citizens. The transformed role of government is not to protect citizens or the precious safety net of public space but to protect and facilitate the flow of capital. So today we speak of free markets, but not of free labor. We speak of an expanding global market, but a diminishing public space, and we hardly speak at all of citizen participation and justice. This is an authoritarian vision where armies police people and nations, so capital might be free.

It is very doubtful that capital, despite advances in technology, would be nearly as mobile without the nationally brokered agreements that have the force of law and the coercive power of the state behind them. But while capital relies on the government to do its bidding, we enjoy freedom as individuals without the power that only comes from the collective action of informed citizens. While it might be true that cities and states, and certainly private individuals, can do little to influence globalism, it is clearly false that nations, especially the United States, are powerless in the face of globalism.

Undermining Social Movements

During the last part of the twentieth century, the Civil Rights Movement, the women's movement, and the environmental movement advanced their claims for inclusion and justice. An attack on the public role of the state is a powerful strategy to limit the aspirations of these groups. They are made impotent

Readings

"Global Finance in the Americas: Wealth & Hunger Revisited," *NACLA Report on the Americas* 33/1 (July/August 1999).

Greider, William. *One World, Ready or Not: The Manic Logic of Global Capitalism.* New York: Touchstone, 1997.

Singh, Kavaljit. *The Globalization of Finance: A Citizen's Guide.* London & New York: Zed Books, 1999.

"The Threat of Globalism," *Race and Class.* 40, no. 2–3 (October 1998–March 1999).

United Nations Development Programme, *Human Development Report 1999.* New York: Oxford University Press, 1999.

Yutzis, Mario J. "A Special Issue on Globalization and Discrimination." Peoples for Human Rights, *IMADR Yearbook.* 6 (1998).

Organizations

- Focus on the Global South, Professor Walden Bello, c/o CURSI Wisit Prachuabmoh Building, Chulalongkorn University, Phyathai Rd., Bangkok, Thailand 10330; 66–2–218–7363/64/65; admin@focusweb.org; www.focusweb.org
- International Forum on Globalization, Building 1062, Fort Cronkhite, Sausalito, CA 94965; 415/229–9350; ifg@ifg.org; www.ifg.org
- Global Exchange, 2017 Mission St., #303, San Francisco, CA 94110; 415/255–7296; www.globalexchange.org
- Foundation for Science, Technology and Natural Resource Policy, Dr. Vandana Shiva, 105 Raipur Road; Dehra Dun 248 001, India; 91–135–23374; vshiva@giasdl01.vsnl.net.in
- People-Centered Development Forum, David Korten, c/o Positive Futures Network, P.O. Box 10818, Bainbridge Island, WA 98110; 206/842–0216; dkorten@bainbridge.net

in a forum where wealth, not votes, dictates policies. These groups are marginalized in an economic arena that transforms the market, with decisions made behind closed doors, not in public and civic spaces.

Destruction of the public space also results in a decline of the public voice. In the United States, this decline in the role and scope of democracy in the relationship to the market occurred just when the Civil Rights Movement began to make significant gains in securing real access to the political process for blacks and other minorities.

This article, then, is not an attack on globalism per se but on the excesses and undemocratic nature of the U.S.-style globalism popular now, which is particularly hostile to people of color and other marginal groups. This style of globalism disempowers average Americans in every way, except as consumers. Globalization has been happening for over a century and will continue. It must be reenvisioned to appropriately protect capital, and also to protect labor, the environment, and people of color. These concerns must be seen as interrelated, not as separate. Furthermore, we must create the necessary international structures with transparency and accountability in order to make this vision a reality and to develop suitable remedies for the plight of marginalized peoples. These steps should not be seen as hostile to business, but as an appropriate cost of doing business in a justice-oriented and sustainable global economy.

Despite the rhetoric about the unmitigated good that can come from U.S.-style globalism, there is an increasing call to look more closely at the process as it relates to people and the environment throughout the world. Some assert that the U.S.-style globalism threatens democracy. Others argue that this style of globalism threatens capitalism itself. Both claims may be right.

We believe it is critical to look more closely at what globalism means for people in general and people of color in particular. Given our more recent history of developing a social compact that includes all people, the United States should not be championing a style of globalism that is blind to the needs of some sectors. If this process continues, we are likely to permanently reinscribe a subordinated, life-threatening status for people of color all over the globe and rationalize it with an invisible hand. We can change this by working to make the invisible visible.

Part 7

President Clinton's Initiative on Race

In May 1997, President Clinton, as part of his commencement address at the University of California-San Diego, a symbolically appropriate locale, given the demographics of our largest state, announced formation of The President's Initiative on Race. Its ambitious mandate was to promote constructive national dialogue on race; understand the nation's racial history; encourage innovative approaches to calming racial tensions; and develop and implement solutions in the areas of education, economic opportunity, housing, health care, and the administration of justice.

One of the President's first steps was appointment of an Advisory Board to the Initiative, to be headed by the distinguished African-American historian John Hope Franklin, author of, among his many books, Reconstruction After the Civil War *(University of Chicago Press, 1995) and* From Slavery to Freedom: A History of African Americans *(Knopf, 2000 - 8th ed.). Although the appointment of this Advisory Board—indeed, the entire Initiative—was apparently planned absent consultation with traditional civil rights leaders and organizations, the move was greeted enthusiastically by the civil rights community. PRRAC was particularly enthused, as the person named to head the Initiative staff, Judith Winston, was a former PRRAC Board member.*

But consternation arose immediately when word leaked out that Professor Franklin and his six colleagues did not plan to issue an independent public report, but rather saw their role as privately and quietly advising the President. Our response was to place pressure on this body to act openly and publicly, else the prestige and wisdom of John Hope Franklin would be dissipated. We commissioned and printed, in two successive issues of Poverty & Race, *a series of short "Advice to the Advisory Board" essays by well-known thinkers and activists (not necessarily mutually exclusive categories). These were sent to all seven members of the Advisory Board and distributed widely beyond the readership of* Poverty & Race, *and are reprinted here.*

*As it turned out, the Advisory Board did issue a report of its own—whether our pressure, added to that of others, was a factor, we will never know. Unfortunately, however, the Advisory Board's September 1998 report—*One America in the 21st Century: Forging a New Future*—was disappointing: the other members of the Advisory Board were no John Hope Franklins. It contained some inspiring rhetoric, some useful history and demographic projections, but the recommendations were very general, and, as could be expected, there was no criticism of the relevant actions and inactions of the Administration that established the advisory body. A full half of the report consisted of appendices, most of which simply recorded the places of and participants in the Board's many community forums, corporate leader forums, religious leader forums, meetings with American Indian tribal governments, other events and activities—nearly 300 listed under that category alone, "One America Conversations," Campus Week* *of Dialogue activities—nearly 600 schools participated in these, Statewide Days of Dialogue in 41 states. Another appendix provided excerpts from the Advisory Board's One America Dialogue Guide, tips for dialogue leaders, basic ground rules for dialogues, and samples of small group dialogues. And there was a short, undigested catalogue of "Promising Practices" around the country, along with accompanying appendices indexing these practices by sector (business, community-building, education, religious, youth, etc.) and by region. The Advisory Board and Initiative staff carried out a whole lot of meetings and produced a whole lot of verbiage, but the product has been deeply disappointing as a concrete, programmatic plan of action. And so we asked these same persons who had earlier proffered their advice to critique the report, and the responses of those who replied also are reprinted here.*

The initiative turned out to be a big bust. Just five days before leaving office, Clinton submitted a long, rambling Message to Congress, "The Unfinished Work of Building One America"—a laundry list of generalities that got little attention and was, of course, toothless, coming from an about-to-be ex-president. Harvard Law professor Randall Kennedy had this to say about the Clinton Race Initiative (see his "The Triumph of Robert Tokenism" in the February 2001 Atlantic Monthly): ". . . [T]he initiative displayed the parochial, shallow self-servingness that besmirches all too much of Clinton's talk about race relations. Portrayed as an effort at dialogue, the President's conversation was from the beginning a tightly scripted monologue that regurgiated familiar nostrums while avoiding discussion of real problems. . . . Because of Clinton's conversation and its embarrassing end, a long time will have to pass before another President invests personal and political capital in pressing for public education about the American race question."

If and when a future administration ever decides it finally is time for the federal government to mount a serious, comprehensive anti-racism campaign, test it against the concerns, admonishments, and proposals of those PRRAC asked for advice, critique, and commentary. In fact, use those yardsticks to test any and all proposed policies and programs, government and private, designed to deal with racism in our society. The most salient questions and issues are:

- How useful is "dialogue," the central approach of the Initiative, and what relation does dialogue bear to institutional racism?
- How do the intersections of race and poverty present distinct issues from racist practices and patterns more generally?
- How important is the country's racial history in understanding and dealing with today's racism? Are reparations for slavery a useful and appropriate approach, and if so, what form should they take? Is a formal government apology for slavery (never made) useful and possible? Congressman John Conyers for years has introduced a bill to create a commission simply to study the question of reparations, but it has never even gotten out

of committee. In June 2000, Congressman Tony Hall re-introduced his earlier resolution to issue a Congressional apology for the institution of slavery, but it likely will get no further than his prior effort.

- *What are the principal programs needed to deal with racism, and what would they cost? Such programs doubtless will require hundreds of billions of dollars—where will these funds come from and what changes then are required in our tax system? Are WPA-like job creation programs—tied to rebuilding schools, housing, and the infrastructure in low-income communities—a critical component? How do we truly end the racial disparities in education that are simply reproducing on an intergenerational basis what has been termed an "underclass"? How do we handle the nation's serious housing problem: slums, overcrowding, lack of affordability, neighborhood defects—and beyond that, the trickiest question of all: what is our approach to racial integration of neighborhoods?*
- *How do we restructure the criminal justice system so as to reduce or eliminate its patently racist aspects, while at the same time providing all Americans with adequate protection from criminal behavior? How do we create structures of education, employment, community and family stability that make criminal behavior less likely?*
- *How can whites, of all social and economic classes, be made to understand what is meant by "white skin privilege"?*
- *How do inevitable and predictable demographic changes in the country's population affect how race and racism are defined and manifested? What changes are demanded in the black-white paradigm of race, and what are the differences and commonalities between the situation of blacks and other racial minorities? What distinct issues and problems arise in relations between various minority groups?*
- *How do we generate honest critiques of current and recent government policies, and achieve recognition of the key role government must play if racism is truly to be attacked.*

These are only some of the questions and issues. What is needed is a coherent program, a timeline, a pricetag, a set of responsibilities, and—above all—a sense of commitment and urgency. Nothing less will accomplish the task.

Notes on the President's Initiative on Race

Chester Hartman

I was in the audience for the second public meeting of the Advisory Board to the President's Initiative on Race, at the Mayflower Hotel in Washington,

September 30, 1997. Both President Clinton and Vice-President Gore attended for about an hour.

The seven-person Board is a demographic triumph—four men, three women; one Asian-American, one Latino, two African Americans; labor (AFL-CIO) and business (Nissan's CEO): a minister; two former governors, one from the North (NJ), one from the South (MS). But aside from its renowned chair, historian John Hope Franklin, a wonderful choice (and we should all be half as energetic and sharp at eighty-two), the Board is composed of relatively unknown figures—selections made, apparently, with little consultation with those civil rights organizations and leaders one would expect to have a say in such appointments. Franklin of course is author of classic works on slavery and the Reconstruction era—and no stranger to society's race bias, not the least manifestation of which was a 1995 incident when he left a Cosmos Club dinner prior to receiving the Presidential Medal of Freedom, only to be mistaken by a white woman for the coatroom clerk.

A Vague Mission

The Board's mission is necessarily on the vague side. Its formal role, as its title indicates, is merely to provide advice to the President "on matters involving race and racial reconciliation." Apparently, and disturbingly, it does not intend to issue its own report, merely transmit its advice to the President, whose White House staff will take it from there.

The Executive Order establishing the Initiative specified four functions:

a) promote a constructive national dialogue to confront and work through challenging issues that surround race;

b) increase the Nation's understanding of our recent [sic] history of race relations and the course our Nation is charting on the issues of race relations and racial diversity;

c) bridge racial divides by encouraging leaders in communities throughout the Nation to develop and implement innovative approaches to calming racial tensions; and

d) identify, develop, and implement solutions to problems in areas in which race has a substantial impact, such as education, economic opportunity, housing, health care, and the administration of justice.

With respect to item d), the Board, Executive Order language notwithstanding, apparently has decided to focus on education and economic opportunity—certainly central issues, but ignoring housing, where most discrimination and segregation occurs and a prime cause of educational segregation and disadvantage, as well as an important factor in job market discrimination. Housing, however, is the toughest nut to crack, race-wise.

Research on the "hypersegregation" phenomenon by Douglas Massey, Nancy Denton, and others shows how widespread and pernicious extreme racial separation is and the impacts of this isolation.

Reviewing the Data

Most of the Mayflower meeting was taken up with reports by outside consultants. Demographer Reynolds Farley of the Russell Sage Foundation ably reviewed data showing what by now should be accepted knowledge: that the United States is becoming an increasingly multiracial society, due to immigration, differential birth rates, intermarriage, and self-identification, and that shortly after 2050 whites will comprise less than half the nation's population (something true in many locales already due to quite different regional impacts of the forces creating this change). Harvard sociologist Lawrence Bobo reviewed the welter of confusing (and to this observer not always reliable) polling data on racial attitudes. Clearly, expressed attitudes toward integration and racial equality have markedly improved in recent decades (but I wonder how honest people are in admitting to views that increasingly are regarded as unacceptable). Stark and important differences show up in how whites and minorities view the prevalence of racial discrimination and disadvantage in our society, and in acceptable levels of residential integration (whites say they would not mind having a few black neighbors, blacks feel they need a far higher proportion of other blacks, in neighborhoods as well as other settings, in order to feel comfortable—proportions that would lead the whites to flee). These polling data doubtless are accurate, and present a massive barrier to solving Myrdal's "American Dilemma." Equally depressing and disturbing is the extent of negative stereotyping of racial minorities (views the culture inculcates in racial minorities themselves) and the deepening pessimism about the future of race relations and the quite understandable alienation felt by the nation's racial minorities.

Other expert witnesses were psychologists James Jones (University of Delaware), John Dovidio (Colgate), and Derald Wing Sue (California State-Hayward). From them came important, but by now well-recognized truths (often proved via cleverly designed experiments): the ways in which race is a social not a biological construct; the problems that ensue if race is ignored (effectively destroying the fatuous "color-blind America" push from the Right); the way that negative expectations elicit poor performance; the subtlety with which racism now manifests itself; the therefore lesser consciousness of racist practices on the part of those who act in a racist manner; the need to acknowledge and recognize normal, expectable biases, stereotypes, and preconceived notions based on race.

The several hours of testimony was all very well done. But it is hard to imagine that the Board members (or most of the 200 or so people in attendance—the majority of whom did not return for the afternoon session, after Clinton and Gore's appearance) learned much new. There was little interaction among Board members and not much came from them other than their prepared statements. No audience participation was allowed. As Steven Holmes observed in his *New York Times* account the next day, "Missing . . . was any crisp talk about what the panel itself would do. . . ." Subsequent *Washington Post* and *New York Times* stories were headed, respectively, "Race Initiative Appears to Be Foundering" and "Critics Say Clinton Panel About Race Lacks Focus."

Dialogue or Beyond?

And that of course raises the Big Question: What Is To Be Done? And is the President's Initiative any more or other than yet another largely time-buying, window-dressing move to give the impression that Something Is Being Done about the country's historic, deeply grounded racism? Vice President Gore told the audience that "this may turn out to be the most important initiative of the Clinton presidency." But little occurred at the Mayflower to back up this claim.

The key buzz-word is "dialogue." But is there evidence that dialogue by itself leads to real change? Most efforts at dialogue are notably shallow. The President and Board Chair Franklin announced there would be a series of "town meetings" around the country. Honest dialogue itself (which realistically cannot happen at a media event like a town meeting), while having the potential to be a healing step, takes an incredible amount of trust and preparation: Letty Cottin Pogrebin, in her contribution to the excellent collection *Struggles in the Promised Land: Towards a History of Black-Jewish Relations in the U.S.*, edited by Jack Salzman and Cornel West, describes the decade (sic) of regular—and eventually failed—meetings among a small, homogeneous, biracial group of women before feelings could honestly and comfortably be put out.

Dialogue of course implies a very personal, individualistic, and interpersonal approach to racism. While individual attitudes and behavior of course are central issues, an exclusive or predominant take on racism from that perspective will slight the larger institutional forces that reflect and undergird the racist character of American society. How do we deal with the enormous, and growing, racial disparities in wealth and income? How do we fix our education system so that it does not reproduce and exacerbate these disparities and create "hypersegregation"? How do we counter the current judicial and legislative moves to undermine and limit the political representation of Blacks, Latinos, and Asian Americans? How do we get the government to effectively enforce its own anti-discrimination laws? How do we face the ways in which racism benefits various groups and entities—including the very corporations deemed so essential to the goal of economic opportunity? Questions such as these—and the list could be expanded greatly—would seem to lie beyond the Board's purview. And even if they were willing to deal with racism at that level, what advice would our not notably courageous President take and go with?

A frequently invoked theme was the need to involve youth (a demographic category absent from the Board's composition). President Clinton pointed proudly to the Fairfax County, Virginia school system as probably the nation's most diverse: 182 nationalities, 100 language groups. But I suspect any honest look at the workings of that system would show all the signs of disparate educational opportunities by race and class, tracking, de facto segregation, and most if not all the other problems that characterize school systems across the country. Ex-Governor William Winter of Mississippi proudly passed around to the President and Vice President photos of his young grandchildren's integrated school in Oxford. But where is the evidence that simply going to an integrated elementary school (a dying institution, given the rapid resegregation occurring in our country) produces positive results later on? (Going through some office materials while waiting for the meeting to start, I was struck by an account from the SouthWest Organizing Project's (SWOP) newsletter of two teachers fired by the Vaughn, New Mexico School Board for using the teaching materials provided by the Southern Poverty Law Center's "Teaching Tolerance" project and SWOP's *500 Years of Chicano History in Pictures*.)

That's History

Then there's the role of history. John Hope Franklin has declared that no progress can be made on the racial front without an understanding of history. Will the Board look beyond "recent" history? The knotty and complex question of the continuing impact of 200-plus years of slavery ought to be raised (something Congressman John Conyers has tried to do for years via a study commission—but the bill has never made it out of committee). Is the reparations issue one to at least consider? And what about the "apology for slavery" resolution recently introduced by a group of White House members? Certainly, by itself it may not mean much; but it could be a start toward dealing with country's racist past—not only slavery, but our treatment of Native Americans, Mexicans, Chinese. "That's history" seems to be a putdown nowadays; we need to understand and come to grips with our history and how it affects the present if ever we are to disprove the "permanent racism" thesis of Derrick Bell and others.

Perhaps it was providential that as the Board wound up the day's proceedings, a noisy birthday party in the adjacent meeting room was heard playing "Somewhere Over the Rainbow."

The Speech President Clinton Should Have Made

Howard Winant

"My fellow Americans of all colors and all national origins: it is an honor to address you all, and to recognize you all, as equals. For a long time, this country has been moving toward that recognition, as we work together to overcome the legacy of a deeply racist past. It is time to acknowledge the pain and suffering that were wrought by African enslavement, by the virtual holocaust of the native peoples who lived here before there was an America, and by the coerced manual labor of millions of immigrants. Where would our country be today if these countless people, of all colors, of all varieties of the one human race, had not expended their toil, their blood, sweat, and tears to build this society? Their contributions were not properly appreciated; indeed, they often worked for nothing or under the lash. What would America be without the enormous contributions that racially-defined minorities have made to our culture? Think of American music and dance and poetry, think of American military achievements, think of the very language Americans speak. Without the efforts and ideas of a people which included not just white folk, but also black, brown, yellow, and red folk, we could not even know ourselves.

"Despite their great gifts, for centuries these givers—these people of color—were mistreated and exploited. Even after African slavery was abolished and the wholesale slaughter of Native Americans came to an end, racial segregation and discrimination, lynching and deportation, denial of the franchise and widespread neglect, all continued. In our own lifetimes we have witnessed tremendous wrongs committed in the name of race. Yet the struggles of these same peoples for justice, combined with the help of many whites, have begun to overcome the legacy of racism. The great pioneers of the movements for emancipation and civil rights, for the rights of working people and the War on Poverty did not labor in vain.

"But even today, as we near the end of the twentieth century, we are not done with the task of achieving racial equality and respect across the color lines that still survive in America. Yes, some would like us to believe that today we live in a 'color-blind' society, where all are judged according to their merit. I too would like to believe this, but I do not.

"Is opportunity equal when ghetto schools spend only half the money suburban schools can spend per pupil? Is it equal when black unemployment remains twice as high as white unemployment? Is there a commitment to civil rights when the Equal Employment Opportunity Commission labors under a backlog of tens of thousands of discrimination cases? Is there a 'color-blindness' in immigration law? If there is equal opportunity housing in America, then why do we still have ghettos and barrios, as well as nearly exclusively white neighborhoods? Is the attack on affirmative action, which is going on at the state and local as well as the federal levels, going to create more equality, or will it return us to the segregated employment and education we thought were being eliminated?

"If, despite all the progress we have made, there is still a lot of racism in America today, then it is my task as President to provide leadership, and to propose policies, that will work to reduce it. Here are some of my suggestions, which I have directed my staff to formulate, as appropriate, into legislative proposals and legal briefs:

"First, we should intervene systematically against racial harassment. The persistence and even growth of racist organizations and cults, often armed and dangerous, must be effectively countered. Many of them call themselves militias and organizations of 'patriots,' but they are little more than modern-era night riders and racist terrorists. We cannot accept their use of the word 'patriot' because nothing could be less patriotic than spreading the bile of racial hatred.

"Second, we should reinforce our commitment to racial integration. Assaults on minority families trying to move into a previously segregated neighborhood are still a flourishing form of racial harassment; they should be prevented by law and by strong community commitments to tolerance. I'm a great believer in the phrase W.I.M.B.Y.—Welcome In My Back Yard.

"Third, the federal government should endorse the principle of equal law enforcement, notably by police and courts. For example, the widespread police harassment of racially-defined minorities, for the crime known as D.W.B.—Driving While Black—must be ended. The federal government could play a big role in training our often beleaguered and bewildered police to respect all citizens regardless of race. Our police have a tough job to do, but they still must do it fairly. The same is often true of judges and juries.

"Fourth, I will dedicate the rest of my second term to developing programs to foster massive investment in urban infrastructure (in the style of a new WPA). A brief visit to the ghettos and barrios of our nation quickly reveals the price of neglect, a price that will be paid by our nation's youth and by future generations in the form of more crime, higher taxes, and a less open society. The investment we make now, both public and private, could restore our cities to their past comfort, safety, efficiency, and economic viability. It will pay off tremendously all across this country. There is certainly plenty of work to be done: schools and facilities need rebuilding; public transport, roads, and sewer systems do, too. Where such need exists, how can we permit, how can we justify, endemic unemployment in our impoverished urban neighborhoods? Once the efforts begin to rebuild our cities, private investment and job creation in the inner cities will start to grow again as well. This is the lesson of my great Democratic predecessor, Franklin Roosevelt: to provide useful work to those in poverty is a sacred duty of government.

"Fifth, I dedicate myself to a renewed commitment to enforcing the civil rights laws, both through the Equal Employment Opportunity Commission and other civil rights agencies. Those who experience discrimination in employment, housing, education, or voting rights must be assured that the federal government will actively intervene to investigate and remedy racial injustice. I also announce my intention to foster racial equality through judicial appointments: I will seek to appoint judges who have demonstrated their interest in and commitment to civil rights and equal opportunity. I will also direct the Justice Department actively to defend existing policies and programs, such as voting rights, against attempts to nullify or weaken them.

"Finally, I want to let you know, my fellow Americans, of my ongoing commitment to affirmative action. Far from being the evil its opponents label it, affirmative action policy is one of the most valuable tools we have in our effort to combat racism. In government and in the corporate world, it has many supporters, but it needs one more supporter very strongly: the President of the United States. In many areas, but particularly in education and employment, affirmative action works, not only to overcome the habits of discrimination developed in the past, but also to forestall discrimination in the present. Research demonstrates over and over again that affirmative action policies do not discriminate 'in reverse.' Affirmative action programs do not need to be used (and are indeed rarely used) as quotas. Rather, they offer one of the only avenues through which racial minorities can advance through the minefields, unfortunately still very much present, of discrimination and inequality. We cannot dispense with them while substantial racial injustice still exists.

"My fellow citizens, we must recognize that race remains, and probably will remain for a long time, a prominent dimension of our social structure and culture. We must accept that although we have made progress in fighting racism, systematic social inequality continues along racial lines. Once we comprehend this, we can stand together as a people and a government for the ideals we most deeply cherish: that all men and women are created equal. And we can do this not only in principle, but in practice."

—— Symposium ——

Advice to the Advisory Board

Public Education, Policy Initiatives, Paradigm Shift

Raúl Yzaguirre

Recommendations

Public Education

The President's Initiative on Race should promote increased public understanding of diverse perspectives on race and related issues. Adoption of this "public education" objective makes sense for three reasons. First, on the merits, we believe improvements in race relations will be predicated in large part on increased public understanding of the diverse views of various communities. The Initiative should, therefore, have an explicit commitment to educating all of us about each others' perspectives.

Second, adoption of a "public education" focus will reduce real or perceived conflict over the Initiative's mission and mandate. In preliminary discussions leading up to the establishment of the Initiative, National Council of La Raza (NCLR) advocated vigorously that the Initiative should be fully inclusive of the issues and perspectives of Latinos. We believe that a re-framing of the issue along the lines we suggest avoids the need to select any single "correct" perspective and permits all legitimate perspectives to be affirmed.

Third, the objective is both measurable and achievable. Organizations such as the National Opinion Research Center, the National Conference (for Community and Justice), the American Jewish Committee, and others poll regularly on issues related to race; perhaps one or more sets of these polls could be adapted to attempt to measure changes in public attitudes and factual understandings on these issues. In addition, this President has demonstrated his ability to use the power of the bully pulpit and his own considerable rhetorical skills to promote and improve public understanding of complex issues.

Policy Initiatives

The Initiative should identify, prioritize, and promote policy objectives that tend to unify, rather than polarize, the public. Many, arguably most, policy issues related to race are the subject of serious ideological and partisan debate. We do not argue that these should necessarily be avoided; NCLR is itself a vigorous advocate on a number of controversial issues. We do argue, however, that policy proposals that can be framed in inclusive, unifying terms have the greatest likelihood of enactment. Specifically, we believe that the Advisory Board should recommend:

- More vigorous enforcement of basic civil rights laws. Even the most vigorous opponents of affirmative action purport to support the enforcement of basic anti-discrimination laws. Given this apparent consensus, we believe it would be highly appropriate for the Advisory Board to recommend substantial increases in funding for the federal government's civil rights enforcement "infrastructure."
- Provision of English language and literacy training to all who need it. Few public policy issues are as divisive and confusing as language policy, in all of its different contexts (English-only laws, bilingual education, bilingual ballots, etc.). However, both "language restrictionists" and "multiculturalists" appear to agree on one theme—it is in the interest of non-English speakers and the society at-large to promote English language acquisition. Despite this apparent consensus, much of the policy debate is focused on the divisive aspects of the issue rather than on the single unifying theme. We believe the Advisory Board can help cut this proverbial "Gordian Knot" by proposing a major new policy initiative that, over time, will assure that every non-English-speaking resident of the U.S. is afforded the opportunity to learn to speak, read and write English.
- Best practices in reducing racial tensions and addressing racial con-

flicts. While most Americans would agree with the notion that we need to do more to reduce racial tension and conflict, there is little agreement about how we should go about doing so. Numerous materials and "diversity consultants" are widely available, and several organizations are attempting to identify, assess, and promote effective "best practices" in promoting healthy race relations. Notwithstanding these efforts, the efficacy of specific approaches to addressing specific types of situations and problems has yet to be demonstrated in a rigorous, empirical manner. We believe that the Advisory Board and the Initiative can be helpful in both identifying and promoting effective best practices by:

- Sponsoring and commissioning literature reviews, research, and expert discussions designed to identify and promote programs, mechanisms, and practices that have proven effective in preventing, reducing, and/or ameliorating racial tensions and conflicts.
- Identifying and supporting private and public agencies capable of assisting governments, corporations, and individuals to appropriately address racial tensions and conflicts, including state-local human relations commissions, university-based programs, religious institutions and other private organizations, the Community Relations Service, and other federal agencies.
- Articulating, and encouraging the President to articulate, a "new ethos" in race relations that explicitly promotes reconciliation and healing. We believe that rational but direct discussions about race are far healthier than the traditional adversarial conversations about race— in which race is used as a weapon to advance an ideological or political agenda.

Paradigm Shift

The Initiative should identify and promote a "new paradigm" for future discussions of race relations in the United States. The traditional "melting pot" paradigm is clearly inapplicable to communities like African Americans, who were excluded from "the pot" by slavery, Jim Crow laws, and persistent discrimination. Latinos believe that other traditional paradigms about race simply fail to adequately capture, explain, or describe the condition of Latinos in the United States. For example, the traditional "black-white" paradigm obviously fails to include most Latinos. Similarly, however, the "immigrant" paradigm in which Latinos are often pigeon-holed cannot account for two-thirds of Hispanics who are native-born and the millions who can trace their ancestry 150 years back to the Treaty of Guadalupe Hidalgo (Mexican Americans) or 100 years back to the end of the Spanish American War (Puerto Ricans, Cubans, residents of Guam). Neither the "slavery" nor "immigrant" paradigms help to explain or promote understanding about these people, who became "Americans by conquest."

But Latinos are by no means alone in feeling excluded or ignored in conversations about race; the condition of Native Americans, Asian Americans, Afro-Latinos, Arab Americans, African and Caribbean immigrants, multiracial people, and many White ethnics are also not fully addressed by traditional paradigms.

We suggest that a new paradigm is needed, one that is sufficiently broad to encompass the condition of all Americans and our relationships to one another. Such a paradigm should include:

- A powerful metaphor, which might include:

  - a symphony orchestra in which each instrument retains its individuality but contributes to the sound of the whole; or
  - a stew, in which the ingredients are partially "melted" (in a pot no less), while retaining their original character; or
  - a mosaic, in which individual pieces of different sizes, colors, and textures combine to form a beautiful, artistic whole; or
  - some other easily explainable, visually appealing graphic image.

- A "language of public discourse" which permits us to discuss racial and ethnic differences and tensions without offending but also without resorting to exclusive use of "politically correct" euphemisms that do not offend but do not illuminate either. While we may make mistakes along the way, the conversation is too important to be avoided; the deliberations of the Advisory Board could be a "safe harbor" for these difficult but essential conversations.

Needed: An Educational "Bible"

Marcus Raskin

The most the Advisory Board can do is make its document into an educational "bible" which would be used in schools, churches, unions, colleges, and universities. It should be taken as the authoritative statement about race with a subtext about class in America. The document should include a number of sections with interweaving themes.

The Board must interpret and reinterpret foundational documents as the basis for its analysis and recommendations. These are not aspirational documents but have immediate and real effect. By this, I mean the Thirteenth through Fifteenth Amendments to the Constitution. It must show how these are to be interpreted in light of present day realities. The Board must also show how the system of criminal justice which the nation and states have formulated over the last decade continues a form of slavery and destruction of the black male population.

The Declaration of Independence should also become a fundamental referencing document, as should Lincoln's definition of the purpose of government. Franklin D. Roosevelt's Bill of Economic Rights can also be referenced as the means of showing the importance of economic and social justice. What I am suggesting is that the nation as a whole needs a rights and equality canon which sets the frame of reference for future consideration of particular policies.

- Historical view of the struggles for racial justice. Here again there must be discussion of slavery and the slave mentality of whites, which included the stealing of land from African American farmers. This section should also include the passage of anti-vagrancy and -loitering laws as a means of contracting out prison labor and reintroducing slavery-like conditions to build factories.

  There should be discussion of the role of the federal government in more recent times in bringing about change of conditions, its failures and successes, emphasizing that positive changes would not have occurred without specific federal intervention, including that of the federal courts—for example, fair employment practices during the wartime New Deal, and desegregating the military and defense contracts. Mention should also be made of the struggles necessary to get rid of the poll tax and advocacy of anti-lynching laws.
- There should be a discussion of the legal onslaught on affirmative action and the present not so subtle backlash in the courts. Note unfair prison sentencing, as evidenced by cocaine/crack cocaine length of prison terms. There should be discussion of *Plessy v. Ferguson* and Justice Harlan's famous dissent, highlighting how the test of color-blind is predicated on white domination. The color-blind story should be hit head-on, including a discussion of what Martin Luther King, Jr. meant when he used the phrase.
- The question of the use of false standards and modes of certification and admission to keep African Americans on the margins of mainstream America should also be considered. It is important to remember that in a democratic and free society which puts emphasis on the future, we

must be prepared to bet on the capacities and talents of people that do not necessarily show up on past or even present performance, especially on tests which emphasize non-cooperative activities, knowledge, and learning processes which are predicated on competition among students.

- The multicultural society should not be seen as an excuse to refrain from undertaking those specific activities and programs within the civil society and governments which are necessary to improve conditions of African-Americans. This means analyzing directly Representative John Conyers's bill, which is predicated on apology and reparations. Presently, government programs that may have been intended to aid African Americans often end up aiding other "minorities," including white women. In other words, the present system pits minorities against one another for jobs, education, and enterprise grants. This situation could turn out to be disastrous.

- This section would deal with why African Americans are not doing better in a period of prosperity. A historical and sociological discussion of fair shares with respect to who built this nation and how they should be compensated for their role should be undertaken. Often it is those who receive the least pay who keep the society going. And often those are jobs held by minorities.

- There should be a section on repairing the national community, which means discussion of why reparations, why an apology, and what the American Constitution must mean for the twenty-first century. This section could talk about advances made toward the Promised Land. There are promises to keep, if not a promised land. There is a long way to go, especially when we look at incarceration and arrest rates for African Americans. These rates are uncomfortably close to an attenuated system of slavery, especially when linked to government programs which ostensibly are to help the person but end up being social control mechanisms.

Plessy v. Ferguson Lives

Jonathan Kozol

The shame of the nation is the fact that, a full century after *Plessy v. Ferguson*, our public schools remain both segregated and unequal. A deeper cause of shame is that the influential press in northern cities has decided to ignore this issue and pretend instead that "innovative" ghetto education ("site-based," "reinvented," bureaucratically "efficient") is a reasonable substitute for any semblance of fair play or equal justice. If the President attempts to skirt this issue, he will leave behind a legacy of moral abdication. The reliance on local property wealth for tax-support of public education and the persistent residential segregation both of cities and their surrounding suburbs guarantee perpetual injustice and must be addressed head-on. John Hope Franklin understands this better than any other scholar I know. The willingness to force this understanding on the public conscience, at whatever political cost to President Clinton, is the formidable challenge that he faces.

Acknowledge, Understand White-Skin Privilege

Julian Bond

Here is one thing—the most important thing—President Clinton's Initiative on Race ought to have done.

It ought to have found a way to get Americans of European descent to acknowledge the privileges they enjoy because of their race.

Acknowledging and understanding white-skin privilege is the vital first step in any honest dialogue on race. A forthright, candid internal exchange among whites is a necessary first phase, the predicate to interracial conversation.

For years, blacks and some whites built a successful Civil Rights Movement by contrasting black inequality with the national promise of justice for all. The stark divide between black and white life chances was a mighty fuel for the Civil Rights Movement of the 1960s.

But what had been a black-led interracial movement in the 1960s largely became a black-led black movement in the 1990s. For many, black life choices are assumed to account for diminished black life chances. Discussions of race focus entirely on the inadequacy or wrongness of existing remedies or on schemes of community uplift. For a variety of reasons, white Americans today demonstrate little interest or involvement in narrowing the great racial divide.

All of us must find some way to engage whites in common struggle with blacks.

I despair that I cannot imagine how this is to be done—perhaps through structured and informal education, public forums, and neighborhood-level discussion groups. But who will come? Who will summon them?

It is remarkable to consider that the Promise Keepers are the only predominately white group I can think of who have adopted achieving racial harmony as a core belief—even if they do not acknowledge that something is wrong between the races in America—and have pledged to do something about it. Why do they stand almost alone?

An Action Agenda

Hugh Price

To be blunt, we worry that the game plan for the Initiative going forward is long on dialogue and short on action. We offer the following recommendations:

- By the middle of the next century, our nation's population will be roughly one half Caucasian, one half people of color. Accordingly, we urge Mr. Clinton and the Advisory Board to remind the American people of these demographic trends, over and over, until we understand the inevitability and accept the clear implication that the opportunity structure of society must be kept wide open to America's growing population of color. We strongly recommend that the President mount a campaign to ensure that this message is repeated in task force reports, town meetings, and in the media.
- We call upon President Clinton and the Advisory Board to keep up the pressure on higher education and employers to stay the course on inclusion. Just as the President has summoned leaders of other sectors to the White House for highly publicized mini-summits, we urge him to invite corporate CEOs, Chamber of Commerce leaders, and university presidents and board chairs to a series of high-profile meetings to affirm their commitments to inclusion.
- We urge the President and the Advisory Board to mount a campaign to pressure state and local educators, policymakers, and elected officials to institute the changes needed in schools and communities to lift the achievement levels of underachieving children. Those key changes include:
  - quality pre-school education;
  - qualified teachers who genuinely believe minority youngsters can learn;

– widespread access to intellectually challenging courses;
– more intimate and autonomous public schools whose core mission is student learning instead of keeping order; and
– constructive programs and caring adults after school and over the summer while parents are earning a living.

This campaign to elevate student achievement should be waged through high-profile White House summits, regional and local town meetings, concerted media outreach, public service advertisement campaigns, and, of course, aggressive use of the bully pulpit.

In addition, President Clinton should review all federal policies and appropriations dealing with pre-K programs, K-12 education, and juvenile justice to make certain they advance these five goals.

We implore the President and the Advisory Board to take up the issue of police/civilian tensions. The Initiative simply cannot and must not sidestep the festering issue of police brutality and abuse toward minority civilians. Mr. Clinton should summon governors, mayors, and state and local police chiefs to call public attention to the urgent need for reform.

Mr. Clinton should underscore his determination by insisting that the Justice Department investigate and prosecute any patterns of abuse. Finally, he should instruct the U.S. Solicitor General to urge the courts to scale back the runaway discretion that has permitted this abuse of civilians who've done little or nothing wrong.

• President Clinton and the Advisory Board should attack the problem of racial isolation by challenging the religious community to reconnect people of different races on a regular basis, for instance through Sunday school exchanges. They should exhort college presidents and student leaders to find ways to bridge the chasms in communications and trust.

• The Clinton administration should pressure school districts and federal courts to stay the course on school integration wherever it's feasible demographically. Finally, the Advisory Board should publicize and disseminate effective curricula for promoting intergroup understanding and tolerance in elementary and secondary schools.

• Lastly, no Initiative to improve race relations can succeed if the federal agency that polices racial discrimination is enfeebled. President Clinton should insist that the Equal Employment Opportunity Commission receive adequate funding to clear up its backlog of roughly 80,000 cases and then stay current with its caseload for a change.

The above was excerpted from a statement of National Urban League recommendations released at an October 7, 1997 press conference.

Focus on the Institutional Barriers

Manning Marable

If the Advisory Board truly wants to understand the contemporary dynamics of institutional racism, it should go first to the prisons and jails across this country, conversing with black, brown, and poor inmates. The criminal justice system today has become our chief means of regulating and controlling millions of unemployed and undereducated black and Latino young men. What lynching was in the South when John Hope Franklin grew up in the 1920s and 1930s, the death penalty and life sentences without parole have become in the 1990s.

As of 2000, there are 2 million inmates in U.S. prisons and jails. In California alone, the number of prisoners, which stood at 19,000 two decades ago, now exceeds 160,000. Prison construction has become a multi-billion dollar business, as small towns compete for new prison sites. Since 1990, the number of prison and jail guards nationwide has grown by 30 percent, to over 600,000. We are constructing about 150 new prison cells *every single day* in the United States.

The social and racial consequences of regulating the poor and minorities throughout the criminal justice apparatus are devastating. One recent study in Washington, DC found that one-half of all African-American males between the ages of eighteen and thirty-five are, on any given day, under the control or direct supervision of the criminal justice system—either in prison or jail, on probation, parole, or awaiting trial. Instead of investing in quality schools and vocational training, we construct new prisons. Instead of providing real jobs at living wages, we pass a crime bill that undermined civil liberties and greatly expanded the possible use of the death penalty. A conversation about race must discuss the connections between poverty, joblessness, and crime. By stigmatizing nearly all young black men as a criminal class, we justify racist stereotypes and reinforce society's racial divide.

Perhaps the Advisory Board should schedule a session at the University of Texas at Austin, where scores of black and Hispanic law students are eliminated with the end of affirmative action programs. Maybe they should interview University of Texas law professor Lino Graglia, who publicly declared that black and Mexican-American students were culturally inferior and "not (as) academically competitive" as whites. Despite the firestorm of criticism generated by Graglia's crude comments, no measures have been taken to reverse the impact of the 1996 *Hopwood* decision, which outlawed the use of race as factor in school admissions criteria and scholarships.

A real conversation about race must examine critically the institutional barriers that have been erected to subordinate people of color, denying them an equal voice in society. Such a conversation would interrogate white politicians and government officials who push for so-called "race-blind" initiatives, which only buttress white racial privilege. As W.E.B. DuBois knew, the struggle to uproot racism requires "race-conscious solutions." Only by talking honestly about the institutions and policies that perpetuate white power and privilege can we begin the long and difficult journey toward reconciliation.

Knitting the Nation

S.M. Miller

The Advisory Board has two audiences, people of color and all Americans. It has educational, policy, political, and community functions. Its contribution should be to provide a new basis for overcoming discrimination and changing the tone of American society. It should provide a report card on the current racial scene, directions to take, and a call to realizing positive American values.

Educationally, the Advisory Board should report on the progress in reducing discrimination and improving racial attitudes. It should then go on to analyze the difficulties that exist, emphasizing the plight of those in the race-poverty intersections and focusing on institutionalized barriers to greater economic and social equality for those in and out of the intersections. Continuing in current directions will not solve the nation's racial problems and tensions. For example, how do educational institutions have to change in order to foster civic learning and employment opportunities for those groups presently not doing well in school?

Institutional barriers include the changes in American industry which limit entry jobs with good pay and promotion potentials, the hidden biases built into selection processes for jobs and higher education, police and judicial treatment of racial-ethnic groups, the maintenance of residential segregation practices, inadequate public and educational services.

If the Advisory Board could open up dialogue about the contemporary interplay of class and race—rescuing "class" from its admissibility that is limited to speaking of "the middle class"—it would be a great contribution.

Many white groups face economic, educational, and social barriers somewhat similar to those experienced by people of color.

Politically, the Advisory Board should seek to widen support for important changes. Since the number of groups now identified as "people of color" is growing and since African Americans will be a declining percentage of people of color, the Board should embrace all people of color (and pay some attention to all poor people). Exclusive focus on African Americans is not an effective political stance today. Promoting interracial political coalitions, locally and nationally, is crucial. Highlighting areas of common interest would be important. The Advisory Board should address the low voting turnout of people of color and what can be done about that as a problem of democracy and representation. Since the majority of the poor are not people of color, stressing common economic conditions and interests would contribute to the possibility of action. Political weakness is economically and socially disabling.

Policy analyses and recommendations should deal with ways of overcoming institutional barriers and promoting greater respect for people of color. The emphasis should be on how the economy and society would improve if the situations of people of color advance. A laundry list of narrow proposals should be avoided: clearly specified lines of action should be offered.

"Civil society" is emphasized in today's political parlance. What it could mean for people of color should be highlighted. With devolution and the enhanced roles of private and nonprofit institutions, inequalities between communities, defined racially and/or economically, will likely grow. Helping to utilize and enlarge community assets of the neighborhoods of people of color is essential. What can government do to strengthen civil society in racial communities, particularly those suffering great economic distress?

The Advisory Board should also speak to people of color and stress the importance of strengthening their communities, developing leaders who can build and strengthen institutions, moving beyond a counterproductive defensiveness which discourages discussing positive and negative responses to ongoing stresses. It should analyze the implications of the debate in African-American circles of integration or separatism.

Finally, the Advisory Board should address the political football of "values." It is important to move discussion of race in the United States from an obsessive focus on issues such as affirmative action to the basic values of this nation about democracy, liberty, equality, and fraternity. Instrumental objectives need a value base.

A Ten-Point Plan

Peter Dreier

The Advisory Board should not wait for direction from the president. Nor should it even direct its recommendations exclusively to the president. Rather it should view its audience as the general public. Of course we'd like our leaders to set the tone and the climate for change, but we shouldn't expect our presidents or Congress to initiate the important changes needed to improve race relations in America. As Harriet Tubman, Frederick Douglass, Ida Wells, Jane Addams, A. Philip Randolph, Walter Reuther, Martin Luther King, Cesar Chavez, and others recognized, improvements in race relations come about when citizens are organized and in motion, demanding justice, not begging for it, forcing government leaders to respond to pressure from below.

What we don't need from the Advisory Board is a sermon (or a 500–page report) calling for greater understanding, "dialogue," or small pilot programs. Nor do we need another massive study of America's racial situation, such as Myrdal's *American Dilemma* or the Kerner Commission report. This would simply be a full employment program for sociologists. Rather, we need a full employment program—at decent wages—for America's workers. If there is one truism about race relations, it is that prejudice, bigotry, and discrimination decline when everyone who wants to work has a job at decent wages. Although it is simplistic to argue that if you give people a job, hearts and minds will follow, it is certainly true that full employment at decent wages makes interracial cooperation much more likely. Otherwise, competition over a shrinking pie (or the crumbs from the economy's table) will lead to resentments, bitterness, and racial tensions. For example, studies have shown that the number of lynchings went up whenever the southern cotton economy declined. In more recent times, economic hard times are correlated with increases in the murder rate, racial violence, and hate crimes.

At a time when the nation's economic prosperity is primarily benefiting the wealthiest 20 percent, we need the Advisory Board to remind us that economic justice is a precondition for racial justice. The Advisory Board should recommend a broad policy agenda that will help unite those Americans on the bottom three-quarters of the economic ladder around a common vision of the American Dream—and a road map explaining how to get there.

Here are ten ideas for the Advisory Board to consider as its recommendations to President Clinton, Congress, and the American people:

1. Require the Federal Reserve to change the definition of "full employment" from 6 percent unemployed to 2 percent unemployed, so that it will no longer boost interest rates whenever working people are doing well, in order to stem Wall Street's misguided fears of inflation.

2. Reform our federal tax structure to return to a more progressive system, especially by raising tax rates on large corporations and very wealthy individuals, so that we have the funds necessary to invest in our nation's future.

3. Invest in a major public works program, similar to the New Deal WPA, to rebuild our nation's crumbling infrastructure of roads, sewers, water systems, bridges, public schools, playgrounds, and parks, which would generate millions of jobs in both the public and private sectors.

4. Enact a universal health insurance program and regulate the cost of medical care, so that our nation's children, in particular, will not needlessly go without preventative medical care.

5. Update the nation's labor laws to level the playing field between employees and employers and give America's working people a fair voice in their workplace lives, to replace the current system biased in favor of management.

6. Replace the current campaign finance system of legalized bribery with a system of public financing, to reduce the influence of big money in American politics—ultimately by appointing Supreme Court justices who will vote to overturn the infamous *Buckley v. Valeo* decision that gives wealthy people an unfair advantage in exercising free speech.

7. At a minimum, equalize the funds we spend (per student) on public education between poor and wealthy school districts. Reform our current over-reliance on local property taxes to fund local schools, a system guaranteeing that poor children will receive a poorer education than their wealthier neighbors.

8. Cash in the "peace dividend" we've been expecting since the end of the Cold War—by reducing the nation's economic dependence on military spending and putting the money to work solving our nation's economic problems. We need a ten-year plan to convert our nation's scientific and technological over-reliance on the military to civilian uses so that the nation's defense contractors, defense workers (including both civilians and soldiers, who are disproportionately people of color), and communities that have long depended on the Pentagon are not the victims of the Cold War's end.

9. Increase the minimum wage to at least the official poverty level, and index it to inflation, so that families who work hard will be able to support their children, while expanding the Earned Income Tax Credit so that all eligible families participate. (Only about 70 percent do so now.)

10. Bring America's family policies—maternity/paternity leaves, vacation time, child care—up to the level of our Canadian and European counterparts.

Needed: A Focus on the Intersection of Race and Poverty

Peter Edelman

I still don't see how President Clinton could have said he was pursuing a completely serious initiative on race relations if he didn't ask his Advisory Board to focus on the intersection between race and poverty. It is of course true that there are important racial issues to be addressed in every area and at every level of the economy and society. But with poverty among African Americans and Latinos consistently at three times the level of poverty among whites, the issue of the impact of discrimination in producing that disparity cries out for attention.

The concentrated poverty of our inner cities is one critical aspect of this. In 1990, there were nearly 11 million people living in census tracts that were over 40 percent poor, about twice the number of the concentrated poor two decades earlier, and they were overwhelmingly African American and Latino. This racial isolation is not accidental. People of color are not trapped the way they were in the 1960s, to be sure. Those with the economic wherewithal to move do so in large numbers. But the isolation of those who remain represents a destructive concatenation of race and poverty. It is devastating in its negative synergy, and it has been getting steadily worse for 30 years. Of particular concern is the appallingly bad quality of schools composed entirely or almost entirely of low-income children of color, because such schools cause the poverty to be transmitted from one generation to the next. These issues of geographic isolation and educational inequality are not merely questions of economics. They demand attention in a serious conversation about race.

Another pervasive problem is employment discrimination against young people of color. I know from my work with the Fair Employment Council of Greater Washington in the early 1990s that young people of color, especially young people without post-secondary education, face pervasive discrimination when they try to get started in the job market. This is not to say that African-American, Latino, and other minority college and professional graduates have an easy time, but the more race is mixed with the economics of the lower end of the labor market, the more powerful the negatives become. Yet this question of what happens to young people looking for their first job is not on any policy scope anywhere. Testing by simulated applicants is a proven way of ferreting it out. Yet the use of such testing is not official policy of any relevant public agenda anywhere, to my knowledge. These are not issues of affirmative action. They represent plain old garden-variety race discrimination. They should be high on the list of anyone who wants to look at race issues.

Conversation Is Far from the Central Issue

Howard Zinn

As a prerequisite, the Advisory Board to President Clinton's Initiative on Race should move away from the emphasis on "conversation" among the races, of which we have heard too much from the White House. Of course, conversation is useful, but that is far from the central issue and a huge diversion of energy and attention from what needs to be done.

It should be obvious that the central issue is the economic condition of black and Hispanic people in this country—which is tied to the economic condition of whites, but is marked by a special desperation. The glowing overall reports on the economy and the overall statistics on unemployment ignore the specific situation within the black and Latino communities. Many studies on unemployment (Lester Thurow's is only one) point to the great underestimation of unemployment. In 1992, the National Urban League estimated that the real unemployment rate—unlike the official statistics—was 13.3 percent for whites and 25.5 percent for African Americans.

True, racism is a complex phenomenon, which can exist independently of economic conditions. But the disease of racism historically came out of the swamp of the profit system. The luxuries of plantation owners required slavery, and then the profits of manufacturers required cheap labor, and today the greed of the stock market requires unemployed and underpaid labor.

The failure of the "free market" to bring real equality to black people has always been part of a larger problem, the failure to bring economic justice to the working-class majority of the population. When, in the post-Civil War years, the freed slaves insisted that their freedom was meaningless without land, they created alarms in the higher circles of the North that such demands might spread to the white underclass. The *New York Times* declared (July 9, 1867): "An attempt to justify the confiscation of Southern land under the pretense of doing justice to the freedmen strikes at the root of property rights in both sections. It concerns Massachusetts as much as Mississippi." *The Nation* said that the "division of rich man's lands among the landless . . . would give a shock to our whole social and political system. . . ."

But only such a "shock," accompanying a more equal division of the nation's wealth, can begin to address the fundamentals of the "race problem." Black leaders historically have understood that. Sociologist E. Franklin Frazier, in an official report on the Harlem riot of 1935 for New York City, insisted that the primary need of African Americans was for jobs, and asked that job discrimination be outlawed for city employees and on city contracts. Mayor LaGuardia suppressed the report; undoubtedly, he would have preferred the suggestion of "a conversation."

Jobs are crucial. That's why A. Philip Randolph threatened his March on Washington in 1941 to get Franklin D. Roosevelt to establish a Fair Employment Practices Commission. And why Martin Luther King turned his attention in his last years, not to feel-good talk on race relations, but to poverty. He planned to use the tools of the Civil Rights Movement: civil disobedience (as in his Poor People's Campaign) and the experience of the labor movement (as in his support of the Memphis strikers just before his death).

In short, the Advisory Board will be wasting its time if it does not address the economic issue. Recent bipartisan legislation diminishes benefits for the poor and foreign-born, builds prisons instead of schools and homes, and legalizes a Dickensian cruelty for huge numbers of children. The victims will be of all races, but the historical legacy of racism will ensure that the greatest pain will be felt by people of color, and that the ensuing racial competition for scarce resources will become more destructive.

The Advisory Board needs to recommend a bold program, costing hundreds of billions of dollars (the money to come out of a severely reduced military and out of a truly progressive tax structure): full employment, giving the market a chance, but with the government the employer of last resort, going even beyond the New Deal programs in its scope; a guaranteed annual income (even Nixon proposed this, but at a very low level) to do away with "welfare as we know it"; using the new labor to build housing, schools, day-care centers, and to clean up the environment.

Surely, John Hope Franklin and some of his colleagues must understand that they will be wasting their time on anything else.

If Not Action on Race, Then Straight Talk

Herbert J. Gans

I agree that the President's Initiative on Race should be devoted to action instead of talk. But if the Initiative is going to be limited to talk, let it at least be straight talk.

I would begin by taking testimony from all the important black leaders— including those invited to testify to the President's Initiative and to White House meetings and dinners—about their chronic inability to get taxis. That session might then continue with a discussion of the continuing slights and harassments black professionals and managers still suffer on the job—the kinds Ellis Cose (*The Rage of a Privileged Class*) and Joe Feagin/Melvin Sykes (*Living With Racism: The Black Middle-Class Experience*) have reported.

Thereafter, the Initiative should hear from representatives of the rest of the black community, middle-class, working-class, and poor, about the far greater slights and harassments that discrimination and segregation make them pay; as well as about the economic and occupational insecurity suffered by the many black workers in declining industries, financially troubled public agencies, and workfare, as well as what's left of welfare.

For a change of pace, the Initiative should ask black children and adolescents, particularly poor ones, what it feels like to sense, at an early age, that their life chances, for all aspects of the American Dream, are already drastically impaired by the poor, overcrowded, underfinanced schools they have to attend.

A related panel should hear from the angriest or most despairing black youngsters—for example, those who were abused as children or grew up hungry and without a supportive family life. They could report on having grown up depressed or enraged, rejecting success in school as "acting white," and consciously or unconsciously heading for sporadic day labor work or careers in crime or violent gangs.

That same panel might also invite testimony from the black young adults imprisoned for long terms, often for minor drug crimes, about the everyday life of blacks in the typical American prison.

A related session should convene young black women who become adolescent single parents because they see no decent jobs or marriageable males in their future, as well as those who are driven into motherhood by jobless young males who have to determine their success in life by the number of their sexual conquests.

A very different panel would hear from social scientists who can estimate the economic and social costs, say, in dealing with malnutrition, mental and other illness, school failure, crime, and other pathological consequences associated directly or indirectly with growing up poor and black. The panel should also include an expert who could determine the costs for both blacks and whites by the white majority's turning blacks into an undeserving race, and into the country's primary scapegoats.

The Initiative would end with a closed-door session in which opponents of affirmative action, job, income, and related programs would be required to formulate detailed and demonstrably effective substitutes for these programs before the doors are reopened.

Fantasy Moral Capital

Benjamin DeMott

The Advisory Board could most usefully begin the process of educating white America about the history of its own retreat from concern with minority problems. Part of that history runs as follows:

Liberal wisdom in the post-Civil Rights era commenced minimizing the impact of the black past—the conditions that made programs of development a necessity. Rearguard racist tirades on black "inferiority" were answered by right-minded whites with assertions, absolute and unqualified, of black-white equality—no acknowledgment of distance resulting from separate caste backgrounds, separate modes of education and training, separate ways of achieving selfhood, separate levels of economic resource. The assertions played well because of the national feeling for the social potency of open-handed, one-on-one warmth. "Personalizing" and sociability were in the American grain: programs of race-wide development were not. Wishfulness—the kind borne in such slogans as "we're all in the same boat, all taking our chances as we must"—took command, undermining the ability of the fair-minded to grasp that "decent" denials of difference obliterated caste history and left the largest sector of African America defenseless.

And then movies, sitcoms, and ad-man culture took over. The society is ceaselessly distracted nowadays with new episodes of brave white dawnings, endless tales of once oblivious or heartless whites who become civil, find astonishing pleasure in the company of an African American, and begin to *understand.* Now playing virtually nonstop in every medium, our national, self-congratulating epic of amity provides whites with unlimited occasions for contemplating their own sensitive antiracist selves—and no occasion for confronting objective race realities. It also provides the majority culture with huge supplies of fantasy capital—fantasy moral capital. Each story of "improved" white attitudes qualifies as a contribution to solving the "black problem"—a daily deposit in a white goodness savings account.

The weaknesses of official policy built on fantasy capital—fantasy denials—will appear only when questioning and criticism lay bare the flaws in that foundation. Because of its detachment, the Advisory Board can point the way toward this utterly vital questioning and criticism. It's the only route left to real action.

Escaping Clinton's Control

Frances Fox Piven

Presidential advisory bodies are not ordinarily created to craft genuinely new policy recommendations. Rather, their purpose is legitimation; they are appointed to delay and defuse popular demands for governmental action on a problem or to justify with studies and reports a policy direction already decided. And sometimes, as seems to be the case with the Advisory Board to the President's Initiative on Race, the intention is merely to adorn with serious studies and lofty thoughts a government determined to do nothing of consequence.

A number of the contributors to this symposium have made the reasonable argument that race relations are not likely to improve unless the economic conditions of poor and working people improve. But the Advisory

Board is the agent of a President who has presided over the unprecedented economic circumstances of the 1990s, when the economy boomed, profits spiralled upward, and wages lagged behind, including for the lowest paid. Bill Clinton responded to these conditions by talking family values and signing a welfare bill that is flooding the low-wage labor market with desperate women, thus tempering the wage gains that a low unemployment rate generates.

I don't mean by these comments that the Initiative on Race should be ignored. Just possibly, the Advisory Board and the dialogue it is overseeing may have consequences the President does not intend, by helping to give courage and voice to the groups and the commitments that have so far been effectively suppressed by this Administration. Except for the evidence of renewed political protest, it is a bleak political moment, and no possibility should be ignored. Still, if this is an opportunity, it is not likely to be realized through polite contributions and good suggestions. My hope rather is that the Initiative on Race sparks enough outrage and indignation so that the temper of the national dialogue rises and escapes Clinton's control.

. . . And Interracial Justice For All

Michael Omi

At the first Advisory Board meeting of the President's Initiative on Race, a debate ensued between the chair, distinguished African American scholar John Hope Franklin, and board member Angela Oh, a Korean American attorney. Franklin argued that the Initiative needed to focus on unfinished business between blacks and whites. Oh argued for a "new paradigm" that would move beyond a bipolar model of race relations to engage the experiences of other racial minorities. While Franklin and Oh have subsequently downplayed their differences, their distinct perspectives have continued to provoke debate within academic and community activist settings. Historian George Fredrickson, in the *New York Review of Books*, says that Franklin has "historical justification" to argue against the multiculturalist approach of President Clinton and to center the Advisory Board's work on "the basic and enduring problem of black-white relations." As an admirer of Fredrickson's work, I regret that his position doesn't give Latinos, Asian Americans, and Native Americans much room to maneuver.

The prevailing black/white paradigm misses the complex nature of race relations in the post-civil rights era and is unable to grasp the complex patterns of conflict and accommodation among multiple racial/ethnic groups. In many major cities, for example, whites have fled to surrounding suburban rings, leaving the core areas the site of turf battles between different racial minorities over housing, educational opportunities, public services, and community economic development initiatives. Unfortunately, changing demographic trends and new political realities have not forced us to reexamine and interrogate our stock assumptions about race in the United States.

There is an urgent political necessity to do so. Political issues are emerging that exploit conflicts and tensions between (and within) racial minority communities. California, a state that should be offering the rest of the nation positive lessons on the transition to a multiracial society, sadly provides examples that illustrate this despicable trend. In the campaign for California's Proposition 187 to restrict immigrant rights, African-American "interests" were framed in popular discourse as counter to that of Latino, and to a lesser extent Asian, immigrants. In debates regarding California's Proposition 209 on affirmative action, Asian-American "interests" were defined in opposition to those of blacks and Latinos. Political issues are increasingly racially coded and framed in a manner that uncritically assumes a zero-sum game of race relations—where one group's gain is perceived to be another group's loss. Herein lies the potential for widespread, and perhaps violent, conflict.

The Advisory Board needs to convene sessions that explicitly deal with conflicts *between* different racial minority groups. These conversations could provide the space and opportunity to rethink race and racial meanings, identify and defuse potential conflicts, consider the possibilities for alliances, and grapple with our collective identity as a people. A starting point for dialogue among racial minorities is to acknowledge the historical and contemporary differences in power that different groups possess. Groups are positioned in unequal ways in a racially stratified society. In a study of perceived group competition in Los Angeles, sociologists Lawrence Bobo and Vincent Hutchings found that whites felt least threatened by blacks and most threatened by Asians, while Asians felt a greater threat from blacks than from Latinos.

Such distinct perceptions of "group position" are related to, and implicated in, the organization of power. Some scholars and activists define racism as "prejudice plus power." They argue that people of color can't be racist since they don't have power. But things aren't that simple. In the post-civil rights era, some racial minority groups have carved out a degree of power in select urban areas—particularly with respect to administering social services and distributing economic resources. This has led, in cities like Oakland and Miami, to conflicts between blacks and Latinos over educational programs, minority business opportunities, and political power.

To acknowledge differences in power between groups, whether real or imagined, has profound implications for the possibilities of coalition-building. Law professor Eric Yamamoto advances a concept of "interracial justice," drawing upon the 1993 campaign by the Hawaii Conference of the United Church of Christ for an Asian American apology to, and reparations to, Native Hawaiians. Interracial justice, Yamamoto argues, reflects a commitment to anti-subordination among nonwhite racial groups—one that acknowledges the ways racial groups have harmed and continue to harm one another, along with affirmative efforts to redress inequalities. Such efforts are not meant to divert attention from the dominant reality of white supremacy and white racism, nor should they be read as minimizing or erasing the class and ethnic heterogeneity of the racial categories that we so glibly refer to as "black," "Latino," "Asian," or "American Indian." The emphasis here, however, is on racial minority groups acknowledging differences and beginning to transform "power over" one another into "power to" coexist, cooperate, and work together politically.

The Advisory Board needs to advance such a conversation. It should convene meetings in cities where conflicts are occurring, encourage groups to articulate their concerns and interests, and consider the ways groups can engage in coalitional efforts to deal with admittedly difficult issues. In situating and interrogating these conflicts, the prevailing black/white paradigm of race relations will be of limited utility as a framework for analysis. But a multiculturalism that merely celebrates cultural "difference," while ignoring inequalities between groups with respect to power, will equally not be up to the task. Moving beyond the debate over paradigms, the Board needs to re-center the discussion on how to advance and achieve interracial justice for all.

First Peoples First

Lillian Wilmore

The principle of "first things first" should compel the inclusion of American Indian and Alaska and Hawaii natives, the indigenous peoples of this country, in any effort to solve the dilemmas of race and racism. The President's Advisory Board contains no representative of these "first peoples." This exclusion is a part of the reason for the floundering and weakness of the dialogue to date. The Initiative is taking place in a vacuum devoid of a sense of place, *this* place, the ground upon which we all stand. Unless you understand the place where you live in terms of its natural systems, you're not going to understand anything, anyplace. The connection to land, the recognition that life resides in everything, and the understanding indigenous peoples have of how the forces and cycles of nature work are good medicine for healing the sickness of racism.

The Advisory Board must create space for the indigenous voices, advocate for them, and be willing to hear and respond to perspectives that are fundamentally different.

But because the tribal-federal relationship is a political relationship, based on the inherent sovereignty of each party, and not a racial one, and because of the genocide that has reduced America's indigenous peoples to small numbers—a false "color-blindness" is often at work, excluding indigenous peoples from the dialogue. The "crisis in black and white" is deep, and reparations are long overdue, but as a nation the United States must understand the difficulty of seeking "common ground" on ground that was forcibly taken from others, and they are still here.

The indigenous red peoples were the original rulers and caretakers of the lands that are today the United States. Originally numbering close to 5 million, Indian people now number roughly 2 million—the smallest minority in their own land. The American Indian holocaust is not acknowledged, taught, or memorialized. Although American Indian people have survived despite overwhelming odds and attempts to destroy their culture, alter their governments, and extinguish their sovereignty, the very survival of the native nations remains a question. Chairman Ronnie Lupe of the White Mountain Apache sometimes wears a button saying, "We are a part of the endangered species."

Ignorance about Indian culture and competition for resources remain the two major reasons for white hostility toward Indian rights. When Europeans arrived in our world, they found communities of red color considerably different from their own. Indian people had (and many still have) a holistic and spiritual approach to life. Their societies were basically communal and nonmaterialistic. Their value systems stressed cooperation, harmony, and responsibility. European culture, on the other hand, emphasized "progress," materialism, individualism, competition, and property. The Europeans considered their own culture to be vastly superior to the indigenous societies. It was incomprehensible to them that these "inferior" tribes did not wish to adopt the newcomers' religion, values, and practices. Europeans considered Indians "children of nature" or "savage beasts." It is telling that Indian people are the only *people* under the Department of the Interior, along with forests and wildlife.

Sharon O'Brien, in her 1989 book *American Indian Tribal Governments*, noted: "The Europeans', and later the Americans', belief in their own superiority helped them to rationalize taking the Indians' lands. The tribes were viewed as intolerable obstacles to progress and Manifest Destiny. Selling Indian lands raised money for the U.S. government's operation and provided homesteads for settlers and resources for industries. To obtain Indian lands, the U.S. government broke treaties, negotiated fraudulent land deals, and passed assimilationist legislation."

The Initiative should act swiftly to include indigenous peoples and should speak directly to the developing termination sentiment among members of Congress. There is a real and present danger that tribes face the greatest threat to their sovereignty since bills to terminate tribal authority were introduced in 1977. Numerous other bills were introduced during 1996, and continue to be introduced, to erode the authority of tribes, make it impossible for them to regulate health and safety, and cripple them economically. Senator Daniel Inouye observed that Washington legislators "have just begun their crusade to strip power from Native American tribes." Senator Ben Nighthorse Campbell says he "cannot remember a time when there was more dialogue about Indians in Washington, nor a time when Indians were consulted less." These continuing threats to the survival of the native nations as nations should be ended by legal assurances of permanence. Prompt and fair settlement of outstanding tribal claims against the United States would help to lay the past to rest with some sense of finality and enable tribes to devote their time to other things.

Education is a priority. The U.S. public education system (in contrast to Canada, for example) has utterly failed to require that students learn any body of consistent, coherent knowledge about the indigenous peoples of this land. Civics classes do not teach (1) the continuing existence of native nations; (2) the government-to-government relationship those nations have with the United States; or (3) the significance of treaty rights. Social studies generally do not teach the lifeways of living Indians, as opposed to the "Dead Chiefs," "Vanishing People," and "Nanook of the North" tidbits now sprinkled here and there in curricula.

The U.S. educational system leaves most children under the impression that all or most Indians died in the 1700s and 1800s, and that those remaining went to reservations, where they serve the tourist industry. It is not taught that at a time when Europeans labored under authoritarian, hierarchical governments, most tribes possessed democratic and responsive governments. Most U.S. citizens are unaware that many tribes practiced universal suffrage and incorporated provisions for recall, referenda, and other political processes thought later to have been developed by American and European political theorists. Few, if any, books deal directly with the subject of tribal government, and only in very recent years have any treated it from an Indian perspective.

White ignorance and misunderstanding of Indians continues to breed contempt and racism. Five hundred years of contact, unfortunately, have done little to reverse non-Indians' ignorance of Indian beliefs, traditions, rights, and tribal life. Caricatures, sentimentalized stereotypes, and racist kitsch about Indians adorn billboards, magazine ads, numerous products, and sports teams. In polls, non-Indians see nothing wrong with these things, despite repeated protests from the Indian community. Many non-Indians still find it difficult to understand why many Indian people wish to retain their culture, their reservations, and their governments instead of just joining mainstream American society.

The notion that we are all striving only to create a society of equality, to "get our piece of the American pie," is at odds philosophically and legally with Indians' desire to be treated differently and to their hard-bargained-for treaty rights to a "measured separateness." We are an unassimilable element. As the Chickasaw poet Linda Hogan has observed, "Synthesis is thought of as positive, but that is not necessarily the case. There is a possibility of separate cultures living side by side, cooperating with each other, without being synthesized. Shared, but not enmeshed."

Not bringing the indigenous people to share in this effort deprives it of uniquely American authenticity. Without the active participation of the first peoples of this land, healing and reconciliation on this land cannot occur.

Conversation Doesn't Pay the Rent

William L. Taylor

Conversation Is Needed But It Doesn't Pay the Rent

Some years ago, Bayard Rustin, the brilliant strategist of the Civil Rights Movement, stated his reservations about the social-psychological approach to race relations. Rustin said he could envision Americans being persuaded figuratively to lie down on the psychiatrist's couch to examine their feelings about race. They would likely arise, he said, pronouncing themselves either free or purged of any bias. And nothing would have changed.

Much history supports Rustin's view. The progress of the last four decades in civil rights did not come about initially through a revolution in public attitudes but through changes in law and public policy beginning with the Supreme Court's 1954 *Brown v. Board of Education* decision. President Eisenhower, a critic of that decision, repeated William Graham Sumner's shibboleth that "law could not change the hearts and minds of men." But ultimately, through a torturous process, the national conscience was aroused and we achieved the will to enforce the principles of *Brown*.

The laws changed behavior, which in turn changed attitudes. I will not forget the days in the Summer of 1964 when I led a group of U.S. Commission on Civil Rights lawyers in an investigation of rights denials in Mississippi. When the Civil Rights Act was passed prohibiting discrimination in public accommodations, we became the first interracial group staying at the Admiral Benbow Inn in Jackson, Mississippi. Each day, as we ate in the restaurant, we could feel the hard stares of local diners. But on the last day of our stay, as I waited on line to pay the bill, I heard an elderly man say to his wife, "I guess this is something we will have to learn to live with." His words were prophetic. The trappings of the seemingly entrenched caste system in the South—the segregated buses, hotels, restaurants—are gone, changed by law, and hardly anyone today gives it a second thought.

In sum, the racial discrimination that persists today, the deprivation that stunts the lives of people who live in concentrated poverty in inner cities, are objective conditions. They will not be cured by conversation, but only by concrete measures that offer opportunity. At the same time, dialogue and debate are clearly needed to establish the political conditions that will lead to policy changes. But it must be focused dialogue, tied to policy, not group therapy or conversation designed mainly to make us feel good about ourselves.

If We Are Going to Have a Conversation, Let Us Talk About the Hard Issues

History tells us that having an honest dialogue about race will be very difficult. From the beginning of the Republic, race has been the issue that has clouded the minds of Americans. From the declarations of black inferiority that sustained slavery to the massive fiction of *Plessy v. Ferguson* that separate really was equal and that if black people thought otherwise they were being overly sensitive, to contemporary claims that segregation is defensible because that's the way most black people prefer to live, opinion leaders have been extraordinarily adept at constructing rationales for the worst injustices.

Today, racial inferiority talk is largely out of fashion (although not completely, since we still have Dinesh D'Souzas and Charles Murrays spouting bigotry). But now the focus has shifted to bashing poor people. Canards that once were addressed to people of color—that they were shiftless, uncaring about their children, amoral, etc.—are now freely said about the urban poor, and those who are on the receiving end are not being paranoiac when they believe that there is a continuing racial element to the charges.

These are stereotypes that must be addressed directly and thrashed out to help establish a political basis for extending genuine opportunity to the poor. Elijah Anderson, William Julius Wilson, Alex Kotlowitz, Elliot Liebow, and others have written clearly about the conditions of life in inner cities. Another example is Fred Wiseman's 1997 documentary about life in Chicago's Ida Wells public housing project. Anyone who gives serious attention to this portrait (offered without any commentary) will understand what a struggle it is to get through a day and accomplish even the minimal things most of us who are middle-class take for granted. People will gain a better understanding of the conclusion that contemporary researchers have drawn—that being poor is bad enough, but that living in concentrated poverty creates barriers and conditions of hopelessness that few can overcome.

Perhaps the most important thing the Race Initiative can do is to find ways to give the American people an understanding of the plight of their fellow men and women. Among the questions that must be asked is why, though poverty affects all races and nationalities, it is only black people and Latinos who live in conditions of concentrated poverty. Surely the answer cannot be choice. I heard a suburban state legislator in Missouri object to a measure designed to give additional education aid to children who live and attend school in concentrated poverty. He asked how he could justify to his constituents giving more money to the education of the poor than to their children. I suggested he ask his constituents whether, if they were offered an extra thousand dollars for each of their children, they would be willing to enroll them in the central city public schools in St. Louis. And of course, state finance systems based on property taxes in fact continue to reward wealthy districts with far more education dollars than are available to the poor.

The Conversation Should Not Let Anyone Off the Hook and Should Lead to Concrete Policy Proposals

Certainly all views should be heard, but people ought to be asked to support their positions with more than glib generalizations. There may be a special burden on those who would discard policies such as affirmative action that have produced real progress in favor of loosely reasoned alternatives that have not been thought through. For example, Abigail Thernstrom and her fellow foes of affirmative action assure us that the place for education initiatives is in elementary schools and the family, and that this would obviate the need for affirmative action in higher education. She fails to acknowledge that affirmative action policies that universities pursued in the 1970s led to educational success for students of color, who then found decent jobs and formed stable families. That success has now created the conditions for the success of their children, who were able to cut the gap between their performance and that of white teenagers in high school in half from the 1970s through 1980s.

Certainly, there are other components of a successful effort to improve public education. But if the need is to improve teaching, how are we to attract the most talented people into the profession now that the once captive pool of talent—women and people of color—have many other opportunities? If we do attract them, how do we assure that the poverty schools that need good teaching most will receive and retain their share of the most able people? For those who believe that more choice will improve public education, the question is how we assure that minorities and the poor will actually benefit from choice programs and avert the possibility that charters or vouchers will lead to more racial and socio-economic isolation than exists right now. And do Ms. Thernstrom and her colleagues favor or oppose the continued racial and socio-economic isolation of poor children in schools in the face of evidence that such isolation is a formidable barrier to the success of the poor?

There are comparable questions to be asked in all areas and of people of liberal as well as conservative views. But people who want to be taken seriously ought to offer reasoned views. Ms. Thernstrom, presumably a supporter of higher order thinking, should be able to hold two thoughts in her head simultaneously: first, that the nation has made great progress in civil rights, and second, that hard work and sacrifice are needed to extend opportunity to the many who have not benefited from the civil rights revolution.

The odds may be against the whole endeavor. Reasoned dialogue about any important public issue (much less the volatile issue of race) is hard to find these days. It may be that the days of Myrdal's *American Dilemma* and the Kerner Commission report and the debates they prompted are over. If so, we will have to devise forums where opinions are not thought to be equivalent to facts and where the competition is not for the best sound bite.

If the Clinton Race Initiative is ever to pay any dividends, it will take more time. The end result must be a comprehensive proposal to extend opportunities to those who, because of continuing barriers of discrimination and deprivation, are worst off in our society.

Postscript: (December 2000) *As the Clinton Administration draws to a close, it is clear that the hopes for his Race Initiative expressed in this essay and others in this volume will not be realized. Mr. Clinton deserves credit for defending affirmative action against its many political assailants and for his rhetorical ability to make people of color feel they are welcomed participants in American society. But the forces operating to widen the opportunity gap are formidable and, while some factors are impersonal, all have racial consequences that stem from neglect of the constitutional imperative of equal justice. Mr. Clinton will soon be freer to speak his mind on the issues, and one hopes he will set forth a bolder vision than he has so far, telling us why it is worth the investments and costs.*

Spotlight Bigotry's Covert Expression

David K. Shipler

The Advisory Board has been charged with a dual mission: to educate and to propose. The two tasks are inextricably linked, and one follows logically on the other. Without a public that is well educated about the insidious workings of racial prejudice, there will be little popular support for proposals that are refined enough to address encrypted bias.

The only consensus on race that now prevails among Americans endorses civil rights laws as tools to attack the most blatant discrimination. But there is no agreement on the finer tools, such as affirmative action and diversity training, because they combat subtler forms of discrimination whose existence many Americans fail to recognize.

Therefore, the Board would do well to throw the presidential spotlight on the covert expressions of anti-black bigotry that pervade American society: the quiet aversions triggered by skin color, hair styles, dress, and accent; the silent assumptions about mental inferiority, dishonesty, and violence; the unequal power relationships implicit in most "integrated" institutions. These images often translate into damaging behavior that obstructs blacks' opportunities. If that process can be documented by the President's Initiative, and if such exposure can raise even some Americans' consciousness of the dynamics of stereotyping, the groundwork may be laid for some serious conversation about remedies. First, the Board has to identify the problems, then it can discuss solutions. It cannot be persuasive about remedies until it lays the problems out before the public.

Prejudice is merely a thought. In this country in this time, it finds its most fertile ground out of the sunlight, in the shadows cast by facades of polite denial. It is not up to any government agency to counter people's thoughts or to interfere with people's speech. Yet if the goal of educating the public is to be met, it is essential for the Board to call attention to discriminatory actions that emanate from prejudicial thoughts. This is best done with personal testimony from blacks and whites, Asians and Hispanics. One telling anecdote makes a more vivid impression than a volume of theory. It can also trigger helpful discussion about decoding action that may or may not be racist.

Then the connection can be made between the recognition of these subtle patterns of discrimination on the one hand, and, on the other, pragmatic steps toward amelioration. The discussion should focus on which mechanisms can legitimately inhibit the conversion of bias into behavior. Society already intervenes with a multitude of tools: ethics and mores, laws and regulations, workshops and training courses. Which of these work? How can institutions and communities be encouraged to use the successful methods? What new tools can be invented?

Taking a close look at the military, many of whose approaches are easily adaptable to civilian life, can be convincing because most Americans have regard for the armed forces and will treat military leaders' discussions of race as credible. It would be dramatic and helpful to contrast the military with police departments, where racism is endemic; one persuasive argument for developing programs to attack police bias is that the tensions among black and white officers, and between white officers and non-white citizens, are undermining the criminal justice system by damaging the credibility of police evidence.

As a blend of both its educational and programmatic functions, the President's Initiative has the potential to create an information network about the disparate trends in diversity training, about programs that teach tolerance in schools, about corporate efforts to deal with racial issues among employees, and other such efforts. There is too little communication now among Americans who work in this field. The Board could make a contribution by finding a way to harness the good will that is now scattered in fragments throughout the land.

A Lesson Plan for Thinking and Talking About Race

Theodore M. Shaw

Our nation's challenge is what it always has been: to find a place where all of its people will stand on equal footing without regard to characteristics that reflect the accident of birth. This goal cannot be reached by mere assertion that America should be "color-blind"; nor does it mean that Americans can or should expect an end to the question of race. The issue is not whether we all see race or color; the issue is, having seen it, how we treat each other. Is it a point of exclusion, or does our consciousness of race lead us to seek inclusion?

Perhaps the discourse led by the President and his Advisory Board can underscore the real nature of our race problem. It is not a matter that will be resolved with finality, as apparently some people are anxious to believe we can do as we enter into the twenty-first century. America's race problem is rooted in the more unfortunate aspects of human nature: the tendency to alienate those who are different—"the others"—and treat them less kindly than those we think are most like us. This is not strictly an American phenomenon. We simply have our own manifestation of a problem that has plagued the human race throughout history.

The United States is a better nation, when it comes to the issue of race, than it was fifty years ago, as are many places around the world. But progress on these issues has been incremental and painfully slow. Perhaps the most valuable service the Race Initiative can render is to promote the idea that each generation will bear its own responsibility to fight bigotry and injustice in its time. Thus, for example, whatever the outcome of the current struggles around affirmative action, racial justice issues will remain with us.

The President's Initiative on Race will not solve "the race problem." It can help us learn how to think about and struggle with it. The issue of race has been and is America's greatest dilemma. The Founding Fathers wrestled with it without conclusion; their unholy compromise with slavery cursed the young country with a stain of original sin that only a civil war would begin to wash away. One hundred years after the Emancipation Proclamation, African Americans were still second-class citizens. The Supreme Court's 1954 decision in *Brown v. Board of Education* and civil rights statutes enacted in the 1960s created a framework for equality. They did not, however, finally resolve America's race problem. Neither will President Clinton's Initiative.

What, then, can it do? First, it can put the issues of race in their proper context, and it can give Americans a lesson plan on how to think and talk about race. The Initiative has a short life in which to accomplish something of lasting significance. We do not need another massive study of race relations. Our libraries are chock full of commission reports, studies, and books on race, ranging from the work of W.E.B. DuBois, Gunnar Myrdal's *American Dilemma*, to the 1968 Kerner Commission report with its dire prediction of what had long been fact ("two societies, one black, one white—separate and unequal"). Among the best of these works are the writings of the chairman of President Clinton's Race Initiative, the eminent scholar John Hope Franklin. From his place among America's leading historians, Dr. Franklin can illuminate how our current struggles occur against a backdrop of practice and policies that created the inequities between black and white people that mark our society today.

Even more valuable would be a national exposition of the historical role of white skin privilege, not for the purpose of assigning blame or summoning guilt but in order to illuminate the nature of current racial inequities that have affected all who are not race-privileged. This lesson will meet strong and vituperative resistance on the part of those who wish to engage in denial and "donothingism" concerning what most honest people acknowledge to be our nation's greatest challenge. Accordingly, the Advisory Board and the President must be prepared for harsh and unfair criticism, and should not compromise the integrity of their conclusions or recommendations in order to placate those who ignore or distort fact and history.

Second, the Advisory Board can attempt to put the present-day discourse on race in an appropriate multi-ethnic perspective. While the old black-white divide remains the core of America's most intractable race problems, a biracial analysis is plainly inappropriate. White supremacy and its legacy was not limited in its purpose or effect to African Americans; nor do African Americans hold claim to any special moral position when it comes to inter-ethnic relationships in a nation where racial conflict runs between many groups.

—— **Symposium** ——

Comments on the Advisory Board Report

Neither Praise Nor Burial

S.M. Miller

I write not to praise and certainly not to bury the Advisory Board's report (for it is likely to be ignored or maliciously treated by the media). Rather, my quest is how to move to the next stages of the long-time fight to improve the conditions of "the others" in American society. The report should be thought of as a beginning measure that requires people to lift it to the next step.

The difficulty faced by the Advisory Board and all of us is that two very different stories or narratives can be told about the last forty years. One story line centers on the considerable success in overcoming prejudice and discrimination and in reducing differences in the well-being of "whites" and African Americans and Latinos. (I concentrate on the two largest groups of "minorities" or "others.") A lot of data support this narrative. Unfortunately, the too frequent lesson is not that further success is possible but that not much more has to be done or that too much in the form of affirmative action has been pursued.

The other story, which many organizations of the "minorities" recount, is that of failure or defeat. Things have not changed enough, and backsliding occurs. Great and sometimes widening differences between "whites" and "people of color" exist. As the Advisory Board stresses, a major task is reducing inequalities (usually expressed as comparisons of whites-minority percentages of selected indicators), not just improving the position of "minorities."

These two contrasting stories or interpretations of American experiences in the last few decades are barriers to the effective dialogues that the Board seeks. "Minorities" should acknowledge successes because they show that improvements are possible. In that context, they can point then to the obstacles that continue to harm them. Struggle and programs have wrested important changes. It has not been one long agony of unrelenting defeat. Such a sigh does not ring true. Nor does that outlook mobilize people; hope is needed, and success ignites hope. Those who only see success and great or disturbing change have to be brought to recognize the limits of what has been achieved and to undertake the further steps that would make us truly "One America."

The Advisory Board's image of "One America" needs filling in and debate. It is not about the "melting pot" where "minorities" presumably shed their pasts and styles of life and where all Americans pretend to follow *the* "mainstream" or "white" way of life in a patriotic jubilee. The main thread of its analyses is about the reduction of inequalities, mainly economic, educational, and police-judicial, between "minorities" and "whites." That is the key objective. Unfortunately, it is not enough to assure social connections and closer relations among people that the Board seeks. A condition of achieving that state is the development of group respect. Economic and educational gains do not automatically assure the emergence of respect for once-dominated groups.

The debate about integration versus separatism and building "the ghetto" is muted for the time being, although important changes occur. Many inner-city areas are building on their assets to improve their conditions and prospects. How successful, how widespread and how well they would weather economic downturns is highly uncertain. While occupational segregation declines, school segregation expands.

A politics of change is needed to achieve the goals of the Board and other important objectives. A disconnect appears between the report's emphasis on dialogue and its legislative and spending objectives. Politicians act when they sense pressure to move. Political muscle is needed. Presidential orders and legislative appropriations are unlikely to happen without pressure demanding them. The unfortunate, disheartening truth that has to be recognized and improved is that "minorities" are not doing an effective job in building political strength. Almost all the "minorities" are not well organized as political actors. For example, African Americans and Latinos vote much less than whites, despite their high stakes in elections. Their communities are seldom organized on a continuous political basis that involves many residents. Leadership is often contentious, narrowly self-serving, and little interested in widening and deepening its base. The various "minorities" do not work closely together. They do not act as though they have a common cause to meet objectives. Gaining allies outside their communities is often neglected.

While most political constituencies are not doing well—the significant exception is politically awakened religious fundamentalists—"minorities" are hardest hit by their lack of political clout. The failure of race and poverty politics demands soul-searching, reaching out, and new grassroots and national designs, activities, and organization.

The report unfortunately ignores gender issues. "Minority" women have improved economically relative to "white" women, but both groups have not gained much if at all when compared to "white" men. Gender discrimination as well as "race" discrimination is important. Many of the difficulties and burdens of this unequal society are borne by women. On the other hand, women are the spark plugs and mainstays of many neighborhood activities and organizations. Improving their situations is important.

The "inner city," "the ghettos," need special attention, for their populations suffer economically and socially. At the same time, stereotypes about minorities are reinforced by what people think occurs in these residential areas.

In progressive circles, a current argument is that is that class (economic) issues have been sidetracked by the focus on identity group issues affecting race and gender. The contention is that concentrating on economic questions would overcome divisiveness among "race-ethnic" groups and attract "whites" who are also hurting economically. Thus, a majority for positive change could develop. There is not room here to examine the effectiveness and morality of this perspective, but one strategic approach can be gained from this outlook—the importance of pushing on economic issues that benefit many, both "whites" and "minorities." Many of the report's recommendations, e.g., raising the minimum wage, have this effect but their cross-"race" benefits are not stressed.

The Board regards its report as a (re)-beginning in a period when we are not likely to be moving toward a Third Reconstruction Era. Whether it plays even that limited role depends less on elected officials taking the initiative than on ordinary people and their leaders pushing strategically and wisely for change.

Where Is the Declaration of War?

Bill Ong Hing

Where is the Declaration of War? We all agree that racism in evil forms continues in the United States. We all agree that racism is wholly and completely unacceptable. Then where is the sense of urgency over this issue? Where is the sense of outrage and indignation? Where is the massive mobilization over the issue? Where is the commitment of billions of dollars to shock the conscience of America on this issue? Where is the Declaration of War?

As reports go, the Advisory Board's report to the President is a good one. The report recognizes the complexities of the issues and the need for multi-faceted approaches to the subject. The Advisory Board knows that we need a combination of leadership, legislation, media work, and focus on the young to begin to influence the actions as well as the attitudes of Americans when it comes to issues of race and bettering race relations. The report does a fine job in pointing out the common history of legal, social, and economic subordination suffered by American Indians and Alaska Natives, African Americans, Latinos, Asian Pacific Americans, and white immigrants. It contains an excellent reminder to readers about the changing diversity of America and the fact that any discussion of race today is inadequate if limited to a discussion about blacks and whites. The Advisory Board and its staff deserve high praise for providing this important foundation for action.

However, the call to action on the issues of racism and race relations must go far beyond the polite letter to be sent from the President to the National Governors Association and other local leaders. The call to action must go far beyond the mild suggestion of a "media campaign that has the capacity to effectively disseminate factual information and inspire creative expression." In June 1998, James Byrd, Jr., a black man in Texas, was chained to the back of a pickup and dragged to death by three white men. That tragedy sparked outrage for a while; but once again that outrage subsided to polite talk over passage of the Hate Crimes Prevention Act. Time and time again, the Advisory Board heard about incidents of this nature, but it too succumbed to polite talk on these issues. The problem with polite talk on these issues is that it lets the vast majority of the nation off the hook. The problem with polite talk, especially about hate crimes, is that it fails to get across to the nation the fact that hate crimes are only the tip of the iceberg. The nation ends up taking these incidents lightly, thinking that those types of incidents are the prime and only target, when in fact the prime target should be the foundation of institutionalized racism that has created an environment that enables subtle and unconscious racism and emboldens perpetrators of hate crimes. Yet all forms of racism are evil and must be vigilantly addressed.

Thus, we need more than a polite "call to action." We need a Declaration of War! The declaration of war on the evils of racism and intergroup tensions must be loud and constant. Just as the Clinton Administration poured millions of dollars into its campaign against drugs through high-profile, shock-the-conscience types of television ads, something just as attention-grabbing, but much more consistent, has to be initiated. Just as organizations and businesses have their motivational mission and vision statements, of which good leaders constantly remind their workers, we need a clear vision or mission statement on these issues that will serve as the moral equivalent of the Declaration of Independence into the new millennium. We must be driven, not politely, because we are beyond politeness on the evils of hate and prejudice that our leaders and Advisory Board members acknowledge are not "American values." Of course, be creative and imaginative in approaches. Call for new laws, enforcement of old laws, smart coalition-building, civility, respect, and approaches to addressing actions and private attitudes, but make that call loud and clear and remind us over and over! Make it part of the national psyche, not just part of the national agenda.

Let us not wait for more hate-motivated beatings and shootings. Let us not wait for more church burnings and house bombings. Let us not wait for more lynchings. Let us not wait for another race riot. We must wake up America now! After we wake up, then we can begin to learn how to say "good morning" to one another.

Not a Word of Criticism of Clinton

Clarence Lusane

Few people consciously appoint their own executioners. This is painfully but not surprisingly evident in the report presented to the President by his Race Initiative Advisory Board, where nary a word of criticism of Bill Clinton is to be found. Indeed, as far as the report is concerned, while racism and racial discrimination still persist, they are practiced by virtually no one except a few skinheads and unreconstructed Klansmen.

The Advisory Board not only does not chastise the current administration, it goes through great contortions to praise Clinton, referring to him as the only president in U.S. history to have "had the courage to raise the issue of race and racism in American society in such a dramatic way." Apparently, the Board members never heard of Lyndon Johnson and his Great Society agenda. While arguably Clinton has distinguished himself from most other recent presidents, such as Reagan and Bush, in giving attention to the need to address race as an issue in U.S. society, look to whom he is being compared. It is disingenuous to pretend that his policies have been a rose garden of racial enlightenment and progress. Highly symbolic acts by the president that generated racial outrage among many (the pre-election execution of Ricky Rector, distancing from former Spelman College President Johnnetta Cole, undermining of Rev. Jesse Jackson with rapper Sistah Souljah, and the conservative-inspired firing of then-Surgeon General Joycelyn Elders) also failed to make the cut.

This undue, indeed unseemly, adulation is rooted in what many suspected was the true purpose of the Race Initiative all along: valorization of Clinton's New Democrat perspective on race. Clinton's affliction for talking left and walking right appears to have had a contagious effect on Board members.

The Congress and the Supreme Court, for the most part, also remain exempt from any condemnation. Congressional actions regarding crime and cuts in social programs, and Court initiatives against affirmative action and majority-minority political districts have not been minor issues in the game of race.

The report's recommendations, when not politically uninspired and timid, border on the farcical. The report notes, for example, the disparities in sentencing and incarceration between racial minorities and whites, in particular drug convictions spurred by the difference generated by the one-hundred to one penalty ratio between crack cocaine and cocaine powder. Clinton is honored for his administration's belated and politically pointless proposal to bring that gap down to ten to one by decreasing the crack penalties and raising the powder ones, a proposal that will do little to ameliorate the problem. It is prudently not mentioned that Clinton signed off on this one-hundred to one ratio year after year, even though he was presented with irrefutable evidence of its racially disparate impact from the day he came in office. The tragic increase, from one-quarter to one-third, of young black males between twenty to twenty-nine being either on parole, on probation, or incarcerated occurred during the Clinton years.

The spread of AIDS is also noted by the report as an increasing problem among African Americans. Yet in Spring 1998, even after admitting that evidence demonstrated that clean needle exchange programs saved lives while not increasing drug use, Clinton went against the wishes of HHS Secretary Donna Shalala and refused to approve funding for these efforts. This occurred at a time when Clinton's approval rating was riding high and he had little to lose.

The report also seems to believe that racism can be and should be attacked a little step at a time. There is no call for massive social intervention on the part of the state similar to the 1930s Works Progress Administration or the 1960s War on Poverty efforts. A substantial, multi-year domestic Marshall Plan is minimally needed if there is to be a significant advance in ending the class dimensions of racism.

The report correctly calls for more data gathering regarding the social and economic status of the nation's racial minorities. For instance, specific information is needed on sub-groups within the larger racial groups.

In the end, however, the report is an intellectual failure of the grandest order. It is less than the sum of its parts. At least half of the report is comprised of lists of meetings, quotes from Board members and others, and endnotes. The overwhelming majority of footnotes consist of journalistic pieces rather than the bevy of academic studies and books on race and racism that have emerged in recent years. Compared to the 1968 National Advisory Committee report, *Common Destiny, An American Dilemma*, or even Reagan-era Civil Rights Commission reports, the Race Initiative Advisory Board report is a throw-away.

After dozens of meetings, hundreds of pages of report, and endless yakking, the report is another gift box in pretty wrapping paper that is empty. Clinton's "One America" remains as elusive as ever.

No Surprises

Frances Fox Piven

There is not much to be surprised by in the report to the President: airy and timid calls for more dialogue, more data, more effort to understand our history, and so on. There is even, in true Clintonese fashion, a list of ten things every American can do to encourage racial conciliation. The Board compliments the nation lavishly on our racial progress—and there has been progress—but it does not frontally address the growing and deep divide that compounds race differences with class differences. Obviously, this new racial and class configuration is the result of the rapid polarization of income and wealth of the past twenty-five years which, given persistent racism together with educational disadvantage, hits racial minorities harder. The rich who get richer are white. The working and middle classes are more diverse, to be sure. But the poor are poorer, and the welfare rolls are increasingly composed of Blacks and Hispanics.

The report offers little in the way of direction or urgency to address these conditions. There is mention of an increase in the minimum wage, expansion of health insurance, and support for organized labor. But these are familiar and vague proposals. There is no bold call for intervening in labor markets, for correcting wealth and tax inequities, or for reforms that might make votes count more than money in electoral politics. Even the *New York Times* seems to sense something is missing. Comparing the Report to the Kerner Commission report issued thirty years ago, it notices the differences and explains the comparative boldness of the Kerner recommendations by pointing out that they were formulated in the context of spreading riots in the nation's major cities. Maybe that is what is required to get egalitarian reform on the agenda in the United States.

A final and curious point still puzzles me. In the wake of the scandal and impeachment that swamped the cautious Clinton reform agenda, Blacks rallied to the President, with a firmness shown by no other group in America, and with talk about the deep cultural affinities between this President and American Blacks: the taste for soul food and the saxophone, the preacher-like Clinton cadences, and so on. No doubt this was partly a reaction to the draconian neo-liberal policies associated with the makers of the intended coup d'etat unfolding in Washington. Perhaps it also reflected fear of the fundamentalist political culture which Right-wing Republicans were trying to foist on the country, to their zealous pursuit of personal and especially sexual morality through state authoritarianism. Think how similar the themes raised in the campaign to oust the president were to the themes of sexual immorality during the campaign against welfare mothers.

Native Nations Won't Rally Around "One Nation" Concept

Lillian Wilmore

The report stresses common ground of shared values and goals. Many Native Americans are dubious about the extent of their shared values and goals with the mainstream culture. They see a materialistic culture, driven by greed, detached from nature or pursuing the illusion that it must and can dominate nature, excessively individualistic, always in a hurry, and untrustworthy.

This view is a product of our experience. The mainstream culture has for 500 years been attempting to destroy or assimilate Native Americans and has not yet learned that it cannot. "Indian-ness" resides in the teachings of the Old Ways and our native languages. The view of the world that our traditions teach has an integrity of its own and represents a sensible and respectable perspective of the world and a valid means of interpreting experiences. In a great many areas, tribal religion defines culture. Yet in the Advisory

Board's section on The Role of Religious Leaders it fails to even mention the need for protection of American Indian religious freedom and sacred places. It is the principle of respect for the sacred that is important. For all these reasons, the native nations—still here—are not likely to rally around a "One America" concept.

However, our elders have taught us that all things are alive and connected. Groundwater contamination knows no boundaries; acid rains falls on all our relations; the disappearance of herbs and medicinal plants can cost lives and add to pain and suffering. Perhaps the best common ground is the ground itself. The spirit of this ground calls for relief from the constant burden of exploitation. The Advisory Board at least identified the "Lack of Environmental Justice" as a critical issue, and that is good.

Native nations are disproportionately impacted by the mining and petroleum industry. They are vastly underfunded in their efforts to protect their lands, air, and waters. Drinking water quality in Indian Country is often abysmal. Native nations are disproportionately impacted by the current crisis of inadequate resources for rural and small drinking water systems. The ongoing devolution of environmental authority to the states, without equal opportunity for the tribes, threatens tribal sovereignty, makes mockery of the federal trust responsibility to the native nations, and is a continuing breach of treaty rights.

The development of indigenous peoples' capability to manage their own natural resources and enforce tribal law, if adequately supported, will produce models of sustainability for all peoples. It is significant that it is native peoples who have, as a group, been among the first to actively organize to address global climate change.

Vine Deloria, Jr. has written: "As long as Indians exist there will be conflict between the tribes and any group that carelessly despoils the land and the life it supports." In sincere efforts to bring people together and heal conflicts, the preservation and restoration of the land and the life it supports should be central, and not peripheral.

"One America" Needs To Be More Than a Nice Slogan

Frank H. Wu

The "One America" race panel has been and should be criticized for many reasons: lack of purpose, attention to feelings over reality, emphasis on talk rather than action, etc. Yet with the release of the Advisory Board's report and its recommendation of continuing public discourse, the Initiative has lived up to at least part of its promise. It has forced people to confront racism as much as race. It is better than benign neglect, but below the level of praise.

The report deserves support from progressives who care about civil rights for two reasons—not to mention that some attacks against it are explicitly also attacks on any systematic efforts to comprehend or address racial discrimination.

First, the report states that historic racial discrimination—primarily imposed on African Americans—must be recognized. It also does not shrink from stating that such subordination continues to have insidious effects. It notes contemporary forms of bias, ranging from the violence of hate crimes to the subtlety of assumptions based on stereotypes.

These might appear to be simple observations of fact. But the dominance of reactionary sentiments on campuses and television and radio talk shows has made even these concessions difficult to gain, other than as rote dismissals of what once was awful but no longer needs to be considered. The pseudo-scientific claims of Richard J. Herrnstein and Charles Murray's *The Bell Curve* (1994) and Dinesh D'Souza's *The End of Racism* (1995) have been thoroughly debunked on their own terms, but the books have achieved a success inversely correlated to their truth. They have persuaded much of the public that people who are suffering are genetically inferior or culturally pathological: they deserve their condition.

Second, the report urges community responses. It manages to defend affirmative action. Its town hall meetings, despite their amateurish group therapy aspects and the media coverage devoted to white supremacists disrupting sessions, display a faith in consensus that may be naive but is needed. The combination of public and private efforts cataloged as "best practices" share the premise that individuals and groups can make meaningful contributions.

This too might seem to be an easy tendency toward justice. But the regressive shifts in public policy have reduced our optimism and even interest in social change. The movements of law and economics and evolutionary psychology, with their popular versions, assure us that self-interest is not only rational but natural; we are doing our best if we care about only ourselves.

In both these respects, the report serves the task of translating. Its findings will be useful to advocates. The document summarizes scholarly research—for example, its discussion of wealth differences related to race and its description of Latinos and Asian Americans—that was cutting-edge long ago. Thanks to the official presentation and the bureaucratic style, however, the academic studies acquire an extra authority.

The "One America" project will have whatever importance we give it. Gunnar

Myrdal's Carnegie Foundation-funded *American Dilemma* and the Kerner Commission's crisis management, both of which this latest endeavor matches in ambition but not stature, are remembered for their general good intentions more than they are acclaimed for their specific positive achievements.

If "One America" is to be better than a nice slogan, it will require resources, work, and committed leadership who will confront the opposition.

Politainment and an Extended Renaissance Weekend

Marcus Raskin

In mid-1997, our National Seminar Leader, President Clinton, wanted to arrange what we might describe as an extended Renaissance Weekend for all of us. It would be about race and civil rights. It would also have the character of an encounter group where all complaints of the national dysfunctional family are supposedly aired. All members would then feel better, "process their issues," take part in a collective "I hear you," and then go on with their lives. The Extended Weekend would have created a new language of politesse, damned certain words as not appropriate in polite company, and end with hugs all the way around by the closing of the event.

The National Seminar Leader would be praised for his openness and his willingness to "hear" all sides while he would be preparing his next "national dialogue" about, say, gutting the Social Security system. On matters of race, the governing process would be reduced to an arm around complainants in which we would hear each other's pain. If we could listen carefully through the static, we might think of government as our personal facilitator, but this conclusion would be mistaken. Government would not be big brother so much as distant cousin talking to us through a bad connection on a long distance telephone wire. We would find, in fact, that there was no cousin on the other end but the syrupy, mechanical sound of a voice telling us to "hold" because our vote was important to the National Leader.

Nevertheless, as a result of the process, if it would work the way it was intended in the mind of the National Seminar Leader, the public would have internalized the idea that democracy is nothing more than poll data and focus groups punctuated by claims that democracy is chatter which goes nowhere and is meant to go nowhere.

But the seminar was interrupted by another, more powerful mode of social communication. It was the coming of age of politainment. The media were not going to take their cue from the style of national encounter groups, which could only give us pictures of talking heads, screaming anguish and dull words. They were going to take their cues from entertainment. What could be better than turning on the National Seminar Leader? He was morphed into the traveling preacher who was caught with his pants down. The Seminar Leader who had attended many Renaissance Weekends explained himself in linguistic ways which would have filled the hearts of medieval casuists with great pride. For the populace, politainment had a price. It meant that all other concerns had to end as the national dysfunctional family yielded to the debate of when, where, and who could give or get what kind of sex. What should be said about them to nonparticipants became the new chatter coin of the realm traded in the media, Congress, and academe.

The errant National Seminar Leader needed all the friends he could get in the politainment play. So he turned to the very part of the community which he did little for: the African-American community. Left behind was our extended Renaissance Weekend on race. It was a vague memory, mush in our minds leading nowhere.

But there is one question left for the rest of us. Do we think we could do better? Let us imagine the following: Suppose all those who claim more wisdom than those who wrote the Franklin report began from the premise that while democracy is a dialogue, it is more than a dialogue. Could we write—and then act on—a national report that would be different, better, more lively, and result in practical projects that would indeed lead to a different covenant among the people? I like to think so. But let's see whether anyone among us will respond. And let's see how the President responds to the Franklin report. Will the combination preacherman and seminar leader remember who in the family stood by him?

Three years later, I am still waiting to see if he can do better. The need is great.

"One America"—To What Ends?

Sam Husseini

The report is 121 pages. I've delved into it. I could immerse myself in it and write a dissertation, but who would read it? For a short piece, it's enough to just look at the cover—and consider how this administration uses this issue as cover.

"One America in the 21st Century" is the title. Not "Finally Overcoming Racism." Not "Towards an America of Equality." "One America"—is that really the point? Should that be the goal of this Race Initiative?

National cohesion is the driving concern here. How can we make these differing ethnicities get along well enough to ensure that this stays one nation is a question elites must ask themselves. We are called to "overcome the burden of race." In some respects, the people—their very genetic makeup and heritage— are implicitly viewed as a threat to the great goal: "One America." Is that more important than reaffirming our humanity with regards to ethnicity? Indeed, humanity is viewed at best as a mere lever, a tactic for national unity, just as racial diversity is viewed as a means to economic success.

There is some truth in the notion that governments should not legislate morality. So the issue foremost on this administration's mind should be: "Are we doing anything that is fostering racism? Are we carrying out the laws that are on the books properly? Or are we applying punishments, such as the death penalty, in a manner that is prejudicial? Are police harassing African Americans on the highways? Are security personnel stopping Arab Americans more than others at airports?" Bill Clinton can ask himself: "Did I do virtually nothing to stop the disaster in Rwanda because their skin was darker than mine?" and "Am I keeping the sanctions in place in Iraq because the greatest victims—4,500 Iraqi children dying every month—belong to a group that has been cast as 'the other'— the great non-American ethnicity?"

Can we really talk about "The President's Initiative on Race" with some seriousness? Clinton lied to—and about—Lani Guinier; he signed the crime and the welfare bills. Clinton—when he had a Democratic majority—did not invoke "one person one vote" to rally support for DC statehood. The president did, however, run down to DC from Martha's Vineyard when he ordered the launching of missiles, in total violation of international law, at a pharmaceutical plant in the Sudan, apparently to distract from his sex scandals. Few recall that this same man, when the Gennifer Flowers sex story was breaking, pulled his first "wag the dog" on the national stage by running down to Arkansas to oversee the frying of a retarded black man.

Of course, "One America in the 21st Century: Forging a New Future" could be used as a title for things other than "The President's Initiative on Race." Say, on economics. What would that title mean in that context? Perhaps on health care, where this administration portrayed itself as challenging the health insurance companies while it was actually in cahoots with the insurance giants as they clashed with the smaller players. The Clinton Administration doesn't seem interested in forging "One America" economically, where we "overcome the burden of economics." "One America" was not of a great deal of concern to the 14 billionaires who gave up their U.S. citizenship to avoid paying taxes a few years back.

Bill Clinton's presumed hero, John F. Kennedy, said, "Ask not what your country can do for you, ask what you can do for your country." Here, we are asked to address the "burden of race"—for the good of the country.

We have accepted a Divine Right of Nations. Walter Mondale said that "America is forever." Wouldn't true religious people view that as idolatry? Nations are made to serve humans. It is people who are born with inalienable rights. It is governments that must not trample on those rights. Patriotism has become less an expression of love for those around you, or a devotion to timeless principles, than blind allegiance.

There's No Racial Justice Without Economic Justice

Peter Dreier

President Clinton had hoped that one of his major legacies would be to foster a new climate of racial reconciliation, but the tepid report of the Advisory Board to his Initiative on Race offered no road map toward that lofty goal.

Waves of social and economic reform typically require three things: a widely-shared analysis of the problem, a policy program for change, and a political vehicle for mobilizing a constituency.

The Advisory Board's report of the President's Initiative on Race offers a very useful analysis of the nation's racial history and current racial conditions, but it failed to focus on the major obstacle to racial conciliation—the widening disparities of wealth and income.

Likewise, the report has lots of good ideas, but the recommendations are all over the map, from urging Americans to be more tolerant, to asking the mass media to eliminate racial stereotypes, to changing our practices regarding such areas as early childhood learning, policing, job training, and housing development. There is no clear sense of priorities.

Finally, it is well known that presidential commissions and blue-ribbon task forces rarely have much impact unless there is a well-organized constituency prepared to mount a campaign to translate the report's recommendations into public policy. The report exhorts Americans to change their ways, but makes no distinctions about who is likely to win and lose in (and thus who is likely to support and oppose) the struggle for racial reconciliation.

Most conspicuous by its absence is any reference to the labor movement as a vehicle for building a majoritarian constituency for racial and economic justice. The report's scattershot approach is understandable, since so many aspects of American life are intertwined with race. But this makes it difficult to get a handle on what to do—what's most important. Indeed, due in part to the lack of a clear focus, the news media barely paid attention to the report when it was released. (It was more interested in the controversies about the panel's deliberations than its conclusions.) This, in turn, makes it difficult to build much political support for the report's recommendations.

The report acknowledges the dramatic racial progress of the past three decades. Thanks to the civil rights revolution, we've witnessed the significant growth of the African-American and Latino middle class and the dramatic decline of the overt daily terror imposed on Black Americans. Racial minorities are now visible in positions of leadership and influence. There are impressive numbers of Black and Latino political leaders who have garnered cross-racial support. We've opened up colleges and the professions to Blacks and Latinos.

The number of minorities in Congress, as well as those at local and state levels of government, has grown significantly. A growing number of large, predominantly white cities have elected Black and Latino mayors—in fact, the number of Black and Latino mayors reached an all-time peak in 1999. Douglas Wilder became the first Black governor. Jesse Jackson ran for President, and Ron Dellums became chair of the House Armed Services Committee. Colin Powell led the Joint Chiefs of Staff.

Thirty years ago there were hardly any minorities on Fortune 500 corporate boards, as TV newscasters and daily newspaper editors, or as presidents and administrators of major colleges and hospitals. That is no longer the case. Although the glass ceiling persists, we have gone beyond symbolic tokenism.

Despite this progress, race remains a divisive issue in America. The poverty rate among Black and Latino Americans is three times that of white America. Almost half of Black children live in poverty. Our residential areas remain racially segregated. At least two out of three white Americans live in essentially all-white neighborhoods. In most major American cities, more than 70 percent of the population would have to move to achieve full integration. Even when Blacks move to the suburbs, they are likely to live in segregated areas—and not because they prefer to do so. Blacks and Latinos still feel the sting of discrimination in the workplace, by banks and real estate brokers, and by the police and the criminal justice system.

Some analysts see these conflicting trends as a paradox. It is not. The essence of America's troubled race relations can be summarized by the following observation: Corporate America has learned to live with affirmative action and laws against racial discrimination. But it steadfastly opposes policies to promote full employment, universal health care, and affordable housing for all. Assimilating some people of color into the professional middle class, and even into the upper class, does not threaten the power and privilege of the corporate elite. But full employment and decent wages, universal health coverage, and an adequate supply of affordable housing for all Americans challenges the foundation of the business elite's power and profits.

Not surprisingly, the report failed to focus on the major obstacle to racial reconciliation: the nation's widening disparities of wealth and income. Today, the top 1 percent have a larger share of the nation's wealth than the bottom 90 percent of the population. The richest 5 percent of the nation own 61.4 percent of total wealth and have 20.3 percent of total income. The most affluent 20 percent of Americans have 84.3 percent of all wealth and 46.8 percent of total income.

We need to remind ourselves that economic justice is a pre-condition for racial justice. We need a broad policy agenda that will help unite Americans who are on the bottom three-quarters of the economic ladder around a common vision of the American Dream. These are the vast majority of Americans—Black, white, brown, yellow, and all shades in between—who are currently not benefiting from the nation's recent economic upturn and who will certainly suffer even more during the next inevitable downturn of the business cycle. If there is one truism about race relations, it is that prejudice, bigotry, and discrimination decline when everyone has basic economic security.

A Role for Organized Labor

Organized labor is the most important vehicle for challenging the widening gap between rich and poor, corporate layoffs, a dramatic increase in temporary and part-time work, major cutbacks in government social programs, and the export of good jobs to anti-union states and to low-wage countries. But the Advisory Board report is silent on the important role that unions have played and can play in addressing racial injustice.

The erosion of America's labor movement is the chief reason for the declining wages and living standards and the nation's widening economic disparities. Union membership has declined to 15 percent of the workforce—the lowest since the Great Depression. (Omit government employees, and unions represent only 11 percent of private sector workers.) Some of American labor's decline is due to the erosion of the nation's manufacturing industry, where unions were strong, and the growth of service-sector employment, where unions have so far made few inroads. Labor's decline is compounded by our outdated labor laws, which give management an unfair advantage in all aspects of union activity; this policy bias has been compounded by the anti-union policies of the National Labor Relations Board (especially during the twelve years of the Reagan and Bush Administrations) which routinely sided with management when overseeing union elections. Labor's decline is also due to the union movement's own failure to put more resources in organizing new workers and new types of workplaces.

After decades of decline, the sleeping giant of American unionism seems to be waking up. A new generation of labor activists, including a growing number of African-American, Latino, and Asian leaders, have been shaking up the labor movement, with a renewed strategy of organizing unorganized workers (especially minorities) and restoring the labor movement's political clout. The new cohort of labor leaders at both the national and local levels intends to rekindle the "movement" spirit of activist unionism, in part by focusing on sectors now composed disproportionately of minorities, women, and immigrants. Since the late 1990s, overall union membership has inched upward for the first time in decades because of innovative organizing drives, such as the nationwide "Justice for Janitors" campaign. In 1999, the Service Employees International Union in Los Angeles won a union election for 75,000 low-wage home care workers, most of them women and immigrants. This was the largest single union victory since the 1930s.

In at least three dozen cities, local unions, working in coalitions with community and religious groups, have mobilized "living wage" campaigns to increase living standards of low-wage workers employed by firms with local government contracts. Labor unions have joined forces with college students through the Union Summer internship program and the growing campus "anti-sweatshop" movement.

Unions have a complex history with regard to race relations. On the one hand, they have often been one of the few institutions where workers of all races have both common interests and somewhat equal footing. Throughout this century, progressive unions have been at the forefront of addressing the "race question." On the other hand, conservative elements within organized labor (primarily but not exclusively craft unions, not industrial unions) often turned a blind eye to racism both within their own unions and on matters of politics and public policy.

Until the Civil Rights Movement of the 1960s, black Americans did not gain their fair slice of the postwar era's economic gains. With organized labor as an ally, the civil rights crusade helped many black Americans move into the economic mainstream. They gained access to good-paying jobs—in factories, government, and professional sectors—that previously had been off-limits.

In unionized firms, the wage gap between Black and white workers narrowed significantly. Whites and Blacks not only earn roughly the same wages, they both earn more than workers without union representation. According to the Economic Policy Institute, unionized Black males earn 19 percent more than Blacks in non-union jobs; for whites, the union "wage premium" is 18 percent.

Unions that have made the most headway in recent years have drawn on the tactics and themes of civil rights crusades and grassroots organizing campaigns. Union drives that emphasize dignity and justice, and that forge alliances with community and church groups, have been the most successful. Surveys consistently show that Blacks and Latinos are more favorably inclined toward unions than whites in similar jobs. In fact, Kate Bronfenbrenner of Cornell University found that since 1980, workplaces with the highest percentage of minority workers are the most likely to win union elections.

Rebuilding the nation's labor movement is not a panacea for racial division, but it is a necessary first pre-condition. It is no accident that those advanced industrialized nations with narrower economic disparities, better health and child care policies, fewer children in poverty, and higher rates of social mobility also have a significantly higher level of unionization.

A stronger labor movement, working with allies among community and religious groups, women's organizations, civil rights groups, and others, is essential if the nation is to mobilize around an agenda of economic prosperity, economic justice, and racial reconciliation. In contrast to the report's scattershot recommendations, we need a coherent program around which to mobilize the vast majority of Americans who are not getting their fair share of nation's economic prosperity.

The labor movement's political agenda looks strikingly similar to the policy prescriptions of most progressive African-American and Latino leaders and organizations. It includes a new wave of job-creating public investment in the nation's crumbling infrastructure; increasing the minimum wage to the poverty level (and indexing it to inflation); protecting social programs like Medicare, Food Stamps, and subsidized housing; universal national health insurance; restoration of progressive taxes; renewed funding for public education; expansion of job training programs; bringing our family policies (maternity/paternity leaves, vacation time, child care) up to the level of our Canadian and European counterparts; and stronger enforcement of workplace safety regulations and anti-discrimination laws like the Community Reinvestment Act.

In his last speech in Memphis shortly before his death, speaking at a union rally, Reverend Martin Luther King, Jr. said that "as a people, we will get to the promised land." With the end of the Cold War, and with our nation again prospering economically, we have an unprecedented opportunity to fulfill the American Dream for all. Achieving that goal as we enter the twenty-first century is akin to entering the promised land. But it will take bold action and political mobilization.

Contributors

Douglas J. Amy (damy@mtholyoke.edu) is a professor at Mount Holyoke College Department of Politics. His latest book is *Beyond the Ballot Box: A Citizen's Guide to Voting Systems* (Praeger Publishing, 2000).

Carl Anthony, executive director of the Urban Habitat Program in San Francisco, California, is an urban planner, architect, and environmental justice organizer.

William Ayers (bayers@uic.edu) is Distinguished Professor of Education and senior scholar at the University of Illinois, Chicago. He is co-director of the Small Schools Workshop and director of the Center for Youth and Society. His latest book is *A Kind and Just Parent: The Children of Juvenile Court* (Beacon Press, 1997).

David S. Bailey (dsbailey@igc.org), a lawyer in private practice in Beaverdam, Virginia, was formerly an attorney with the environmental justice team at the Lawyers' Committee for Civil Rights Under Law in Washington, DC.

Chip Berlet is a senior analyst at Political Research Associates in Somerville, Massachusetts, where he specializes in investigation of far right hate groups.

Jared Bernstein (jbernstein@epinet.org) is a labor economist with the Economic Policy Institute in Washington, DC. In 1995–1996, he was deputy chief economist at the U.S. Department of Labor.

Julian Bond (hjb7g@virginia.edu) is chairman of the board of the NAACP,

Distinguished Professor at American University, and professor in the University of Virginia's History Department. He was communication director for the Student Non-Violent Coordinating Committee and served more than twenty years in the Georgia General Assembly.

John C. Bonifaz (nvri@nvri.org) is the founder and executive director of the National Voting Rights Institute, Boston, Massachusetts, a nonprofit litigation and public education organization dedicated to challenging the campaign finance system on voting rights grounds and to defending meaningful campaign finance reform laws at the state and local level across the country.

Bunyan Bryant (bbryant@umich.edu) is a professor at the University of Michigan School of Natural Resources and Environment. He is author of *Environmental Advocacy: Concepts, Issues and Dilemmas* (Caddo Gap Press, 1990) and *Race and the Incidence of Environmental Hazards: A Time for Discourse* (Westview Press, 1992; edited with Paul Mohai).

John Calmore (jcalmore@email.unc.edu) is the Reef C. Ivey II Research Professor in the School of Law at the University North Carolina at Chapel Hill. Previously, he was an attorney at the National Housing Law Project, Western Center on Law and Poverty, and Legal Aid Foundation of Los Angeles. He also taught at Loyola Law School in Los Angeles and was a Program Officer at the Ford Foundation.

Bebe Moore Campbell is the author of the novel, *Singing in the Comeback Choir.*

Stephen Carpenter (scarpenter@flaginc.org) is a staff attorney at Farmers' Legal Action Group in St. Paul, Minnesota. FLAG works on behalf of financially distressed family farmers nationwide. His article was originally written in 1999.

John Cawthorne (cawthorn@bc.edu) is an assistant dean at Boston College Lynch School of Education and former vice-president for education at the National Urban League.

Luke W. Cole, an environmental justice lawyer, is director of California Rural Legal Assistance Foundation's Center on Race, Poverty & the Environment. He is co-author of *From the Ground Up: Environmental Racism and the Rise of the Environmental Justice Movement* (New York University Press, 2000), which chronicles the transformative politics of the movement and its impact on American life.

Yvonne Combs (yjcombs@ufl.edu) is a graduate minority fellow in sociology at the University of Florida. Her doctoral research deals with the intersections of race, health, and aging among African-American women.

Don DeMarco (open@libertynet.org) is president and executive director of Fund for an OPEN Society, Philadelphia, Pennsylvania, a pro-integrative mortgage, housing counseling, and consulting nonprofit organization.

Benjamin DeMott is the author of fourteen books and scores of essays on American history and culture, including *The Trouble With Friendship: Why Americans Can't Think Straight About Race* (Yale University Press, 1998). His most recent book is *Killer Woman Blues: Why Americans Can't Think Straight About Gender and Power* (Houghton Mifflin, 2000).

Sheryl Denbo (sdenbo@maec.org) is president of the Mid-Atlantic Equity Consortium, a nonprofit organization in Chevy Chase, Maryland, working on education equity and school reform issues.

Ty dePass (maceito@aol.com) is associate editor for *The NonProfit Quarterly*, a magazine for the exchange of ideas, opinions, and information among nonprofit and neighborhood-based organizations.

Barbara Diggs-Brown, a journalism historian, is an associate dean and associate professor at American University School of Communication and is co-author of *By the Color of Our Skin: The Illusion of Integration and The Reality of Race* (Plume, 2000).

Peter Dreier (dreier@oxy.edu) is E.P. Clapp Distinguished Professor of Politics and director of the Urban & Environmental Policy Program at Occidental College in Los Angeles, California. He formerly was senior policy advisor to Mayor Raymond Flynn of Boston, Massachusetts, and is co-author of *Regions That Work* (University of Minnesota Press, 2000) and *Place Matters: Rethinking Urban Policy* (University Press of Kansas, 2001).

Cynthia M. Duncan, a former PRRAC Social Science Advisory Board member, is director of Community and Resource Development at the Ford Foundation. Before joining Ford, she was chair and professor at the University of New Hampshire Department of Sociology.

James Early (james@folklife.si.edu) is director of Cultural Heritage Policy at the Smithsonian Institution Center for Folklife and Cultural Heritage, Washington, DC.

Marian Wright Edelman is founder and president of the Children's Defense Fund and author of five books: *Families in Peril: An Agenda for Social Change* (Harvard University, 1987); *The Measure of Our Success: A Letter to My Children and Yours* (Beacon, 1992); *Guide My Feet: Meditations and Prayers on Loving and Working for Children* (Beacon, 1995); *Stand for Children* (Hyperion Books for Children, 1998); and *Lanterns: A Memoir of Mentors* (HarperPerennial, 2000).

Peter Edelman is a professor at the Georgetown University Law Center. He served as an assistant secretary in the Department of Health and Human Services during the first Clinton Administration. His recent book is *Searching for America's Heart: RFK and the Renewal of Hope* (Houghton Mifflin, 2001).

Joe Feagin (feagin@ufl.edu) is graduate research professor in sociology at the University of Florida and immediate past president of the American Sociological Association. His most recent books are *Racial and Ethnic Relations* (Prentice-Hall, 1999; with Clairece Booher Feagin); *White Racism: The Basics* (Routledge, 1995; with Hernan Vera); and *Double Burden: Black Women and Everyday Racism* (M.E. Sharpe, 1998; with Yanick St. Jean).

George C. Galster (aa3571@wayne.edu) is the Clarence Hilberry Professor of Urban Affairs at Wayne State University. He is currently engaged in a national study of housing market discrimination with a team of researchers at the Urban Institute.

Herbert J. Gans is the Robert S. Lynd Professor of Sociology at Columbia University and a past president of the American Sociological Association. His most recent books are *War Against the Poor* (Basic Books, 1995); *Making Sense of America* (Rowman & Littlefield, 1999); and a new edition of *Popular Culture and High Culture* (Basic Books, 1999).

Arnoldo García (agarcia@igc.org) is a long-time cultural worker and activist based in the Mexican-Chicano community. Formerly with the Urban Habitat Program, he now works for the National Network for Immigrant and Refugee Rights, heading up its campaign on the UN's 2001 World Conference Against Racism.

Barbara Gault (gault@iwpr.org) is the associate director of research at the Institute for Women's Policy Research in Washington, DC, a nonpartisan, scientific research institute devoted to providing resources to inform policy debates affecting women.

Rachel Godsil (godsilra@shu.edu) is an associate professor at the Seton Hall University School of Law. She formerly was an Assistant U.S. Attorney for the Southern District of New York, and Assistant Counsel of the NAACP Legal Defense and Educational Fund, where she coordinated the environmental justice docket.

Marian (Meck) Groot (meck@world.std.com) is co-director of the Women's Theological Center in Boston, Massachusetts. The Center's mission is to nourish women's spiritual leadership and communities for liberation movements.

Bristow Hardin (bhardin@tui.edu) directs The Union Institute's Center for Public Policy in Washington, DC. The Center conducts applied research focused primarily on the roles of nonprofit organizations and community groups play in strengthening democracy and increasing social justice.

Phyllis Hart is executive director of The Achievement Council in Los Angeles, California, a nonprofit organization whose mission is to improve kindergarten through twelfth grade academic outcomes for African American, Latino, Native American, and low-income youth so that all students are eligible to enter a four-year college.

Chester Hartman (chartman@prrac.org), an urban planner, is president/ executive director of the Poverty & Race Research Action Council in Washington, DC, and editor of *Poverty & Race*. His most recent books are *City for Sale: The Transformation of San Francisco* (University of California Press, 2001) and *Between Eminence and Notoriety: Four Decades of Radical Urban Planning* (Rutgers Center for Urban Policy Research, 2001).

Kati Haycock (khaycock@edtrust.org), a PRRAC Board member, is director of The Education Trust, Inc., a nonprofit organization that assists school districts and institutions of higher education to launch simultaneous reform efforts aimed at improving teaching and learning, especially for minority and low-income students, and provides policy leadership at the national level. She formerly was executive vice-president of the Children's Defense Fund and director of the University of California Outreach and Student Affirmative Action programs.

Thomas J. Henderson (thenders@lawyerscomm.org), a PRRAC Board member, is chief counsel and senior deputy director at the Lawyers' Committee for Civil Rights Under Law, Washington, DC, where he is primarily responsible for fair housing, education, environmental justice, and other civil rights claims.

Jay P. Heubert (jay.heubert@columbia.edu) is Associate Professor of Education at Teachers College, Columbia, and Adjunct Professor of Law at Columbia Law School. He directed the congressionally mandated study, *High Stakes: Testing for Tracking, Promotion, and Graduation* (National Academy Press, 1999), and served for five years as a trial attorney in the education section of the Civil Rights Division, U.S. Department of Justice.

Bill Ong Hing (bhing@ucdavis.edu) is professor of law and Asian American Studies at the University of California, Davis. He is founder and volunteers as general counsel of the Immigrant Legal Resource Center. Among his books are *To Be An American—Cultural Pluralism and the Rhetoric of Assimilation* (New York University Press, 1997) and *Making and Remaking Asian America Through Immigration Policy, 1850–1990* (Stanford University Press, 1993).

Lyman Ho (lho@ci.aurora.co.us) is a parent member of a site-based governing committee for South High School in the Denver Public School District and a member of the Cross City Campaign for Urban School Reform.

Hollywood Women's Political Committee was a major liberal Political Action Committee which dissolved in April 1997, as a protest against the campaign finance system. For further information on the HWPC action, contact Lara Bergthold, Act III Communications, 1999 Ave. of the Stars, #500, Los Angeles, CA 90067; 310/551–4004.

Sam Husseini (sam@accuracy.org) is communications director for the Institute for Public Accuracy, a consortium of public policy experts. He has also worked with the American-Arab Anti-Discrimination Committee and Fairness & Accuracy in Reporting.

Noel Ignatiev (ignatiev@fas.harvard.edu) is co-editor of *Race Traitor* (Routledge, 1995), author of *How the Irish Became White* (Routledge, 1996), and a member of the New Abolitionist Society (www.newabolition.org). He teaches in the Department of Critical Studies at the Massachusetts College of Art, and is a fellow of Harvard's W.E.B. DuBois Institute for Afro-American Research.

Robert Jensen (rjensen@uts.cc.utexas.edu), a former journalist, is professor at the University of Texas at Austin Department of Journalism. His essays on politics and white privilege are available online at http:// uts.cc.utexas.edu/~rjensen/home.htm.

Richard D. Kahlenberg (rkahlenberg@tcf.org) is a Washington, DC-based senior fellow at The Century Foundation (formerly the Twentieth Century Fund), where he writes about education, equal opportunity, and civil rights. He is the author of *All Together Now: Creating Middle-Class Schools through Public School Choice* (Brookings Institution Press, 2001); *The Remedy: Class, Race, and Affirmative Action* (Basic Books, 1996); and *Broken Contract: A Memoir of Harvard Law School* (Hill & Wang, 1992).

David Kairys (dkairys@vm.temple.edu), a civil rights lawyer for over twenty-five years, is professor at Temple University Beasley School of Law. He is the editor of *The Politics of Law* (3rd ed., Basic Books, 1998) and the author of *With Liberty and Justice for Some* (New Press, 1993).

Walda Katz-Fishman (wkatzfishman@igc.org) is professor of sociology at Howard University, board chair of Project South: Institute for the Elimination of Poverty & Genocide, board member of Ecumenical Program on Central American and the Caribbean, and is active in the Association of Black Sociologists and the American Sociological Association.

Surina Khan (surina@iglhrc.org) is executive director of International Gay and Lesbian Human Rights Commission in San Francisco, CA. Prior to that, she was a research analyst at Political Research Associates (PRA), a national progressive think-tank. She is co-chair of the board of directors of the Funding Exchange, a national network of progressive community foundations.

Jonathan Kozol is the author of *Death at an Early Age* (New American Library, 1985); *Rachel and Her Children* (Ballantine Books, 1989); *Amazing Grace* (HarperPerennial, 1996); and most recently *Ordinary Resurrection: Children in the Years of Hope* (Crown Publishers, 2000). He lives in the village of Byfield, Massachusetts.

D. Bambi Kraus (bambi@itc.org) is the president of the National Association of Tribal Historic Preservation Officers in Washington, DC. She served as senior advisor on American Indian and Alaska Native affairs to the executive director of President Clinton's Initiative on Race.

Greg LeRoy (goodjobs@ctj.org) directs Good Jobs First, a project of the Institute on Taxation and Economic Policy. He is author of *No More Candy Store: States and Cities Making Job Subsidies Accountable*, published by ITEP, and 1998 recipient of the Stern Family Fund Public Interest Pioneer Award.

John Lewis represents Georgia's 5th Congressional district, first elected in 1986. From 1963–1966 he was Chairman of the Student Nonviolent Coordinating Committee and was one of the original 1961 Freedom Riders, challenging segregation at interstate bus terminals across the South. His autobiography, *Walking With the Wind: A Memoir of the Movements*, was published by Harvest Books in 1998.

James W. Loewen (jloewen@zoo.uvm.edu) taught race relations for twenty years at the University of Vermont and is the author of *Lies Across America: What Our Historic Sites Get Wrong* (New Press, 1999) and *Lies My Teacher Told Me: Everything Your High School History Textbook Got Wrong* (New Press, 1995).

Clarence Lusane is a professor at the American University School of International Service and author of *Race in the Global Era: African Americans at the Millenium* (South End Press, 1997).

Fred McBride (cvdmcbride@aol.com) is a doctoral candidate in the Political Science Department at Clark Atlanta University. He recently served as Southern Regional Director for the Center for Voting and Democracy and was extensively involved in the NAACP National "Lift Every Voice and Vote" campaign.

Cynthia A. McKinney, Georgia's first African-American Congresswoman, elected in 1992, is an internationally renowned advocate for voting rights, human rights, and the strengthening of business ties between Africa and the United States.

Ellen Malcolm (bdavidson@emilyslist.org) is the founder and president of EMILY's List, Washington, DC, a donor network that supports pro-choice Democratic women candidates for governor, U.S. House and U.S. Senate. EMILY's List, an acronym for "Early Money Is Like Yeast," has become the nation's largest financial resource for congressional candidates.

Robert D. Manning (ccnation@hotmail.com) is Senior Fellow, Institute for Higher Education Governance and Law, University of Houston Law Center. He is author of *Credit Card Nation: The Consequences of America's Addiction to Credit* (Basic Books, 2000) and the financial education website www.creditcardnation.com.

Manning Marable (mm247@columbia.edu) is professor of history and political science and the director of the Institute for Research in African American Studies at Columbia University. He is the author of fourteen books, most recently *Dispatches from the Ivory Tower* (Columbia University Press, 2000). His "Along the Color Line" column is distributed free of charge and regularly appears in over 325 black and progressive publications worldwide.

Paul Marcus (pmarcus@mcimail.com) is co-director of Community Change, Inc., a thirty-two-year-old Boston-based nonprofit which focuses on issues of institutional racism.

S.M. Miller (fivegood@aol.com), a PRRAC Board member, is an economic sociologist and research professor of sociology at Boston College. He directs the Project on Inequality and Poverty at the Commonwealth Institute, Cambridge, Massachusetts. He is also on the board of directors of United for a Fair Economy. His current book projects focus on class and identity group respect as political issues, and the implications for progressive politics of economic and social change.

Kary L. Moss (kmossaclu@aol.com) is executive director of ACLU of Michigan. Formerly, she was executive director of the Sugar Law Center for Economic and Social Justice, a project of the National Lawyers Guild. Her writings include: *The Rights of Women and Girls* (Puffin Books, 1997); *Women's Health Care, Public Policy and Reform*, (Duke University Press, 1995); and *The Rights of Women* (Southern Illinois University Press, 1993).

Peter Negroni (pnegroni@collegeboard.org) is vice president for Teaching and Learning at The College Board, Princeton, New Jersey, and formerly superintendent of schools in Springfield, Massachusetts.

Monty Neill (monty@fairtest.org) is executive director of the National Center for Fair & Open Testing in Cambridge, Massachusetts. He is co-author of *Implementing Performance Assessments: A Guide to Classroom School and System Reform* (FairTest, 1995) and *Testing Our Children: A Report Card on State Assessment Systems* (FairTest, 1997), the first comprehensive evaluation of all fifty state testing programs.

Angela E. Oh (aeola@earthlink.net), a former member of the Advisory Board to President Clinton's Initiative on Race, is writing a book based on race relations conversations. She is Chancellor's Fellow at the University of California, Irvine for 2000–2001.

Michael Omi (omi@socrates.berkeley.edu) is professor of ethnic studies and acting director of the Institute for the Study of Social Change at the University of California, Berkeley. He is the co-author (with Howard Winant) of *Racial Formation in the United States: From the 1960s to the 1990s* (Routledge, 1994).

Frances Fox Piven (FFox-Piven@gc.cuny.edu) is Distinguished Professor of Political Science and Sociology at the Graduate Center of the City University of New York. She is co-author with Richard Cloward of *Why Americans Still Don't Vote* (Beacon Press, 2000); *The Breaking of the American Social Compact* (New Press, 1997); and *Regulating the Poor* (Vintage Books, 1993).

john a. powell (irpetc.umn.edu), secretary of the PRRAC Board, is professor director of the Institute on Race & Poverty at the University of Minnesota Law School. He formerly was legal director of the American Civil Liberties Union, executive director of Greater Miami Legal Services, and on the staff of Evergreen Legal Services.

Hugh Price is President of the National Urban League in New York City.

Jamin B. Raskin (raskin@wcl.american.edu) is professor of constitutional law and the First Amendment at American University's Washington College of Law. He formerly was Assistant Attorney General of Massachusetts and General Counsel of the National Rainbow Coalition. His most recent book, *We the Students: Supreme Court Cases For and Against Students* (CQ Press, 2000), analyzes the twenty-five most important Supreme Court cases affecting America's high school students.

Marcus Raskin (mraskin@igc.org) is co-founder of the Institute for Policy Studies, professor of public policy at George Washington University, and author or editor of eighteen books on political theory, politics, and international affairs. His forthcoming book, *On Liberalism*, will be published in 2001 by Rowman & Littlefield. He is on the editorial board of *The Nation*.

Robert Richie (fairvote@compuserve.com) is co-founder and executive director of the Center for Voting and Democracy, Takoma Park, Maryland, a nonprofit organization that researches and distributes information on election reforms promoting voter participation, accountable government, and fair representation.

Florence Wagman Roisman (froisman@iupui.edu), a founding PRRAC Board member, is professor of law at the Indiana University School of Law in Indianapolis, Indiana. She worked for almost thirty years with the National Housing Law Project and the District of Columbia Legal Services Program.

Steve Savner (ssavner@clasp.org) is a senior staff attorney at the Center for Law and Social Policy, Washington, DC. CLASP is a national nonprofit organization addressing issues of family poverty through research, policy analysis, technical assistance, and advocacy.

Tom Schlesinger (tom@fmcenter.org) is executive director of the Financial Markets Center, a nonprofit institute that provides research and education resources to citizen groups, labor unions, journalists, policymakers, and others interested in the Federal Reserve and the financial sector.

Jerome Scott (projectsouth@igc.org) is director and past board chair of Project South: Institute for the Elimination of Poverty & Genocide in Atlanta, Georgia, southern regional organizer for Up & Out of Poverty Now!, board member of Fund for Southern Communities and Georgia Black United Fund, and past board chair of the Funding Exchange.

Theodore M. Shaw (tshaw@naacpldf.org), a PRRAC Board member, is associate director-counsel at the NAACP Legal Defense & Educational Fund, Inc. in New York City, and previously was counsel for the Fund's Western Regional office in Los Angeles, California. He formerly was on the faculty of the University of Michigan Law School and served in the Civil Rights Division of the U.S. Department of Justice.

David K. Shipler, a Pulitzer Prize-winning author and former *New York Times* correspondent, participated in President Clinton's first town meeting on race in December 1997. His most recent book, *A Country of Strangers: Blacks and Whites in America* (Vintage Books, 1998), explores the subtle and explicit patterns of racial stereotyping and their impact on Americans' lives.

Selena Mendy Singleton (ssingleton@transafricaforum.org) is senior policy advisor for TransAfrica Forum. Prior to that, she was a senior research associate for former U.S. Senator Bill Bradley, an environmental justice attorney for the Lawyers' Committee for Civil Rights Under Law, and a legislative assistant to District of Columbia U.S. Congressional Representative Eleanor Holmes Norton.

Leonard Steinhorn (lsteinh@american.edu), a professor at the American University School of Communication, is co-author of *By the Color of Our Skin: The Illusion of Integration and The Reality of Race* (Plume, 2000). He is contributing editor of the internet magazine *TomPaine.com*. Before joining the American University faculty, he spent years as a political speechwriter, media strategist, and civil rights advocate.

Rich Stolz (richs@commchange.org) is a policy specialist at the Center for Community Change in Washington, DC, where he staffs the Transportation Equity Network as well as the Center's other transportation and welfare-related initiatives.

William L. Taylor (williamtaylor@wltlaw.com), a PRRAC Board member, teaches education law at Georgetown University Law Center and is vice-chair of the Leadership Conference on Civil Rights and of the Citizens Commission on Civil Rights. He has also been a civil rights lawyer for more than four decades.

S.P. Udayakumar (spudayakumar@yahoo.com) is research associate of the Institute on Race & Poverty at the University of Minnesota Law School.

Annisah Um'rani was a research fellow at the Institute for Women's Policy Research during the 1999–2000 academic year. Beginning in the fall of 2000, she is a graduate student at the University of Chicago.

Paul L. Wachtel (plwachtel@hotmail.com) is Distinguished Professor of Psychology at City College and the Graduate Center of the City University of New York. His most recent book is *Race in the Mind of America: Breaking the Vicious Circle Between Blacks and Whites* (Routledge, 1999).

Margaret Walsh (mwalsh@keene.edu) is assistant professor of sociology at Keene State College in Keene, New Hampshire.

Joyce Germaine Watts is associate director of The Achievement Council in Los Angeles, California. The Achievement Council is a nonprofit organization aimed at increasing academic achievement among minority and low-income students.

Byron Williams is the author of *Puerto Rico: Commonwealth, State or Nation?* (Parents' Magazine Press, 1972); *Continent in Turmoil: A Background Book on Latin America* (Parents' Magazine Press, 1971); *Cuba: The Continuing Revolution* (Parents' Magazine Press, 1969). He passed away in 1999.

Lillian Wilmore (NAEcology@aol.com), a lawyer of Kiowa and Scottish heritage, is a founder and executive director of Native Ecology Initiative, Inc. in Brookline, Massachusetts. NEI's purpose is to assist native nations and indigenous peoples in protecting and restoring Mother Earth.

Howard Winant (hwinant@nimbus.temple.edu) is professor of sociology at Temple University. He is the author of *Racial Conditions: Politics, Theory, Comparisons* (University of Minnesota Press, 1994), and co-author (with Michael Omi) of *Racial Formation in the United States: From the 1960s to the 1990s* (Routledge, 1994). His forthcoming book concerns the comparative historical sociology of race, with emphasis on selected European, African, and American countries.

John Woodford (johnwood@umich.edu) is executive editor of *Michigan Today*, former editor-in-chief of *Muhammad Speaks Newspaper*, and a contributor to *The Black Scholar*. He also worked an an editor and writer for *Ebony* magazine, the *Chicago Sun-Times*, and the *New York Times*.

Frank H. Wu (fwu@law.howard.edu) is an associate professor at Howard University School of Law. Basic Books will publish his *Yellow: Race Relations Beyond Black and White* in 2001.

Raúl Yzaguirre is president of the National Council of La Raza in Washington, DC, the largest constituency-based national Hispanic organization and leading Hispanic "think tank."

Howard Zinn (hzinn@bu.edu) is professor emeritus at Boston University. Formerly, he taught at Spelman College in Atlanta, Georgia, and was an advisor to the Student Non-Violent Coordinating Committee. He is author of *A People's History of the United States* (HarperCollins, 1999); *The Zinn Reader: Writings on Disobedience and Democracy* (Seven Stories Press, 1997); and *Marx in Soho: A Play on History* (South End Press, 1999).

PRRAC Board of Directors and Social Science Advisory Board

Index

Environmental justice,
sustainable communities and *(continued)*
policy strategies, 208–9
poverty, 205, 206–8
racism, 207
smart growth, 205, 207
suburban sprawl, 206–7, 208, 209
technology, 207, 208
Equality politics
bottom-up movement, 46
civil rights movement, 45
class division, 45
income distribution gap, 45–46
international policy and, 46
welfare reform, 46
Equality versus integration
assimilation, 47
civil rights movement, 46–47
economics, 47, 48
housing, 47
intermarriage, 47–48
politics, 47, 48
societal, 47–48
Ethnocentrism, 14
Exclusionary zoning, 22, 24–25
Executive Order 12898, 210, 216, 218,
219, 250

Fair Housing Act (1968), 24
Family farms
African Americans and, 124, 126,
128–29
dispossession impact, 125–26
Farmers' Legal Action Group (FLAG),
128–29
Farm Service Agency (FSA), 127–28
Federal Agriculture Improvement and
Reform Act (1996), 127
government discrimination, 128–29
government policy, 126–29
off-farm income, 124, 125
ownership rates, 123–24
poverty rates, 124, 126
production rates, 125
whites and, 124, 126
Family policy, 313

Federal Agriculture Improvement and
Reform Act (1996), 127
Federal Highway Administration, 250,
251
Federal Housing Administration (FHA),
20, 22
Federal policy. *See* Government policy
Federal Reserve System
influences on
community development, 267
consumer debt, 266, 267
economic growth, 267–68
employment, 266
income distribution, 266
lending practices, 267
politics, 267
reform strategies, 268–70
community development, 269
governance, 269–70
monetary policy, 269
South Carolina, 269
structure of, 268
Virginia, 268–69
Federal Transit Administration, 251
Felton, Rebecca, 30
Feminist theory, 17
Financial services
ACE Cash Express, 240–41
automated teller machines (ATMs), 235,
241
car title loans, 244, 246
Cash America Investments, 239–40
Cash America Pawn, 239–40
cash leasing, 243, 245, 246
Central Rents, 243
check cashing outlets
ACE Cash Express, 240–41
auto insurance, 241
automated teller machines (ATMs),
235, 241
consumer loans, 241
interest rates, 243, 244, 246
Internet service, 241
mergers, 241
minority impact, 243–44
money orders, 241

Financial services,
rent-to-own *(continued)*
Thorn Americas, 243
research resources, 246, 254
revenues, 247
check cashing outlets, 240, 241, 244
deregulation impact, 235–36
pawnshops, 239, 240
rent-to-own, 242, 243
second tier defined, 235
Thorn Americas, 243
United Credit National Bank Visa, 245,
247
white impact and
deregulation, 236–37
financial costs, 239–40
pawnshops, 239–40
Financial Services Modernization Act
(1999), 236
Fire Next Time, The (Baldwin), 19
Florida
democratic participation, 173
immigration, 277
Food stamps, 96, 104
Franklin, John Hope, 32, 289, 292, 294,
295, 319, 330–31
*From Slavery to Freedom: A History of
African Americans* (Franklin), 289

Gamaliel Foundation, 252
Geographic Information Systems (GIS), 255
Georgia, 201–2
Germany, 173
Glass-Steagall Act (1933), 236
Globalization
civil rights organizations, 283–85
defined, 280–81
democracy and, 282–83
economic disparity and, 279–80
minority impact, 279–85
research resources, 284
trade policy and
capital, 281–83
free trade, 281–83
government organizations, 281, 283
location-dependent industry, 280–81

Globalization,
trade policy and *(continued)*
sweatshop labor, 280, 282
taxation, 282
technology, 281, 283
women and, 280, 282
Goals
integration alternatives
community control, 68–69
institutionalized racism and, 68
integration defects and, 69
self-development, 68–69
integration objectives
progress perspective, 76
racism defeat, 64, 66
Good Jobs First, 256, 257–58, 259
Government policy
deregulation, 5
environmental justice
Environmental Impact Statement (EIS),
215, 217, 218, 220–22, 224
Executive Order 12898, 210, 216,
218, 219
hazardous sites, 210, 215, 216, 217,
218, 219
incinerator sites, 220–22, 224
National Environmental Policy Act
(NEPA), 215, 217, 218, 219
Supplemental Environmental Impact
Statement (SEIS), 220, 222,
223–24
globalization and, 281, 283
immigration, 275–76, 277–79, 320
metropolitan segregation
Federal Housing Administration
(FHA), 20, 22
historically, 21–22
Veterans Administration (VA), 20
poverty
children, 111–12
family farms, 126–29
Native Americans, 114, 116–17
transportation, 249, 250, 251, 253–55
See also Clinton administration; *specific
legislation*; Supreme Court
Greenhow, Rose, 32